Radical Atlas

of Ferguson, USA

Patty Heyda

More Praise for *Radical Atlas of Ferguson, USA*

"I can't think of a more wide-ranging, rigorous, and artfully produced portrait of how decades of discriminatory policy, planning, and real estate practices played out on a particular stage. Armed with an impressive array of data, Heyda uses exquisitely crafted maps to illustrate the causes, consequences, and persistence of uneven development. It's hard not to walk away from this book and see how pervasively inequality is structured into the built environment. I will hold *Radical Atlas of Ferguson, USA* up as a gold standard for spatial analysis, critical mapping, and visual storytelling."

—Daniel D'Oca, Principal of Interboro Partners, Associate Professor in Practice at Harvard Graduate School of Design, and coauthor of *The Arsenal of Exclusion & Inclusion*

"This singular book makes it possible to see St. Louis and the Ferguson Uprising in a new way. Map by map, it both extends and deepens our account of the deep structures and emergent histories that framed both the murder of Michael Brown and the revolt that followed."

—Walter Johnson, Winthrop Professor of History and professor of African and African American Studies at Harvard University, and author of *The Broken Heart of America: St. Louis and the Violent History of the United States*

"Patty Heyda brings Ferguson into sharper focus in *Radical Atlas of Ferguson, USA*. In dozens of richly annotated maps, she makes a convincing case that first-ring suburbs are increasingly where tensions over space, capital, and justice come to a head."

—Amanda Kolson Hurley, author of *Radical Suburbs: Experimental Living on the Fringes of the American City*

"In this pathbreaking volume, Patty Heyda elaborates a brilliantly comprehensive spatial forensics of class and racial injustice in the contemporary neoliberal American city. *Radical Atlas* provides a systematic dissection of the multilayered processes of spatial dispossession, institutionalized disenfranchisement, inequality-by-design, neocolonial extractivism, and militarized violence that underpin life and death in poor communities of color in Ferguson, North St. Louis County and the metropolitan region of St. Louis. It will inspire scholars, cartographers, citizens, and activists to imagine—and to construct—alternative forms of urbanism in which public institutions actively support, protect, and sustain the conditions for social and spatial justice for all."

—Neil Brenner, Lucy Flower Professor of Urban Sociology at the University of Chicago, and author of *New Urban Spaces: Urban Theory and the Scale Question*

Printed in the United States of America
First edition 2024

123456789

ISBN: 978-1-953368-75-1

Belt Publishing
13443 Detroit Avenue, Lakewood, OH 44107
www.beltpublishing.com

Cover Design: Patty Heyda, David Wilson
Graphic Design: Isabella Levethan
Book Design: Patty Heyda and Isabella Levethan

Table of Contents

List of maps

04 Politics

05 Justice

Sources

Acknowledgments

Foreword

Radical Mapping: Critical Proximity

We write from a particular geography of conflict, the San Diego-Tijuana border region, where expanding infrastructures of violence have transformed this contested zone into a microcosm of an increasingly walled world. The US-Mexico border is a physical barrier that divides two countries. But the division and control it exemplifies, and the racism it stokes, radiate far beyond the borderline itself, moving deep inside cities across the US, including in places like Ferguson, Missouri, where histories of racism, marginalization, inequality and public disinvestment reproduce urban borders everywhere.

For us, "radicalizing the local" has always meant investigating how global dynamics manifest in local contexts, and recognizing that geopolitics is always an intensely local experience. We believe that scholars, designers and cultural producers who wish to confront global injustice must move from a critical distance (engaging an abstract "out there" in the world somewhere) to a critical proximity (engaging with the "here and now" of the local territory and its immediate social and political context). For this reason, we have rooted our own practice in local dynamics to expose the drivers of injustice, discriminatory public policy and unscrupulous actors in the border region. Our work is grounded in, and fortified by, the voices and practices of the marginalized and their stories of struggle, solidarity and resistance. Patty Heyda's *Radical Atlas of Ferguson, USA* brings the American suburb into critical proximity with a focus on Ferguson and North St. Louis County, Missouri. Maps upon maps build layers of violent contradiction inflected on space and people by the extra-local priorities of capital and its agents.

Only the most myopic and regressive of politics could see "law and order" and wall-building as a solution to violence in our cities. It has been demonstrated time and again that urban violence is rooted in social and economic inequality and that it is exacerbated by accelerating privatization and public disinvestment from already vulnerable communities. In other words, privatization, public defunding, social exclusion and urban violence are causally intertwined, and this cocktail of urban dysfunction has ignited conflict in cities across the US and the world, notably in Ferguson, just as it has in the border zone where we live and work.

We believe that urban justice must begin with recognizing the contested spatial, political and cultural dynamics that reproduce injustice in the city, recontextualizing histories of racism and urban violence, and piecing together forensically the ways that historical macroagressions have been naturalized within the official processes of knowledge construction and urban development. *Radical Atlas of Ferguson, USA* shares this aim. An *urban forensics* thus entails filling in the voids hollowed out by oppression and reconstructing facts that have been erased, silenced and tamed to benefit markets and economic growth, which always demand that urban antagonism is camouflaged and difference is smoothed and banalized.

Exposing missing information enables us to reconstruct a more accurate, accountable, anticipatory and indeed radical urban research and design intervention. No architectural and urban intervention in the city should begin without investigating the contested histories inscribed in a site, the lineages of racism and marginalization, displacement and disinvestment and the politics of ownership and belonging that have defined it. In other words, the conditions themselves can be the materials for urban design, rendering conflict a creative tool for reimagining the city—a generative platform from which to develop policy proposals, unanticipated collaborations and urban development strategies. What emerges is a space for more experimental architectures that is committed to exposing, visualizing and engaging urban conflict as the radical context from which to problematize and reconsider relations between the social, the political, and the aesthetic.

The atlas might also be a radical visual project that daylights social memory. The histories, structures and policies of systemic racism and their spatial implications in the city are documented and visualized through maps and diagrams to elucidate complexity, stimulate awareness and critical reflection and reconstruct a new social and political ground. As Patty Heyda demonstrates, this kind of forensics is urgent today not only in war-torn zones across the world but also in mundane suburban landscapes, whose relentless banality masks histories of violence and exclusion. New visual and conceptual tools can serve to expose and communicate these hidden histories and institutional mechanisms that have inflicted so much harm. *Radical Atlas of Ferguson, USA* reveals the violence of privatization within the picturesque and the quotidian and its intersections with racism. The atlas illuminates the complicity of the design fields, and opens spaces for recognition, accountability and resistance.

Too often, our creative design fields align uncritically with neoliberal agendas that spatialize and materialize a consensus politics of free-market economics into apolitical formalist projects that camouflage disparity through relentless homogeneity. *Radical Atlas of Ferguson, USA* will be inspired reading for architects, urbanists and planners who seek a different path. And it will be essential reading for those who perpetuate injustice— unwittingly or not—by riding the currents of the status quo, too often carried by flows of global capital that do not accommodate critical proximity.

Teddy Cruz and Fonna Forman
Principals of Estudio Teddy Cruz + Fonna Forman,
a research-based political and architectural practice
San Diego / Tijuana

Introduction

Contradiction as context

1 See Fox Piven, Francis, "Poverty, Inequality and the Shredded Safety Net," in Glen Muschert et al., ed. *Agenda for Social Justice: Solutions* 2012 (Knoxville, TN, The Society for the Study of Social Problems, 2012).

2 These partnerships go farther. They now constitute an entire additional sector of nonpublic—nondemocratic—government run by nonprofit organizations, redevelopment corporations and other quasi-public commissions backed by the region's most powerful institutions and corporations.

3 This is the basis of what sociologist George Lipsitz calls the "white spatial imaginary," an ideology "based on exclusivity and augmented exchange value...(that) makes the augmentation of private property values the central purpose of public associations." (Instead of making, for example, social programs as central public purpose). George Lipsitz, "The Racialization of Space and the Spacialization of Race: Theorizing the Hidden Architecture of Landscape," Landscape Journal 26:1-07, 2007.

In 2019, the Boys & Girls Clubs of Greater St. Louis opened a new Teen Center of Excellence on West Florissant Avenue in Ferguson, Missouri, a first-ring suburb ten miles northwest of St. Louis City. The new building represented $12.4 million of investment in an otherwise car-oriented, asphalt-heavy commercial strip. It was the same strip where eighteen-year-old Michael Brown was spending time with a friend on a sweltering August day in 2014 before he was shot to death some blocks over by Darren Wilson, a white police officer. The strip is also where the greater community came out to protest that murder and the decades of accumulated injustices leading up to it. The Boys & Girls Clubs Teen Center, together with the Urban League's new Ferguson Empowerment Center a few doors down, is indeed proof that community organizing can bring change—or in this case, investment.

The two buildings and their programs were funded by the efforts of local nonprofit organizations and supported by the region's most powerful corporations, banks and institutions. The projects contribute physical and social amenities to an underserved community in dire poverty, a community that has long been racially targeted, on a street long degraded.

Yet despite the improvements, and nearly ten years after the 2014 events, many people in Ferguson and North St. Louis County live in worsening precarity, working multiple jobs with difficult access to transportation. They live in "affordable" housing built in a flood zone separated from other parts of the city. Their kids attend schools that are underfunded and at risk of deaccreditation. The physical environment, apart from the new buildings, is brutal for pedestrians: it is car-centric, starkly fragmented, segregated, and toxic. The air contains dangerous particulate matter that causes asthma and other respiratory problems. The creek and soil nearby are radioactive. So while it is clear that some kids now have access to valuable after-school programs at the Teen Center that they did not have before, it is also clear that those kids return home to a structural socioeconomic situation that has remained largely unchanged for decades. And for every teenager with access to the new resources, there are others nearby who are without them.

The Boys & Girls Clubs Teen Center of Excellence represents the impossible setup for planning in American cities. On the one hand, the new building signals positive, urgently needed investment in physical and social amenities in a disenfranchised community. On the other hand, the very story of the Teen Center's existence, brought into being with the help of the region's wealthiest corporations and most powerful actors, is why it landed in Ferguson as a response to the protests, and also why it may never bring true structural change.

Radical Atlas of Ferguson, USA remaps the city as a political economic construct to understand how and why inequality is structured into the built environment, and how and why such limited improvement persists.

The political economic background

For context, it is useful to understand the capitalist market-based ideology cities have been subject to for more than half a century. This ideology, referred to as "neoliberalism," was championed in the late 1970s, when local governments were stripped of funding for public programs, and projects and services shifted to a reliance on public-private partnerships. These shifts focused public spending on redevelopment systems that built private wealth instead of elevating public welfare.[1] The justification for privatization was that private-sector growth could produce efficient market competition for development that would generate tax revenues, jobs and other spending that "trickles down" to support people.[2] But this model has only compounded public needs, as demonstrated by the built environment immediately surrounding the new Teen Center. In weak-market regions like Ferguson and St. Louis, Missouri, in particular, years of neoliberalism have created policies to lure investment where the market isn't robust enough to support it. This has led to extreme policy steering, as cities align benefits not for the public good but to attract powerful development interests. As austerity and privatization feed the erosion of public services—the environment and institutions meant for all—private investment skyrockets to benefit a limited few.[3] See 0.1.01.

↳

The Boys & Girls Clubs of Greater St. Louis on West Florissant Avenue in Ferguson, Missouri, in context. Photo by Jeff Roberson, Associated Press (July 2019).

0.1.01

A diagrammatic
timeline
highlighting
key U.S. urban
policies over the
last 100 years,
with presidential
administrations,
R: Republican,
in orange; and
D: Democrat, in
blue. The graphic
shows the shift
from federally
sponsored social
programs (in blue)
to public-private
trickle-down
models favoring
business growth
and private wealth
accumulation
(in orange). The
policy shifts are
shown against a
register of income
disparity and
tax rates on the
wealthiest 1% in
the U.S.

Privatization of public policy

Neoliberalism subjects public policy, democratic rights and space to the unaccountable private market. In the U.S., the privatization of federal government programs under this ideology has led to extreme wealth disparity (and racialization and environmental ruin). The timeline demonstrates that both political parties effectively advanced the gutting of public-sector capacity since the 1970s.

This diagram illustrates the political economic context underlying conditions shown in this atlas.

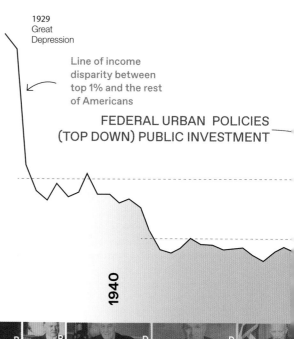

Neoliberal, or market-based,
governance exists at federal, state and
local levels. The resulting situation
means that urban social programs
and services are put into the hands
of private-sector actors to advance.
This has led to intensified, uneven
patterns of racialized exploitation of
urban and suburban space, particularly
in weak-market contexts where
companies still demand returns on
investment. The combination of a
disempowered public-sector and an
undemocratic, private system of city
making is what drives the crisis of the
American city, with amplified impacts
in the first ring.

The striking comparative
index of tax rates on the 1%
and wealth disparities are
adapted from Teddy Cruz,
Fonna Forman (from Saez
and Piketty), *Spatializing
Justice* (Berlin: Hatje Cantz
Verlag and Cambridge: MIT
Press, 2022).

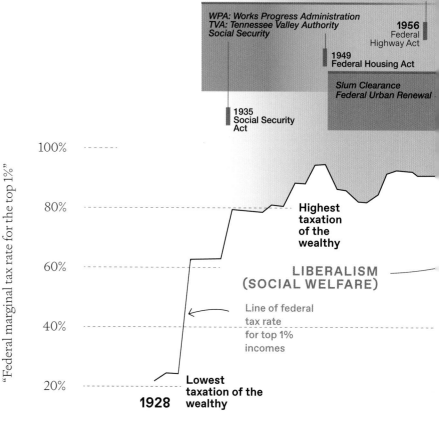

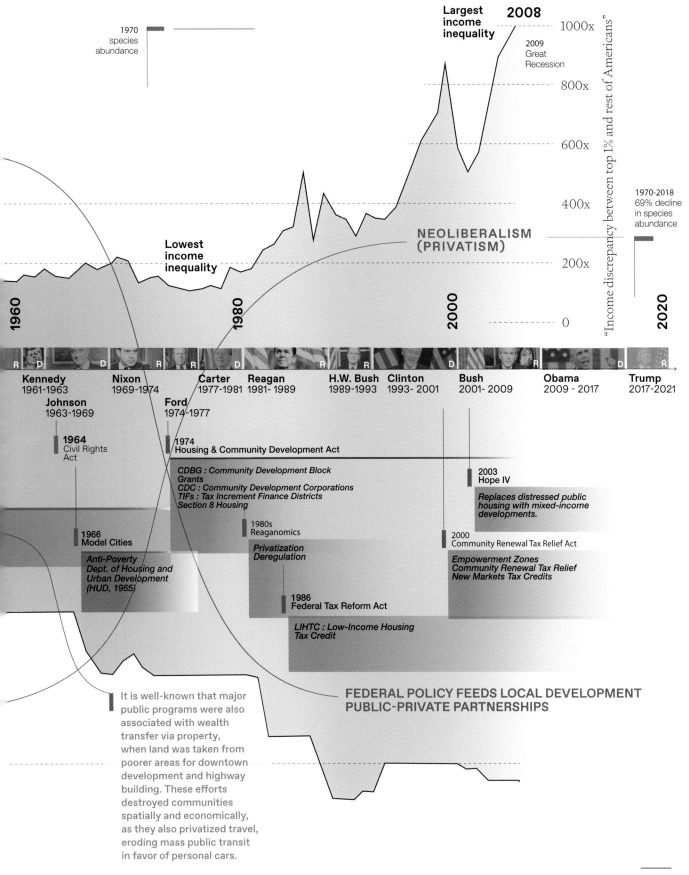

1970 species abundance

Largest income inequality

2008

1000x

2009 Great Recession

800x

600x

NEOLIBERALISM (PRIVATISM)

400x

1970-2018 69% decline in species abundance

Lowest income inequality

200x

0

"Income discrepancy between top 1% and rest of Americans"

1960   1980   2000   2020

R D   D   R R   R D   R   R R   D   R   D   R

Kennedy
1961-1963

Nixon
1969-1974

Carter
1977-1981

Reagan
1981- 1989

H.W. Bush
1989-1993

Clinton
1993- 2001

Bush
2001- 2009

Obama
2009 - 2017

Trump
2017-2021

Johnson
1963-1969

Ford
1974-1977

1964
Civil Rights Act

1974
Housing & Community Development Act

CDBG : Community Development Block Grants
CDC : Community Development Corporations
TIFs : Tax Increment Finance Districts
Section 8 Housing

2003
Hope IV

Replaces distressed public housing with mixed-income developments.

1966
Model Cities

1980s
Reaganomics

2000
Community Renewal Tax Relief Act

Anti-Poverty
Dept. of Housing and Urban Development (HUD, 1965)

Privatization Deregulation

Empowerment Zones
Community Renewal Tax Relief
New Markets Tax Credits

1986
Federal Tax Reform Act

LIHTC : Low-Income Housing Tax Credit

It is well-known that major public programs were also associated with wealth transfer via property, when land was taken from poorer areas for downtown development and highway building. These efforts destroyed communities spatially and economically, as they also privatized travel, eroding mass public transit in favor of personal cars.

FEDERAL POLICY FEEDS LOCAL DEVELOPMENT PUBLIC-PRIVATE PARTNERSHIPS

13

4 Heyda, Patty, "The Façade of Redevelopment," eds. Iver Bernstein, Heidi Kolk, *Common Reader: The Material World of Modern Segregation* Volume 6, No. 1 (St. Louis: Washington University, 2022). See also Brown, Wendy, *Undoing the Demos: Neoliberalism's Stealth Revolution* (New York: Zone Books, 2015).

5 Cruz, Teddy, and Forman, Fonna, *Spatializing Justice: Building Blocks* (Berlin: Hatje Cantz Verlag and Cambridge: MIT Press, 2022).

6 "Accumulation by dispossession" is the state-enabled exploitation and transfer of private land and revenues to private and corporate entities. Coined by Harvey, David, "The New Imperialism: Accumulation by Dispossession," *The Socialist Register*, 2004. "Profiting off of poverty" refers to the state-enabled exploitation of human and civil rights via a system of unjust tickets and fines to make up for revenue shortfalls targeting residents who are Black—while continuing subsidies to corporations. These practices have been called out by many since the Ferguson Uprising in 2014, including by St. Louis legal advocacy firm Arch City Defenders.

Neoliberalism was enshrined during the Reagan administration, but both Democratic and Republican-led administrations have advanced it ever since. The political economic ideology has become so entrenched that many fundamental aspects of social welfare, design and our everyday lives are subjected to market terms and commercialized, even when they shouldn't be.[4] Even more striking is the evidence that shows how this form of capitalism has created the highest level of income inequality in the U.S. since the time of the Great Depression and the New Deal response, arguably the last significant moment of public civic imagination in the U.S.[5] The timeline on the previous page illustrates how the very system that builds wealth for the powerful few in American cities is the same system that perpetuates structural poverty for so many.

Filling out the contours of these politics are ongoing constructions of race and class that play out in profound ways in urban and suburban space, and they are why we should pay attention to places like Ferguson. Instruments of neoliberalism have become state-enabled tools for the racialized exploitation of land and people, to an extreme of reproducing "accumulation by dispossession" and "profits off of poverty."[6] The earlier-built "first-ring" suburbs that are fairly close to downtown—but are now aging and transitioning demographically—are where these politics shape lived space with tensions that the farther suburbs or central business districts (both well aligned by now with white and corporate imaginaries) don't experience in the same way.[7] As the first ring transitions, the logics of individualism and privatization that marked the suburban separation of properties, neighborhoods, and the way people move around in personal cars, have now diminished ideas of public space, public transit, human rights and the city as a just social construct.

While the farther-out, wealthier exurban enclaves maintain the project of suburban segregation, the first ring is compounded by pockets of extreme poverty and multiple forms of resulting predatory policy. Predatory practices range from the police's targeting of residents for revenue via excessive tickets and fines, to lending companies' subprime mortgage schemes—and even erasure—as part of the aggressive refinancialization of declining older suburbs.

The near-urban periphery is the new battleground, as growth machine actors vie for access to cheap land where low- and middle-income communities still live amidst austerity and targeted disinvestment.

Radical Atlas of Ferguson, USA is a cautionary reference book for understanding the spatial and human implications of political economic austerity and privatization, systems that are racialized. It examines conditions of inequality—injustice—that are produced in part by urban planning, and the policies aligned with these vectors. It maps how the varied instruments of market-based city-making reinforce notions of private over public government. The maps reveal how neighborhoods and core institutions are gutted by deliberate economic exploitation or left out of already austere budgets, even as community development projects like the Boys & Girls Clubs building ameliorate localized moments of longer-term structural crisis.[8]

Ferguson in context

The atlas draws on Ferguson, Missouri, a typical first-ring American suburb, for lessons on inherited planning tools that professionals and students may take for granted. But when closely mapped, Ferguson becomes a useful case with which to recast the "suburban problem." After Michael Brown was killed—and then left on the street for four hours—by a white police officer in the low-income community just blocks from a Fortune 500 company, it became clear (to those who did not already live the injustices every day) that additional layers of racial capitalism were entangled with scenes of cookie-cutter houses, strip malls and suburban politics.[9] The bedroom community also emerged as an unexpected center of citizen organizing, social connection and productive public debate. While Ferguson represents every aging first-ring suburb, it is in fact (and perhaps because of that) a timely story of politicized design and investment amidst fragmentation, exploitation, extraction and mobilization.

↳
Kids watch organizers march for social justice on a typical first-ring suburban residential street in Ferguson during the 2014 uprisings. Photo by Charlie Riedel, Associated Press (August 2014).

7 To understand how American urban downtowns have acquiesced, on political and design terms, to corporate imaginaries, see Loukaitau-Sideris, Anastasia and Banerjee, Tridib, "The Corporate Production of Downtown Space," Urban Design Downtown (Berkeley: University of California Press, 1998).

8 This concept is made clear in the work of Piven, Francis Fox, "Poverty, Inequality and the Shredded Safety Net," in Glen Muschert et al., ed. *Agenda for Social Justice: Solutions 2012* (Knoxville, TN, The Society for the Study of Social Problems, 2012).

9 Johnson, Walter, "Ferguson's Fortune 500 Company," *The Atlantic*, April 26, 2015. Accessed May 2016. https://www.theatlantic.com/politics/archive/2015/04/fergusons-fortune-500-company/390492/.

10 U.S. Census, Quickfacts: Ferguson, MO. https://www.census.gov/quickfacts/fergusoncitymissouri; and Census Reporter, Pine Lawn, MO. https://censusreporter.org/profiles/16000US2957800-pine-lawn-mo/.

11 Hudnut, William H. III, *Halfway to Everywhere: A Portrait of America's First-Tier Suburbs* (Washington, D.C.: ULI-the Urban Land Institute, 2004).

12 Mumford, Eric, "National Defense Migration and the Transformations of American Urbanism, 1940–1942," *Journal of Architectural Education*, Volume 61, Issue 3 (January 2008). Accessed July 2023. https://doi.org/10.1111/j.1531-314X.2007.00166.x; Nodjimbadem, Katie, "The Racial Segregation of American Cities Was Anything but Accidental," *Smithsonian Magazine*, May 30, 2017. Accessed July 2023. https://www.smithsonianmag.com/history/how-federal-government-intentionally-racially-segregated-american-cities-180963494/

13 Gordon, Colin, *Mapping Decline: St. Louis and the Fate of the American City* (Philadelphia: University of Pennsylvania Press, 2009). http://mappingdecline.lib.uiowa.edu/map/.). http://mappingdecline.lib.uiowa.edu/map/.

14 Johnson, Walter, "Ferguson's Fortune 500 Company," *The Atlantic*, April 26, 2015. Accessed May 2016. https://www.theatlantic.com/politics/archive/2015/04/fergusons-fortune-500-company/390492/.

Thus, while centered on "Ferguson," the maps and stories in this atlas are about all of North County, and much of the United States. The maps include municipalities surrounding Ferguson that share similar, if starker, situations. Indeed, the 2014 "Ferguson Uprising" happened equally in Dellwood, along the indistinguishable commercial retail strip it shares with Ferguson (the same strip where the Boys and Girls Clubs project is located). But as a reference point, Ferguson is one of the oldest, one of the largest, and one of the relatively more "stable" municipalities in North County. It had a 2021 median household income of $40,195, with 26.4 percent of the population living in poverty, compared to $23,310 in neighboring Pine Lawn, with 45.8 percent of residents in poverty.[10] But like the St. Louis region, Ferguson is a racially and economically divided city despite this aggregate reading of "relative stability." The maps show spatial manifestations of this division in the creek and elevated rail line that slice across the southern part of the city, dividing rich and poor, Black and white populations, single-family homes and multifamily complexes. The uneven production of space is equally apparent, if more extreme, in neighboring Kinloch, Berkeley, and other North County municipalities featured in the atlas.

First-ring suburbs in context

North St. Louis County sits in the northern half of St. Louis County, a highly politically fragmented region with over eighty municipalities. These range from the wealthiest cities in the entire state to the impoverished municipalities that make up North County.

North County exemplifies the quintessential older first-ring suburb that was built at the time of early to mid-twentieth-century suburbanization.[11] Growth outward from dense city centers provided white middle-class workers and veterans access to new housing right outside the city, a project of segregation, national security and industrial expansion that was amplified by the completion of the highways and federal housing programs.[12] Many of these early communities eventually incorporated into municipalities to leverage legal planning mechanisms like single-family residential zoning and other exclusionary tactics to avoid racial integration.

When affordable, multifamily housing—and fair housing rights—finally came to the suburbs in the 1960s and 1970s, efforts were met with major public-sector funding cuts and the shifts to privatization, a conflict with spatial implications that the maps reveal. White suburban residents began leaving, and many parts of North County transitioned from majority white to majority Black neighborhoods, a demographic that is still shifting.[13] As the larger metropolitan area spreads out and the county population grows, the first-ring suburbs have become pockets of shrinkage and disinvestment.

Paradoxically, North County is home to three Fortune 500 companies.[14] Some, like Emerson Electric in Ferguson, and Boeing Industries in neighboring Berkeley, were there since the 1940s and spurred the suburbs' early growth. They were much like company town anchors, with resident workforces living in affordable housing nearby. When demographic, economic and labor changes came about between the 1970s and 1990s, the major corporate campuses became enclaves in their immediate deurbanizing contexts. To shore up their economic base, North County municipalities incentivized industries to stay, and they looked for new industries to attract using various financial "carrots." In extreme—or typical—cases, Ferguson's neighboring municipalities—Kinloch, Berkeley, Bridgeton and Hazelwood—all became targets of corporate capital. This ultimately led to the urban erasure of the Carrollton subdivision in Bridgeton, most of the city of Kinloch, and the Robertson community in Hazelwood. Each was systematically razed and rebuilt as logistics warehouses or infrastructure to serve the nearby airport.[15]

The changes that continue to undergird the spatial production of North St. Louis County are based on many complex, interrelated political economic and spatial processes, which are not limited to racial exclusion. This becomes evident again when we examine the "solutions" to the poverty exacerbated by these processes. Solutions touted as "progress," like the isolated Boys & Girls Clubs Teen Center, the celebrated new Ferguson Starbucks, charter schools, and other privatized models of improvement, all "help" in different ways by effectively maintaining racialized root systems of inequality and corporate power. [16]

Ferguson events in context

This atlas aims to deny simplified narratives of "Ferguson," the 2014 events and the place that have been reduced into stories of poverty and police violence as "symbol[s] of all that must be fixed in Black America."[17] By mapping Ferguson through layers of spatio-political complexity and contradiction, the atlas unravels stories that underline how and why the event and its urban responses came to be, with glimpses of how and why people are so resilient and creative in the face of such systemic oppression.

Ferguson professional and scholarly efforts in context

Since the 2014 events, there have been detailed reports, data collected and academic scholarship that have contextualized and theorized conditions shaping inequality in Ferguson.[18] There have also been organizations on the ground fighting for accountability and justice. These efforts point to and confront structures perpetuating harm. Yet none of these accounts have fully mapped the spatial-material dimensions of those structures for critical design appraisal. If maps themselves are instruments of power, such as we see in the 1937 Home Ownership Loan Corporation (HOLC) Residential Security "redlined" maps that legitimized neighborhood rating systems and land clearances, then the maps of *Radical Atlas of Ferguson, USA* are also instruments of resistance that can render visible the tools and motivations of those wielding power to control access to the city. As a "radical atlas," this book supports existing efforts to challenge the system by reclaiming the politics of the map.

Form, urban design and planning have been used throughout time to advance agendas of power and control. Historians, landscape and urban geographers and others have written extensively about past exclusionary practices in St. Louis, in American planning and the suburbs.[19] The impacts of historic exclusions still reverberate today, and many are included here. But the maps of *Radical Atlas of Ferguson, USA* are mostly situated in the present day (approximately 2014–2024), with the message that injustices are not only legacies of the past but stem from ongoing policies perpetuating the same logics of exclusion. One key difference today is in how exclusionary tactics are harder to see amidst dominant discourses of private interests that mask as public-private collaboration, a point highlighted by

15 Heyda, Patty, "Erasure Urbanism," eds. Esther Choi, Marrikka Trotter, *Architecture is All Over* (New York: Columbia Books on Architecture and the City, 2017).

16 Jan, Tracy, "The Forgotten Ferguson: Four years after Michael Brown was shot by police, the neighborhood where he was killed still feels left behind," *The Washington Post*, June 21, 2018. Accessed March 2021. https://www.washingtonpost.com/graphics/2018/business/is-racial-discrimination-influencing-corporate-investment-in-ferguson/.

17 Parikh, Shanti, and Jong Bum Kwon, "Introduction: Still here in the afterlives," *American Ethnologist*, Volume 47, No. 2, May 2020.

18 Historian Walter Johnson's seminal *Broken Heart of America* (Basic Books, 2020) and "Ferguson's Fortune 500 Company" (*The Atlantic*, 2015) inspired a number of the maps in the atlas, particularly in the "Politics: Power" section. Scholarly work on Ferguson by Jodi Rios, Colin Gordon, Richard Rothstein, Kimberly Norwood, Clarissa Hayward, Shanti Parikh and Jong Bum Kwon, and Thomas Harvey and Brendan Roediger has all been foundational to this book.

David Harvey, among others.[20] Some of the hidden modalities of this discourse include the civic, nonprofit and philanthropic organizations that promise to supplement government deficiencies with strategic projects like the Boys & Girls Clubs building. They also include the corporate-backed think tanks that steer public debate with well-funded campaigns and spin. The book maps the contemporary reproduction of structural violence while literally making visible these entangled spaces of hidden private influence.

Engagements

Radical Atlas of Ferguson, USA samples the interconnected structures shaping contemporary North St. Louis County to start conversations about what a radically realigned set of priorities for American first-ring suburbs might look like. Through the lens of the Boys & Girls Clubs building and other interventions, the atlas offers a window into the ways planners, policymakers and designers have become complicit in the reproduction of inequality, captured by the public-private project. The atlas models critical ways to reconceptualize "site specificity" for design, based on political realities undermining sites, to help the professions rethink—reposition— their relationship to systems of race and power. Designers, for example, may gain community trust if they acknowledge the uneven power structure that undergirds and even maintains low community capacity that residents experience. For civic leaders, the atlas provokes a critical reconsideration of the inherited neoliberal framework still guiding public policy and advancing the project of segregation and privatization. For those residents and others engaged in bringing meaningful transformation, the drawings provide spatial evidence of complexities they already know and what they struggle to change: that the city-suburb has been shaped this way for a reason.

Organization of the book

The maps in the atlas are organized so that each focuses on a discrete feature of neoliberal planning and design. These features are often policy and design instruments, but they also include practices and attitudes that shape lived conditions elaborated in the drawings. The map scales and locations vary in order to best depict the topic being examined, depending on where patterns are most pronounced. The "Atlas Guide" orients the reader to the exact frame, scale and location in the region of each map.

The maps exist in four primary scales and frames. These are:

- 1 inch=20,000 feet, showing the region with St. Louis County and St. Louis City;
- 1 inch=10,000 feet, showing the entire North St. Louis County area;
- 1 inch=5,000 feet, showing selected clusters of North St. Louis County municipalities in relation to each other; and
- 1=2,500 feet, or similar scales that show close-up views of Ferguson or neighboring municipalities like Berkeley, Kinloch, Bel-Ridge or Calverton Park and others.

There are also charts and other graphics that depart from strict scales to elaborate particularities of impacts on people or places. Quotes and citations are included with each map, but note that all sources, including for the call-out statistics and other references, are listed, by chapter and map number, in the "Sources" section at the end of the book.

19 Including, but not limited to, Gordon, Colin, Mapping Decline: St. Louis and the Fate of the American City (Philadelphia: University of Pennsylvania Press, 2009) and Rothstein, Richard, Color of Law (New York: Liveright, 2017) and others. See also, for example, the seminal work on suburbs, politics, meaning and form by designers/design historians Margaret Crawford, Delores Hayden, Peter Rowe, John Stilgoe, Jacqueline Tatom, and others.

20 Harvey, David, *A Brief History of Neoliberalism* (Oxford: Oxford University Press, 2011).

21 Johnson, Walter, *The Broken Heart of America: St. Louis and the Violent History of the United States* (New York, Basic Books, 2020).

22 Interboro, *The Arsenal of Exclusion and Inclusion* (New York and Barcelona: Actar Publishers, 2017).

The maps sample a wide cross-section of topics in order to show the reach of privatization and austerity, but they are organized into five overarching chapters: Territory, Space, Opportunity, Politics, and Justice. Each chapter includes sections made up of further-grouped sets of related maps. In some cases, a "Mobilize" set of maps appears at the end of the chapter to highlight policies already in place with promise of furthering a more just city. The chapters and their sections are described below:

01 Territory—*Contestation* —*Separation*
This chapter briefly contextualizes St. Louis in Missouri, and in the larger U.S. geographical and historical context. The maps cover the widest range of scales and time frames, from continent to community. The first section, titled "Contestation," situates Missouri as a battleground state dating back to the time of the nation's violent growth, something historian Walter Johnson elaborates through the frame of racial capitalism.[21] Missouri holds a lucrative position as a transition zone in the U.S., where major divergent ecological conditions and political positions converge. The maps introduce early colonialist expansion in this context. Still today, Missouri occupies a contested "both/and" position. It exemplifies the politically "red" state of right-wing conservatism framed by "blue," quasi-progressive urban metro regions.

The next section, "Separation," chronicles various strategies of historical and contemporary boundary making. Both contestation and separation have shaped access to new territories for capital accumulation at different scales over time, in ways that reinforce constructions of race and power. Many of the themes and maps in this first section of the book are historical in nature. These are important because they resurface in later maps that show current expressions of colonialism and extraction.

02 Space
This chapter delves into scales of municipal and homeowner association-led exclusions that further the projects of wealth hoarding and racial segregation. Mechanisms like single-use zoning and minimum lot sizes exist in every American city, and how they exclude or include depends on who has access to them.[22] But they remain particularly legible in the first-ring context.

The chapter then traverses the material world of neoliberal efficiency and "convenience" in the already strained weak market. The maps show the violence of suburban codes, franchise models and commercial public realms dictated by development metrics that pit returns over the environment. These spaces are degraded by parking minimums, the lack of robust transit, and the unshaded expanses of asphalt and discontinuous sidewalks.

03 Opportunity—*Property*—*Education*
This chapter speaks to the common urban and suburban policies that maintain access to life opportunities for some and not others.[23] The maps here further the themes in the Space chapter to highlight systems that provide or prevent access to land as access to opportunity.[24] The "Property" section delves into the ways housing and property have been financialized so that people no longer think of them as basic rights but as instruments of investment—opportunities to build wealth. The maps show who controls access to these opportunities. The maps point to institutions involved in the profit markets of homeownership and rental units, like lending institutions then and now, or landlords who actually dictate where Section 8 renters have a supposed "choice" in where to live. The property crime

map in this series calls out contradictions in the kinds of available data that reproduce narratives about financial risk in minority spaces. Urban data is, like policy, an instrument often mobilized to control spatial reproduction. In this case, the crime map intentionally pits physical property crime against the property crimes enabled by the subprime mortgage-lending violations of the last decade, crimes that effectively reproduced conditions of housing instability in North County.

The next section looks at access to opportunity through education, which, because of how public-school funding sources rely on local property tax, is an extension of access to property, which is shown in the preceding set of maps. Education funding in low-income, low-land-value areas is further bound by state austerity measures, causing a host of complications. The neoliberal "solutions" only make things harder for those trying to access education. One of these "solutions" is the charter school movement that, until very recently, was limited in Missouri to St. Louis City and Kansas City, though as of 2022, has infiltrated the county. Charter schools represent both the fallout of neoliberal funding cuts to public services and the creep of corporate ideology and influence into core public institutions, marketed as choices for families in otherwise underfunded districts.

The maps touch on other education dynamics like state deaccreditation processes and the inter-district transfer options offered to students in affected districts. These protocols are presented as objective solutions but are, in fact, interrelated political—politicized—tools.[25] When deaccreditation facilitates a state takeover of school boards, the process, like with charter schools, plugs in unaccountable, unelected, outside leadership that has no obligation to respond to the community.[26] At the end of this chapter, we return to the Ferguson Boys & Girls Clubs Teen Center to understand empowerment centers that concentrate in North St. Louis County. "Empowerment" comes in the form of nonprofit institutions supported by corporations to supplement the gutted public schools, a situation caused in large part by the corporate privatization of the public sector to begin with.

04 Politics—*Government—Development—Power*
The first section of the Politics chapter, "Government," provides context on what public-sector leadership in Ferguson and the St. Louis region looks like. Apart from the fact that the City of St. Louis is itself a separate entity from St. Louis County, the maps show how fragmented the entire St. Louis Metropolitan Statistical Area (MSA) is. It ranks fifth for the most governments in the United States. That means it has over 1,000 total "general and special-purpose units of government" (2012).[27] Those units include municipalities but also special districts, like school and fire districts. This is compared to the peer average of 380 separate governments within a typical MSA.[28] Maps show how governments are categorized and who really has administrative power in the weak-mayor form of government in Ferguson.

"Development" maps the kinds of public financial incentives neoliberal governments make available in their tool kit, most of which predictably subsidize local private development to build "regional growth."[29] It may be no surprise to see that the deciding public boards and commissions behind these incentives are stacked with appointed people from the

23 Lipsitz describes access to opportunity in context of the white spatial imaginary construct that "functions as a central mechanism for skewing opportunities and life chances in the United States along racial lines." George Lipsitz, "The Racialization of Space and the Spacialization of Race: Theorizing the Hidden Architecture of Landscape," *Landscape Journal* 26:1-07, 2007, p. 13.

24 The maps advance "geography of opportunity" discourse by focusing on the particular private instruments that maintain spatial inequality and access to opportunity for low-income communities. Other maps in the Mobilizing series of the atlas highlight important local institutions, mapping what Terrance Green calls "opportunity in geography . . . not only places of inequality but places of possibility." Green, Terrance L., "Places of Inequality, Places of Possibility: Mapping 'Opportunities in Geography' Across Urban School-Communities," *The Urban Review* Volume 47, Number 2 (November 2015). Accessed February 2022. https://doi.org/10.1007/s11256-015-0331-z.

25 Robertson, Brett, in conversation with the author, July 14, 2023.

region's leading corporations and nonprofit organizations (in this case, the graphic depicts development boards of St. Louis City). The maps show aspects of "government" that are hardly democratic. Additional graphics excavate the boards of the region's leading nonprofit organizations that are part of the privatized system of "support" for urban projects and services.

The "Development" section then follows with a longitudinal case study of erasure suburbanism in Kinloch, Missouri, on Ferguson's west side, and the communities of Robertson and Carrollton, in Hazelwood and Bridgeton, Missouri, respectively, on the other side of the St. Louis Lambert International Airport from Kinloch.[30] The case highlights years of airport-related redevelopment policy that has been pitched in terms of "revitalization" for Kinloch and Robertson, two long-neglected historic African American communities.[31] The maps read as colonialism 2.0: suburban space, where Black residents have lived and thrived, is destabilized, then reterritorialized through state-enabled "revitalizations" that bring entirely new infrastructures (irrelevant to residential living) and massive distribution warehouses. The warehouses accumulate capital that flows outward, disconnected from the towns in which they sit.[32] Meanwhile, to the airport's southwest, another unlikely but associated suburban erasure has played out. This time, Carrollton, a largely white middle-class subdivision— arguably the very model of financialized suburban single-family life—is erased under the same processes of economic recolonization.

The last section in the Politics chapter is "Power." These maps elaborate the influence of major companies in North County and the region. The chapter opens with a map of the concentrated corporate wealth in North County's space of concentrated poverty. We see in more detail how the three major Fortune 500 companies in Ferguson and vicinity accumulate capital through low taxation, major incentive programs and other legal loopholes; capital that is diverted revenue from public schools and other gutted services.[33] There are rhetorical claims that the subsidized initiatives of these and other new industries like those in Kinloch will bring jobs. But many of the jobs are managerial or require advanced training (i.e., they are based on the kinds of educational opportunities that have been difficult for most people here to access). If anything, local communities are left with the environmental consequences of having industry in their backyard, if they still have homes and backyards at all.

05 Justice—*Liberty—Health—Environment*
In the Justice chapter, the ultimate toll of social, human and environmental extraction is shown in sections that cover liberty, health and environment. The "Liberty" section speaks to the excessive and racialized policing and issuing of tickets and fines by police in North County municipalities trying to make up revenue shortfalls. This section includes maps of the lived experience of two women trapped in this system, Nicole and Jocelyn, who were each jailed for absurd amounts of time and charged exorbitant fees to be freed, after infractions that were not their fault. While there have been improvements to these practices thanks to the work of advocates on the

26 When parents and schools resist accepting state-mandated transfer students from unaccredited districts, those districts regain accreditation without substantial evidence of having changed. This practice calls into question the initial decisions and exact metrics that are used to deaccredit districts in the first place. See also, Tate, William F., Christopher Hamilton, William Brett Robertson, et al., "Who is my Neighbor? Turner v. Clayton: A Watershed Moment in Regional Education," *The Journal of Negro Education*, Volume 83 No. 3, Summer, 2014. Accessed July 14, 2023. https://doi.org/10.7709/jnegroeducation.83.3.0216.

27 East-West Gateway Council of Governments, "Where We Stand," 8th Edition Report, 2018. Accessed July 2023. https://www.ewgateway.org/research-center/where-we-stand/.

28 Ibid.

29 There will always be missing maps and additional layers that could be included in each set, and transit policy is one of these. See the Mobilizing series. While the suburbs are notorious for lacking robust systems of public transportation, there are viable proposals for bus rapid transit or light rail expansion to parts of North County, and those should be supported and nurtured.

30 Maps in the case study draw from, and then expand upon and update, concepts introduced in Patty Heyda, "Erasure Urbanism," eds. Esther Choi, Marrikka Trotter, *Architecture is All Over*, (New York: Columbia Books on Architecture and the City, 2017). The atlas pulls out a distinction unremarked in the original *Erasure Urbanism* work that described erasure urbanism as "a mainstream mechanism that disrupts architectural notions of site as a physical space and draws our attention to notions of site as a processual locus of law and power," but that left out the critical fact that erasure preys on the aging, transitioning first ring where instability sets the conditions for an uneven power grab—and where these investments can still be labeled "revitalization."

31 Cloud, Kristen, "Schnucks Building New DC In Kinloch, Missouri," *The Shelby Report*, May 28, 2015. Accessed December 2022. https://www.theshelbyreport.com/2015/05/28/schnucks-building-new-dc-in-kinloch-missouri/.

32 Heyda, Patty, "Food Desert: Feeding the Regional Imaginary," *Journal of Architectural Education* Volume 77:2, October 2023.

33 This juxtaposition was brought to light very clearly in Walter Johnson, "Ferguson's Fortune 500 Company," *The Atlantic*, April 26, 2015. Accessed May 2016. https://www.theatlantic.com/politics/archive/2015/04/fergusons-fortune-500-company/390492/.

34 Kite, Allison, "Records reveal 75 years of government downplaying, ignoring risks of St. Louis radioactive waste," *Missouri Independent*, July 12, 2023. Accessed July 2023. https://missouriindependent.com/2023/07/12/st-louis-radioactive-waste-records/.

35 Kutik, William M., "Mallinckrodt Gift Funds Six Chairs," *Harvard Crimson*, March 16, 1968. Accessed July 2023. https://www.thecrimson.com/article/1968/3/16/mallinckrodt-gift-funds-six-chairs-ppresident/.

36 Neil Brenner, ed. *Implosions / Explosions: Towards a Study of Planetary Urbanization*, (Berlin: jovis Verlag, 2014).

ground, many aspects of the predatory profit-based criminal justice system are still complicating life for many. The atlas does not begin to cover all the dimensions of this complex topic, but it aims to show how far basic civil rights have been eroded in the first-ring suburb and how systems of extraction and exploitation have been filling the void.

The second section in this chapter is "Health." The maps here paint a regional picture of the disparities in health and life expectancy between North St. Louis County and other parts of the region. These are disparities we have seen before, but they point to people's low access to health insurance, a largely privatized system, and their low access to healthy food, a situation complicated by hot commercial first-ring corridors with little public transit and dangerous pedestrian conditions.

The "Environment" section links health to the role of land uses that allow industrial pollution and emissions-laden highways near communities. Maps point to neoliberalism's underlying deregulation by representing the connections between compromised water quality and destructive river policies that promote incompatible commercial priorities. Tied to deregulation, there is also the story of the St. Louis-based Mallinckrodt Chemical Company that, between the 1940s and 1970s, spent decades illegally dumping radioactive uranium waste just west of Ferguson in North St. Louis County by the airport. Those crimes have contaminated air and water over at least a seven-mile radius, elevating cancer rates among people who grew up there and compromising entire ecosystems of plant, human and animal life. Establishing accountability for the cleanup has taken decades, largely because of the public-private charade that characterized, as it clouded, the actions of a private company in service of a government-sponsored project (the Manhattan Project of wartime uranium production). As the Mallinckrodt Company is let off the hook for its cleanup and other ethical violations,[34] its nonprofit foundation paradoxically funds a radiation center in its name at St. Louis's Barnes Jewish Hospital, among other philanthropic gestures near and far.[35] The company still maintains access to loopholes that allow them to evade crucially needed taxes by moving their headquarters overseas. With these stories, the maps point again to economic and ethical spatial dislocations between company and town enabled by contemporary neoliberal power regimes. The conditions illustrate an inversion of what Neil Brenner describes as "explosion/implosion" between cities as financial centers and the extractive, collapsing hinterlands that feed them. Here, the global headquarters are miles away, benefiting from exploitation, breakdown and contamination that remain hyper-local.[36]

The "Environment" section concludes with regional maps on current energy policy, since in St. Louis, the electric utility, too, is a quasi-public-private construct. The maps show how the investor-owned Ameren Electric company has no financial incentive to lower profits and transition to renewable energy, despite high rates of childhood asthma from its coal-burning plants, and despite the grave costs of global heating the fossil industry fuels worldwide. As Ameren dangerously delays energy transition, its charitable trust is a major donor to community programs across the region.

Grounding

Radical Atlas of Ferguson, USA only scratches the surface of these complicated issues of place and power. To bring some of the sites of the maps to life, and to break up the serial 10,000-foot views, there are photos interspersed between maps. These bring us to the ground at human and building scale to spotlight contested spaces with qualitative views of political economic contradiction—or to highlight small but important moments of resistance from within the system.

Mobilizing

Radical Atlas of Ferguson, USA is a book that urges readers to consider questions of accountability and agency in light of the powerful forces of capital that complicate the production of public and private space. It points to what sociologist Francis Fox Piven calls the "fight to reclaim a moral economy."[37] As a way to start this conversation, the Mobilize series of maps at the end of each chapter highlight policies already in place, or that could be prioritized, that model a vision of public capacity. These include common sense ideas that could change the rules of government spending and help people, such as bringing public transit to North County. Or, they show more immediately available subversions that communities have pulled off within the rules, such as the creation of an official historic district by Kinloch leaders in the face of erasure. These maps highlight instruments that could and should be nurtured and amplified.

In the spirit of abolitionism and design thinking, *Radical Atlas of Ferguson, USA* ultimately urges urban planning and design to push for political economic systems that are socially democratic, truly public, and well-funded free of private influence. Is it possible to mobilize a lucid design politics that confronts difficult public-private realities, to critically rethink the making of social, human and environmental rights for all? Given the compounding ecosocial crises exemplified by extremes in the first-ring suburb (and increasingly bearing down everywhere), we have no choice but to engage in this radical reimagination. Beyond buildings and blocks alone, the necessary territory for engagement is social and processual, political and politicized. *Radical Atlas of Ferguson, USA* reframes, as it remaps, the root structures below as the terrain ahead. As activists said, *Ferguson is everywhere.*

37 Piven, Francis Fox, "Poverty, Inequality and the Shredded Safety Net," in Glen Muschert et al., ed. *Agenda for Social Justice: Solutions 2012* (Knoxville, TN, The Society for the Study of Social Problems, 2012), p. 84.

0.1.02

A timeline of St. Louis City and County's political history, situating the region's population growth and decline (and relative leveling) alongside major economic and world events. The relationships highlight correlations between periods of national civil rights gains; population redistributions from city to county; public programs; and related efforts of private nonprofit organizations.

The bottom of the chart shows the same topics in the context of St. Louis, including the many private-led initiatives and reports produced to influence policy.

"Mobilization" meanwhile reflects various efforts of those who have advocated for justice within or against current systems.

↳

Neil Brenner reminds us that conceptualizations of the urban in terms of population growth alone are limited and misleading, since they don't account for the destructive processes of urbanism farther afield, like resource extraction, labor exploitation, and disinvestments elsewhere. 1 The first-ring suburb fits into that wider conceptualization, even as it grows, transitions, or stagnates,

1 Neil Brenner, ed. Implosions/Explosions: Towards a Study of Planetary Urbanization, (Berlin: jovis Verlag, 2014).

Timeline: Civil rights & policy reactions 1820-1960

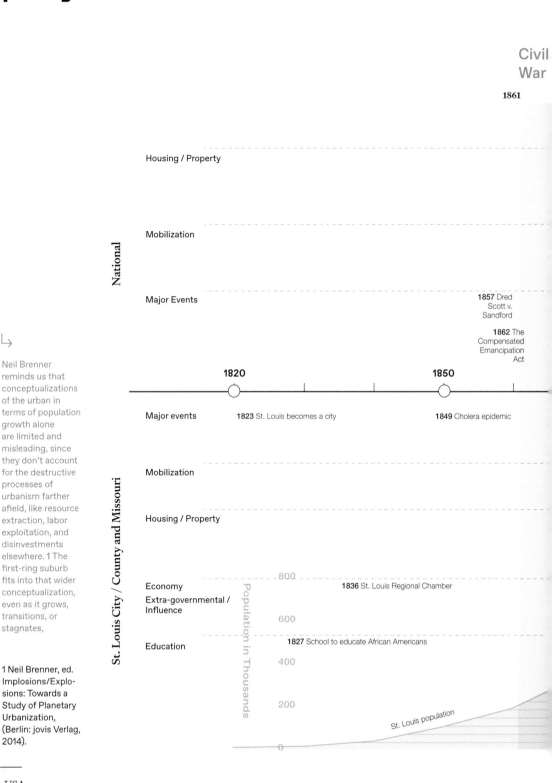

Civil War

1861

Housing / Property

Mobilization

National

Major Events
1857 Dred Scott v. Sandford
1862 The Compensated Emancipation Act

1820 ○   1850 ○

Major events   1823 St. Louis becomes a city   1849 Cholera epidemic

Mobilization

Housing / Property

St. Louis City / County and Missouri

Economy
Extra-governmental / Influence   **1836** St. Louis Regional Chamber

Education   **1827** School to educate African Americans

Population in Thousands
800
600
400
200
0

St. Louis population

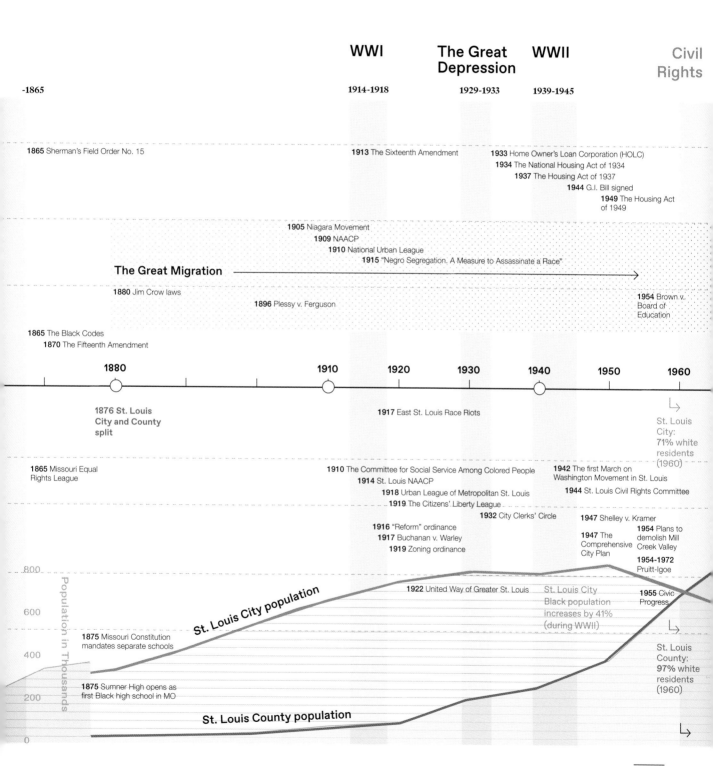

WWI

The Great
Depression

WWII

Civil
Rights

-1865

1914-1918

1929-1933

1939-1945

1865 Sherman's Field Order No. 15

1913 The Sixteenth Amendment

1933 Home Owner's Loan Corporation (HOLC)
1934 The National Housing Act of 1934
1937 The Housing Act of 1937
1944 G.I. Bill signed
1949 The Housing Act of 1949

1905 Niagara Movement
1909 NAACP
1910 National Urban League
1915 "Negro Segregation. A Measure to Assassinate a Race"

The Great Migration ⟶

1880 Jim Crow laws

1896 Plessy v. Ferguson

1954 Brown v. Board of Education

1865 The Black Codes
1870 The Fifteenth Amendment

1880   **1910**   1920   1930   1940   1950   1960

1876 St. Louis City and County split

1917 East St. Louis Race Riots

St. Louis City: 71% white residents (1960)

1865 Missouri Equal Rights League

1910 The Committee for Social Service Among Colored People
1914 St. Louis NAACP
1918 Urban League of Metropolitan St. Louis
1919 The Citizens' Liberty League
1932 City Clerks' Circle

1942 The first March on Washington Movement in St. Louis
1944 St. Louis Civil Rights Committee

1916 "Reform" ordinance
1917 Buchanan v. Warley
1919 Zoning ordinance

1947 Shelley v. Kramer
1947 The Comprehensive City Plan

1954 Plans to demolish Mill Creek Valley
1954-1972 Pruitt-Igoe

800

Population in Thousands

St. Louis City population

1922 United Way of Greater St. Louis

St. Louis City Black population increases by 41% (during WWII)

1955 Civic Progress

600

1875 Missouri Constitution mandates separate schools

St. Louis County: 97% white residents (1960)

400

1875 Sumner High opens as first Black high school in MO

200

St. Louis County population

0

25

0.1.03

Timeline 1960-
2020: Civil rights
gains & reactive
policy protecting
access to wealth
and power.

Civil rights &
policy reactions 1960-2020

Civil
Rights

The Great
Economic
Recession

2008-2010

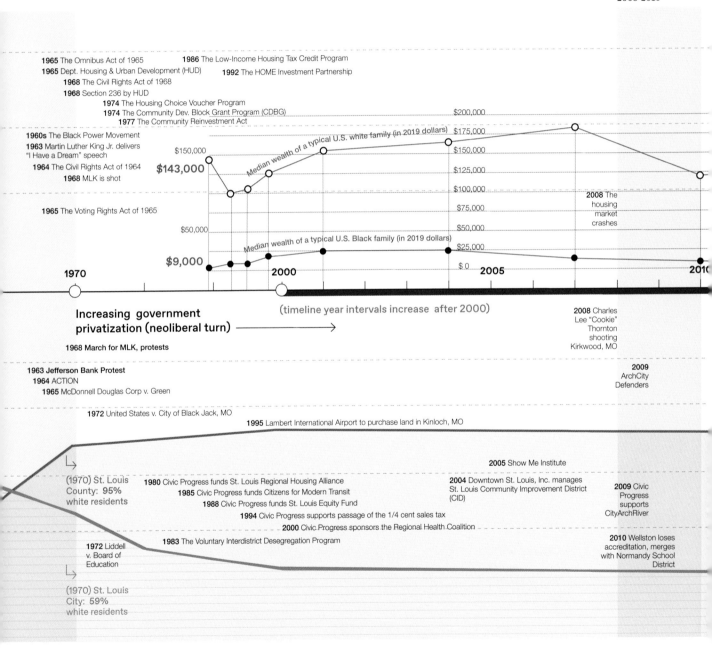

1965 The Omnibus Act of 1965
1965 Dept. Housing & Urban Development (HUD)
1968 The Civil Rights Act of 1968
1968 Section 236 by HUD
1974 The Housing Choice Voucher Program
1974 The Community Dev. Block Grant Program (CDBG)
1977 The Community Reinvestment Act

1986 The Low-Income Housing Tax Credit Program
1992 The HOME Investment Partnership

1960s The Black Power Movement
1963 Martin Luther King Jr. delivers
"I Have a Dream" speech
1964 The Civil Rights Act of 1964
1968 MLK is shot

1965 The Voting Rights Act of 1965

$200,000

Median wealth of a typical U.S. white family (in 2019 dollars) $175,000

$150,000

$150,000 $125,000

$143,000 $100,000

$75,000

$50,000 $50,000

Median wealth of a typical U.S. Black family (in 2019 dollars) $25,000

$9,000 $0

1970 **2000** **2005** **2010**

2008 The
housing
market
crashes

**Increasing government
privatization (neoliberal turn)** ⟶

(timeline year intervals increase after 2000)

2008 Charles
Lee "Cookie"
Thornton
shooting
Kirkwood, MO

1968 March for MLK, protests

1963 Jefferson Bank Protest
1964 ACTION
1965 McDonnell Douglas Corp v. Green

2009
ArchCity
Defenders

1972 United States v. City of Black Jack, MO

1995 Lambert International Airport to purchase land in Kinloch, MO

2005 Show Me Institute

**(1970) St. Louis
County: 95%
white residents**

1980 Civic Progress funds St. Louis Regional Housing Alliance
1985 Civic Progress funds Citizens for Modern Transit
1988 Civic Progress funds St. Louis Equity Fund
1994 Civic Progress supports passage of the 1/4 cent sales tax
2000 Civic Progress sponsors the Regional Health Coalition

2004 Downtown St. Louis, Inc. manages
St. Louis Community Improvement District
(CID)

2009 Civic
Progress
supports
CityArchRiver

1972 Liddell
v. Board of
Education

1983 The Voluntary Interdistrict Desegregation Program

2010 Wellston loses
accreditation, merges
with Normandy School
District

**(1970) St. Louis
City: 59%
white residents**

Do we measure
progress as justice or
growth?

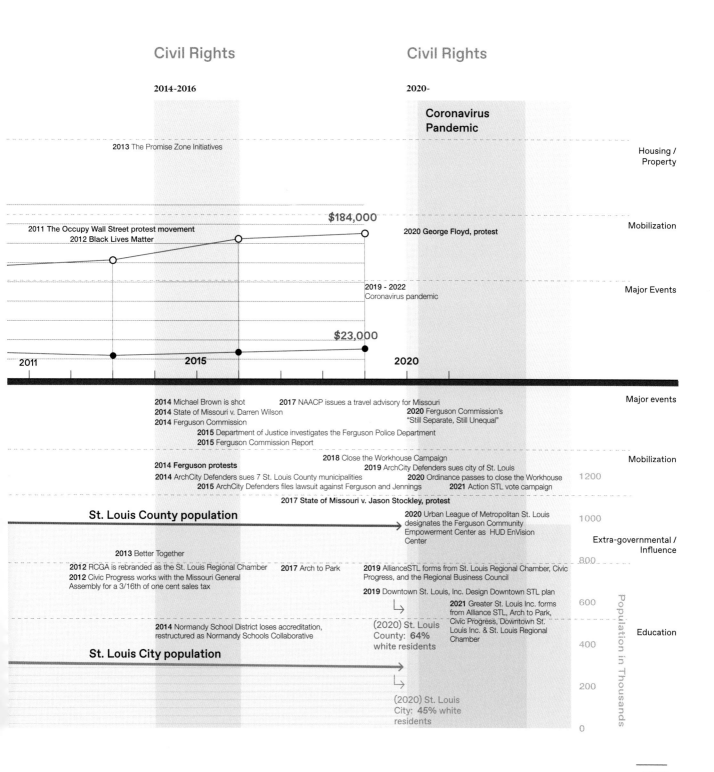

Civil Rights

2014-2016

Civil Rights

2020-

**Coronavirus
Pandemic**

2013 The Promise Zone Initiatives

Housing /
Property

$184,000

2011 The Occupy Wall Street protest movement
2012 Black Lives Matter

2020 George Floyd, protest

Mobilization

2019 - 2022
Coronavirus pandemic

Major Events

$23,000

2011   2015   2020

Major events

2014 Michael Brown is shot   2017 NAACP issues a travel advisory for Missouri   2020 Ferguson Commission's
2014 State of Missouri v. Darren Wilson   "Still Separate, Still Unequal"
2014 Ferguson Commission
          2015 Department of Justice investigates the Ferguson Police Department
          2015 Ferguson Commission Report

2014 Ferguson protests   2018 Close the Workhouse Campaign   Mobilization
2014 ArchCity Defenders sues 7 St. Louis County municipalities   2019 ArchCity Defenders sues city of St. Louis
          2015 ArchCity Defenders files lawsuit against Ferguson and Jennings   2020 Ordinance passes to close the Workhouse
                                                                                 2021 Action STL vote campaign
1200

2017 State of Missouri v. Jason Stockley, protest

St. Louis County population
2020 Urban League of Metropolitan St. Louis
designates the Ferguson Community
Empowerment Center as HUD EnVision
Center

1000

Extra-governmental /
Influence

2013 Better Together

800

2012 RCGA is rebranded as the St. Louis Regional Chamber   2017 Arch to Park   2019 AllianceSTL forms from St. Louis Regional Chamber, Civic
2012 Civic Progress works with the Missouri General   Progress, and the Regional Business Council
Assembly for a 3/16th of one cent sales tax
                                                             2019 Downtown St. Louis, Inc. Design Downtown STL plan
                                                                                     2021 Greater St. Louis Inc. forms   600
                                                                                     from Alliance STL, Arch to Park,
2014 Normandy School District loses accreditation,   (2020) St. Louis   Civic Progress, Downtown St.
restructured as Normandy Schools Collaborative   County: 64%   Louis Inc. & St. Louis Regional   Education
                                                            white residents   Chamber   400

St. Louis City population

200

(2020) St. Louis
City: 45% white
residents

0

Population in Thousands

27

0.1.04

Key to the maps
in the atlas
according to scale
and area featured.

Atlas guide

Broader region MSA
4.1.01

St. Louis County
and City region
1" = 20,000 ft

1.1.03	
1.2.04	
1.2.07	
3.1.01	
3.1.04	
3.1.05	
3.1.07	
3.1.08	
3.1.10	
3.2.12	
3.2.13	
3.2.16	
3.2.17	
3.M.01	
3.M.03	
4.1.07	
4.2.09	
4.2.10	5.1.02
4.3.20	5.1.08
4.3.28	5.2.09
4.3.29	5.2.10
4.3.30	5.3.12
4.3.31	5.3.14
4.3.32	5.3.15
4.3.33	5.M.01
4.M.02	5.M.02
4.M.03	5.M.04

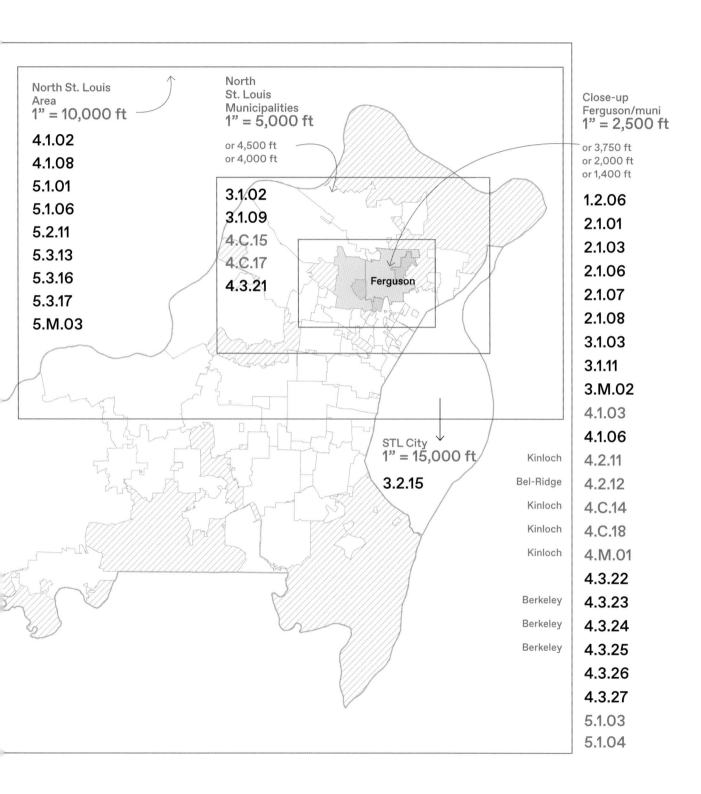

North St. Louis
Area
1" = 10,000 ft

4.1.02
4.1.08
5.1.01
5.1.06
5.2.11
5.3.13
5.3.16
5.3.17
5.M.03

North
St. Louis
Municipalities
1" = 5,000 ft

or 4,500 ft
or 4,000 ft

3.1.02
3.1.09
4.C.15
4.C.17
4.3.21

Ferguson

Close-up
Ferguson/muni
1" = 2,500 ft

or 3,750 ft
or 2,000 ft
or 1,400 ft

1.2.06
2.1.01
2.1.03
2.1.06
2.1.07
2.1.08
3.1.03
3.1.11
3.M.02
4.1.03
4.1.06
Kinloch   4.2.11
Bel-Ridge   4.2.12
Kinloch   4.C.14
Kinloch   4.C.18
Kinloch   4.M.01
             4.3.22
Berkeley   4.3.23
Berkeley   4.3.24
Berkeley   4.3.25
             4.3.26
             4.3.27
             5.1.03
             5.1.04

STL City
1" = 15,000 ft

3.2.15

01
Territory

Situating contestation and separation

The maps in this chapter cover the widest range of scales and time frames, from continent to community.

The first section, *Contestation*, situates Missouri in the wider context of the United States through the lenses of confluence and contradiction. The following section, *Separation*, chronicles various strategies and scales of historical and contemporary boundary making.

Both *contestation* and *separation* have shaped access to territories for capital accumulation at different scales over time, in ways that reinforce constructions of race and power.

1.1.01

Map of the United
States showing
the location of
St. Louis and
Missouri at the
confluence of
several national
scaled natural
systems and
transition points.
The rivers
are depicted
according to
average flows, and
the Mississippi
River watershed
outlined in
orange.1

Confluence

The St. Louis
region lies at the
confluence of
two major river
systems in the
United States. It is
where continental
ecological
conditions meet
and overlap; and
it was historically
the north-south
point at which the
Mississippi River
froze in winter.
Because of these
confluences, the
city became a
transfer point for
river to land/rail
commerce. As
'gateway to the West'
the city's unique
location facilitated a
multi-modal project
of profiteering off of
the region's specific
geography and
natural resources
during the earlier
periods of American
history.

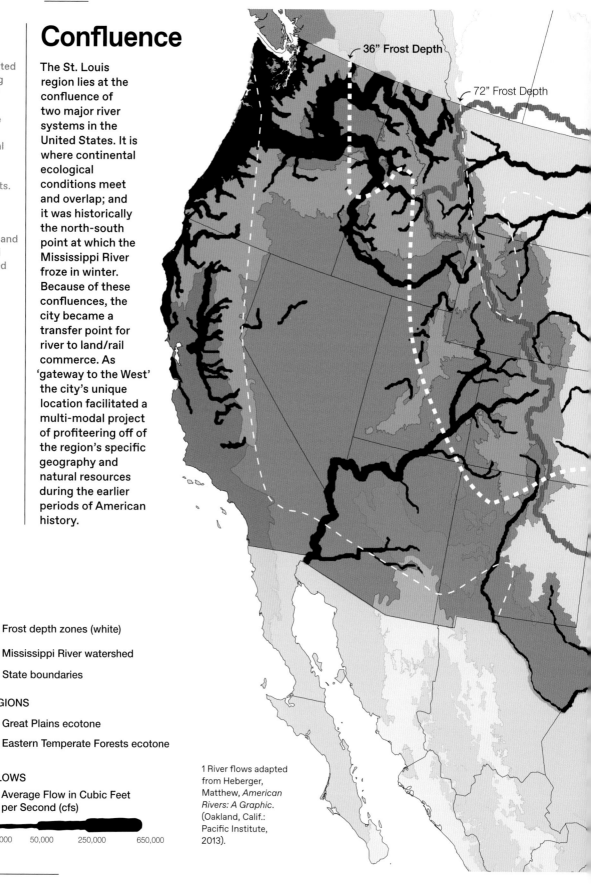

36" Frost Depth

72" Frost Depth

- - -   Frost depth zones (white)

▦▦▦▦   Mississippi River watershed

———   State boundaries

ECO-REGIONS

☐   Great Plains ecotone

■   Eastern Temperate Forests ecotone

RIVER FLOWS

Average Flow in Cubic Feet
per Second (cfs)

2,500   10,000   50,000   250,000   650,000

1 River flows adapted
from Heberger,
Matthew, *American
Rivers: A Graphic.*
(Oakland, Calif.:
Pacific Institute,
2013).

See also   3.1.03   5.3.14

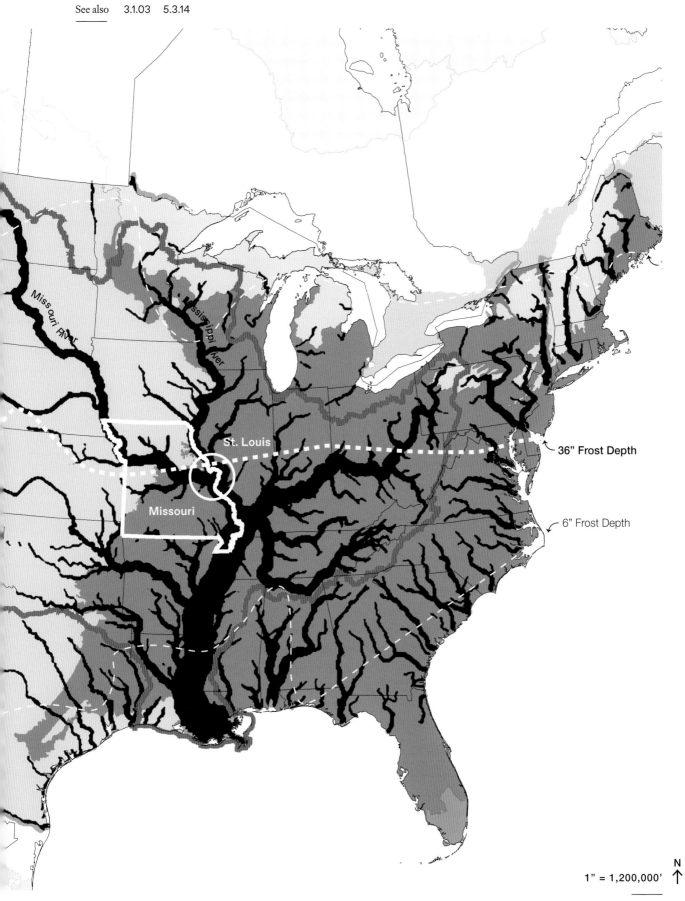

Missouri River

Mississippi River

St. Louis

Missouri

36" Frost Depth

6" Frost Depth

1" = 1,200,000'

N

1.1.02

Map of the United States in 1861, at the start of the Civil War, showing Missouri in the geographic and ideological crossroads between North and South "slave" and "free" states and between the eastern and western United States. In the century preceding the Civil War, Missouri represented the leading edge of the U.S.'s east-west territorial expansion. The current railroad system (2020) is shown in reference, since its 1869-era construction largely enabled that expansion.

↳

Map at right shows Missouri's political ideology in 2022: A conservative "red" state with progressive, "blue" urban centers.

In the St. Louis region alone, residents in 2022 were simultaneously represented in the U.S. Congress by a radically right leaning conservative senator (Josh Hawley-R) and an activist, liberal House Representative from North County (Cori Bush-D), politicians that hold widely opposing positions and agendas.

Contradiction

Missouri has long embodied a contradictory, contested "both/and" condition defined by simultaneous, competing ideologies vs. realities.

During the Civil War, Missouri was *both* a slave-owning state and a member of the "free" Union states. As 'gateway to the west' years earlier, the St. Louis region anchored *both* access to new trade opportunities and profound violence for Native people long settled there. The contradictions defining Missouri represent the contradictions facing cities and regions everywhere under the current political economy. Economic pursuits reproduce desired growth, but with lasting ruin.

Legend:

- - - Boundary (approximate) of Louisiana purchase (1804)

Union / Free states

Union / "Slave states"

"Slave states" pre-1861

Territories (1861)

Boundary of Confederacy (1861)

U.S. Railroads (2020)

Missouri (2020)

See also   4.C.17   4.3.21   5.3.19

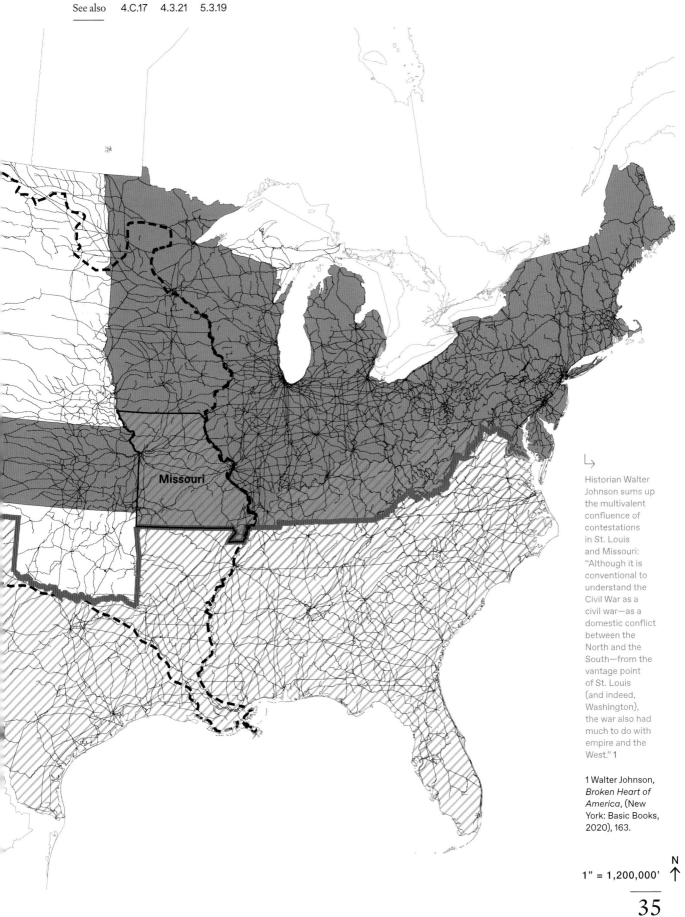

Missouri

↳

Historian Walter
Johnson sums up
the multivalent
confluence of
contestations
in St. Louis
and Missouri:
"Although it is
conventional to
understand the
Civil War as a
civil war—as a
domestic conflict
between the
North and the
South—from the
vantage point
of St. Louis
(and indeed,
Washington),
the war also had
much to do with
empire and the
West." 1

1 Walter Johnson,
*Broken Heart of
America*, (New
York: Basic Books,
2020), 163.

1" = 1,200,000'

N
↑

1.1.03

Map of St. Louis City and County showing the extent of ancient pre-Columbian Native American civilizations, according to the "mound" settlements they built (700-1350 A.D.) and including the largest and most intact today, the UNESCO heritage site called Cahokia Mounds, in Illinois. The blue overlays denote where Native American people lived after the Cahokians, from about the 1600s to the early 1800s, when they were dispossessed of their territory.

Manifest destiny

Thousands of years before Ferguson was "founded" and "incorporated," the region was home to the Cahokian, then Osage and Illini people. "Manifest destiny" was the early economic growth mandate that entitled white settlers and business prospectors to move into the region in search of land and natural resources to capitalize on.

Access to individual destiny was enabled by the state via myriad tools of dispossession and reallocation. The tools included physical violence but also bureaucratic assaults, like the treaties many were coerced into signing.

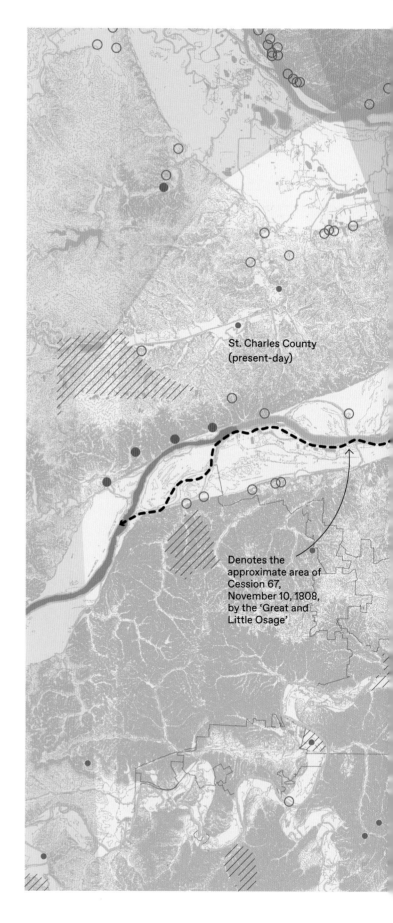

St. Charles County (present-day)

Denotes the approximate area of Cession 67, November 10, 1808, by the 'Great and Little Osage'

- - - Boundary of Native peoples' territory ceded as "Cession 67" (1808)

• Current population of American Indian / Alaska Native people: 1 dot = 10 people (2020)

◖ Ancient Native mounds (700-1350 AD) now public sites (2023)

○ Ancient Native mounds (700-1350 AD) now private property (2023)

—— Municipalities (2023)

—— Major streams (ca 2020)

▨ Major rivers and lakes (ca 2020)

▨ State parks or forests (ca 2020)

▨ (Blue overlay) Area belonging to Native peoples listed (1600-1800s)

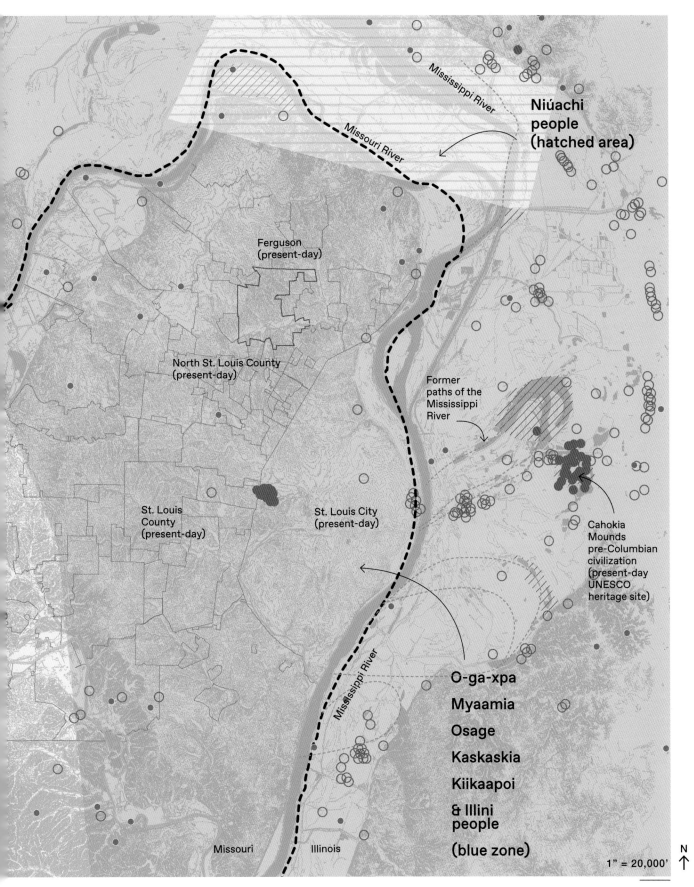

Niúachi
people
(hatched area)

Mississippi River

Missouri River

Ferguson
(present-day)

North St. Louis County
(present-day)

Former
paths of the
Mississippi
River

Cahokia
Mounds
pre-Columbian
civilization
(present-day
UNESCO
heritage site)

St. Louis
County
(present-day)

St. Louis City
(present-day)

O-ga-xpa

Myaamia

Osage

Kaskaskia

Kiikaapoi

& Illini
people

(blue zone)

Mississippi River

Missouri   Illinois

1" = 20,000'

N
↑

1.2.04

Adaptation of the Higgins' Road Map of St. Louis and Vicinity (1895) showing St. Louis City and County, with St. Louis City's successive boundary changes over time, noted by year. The map shows the current-day St. Louis City boundary that was created by the "Great Divorce" (1876), when the city legally separated from St. Louis County that it had been a part of. The town limits of Ferguson, Florissant and St. Charles, MO, during that time period are also shown.

Urban divorce (1876)

The "Great Divorce" of 1876 legally separated the City of St. Louis from St. Louis County, at a time when the city was rapidly growing (and vying for status among the largest U.S. cities). It represents an early, regional-scaled maneuver to hoard taxable land and avoid wider infrastructure costs. The system of separate governments continues to this day, despite numerous reunification efforts over the decades.

Politicized court

The "Great Divorce" actually failed at the ballot box in 1876 when citizens voted "no" to the split. But it was pushed through the court, who threw out enough "no" votes to "pass" the measure.

Home rule (1875)

"Home rule" legally grants cities the ability to create their own charters without the usual state legislative permission. The rule reinforces an idea that local governments can respond better than states to their city's needs.

In 1875, Missouri was the first state in the nation to extend the home rule privilege to St. Louis. 1 A year after being granted that autonomy, the city pursued separation from the county.

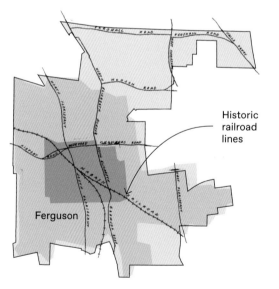

Historic railroad lines

Ferguson

↳
Underlay map adapted from Higgins & Co., *Road Map of St. Louis and Vicinity*, Higgins & Co., (St. Louis, 1895) Collection of the St. Louis Public Library.

↳
At the time of St. Louis' divorce, Ferguson was a small town in St. Louis County. Its largest period of growth came after the divorce, between 1880 and 1890, when the population grew by

300%

Ferguson City Limit

▨	1894
▨	1969
☐	Today

1 Henry J. Schmandt, *Municipal Home Rule in Missouri*, 1953 WASH. U. L. Q. 385 (1953).

See also   0.1.02   0.1.03   4.1.01

Florissant
city limits in:
1895

St. Charles
city limits in:
1885

Current
St. Louis
Lambert
Airport
(belongs to
the city of
St. Louis)

Ferguson
city limits in:
1895

St. Louis City
limits in:

1876

1870

1841

1839

1780

1876 Great Divorce

St. Louis County   St. Louis City

S T . L O U I S

In **1870** the St. Louis
City population was

310,864

Approx. 5%
are of 'African
descent' (1870s)

St. Louis City population
peaked in **1950** at

856,796

In **2020** the St. Louis County
population was

1,004,125

25% African
American (2022)

In **2020** the St. Louis
City population was

301,578

44% African
American (2022)

N

1" = 20,000'

1.2.05

Map of Ferguson and selected surrounding North St. Louis County municipalities according to when they incorporated as small cities.

Municipal incorporation

As suburbs grew in the 1940s-1950s, municipal incorporation provided a means to exclude low-income marginalized populations by preventing multi-family housing in the zoning code of the new city. Municipal incorporation was also how Kinloch, Missouri's "first all-Black city," mobilized to become a town in 1948 after its majority white neighbor Berkeley spun off to avoid integrating schools. 1

Areas are still incorporating to control policy and zoning.

⌐

Over 50 municipalities emerged between 1945 and 1952 in St. Louis County. As historian Colin Gordon points out, the motivations to keep taxes and decisions local that led St. Louis City to split from the county became the same motivations for many of the small cities that emerged later. 2 Since that earlier period of incorporations, some municipalities have merged or dissolved. And some still incorporate. Wealthier Wildwood, MO, incorporated in 1995 to control the leveling of its hilly terrain by encroaching developers. 3 Kinloch in the 1990s was meanwhile destabilized and virtually erased by state and regional development dynamics it was unable to stop.

↳

When it incorporated in 1995, Wildwood, MO, kept its three-acre minimum lot sizes. This was an exclusionary tactic, but also a strategy for maintaining septic systems, since hills were too steep to add sewers. 3

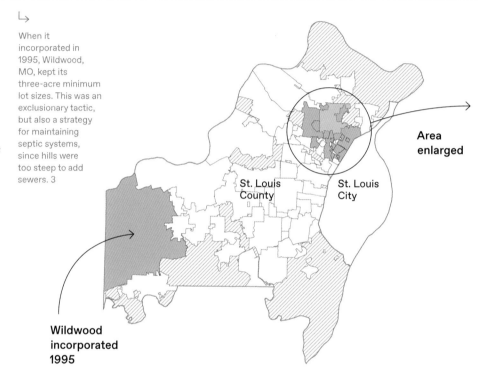

St. Louis County

St. Louis City

Area enlarged

Wildwood incorporated 1995

1 John A. Wright Sr., *Kinloch: Missouri's First Black City,* (Charleston: Arcadia, 2000).

2 As mentioned in: Kenya Rosabal, "Taxation led to original St. Louis City and County divide," *The Journal,* April 3, 2009.

3 Conversation with Dan Vogel, Patty Heyda, *Metropolitan Development,* Washington University in St. Louis, February, 2011.

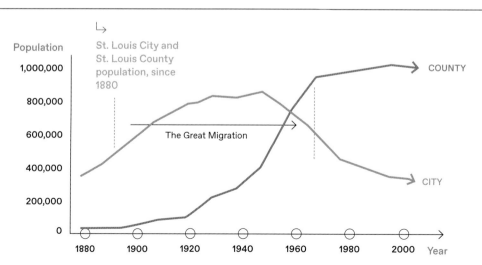

Population

↳

St. Louis City and St. Louis County population, since 1880

1,000,000

800,000

600,000

400,000

200,000

0

The Great Migration

COUNTY

CITY

1880   1900   1920   1940   1960   1980   2000   Year

See also   2.1.01-02   4.2.12

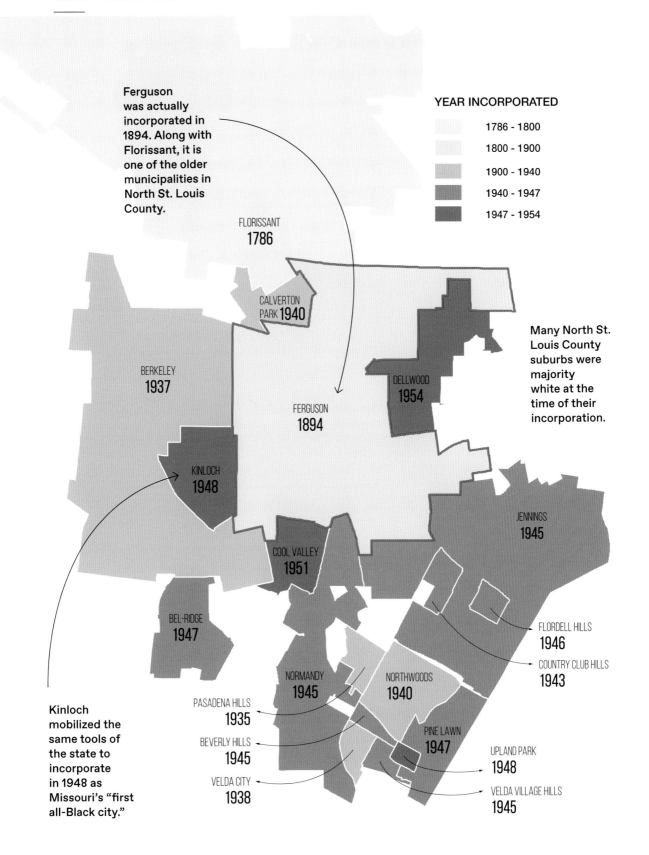

Ferguson was actually incorporated in 1894. Along with Florissant, it is one of the older municipalities in North St. Louis County.

YEAR INCORPORATED

1786 - 1800
1800 - 1900
1900 - 1940
1940 - 1947
1947 - 1954

FLORISSANT
1786

CALVERTON PARK 1940

Many North St. Louis County suburbs were majority white at the time of their incorporation.

BERKELEY
1937

DELLWOOD
1954

FERGUSON
1894

KINLOCH
1948

JENNINGS
1945

COOL VALLEY
1951

FLORDELL HILLS
1946

COUNTRY CLUB HILLS
1943

BEL-RIDGE
1947

NORMANDY
1945

NORTHWOODS
1940

Kinloch mobilized the same tools of the state to incorporate in 1948 as Missouri's "first all-Black city."

PASADENA HILLS
1935

PINE LAWN
1947

UPLAND PARK
1948

BEVERLY HILLS
1945

VELDA CITY
1938

VELDA VILLAGE HILLS
1945

1.2.06

Map of Ferguson showing its origins as a railroad town, with property parcels according to the year built, overlaid with a drawing of the historic rail lines that converged where Ferguson's oldest commercial center still is today. The city became an alternative option for people leaving St. Louis City or looking to live in a small town and commute to the bigger city.

Below right, a snapshot of three commercial corridors in Ferguson according to the eras they were built. The parcelization reveals how the original downtown buildings (left) defined the streets and the train depot and how the newer car-based commercial areas became more spread out and set back from the street.

Community of choice

City formation as free-market ideology dates back well before the flurry of incorporations that swept St. Louis County in the late 1930s to the 1950s. Ferguson's motto, "Community of Choice," reinforces the basic market principle of choice, as it characterized the emerging white commuter suburb that in the later 1800s was an alternate option to living in downtown St. Louis.

Civic hub

The commuter suburb at the time of incorporation revolved around mass transit and the train station, which reinforced a well-built, walkable urban fabric that formed a civic hub, unlike the car-based commercial strips that came later with austerity and market "efficiencies" that eroded possibilities for public life.

The diagrams below show how the newer (modern and neoliberal-era) commercial buildings on West Florissant Avenue became larger and more set back from the road than the older-built commercial South Florissant Road corridor.

———	Ferguson
———	Municipal boundaries
++++	Historical railroad

YEAR BUILT

▆	1790 - 1920
▆	1921 - 1940
▆	1941 - 1950
▆	1951 - 1960
▆	1961 - 1970
▆	1971 - 1980
▆	1981 - 1990
▆	1991 - 2017

1 S. Florissant Rd

2 W. Florissant Ave

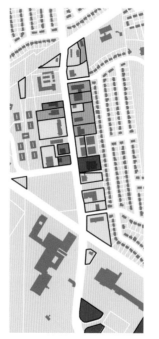

3 W. Florissant Ave & Chambers Rd

(Dellwood)

See also   2.1.06   4.1.02

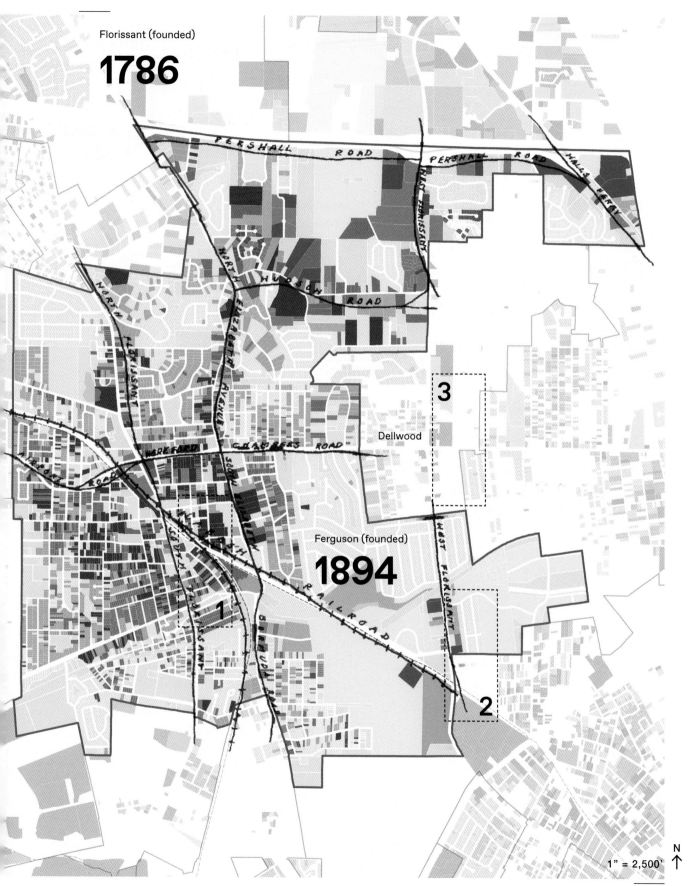

Florissant (founded)

1786

Dellwood

Ferguson (founded)

1894

1" = 2,500'

N

1.2.07

Map of St. Louis City and County showing the population distribution by race and ethnicity according to the U.S. Census (2020) and highlighting the existing (north-south) racial divide and the emerging (east-west) racial melding happening in the region.

Division

'Race' is a social construct,1 yet it is continually reinforced in urban metrics, and by the social, political and economic policies and behaviors, fears or exploitations that follow.

Stark 'racial' divisions are visible between north and south in the St. Louis region; notably at Delmar Boulevard. These same patterns play out in the many disparities and patterns in maps throughout this atlas. But stark 'racial' transition zones are also visible between east and west, notably in the first-ring North County suburbs.

Once majority white at the time of mid-century municipal incorporations, North County is increasingly home to a rich mix of people with different ethnicities and backgrounds. This diversification, among other factors, has made North St. Louis a battleground for redevelopment between state-backed business interests and residents.

Ferguson, MO population (2022)
Based on the American Community Survey five-year estimates (U.S. Census Bureau)

White alone	22.7%
Black or African American alone	71.7%
Asian alone	0.1%
Two or more races	3.8%
Hispanic or Latino	1.0%

1 Angela Onwuachi-Willig, "Race and Racial Identity Are Social Constructs." The New York Times, September 6, 2016.

2 See for example: "Crossing a St. Louis street that divides communities." BBC Magazine, March 14, 2012.

—— Ferguson

RACE AND ETHNICITY (2020)

One dot = 10 people
Based on the U.S. Census (2020)

- Non-Hispanic or Latino Population: African American or Black alone

- Non-Hispanic or Latino Population: White alone

- ● ● Hispanic or Latino population, Asian population, or Alaska Native or American Indian

See also   1.1.02-03

Ferguson

North St. Louis County

Delmar Blvd

St. Louis County

St. Louis City

**The
First-ring
Front Line**

Emerging zone
of economic and
demographic
transition
(and territorial
contestation)

**The
"Delmar
Divide"** 1

Existing zone of
economic and
demographic
division

1" = 20,000'

N
↑

45

02

Space

Material forms of neoliberalism

The Space chapter traverses the material world of neo-liberal efficiency, 'convenience' and externalization in the already strained weak-market context.

The maps in this chapter show the weaponization of multi-family housing codes and cul-de-sacs. Maps then explore the violence of the commercial public realm that is degraded by parking minimums, lack of public transit and unshaded expanses of impermeable asphalt. The fast food franchise models a form of externalization on the strip.

The chapter concludes with a view of West Florissant Avenue, the indistinct, inhospitable strip where the 2014 uprising played out that reclaimed, as it took advantage of, the undefined spatial condition.

2.1.01

At right, zoning map of Ferguson showing the different types of R (Residential) districts (in greens and blues) with parcels, and other separated uses. Below, a diagram compares the minimum required sizes of R-1 single-family lots in Ferguson to those in Wildwood, Missouri, a newer wealthy suburb further west.

At right, Wildwood was incorporated to protect its large lot sizes and wooded environmental integrity from predatory development that threatened to level the hills and build more densely. Denser housing settlements are more sustainable, although there is no public transit out in the farther suburbs to truly gain the benefits of density. Ecological integrity is ultimately still at risk when the large lot sizes remain private.

Minimum lot sizes

Single-family zoned minimum lot sizes may provide visual uniformity in a neighborhood. But when large lots are mandated as a minimum standard, the tool is both exclusionary and exploitative. Farther-out subdivisions tend to have larger minimum lot sizes than the dense first-ring suburbs.

Ferguson is a historic city, but it is considered a first-ring suburb since it grew during the inter-war and post-war era, as new housing was built for returning veterans and workers in the industries nearby. That early growth was made up of quite modest and small houses and lots. The smaller the lots, the more dense the neighborhood, even in the 'suburban' context.

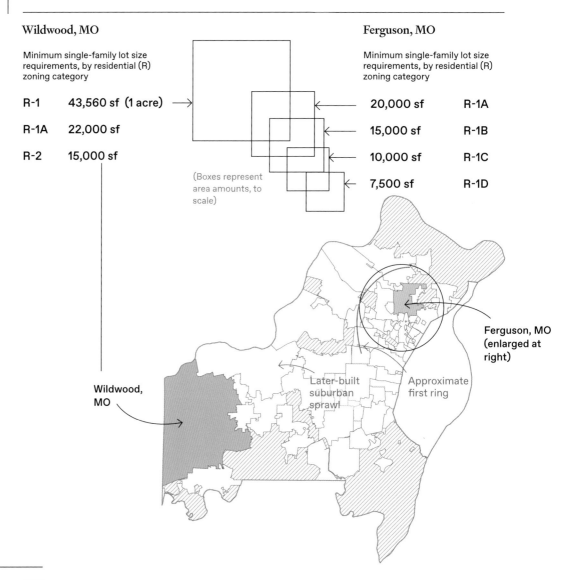

Wildwood, MO

Minimum single-family lot size requirements, by residential (R) zoning category

R-1	43,560 sf (1 acre)
R-1A	22,000 sf
R-2	15,000 sf

(Boxes represent area amounts, to scale)

Ferguson, MO

Minimum single-family lot size requirements, by residential (R) zoning category

20,000 sf	R-1A
15,000 sf	R-1B
10,000 sf	R-1C
7,500 sf	R-1D

Ferguson, MO (enlarged at right)

Later-built suburban sprawl

Approximate first ring

Wildwood, MO

See also 1.2.05 2.M.03 3.1.03

Single-use zoning

Zoning made the suburb into a means of property protection and racial exclusion by preventing the mixture of uses, and by separating residential types.

Multi-family zoning (R-2 to 4) was relegated largely to the southeast quadrant of Ferguson, with some exceptions near the highway or in other flood-prone zones. Retail zoning now allows for a mixed-use "form based" code, but it is limited to the historic center, where buildings and blocks are already pedestrian-friendly.

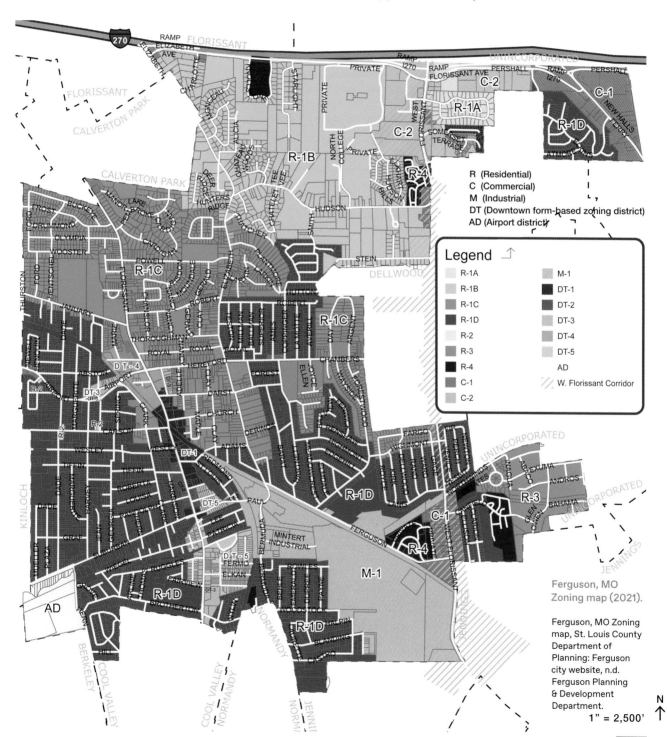

R (Residential)
C (Commercial)
M (Industrial)
DT (Downtown form-based zoning district)
AD (Airport district)

Legend

R-1A
R-1B
R-1C
R-1D
R-2
R-3
R-4
C-1
C-2

M-1
DT-1
DT-2
DT-3
DT-4
DT-5
AD
W. Florissant Corridor

Ferguson, MO Zoning map (2021).

Ferguson, MO Zoning map, St. Louis County Department of Planning: Ferguson city website, n.d. Ferguson Planning & Development Department.

1" = 2,500'

N

2.1.02

Below, a map of Ferguson, MO, showing residential building footprints, with four residential zoned areas called out for comparison. At right, a close-up of the housing found in those four areas, with typical building and block typologies and cost and size metrics.

The close-up views show the extent of variation of suburban housing, which is not monolithic but varies over time. The close-ups include the R-4 planned district tool that is weaponized to allow urban design freedom outside of the established rules of the code for greater exclusivity—or for delivering lower-quality urbanism to save money.

1 Sandra M. Moore, "Transformation opportunity in Canfield Green," *The St. Louis American,* July 14, 2016.

Residential zoning

All residential zoning categories do not protect design quality, but some actually exacerbate unequal access to different urban design standards. In R-4 "planned residential districts," wealthier areas reflect different urban and architectural design features more than "efficient" low-income areas. This quality discrepancy was noted by Sandra Moore in the *St. Louis American,* where she points out that many of the low-income apartments in Ferguson's southwest R-4 area (apartments developed with Low Income Housing Tax Credits nonetheless) have lower architectural standards, like they lack a space to put a dining table for family meals together. She asks, "Is family housing without space for family dining decent? Is such housing adequate?" 1

Residential (R) zoning categories range from R-1A through D single family houses; to R-2 two-family duplexes; R-3 multi-family housing; and R-4 planned districts that can be single, double or multi-family housing. In Ferguson, the categories and housing designs within them generally correlate to when the buildings and blocks were constructed, and for what market segment of buyers. Types range from 1930s to 40s-built single-family worker housing (Area B below) to 1950s-and 60s-era ranch houses (Area A below); to R-4 planned unit developments of widely ranging designs—and prices (Areas C and D, below).

PRDs
(Planned Residential District)

The special R-4 PRD, or Planned Residential District—also sometimes called 'Planned Unit Development (PUD)'—allows subdivisions to be designed more freely within their overall boundary than what the zoning code otherwise dictates. PRDs enable exclusive neighborhood designs to follow separate rules, or low-income neighborhood designs to remain outside of the standards, so developers save costs. R-4 could be a solution to bring responsible vibrant dense neighborhoods to otherwise low-density single-family suburbs. Instead, it is weaponized to reproduce pockets of unequal standards for wealthier or poorer areas.

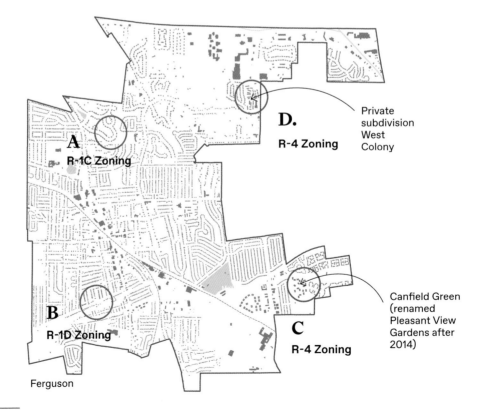

D.
R-4 Zoning

Private subdivision West Colony

A.
R-1C Zoning

B
R-1D Zoning

C
R-4 Zoning

Canfield Green (renamed Pleasant View Gardens after 2014)

Ferguson

N

1" = 4,875'

See also   2.1.04   2.M.02

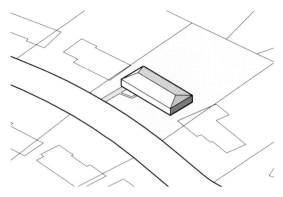

A. (R-1C)   HOA $300/month

Pembroke (Private) Community

Built: 1953
Single-family house
ca $197,000-$300,000 (2022)
3 beds, 2 baths
1500-1900 sq ft

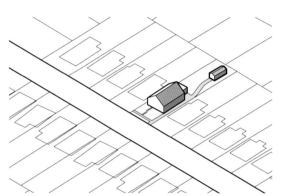

B. (R-1D)

Bertha Place Subdivision

Built: 1936
Single-family house
ca $54,000- $99,000 (2022)
2 beds, 1 baths
650-1100 sq ft

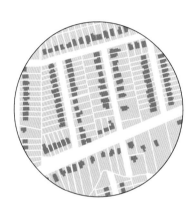

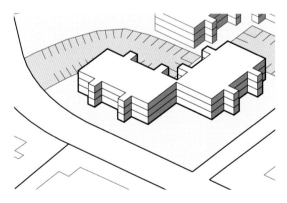

C. (R-4) ↵

Pleasant View Gardens (formerly Canfield Green)

Built: 1970
Multi-family/rental units
ca $625-$800/month
2 beds, 1 bath (2022)
630-880 sq ft (unit)

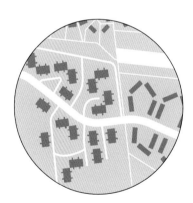

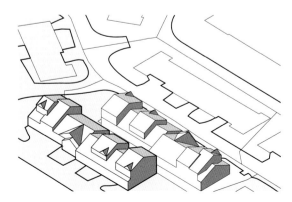

D. (R-4) ↵   HOA $300/month

West Colony (Private) Community

Built: 1988
Single-family/attached units
ca $200,000 (2022)
2 beds 3.5 bath
1568 sq ft (unit)

Radical Atlas of Ferguson, USA

R-4 Zoning: Planned Residential District

Photo by author, 2023
The private West Colony middle-income subdivision in North Ferguson (Labeled D in map 2.1.02) has restricted road access, additional security; attached homes have pitched roofs, dormer windows, individual entries facing the social life of the street, and cars hidden in garages. Landscape amenities are varied and abundant (and likely maintained by the HOA).

R-4 Zoning: Planned Residential District

Photo by author, 2023
Pleasant View Gardens (formerly called Canfield Green) is a low-income residential subdivision in Southeast Ferguson (Labeled C in map 2.1.02) where Michael Brown was killed. It has large exposed parking lots with trash dumpsters in the front, preventing the street from feeling like a place to gather. The flat roofs and entries have no direct relationship to the street, nor to an inner courtyard space. Landscape and shade features are scarce.

2.1.03

Map of Ferguson shows (areas outlined in bold) properties with restricted covenants in the chain of title, with current-day subdivisions that restrict access by closed or limited road connections.

The same subdivision approach is used for multi-family low-income enclaves owned by large-company corporate owners and landlords. These practices compound the fragmentation and exclusions that already exist between so many tiny municipalities.

Subdivision

Subdivisions insulate property for wealth accumulation and / or to shut others out. Many suburban subdivisions were made when builder-developers divided larger land areas (often what used to be rural tracts) into individual lots for homes or apartment complexes. The city does not require subdivisions to connect to each other. The resulting condition is a patchwork of many small segregated communities with restricted access and little diversity.

The R-4 Planned Residential District (PRD) code allows a subdivision to be designed more freely within its boundaries than what the zoning code otherwise dictates for parcel size, set-backs, height, array and other standards. See 2.1.02.

HOAs

Homeowners associations hoard control as they uphold a private system of hyper-localized taxation and rules that benefit only those within the HOA boundary.

When subdivisions are private, a legal entity called an HOA (Homeowners association) is sometimes used for additional restrictive regulation and governance. An HOA fee operates as a private tax to cover services and maintenance for that area. Residents are required to be members of the HOA, and most HOAs restrict the ways streets and lawns can be used, and how they must look, among other things.

HOAs are restrictive covenants 2.0.

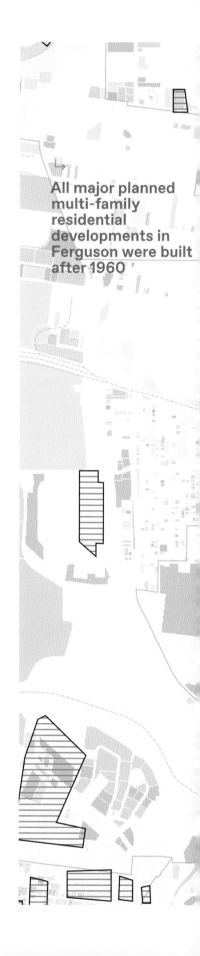

All major planned multi-family residential developments in Ferguson were built after 1960

YEAR BUILT

⬛	1790 - 1920
⬛	1921 - 1940
⬛	1941 - 1950
⬜	1951 - 1960
⬜	1961 - 1970
⬜	1971 - 1980
⬛	1981 - 1990
⬛	1991 - 2017

———— Physically disconnected single-family PRD subdivisions

━━━━ Physically disconnected *and* Private PRD subdivisions with HOA management

━━━━ Limited access or partially disconnected PRD rental apartment subdivisions under company ownership / management

⬡ Approximate areas of properties with historic restrictive covenants in chain of title

See also   1.2.04-05   2.1.02   3.1.02   3.1.06

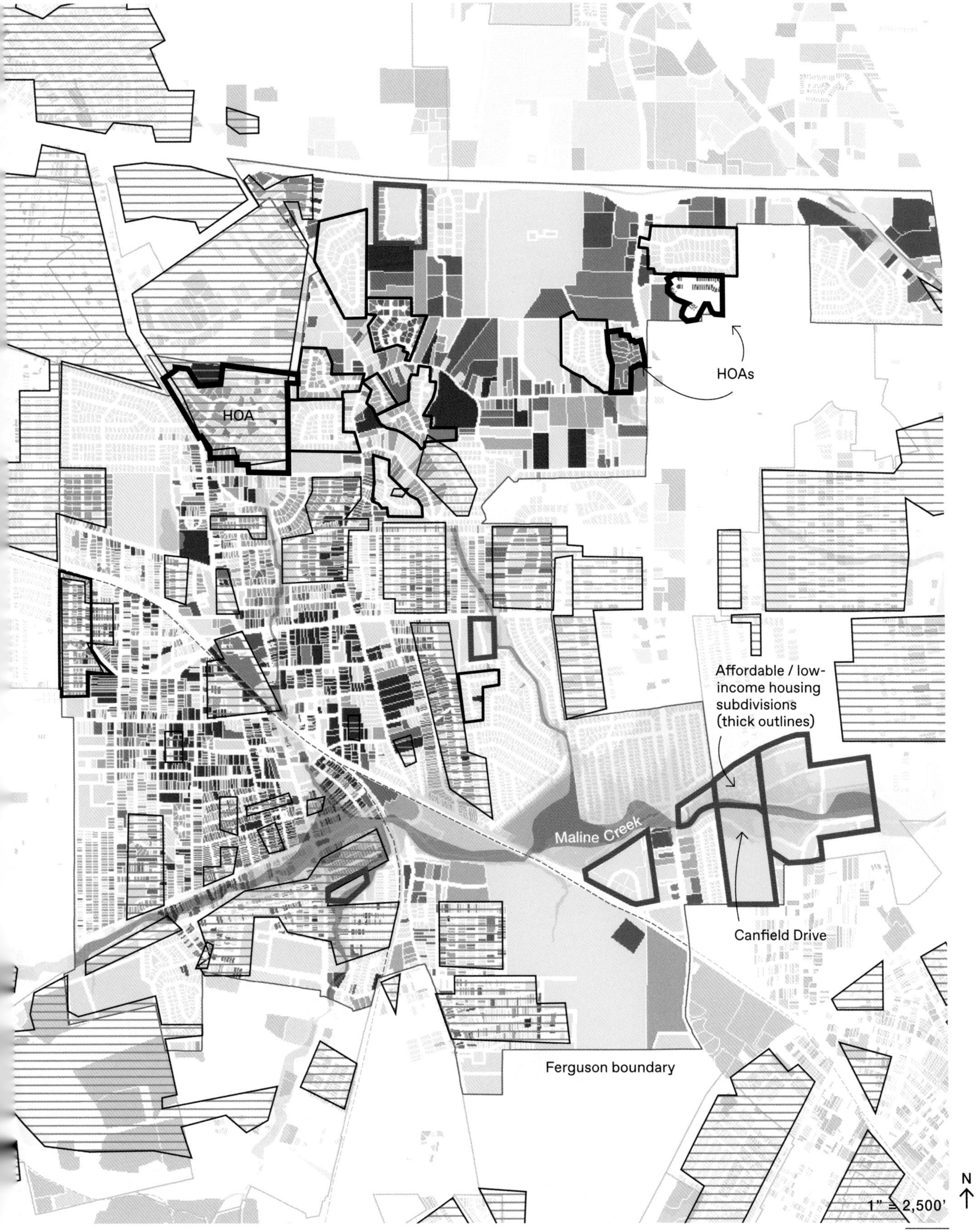

HOAs

HOA

Affordable / low-income housing subdivisions (thick outlines)

Maline Creek

Canfield Drive

Ferguson boundary

N

1" = 2,500'

More connected
neighborhoods could
be linked to robust
public transit to reduce
through traffic and
make streets safer,
while still fostering
public life and easier
commutes for school
kids across and be-
tween subdivisions.

From covenants to cut-offs: Isolating neighborhoods

Photo by author, 2023
Pembroke Lake
Drive in the private
subdivision by the
same name does not
go through at its
boundary with the
next neighborhood.
Subdivided areas like
these create even more
hyper-fragmented
conditions of exclusion
in North St. Louis,
beyond the many small
municipalities.

Isolating neighborhoods

Photo by author, 2024
The corollary to wealthy subdivision exclusion is affordable subdivision isolation. The affordable multi-family rental units in Ferguson are isolated from each other and from the rest of the city. Fences, a stream and barricades cut access on Exuma Dr between Oakmont Townhomes and Northwinds Estates (called Park North in 2023).

2.1.04

Comparative aerial views of two R-4-zoned Planned Residential District subdivisions in Ferguson, MO (2022), with trees circled. The medium-income-level, HOA-governed private West Colony subdivision is at left, and the low-income, landlord-managed Pleasant View Gardens (formerly Canfield Green) subdivision is at right. By a measure of trees alone, the graphics show the discrepancy in how each PRD meets the "adequate landscaping" regulation that calls for vegetation to offset environmental and aesthetic impacts of buildings and pavement.

Adequate landscaping

The qualitative "adequate landscaping" requirement of the Ferguson, MO, zoning code is meant to "buffer adjacent land uses, mitigate the impacts of vehicular traffic and parking lots, minimize the adverse effects of heat and glare, reduce topsoil erosion and storm water runoff, increase the compatibility of adjacent uses, and preserve the integrity of the City and its neighborhoods."[1] According to the code, the property owner is responsible for maintaining the landscape.

In practice, it provides guidance for environmental integrity—or cover, when developers and large landlords implement superficial versions of it to save costs. The harms of this practice—and lack of enforcement—are aesthetic and environmental but social too, since landscape architecture shapes outdoor space where people can or cannot comfortably gather.

1 Ferguson, MO Zoning code, Ord. No. 2009-3416, 12-8-09; 11.10. -LANDSCAPING. (2021)

Imagery, Google Earth Pro, 2022.

Approx 1 tree per 1 unit

R-4 Zoning: West Colony subdivision

See also   2.1.02   2.1.06   5.M.02

Approx 1 tree per 24 units

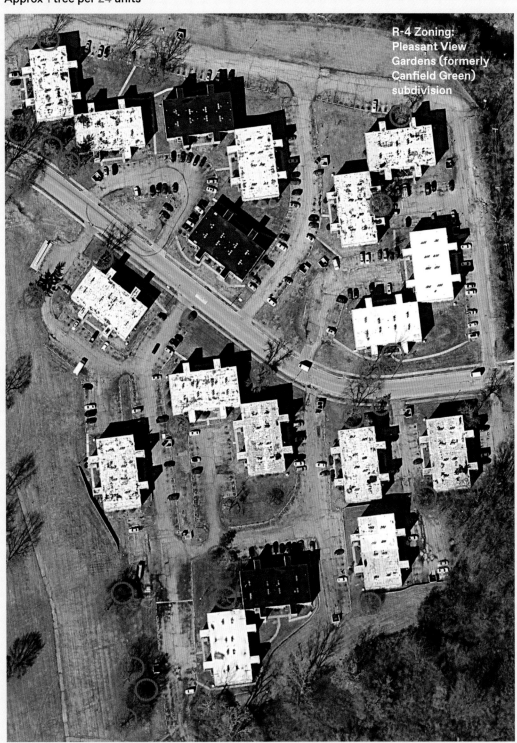

R-4 Zoning:
Pleasant View
Gardens (formerly
Canfield Green)
subdivision

↳

Trees are crucial in
summer months
for their shade and
cooling effects in
urbanized areas.
They also absorb
carbon in the atmo-
sphere and clean
the air damaged by
emissions from cars
and industry.

2.1.05

Map of the small municipality of Calverton Park, MO, located just north of Ferguson, MO. The map shows locations of amenities that concentrate along the interstate at the north, with land-use designations and the town's "walk score," of 30/100—not walkable.

Walkability

The American suburb of single-use zoning, combined with market logics that privilege regional-based retail, is a sacrifice zone of walkability. Even in the (relatively) more economically stable parts of North County, like the tiny city of Calverton Park, amenities concentrate at the interstate rather than in neighborhoods to prioritize customers outside of town. Calverton Park is 99% residential and still only 30% walkable.

Most residents of the first ring, whether poorer or wealthier, cannot easily walk to places. This is also true in much whiter, wealthier suburbs and exurbs. But when issues of food and transportation insecurity are added, like in southeast Ferguson and parts of surrounding North County, the lack of walkability is a form of violence that prevents access to jobs, schools and nutritional health.

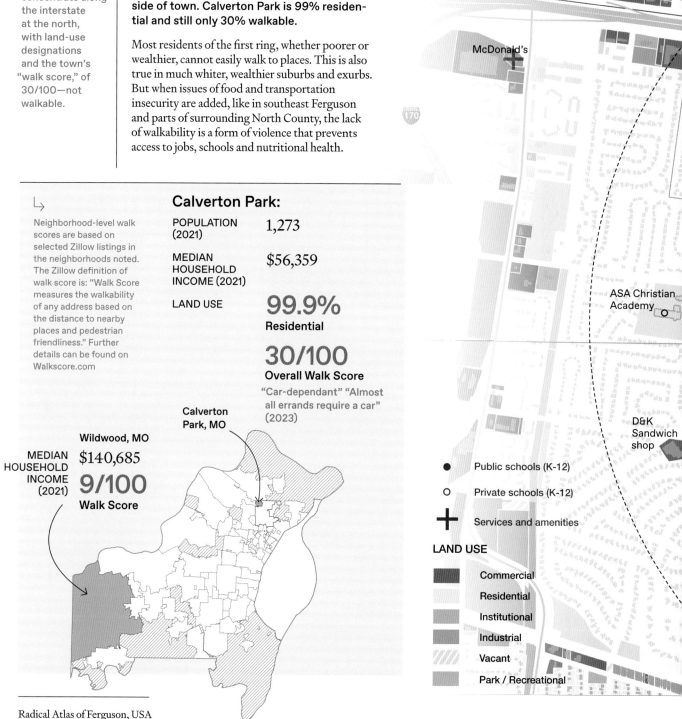

↳

Neighborhood-level walk scores are based on selected Zillow listings in the neighborhoods noted. The Zillow definition of walk score is: "Walk Score measures the walkability of any address based on the distance to nearby places and pedestrian friendliness." Further details can be found on Walkscore.com

Calverton Park:

POPULATION (2021)	1,273
MEDIAN HOUSEHOLD INCOME (2021)	$56,359
LAND USE	**99.9%** Residential
	30/100 Overall Walk Score

"Car-dependant" "Almost all errands require a car" (2023)

Calverton Park, MO

Wildwood, MO

$140,685

MEDIAN HOUSEHOLD INCOME (2021)

9/100 Walk Score

Starbucks

Dollar Tree

Arby's

7- Eleven

Omnicare

McDonald's

170

ASA Christian Academy

D&K Sandwich shop

● Public schools (K-12)

○ Private schools (K-12)

✚ Services and amenities

LAND USE

Commercial

Residential

Institutional

Industrial

Vacant

Park / Recreational

See also   1.2.06   2.1.06   4.3.22   5.2.11   5.M.01

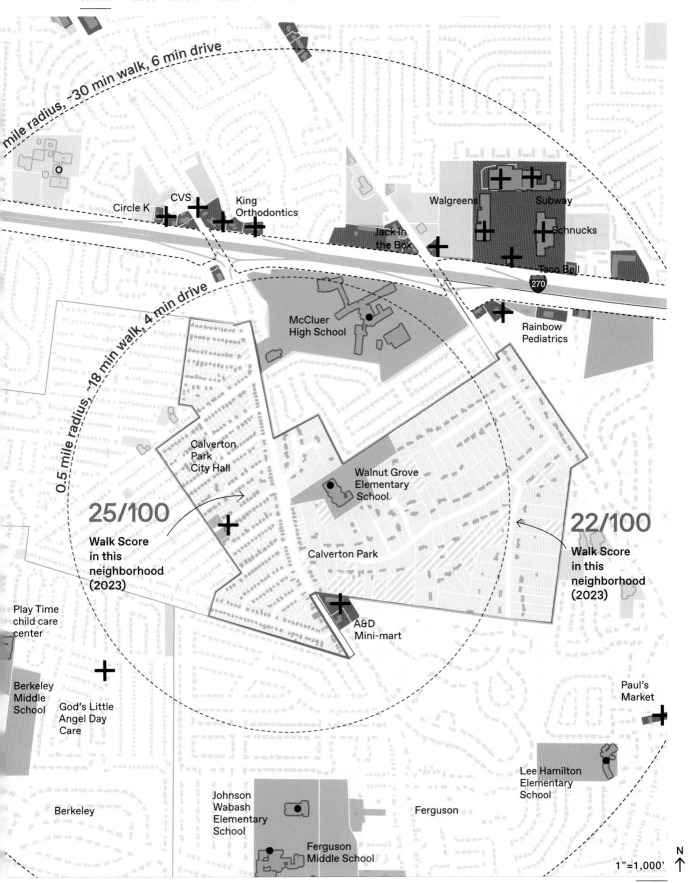

mile radius, ~30 min walk, 6 min drive

0.5 mile radius, ~18 min walk, 4 min drive

Circle K

CVS

King Orthodontics

Walgreens

Subway

Schnucks

Jack in the Box

Taco Bell

270

Rainbow Pediatrics

McCluer High School

Calverton Park City Hall

Walnut Grove Elementary School

25/100

Walk Score in this neighborhood (2023)

Calverton Park

22/100

Walk Score in this neighborhood (2023)

Play Time child care center

A&D Mini-mart

Paul's Market

Berkeley Middle School

God's Little Angel Day Care

Berkeley

Johnson Wabash Elementary School

Ferguson

Lee Hamilton Elementary School

Ferguson Middle School

1"=1,000'

N

2.1.06

Map of Ferguson, MO, highlighting all paved and impervious surfaces along the West Florissant Avenue commercial strip and surrounding area. Two retail zones are called out along this road, with details about their paved parking lots and zoning requirements. The two areas include a big-box development in the north to attract interstate customers, and older retail establishments in the south that cater to more local customers. These retail areas have very few trees to offset the intense heat island effect of so much paving.

↳

A: Commercial Retail Space:
483,511 ft2
Impervious asphalt:
1,338,606 ft2
(16,526 cy3)

↳

B: Commercial Retail Space:
12 Businesses, approx.145,000 sq ft
Impervious asphalt:
297,302 ft2
(3,670 cy3)

297,302 sq feet of impervious asphalt for 12 businesses

Parking requirements

The suburban spatial condition is shaped by efficiency and market preferences for relentless car-based paved landscapes of 'convenience,' despite the health and environmental crises these patterns cause.

The suburban retail parking code upholds this destructive logic. In Ferguson, it requires 5 cars per 1,000 square foot of building that, together with required building setbacks, creates an inhospitable public realm of the street. Expanses of impervious asphalt don't allow rainwater to percolate back in the ground (a process that helps clean it of toxins from the cars and prevents flash flooding and other impacts). Parking increases heat and degrades aesthetic quality. These spatial features keep people from using the space for anything except cars.

Heat islands

Areas with extensive impermeable hard surfaces and buildings (and no trees) create a heat island effect, where temperatures become 1-7°F hotter than outlying areas during the day (and 2-5°F higher at night).

Removing cars is a tall order in the suburbs, but adding public transit and mandating shade trees and pervious surfaces to control (and clean) water run off would be a start. A "Great Streets" project along West Florissant Avenue that will repair sidewalk and edge conditions is in the works, but it requires needed public funding that is not available in this political economy. Any redesign of the street should also require much more from commercially owned parking lots and buildings via code changes.

~7 acres of asphalt paving at Sam's Club alone

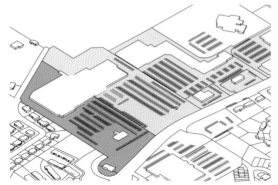

A   North County Festival at West Florissant Avenue (including Sam's Club)

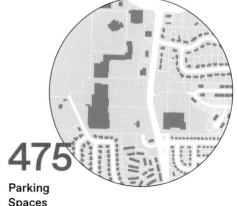

475 Parking Spaces

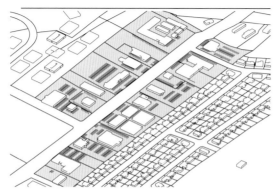

B   Retail Strip at West Florissant Avenue & Ferguson Avenue

See also   2.1.05   5.3.15   5.M.01

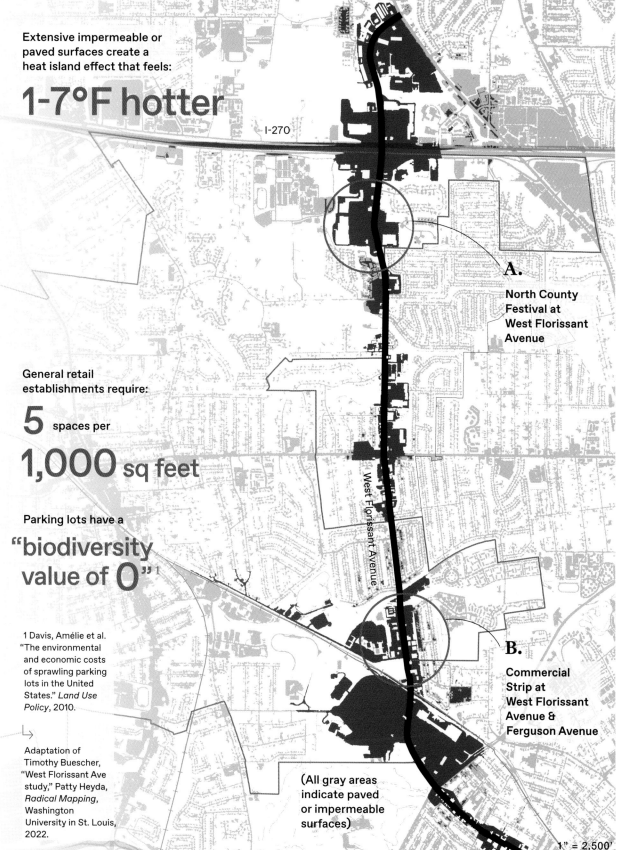

Extensive impermeable or paved surfaces create a heat island effect that feels:

1-7°F hotter

I-270

General retail establishments require:

5 spaces per
1,000 sq feet

Parking lots have a

"biodiversity value of 0"[1]

1 Davis, Amélie et al. "The environmental and economic costs of sprawling parking lots in the United States." *Land Use Policy*, 2010.

↳

Adaptation of Timothy Buescher, "West Florissant Ave study," Patty Heyda, *Radical Mapping*, Washington University in St. Louis, 2022.

West Florissant Avenue

A.

North County Festival at West Florissant Avenue

B.

Commercial Strip at West Florissant Avenue & Ferguson Avenue

(All gray areas indicate paved or impermeable surfaces)

1" = 2,500'

N
↑

Public space

Photo by author, 2023
Looking south down West Florissant Avenue. When public funding for infrastructure is gutted under neoliberal austerity, the street and public life fall into spatial, aesthetic and social disrepair. A major "Great Streets" plan to remake this avenue as pedestrian friendly—and safer—has been in the works since 2014, but as of 2023, it still awaits the full funding necessary to carry it out.

2.1.07

Fast food / Franchise

Map of Ferguson, MO, and surrounding areas, showing commercially zoned areas, with locations of McDonald's and other fast food chains.

The diagrammatic drawing below shows the ubiquitous urban footprint of a McDonald's—the one shown was on West Florissant Avenue in southeast Ferguson, MO, until early 2022.

↳

The former Ferguson McDonald's on West Florissant Avenue near Ferguson Ave.

Global franchise brands like Mc-Donald's define the architecture and urbanism of the suburban commercial strip. But they also define the extractive economics of the strip. Franchising is not a public policy, but it exemplifies the system of corporate externalizations that accumulate profit in distant global—not local—spaces, despite a restaurant's specific context. Money that flows outward does not feed back into a local economy. Franchises generate significant rent revenue for the corporation while absorbing the operating costs of running the business. McDonald's extracts more money from local real estate than from the sale of food. 1

95% of McDonald's globally are franchises. Franchisees leverage the brand of the company to draw customers, but to generate profit, they often pass costs off further, onto low-wage or part-time workers, or by promoting highly profitable, very cheap but very unhealthy—predatory—soft drinks. Cities attract franchises and chain retail stores because they generate high volumes of sales taxes.

The Ferguson McDonald's on West Florissant Road was an important gathering spot for protestors during the 2014 uprisings and for residents who came in to watch TV for the latest news updates. Contested sites are nonetheless still inscribed by lived experiences and carry meaning for communities. This is the complexity of the first-ring suburb. The McDonald's has since been torn down, and the site remains empty as of 2023.

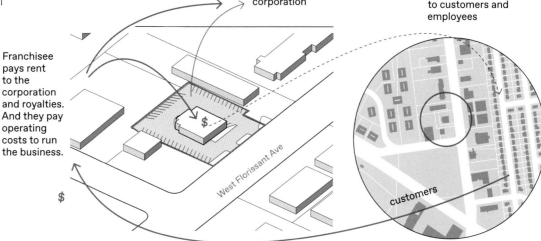

Profits: external

Land on the strip is owned by the global corporation

Franchisee pays rent to the corporation and royalties. And they pay operating costs to run the business.

$

$

West Florissant Ave

customers

Costs: local

Costs are passed on to customers and employees

Supersize

Fast food franchises market *supersize* bargain soft drinks because they are the biggest money maker for restaurants, despite the fact that these drinks are the leading cause of diabetes and obesity in the U.S. Burdens on public health are another hidden externality—or cost—of fast food.

softdrinks generate up to a 90% profit margin

for restaurants, so they can be offered large and cheap. The bargains draw customers in.

Super-sized sugary drinks have no nutritional value and are considered among the

leading causes of diabetes and obesity in the U.S.

1 Claire Nowak, "The Real Way McDonald's Makes Their Money—It's Not Their Food," *Reader's Digest*, July 19, 2021.

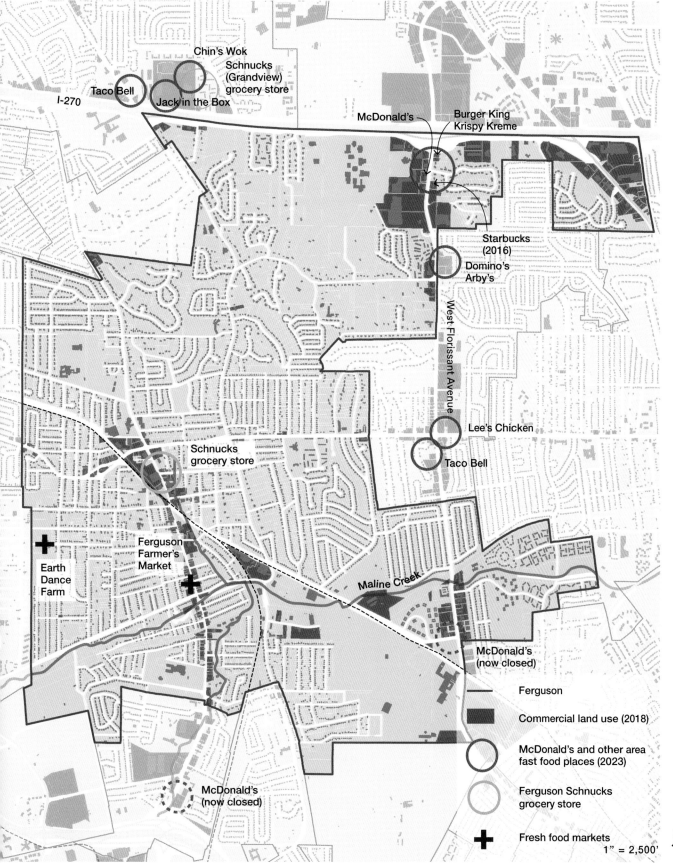

Chin's Wok

Schnucks
(Grandview)
grocery store

Taco Bell

I-270

Jack in the Box

McDonald's

Burger King
Krispy Kreme

Starbucks
(2016)

Domino's
Arby's

West Florissant Avenue

Lee's Chicken

Schnucks
grocery store

Taco Bell

Earth
Dance
Farm

Ferguson
Farmer's
Market

Maline Creek

McDonald's
(now closed)

McDonald's
(now closed)

Ferguson

Commercial land use (2018)

McDonald's and other area
fast food places (2023)

Ferguson Schnucks
grocery store

Fresh food markets

1" = 2,500'

N

2.1.08

Map of West Florissant Avenue in Ferguson, MO, showing events during the "Ferguson Uprising" from August 9-14, 2014. The map reveals that much of "Ferguson" actually happened in Dellwood, MO, the neighboring municipality. At left of drawing, a chart of social media activity during the same time period. These two views of the protest show how suburban space—and social movements for change—are not bound by political borders. Suburban civic space—and its technological extensions—can be mobilized for civic democratic agendas.

Drawing by Ethan Miller, "Ferguson social movements" Patty Heyda, *The Problem of the Suburb*, Washington University in St. Louis, 2016.

Ferguson protest

The Ferguson uprising really also happened in Dellwood, MO (and in digital space).

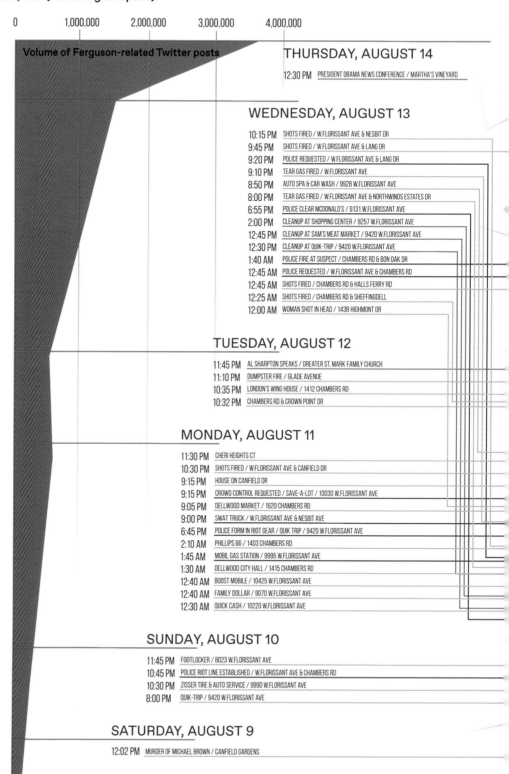

Volume of Ferguson-related Twitter posts

0   1,000,000   2,000,000   3,000,000   4,000,000

THURSDAY, AUGUST 14

12:30 PM — PRESIDENT OBAMA NEWS CONFERENCE / MARTHA'S VINEYARD

WEDNESDAY, AUGUST 13

10:15 PM — SHOTS FIRED / W.FLORISSANT AVE & NESBIT DR
9:45 PM — SHOTS FIRED / W.FLORISSANT AVE & LANG DR
9:20 PM — POLICE REQUESTED / W.FLORISSANT AVE & LANG DR
9:10 PM — TEAR GAS FIRED / W.FLORISSANT AVE
8:50 PM — AUTO SPA & CAR WASH / 9928 W.FLORISSANT AVE
8:00 PM — TEAR GAS FIRED / W.FLORISSANT AVE & NORTHWINDS ESTATES DR
6:55 PM — POLICE CLEAR MCDONALD'S / 9131 W.FLORISSANT AVE
2:00 PM — CLEANUP AT SHOPPING CENTER / 9257 W.FLORISSANT AVE
12:45 PM — CLEANUP AT SAM'S MEAT MARKET / 9420 W.FLORISSANT AVE
12:30 PM — CLEANUP AT QUIK-TRIP / 9420 W.FLORISSANT AVE
1:40 AM — POLICE FIRE AT SUSPECT / CHAMBERS RD & BON OAK DR
12:45 AM — POLICE REQUESTED / W.FLORISSANT AVE & CHAMBERS RD
12:45 AM — SHOTS FIRED / CHAMBERS RD & HALLS FERRY RD
12:25 AM — SHOTS FIRED / CHAMBERS RD & SHEFFINGDELL
12:00 AM — WOMAN SHOT IN HEAD / 1438 HIGHMONT DR

TUESDAY, AUGUST 12

11:45 PM — AL SHARPTON SPEAKS / GREATER ST. MARK FAMILY CHURCH
11:10 PM — DUMPSTER FIRE / GLADE AVENUE
10:35 PM — LONDON'S WING HOUSE / 1412 CHAMBERS RD
10:32 PM — CHAMBERS RD & CROWN POINT DR

MONDAY, AUGUST 11

11:30 PM — CHERI HEIGHTS CT
10:30 PM — SHOTS FIRED / W.FLORISSANT AVE & CANFIELD DR
9:15 PM — HOUSE ON CANFIELD DR
9:15 PM — CROWD CONTROL REQUESTED / SAVE-A-LOT / 10030 W.FLORISSANT AVE
9:05 PM — DELLWOOD MARKET / 1620 CHAMBERS RD
9:00 PM — SWAT TRUCK / W.FLORISSANT AVE & NESBIT AVE
6:45 PM — POLICE FORM IN RIOT GEAR / QUIK TRIP / 9420 W.FLORISSANT AVE
2:10 AM — PHILLIPS 66 / 1403 CHAMBERS RD
1:45 AM — MOBIL GAS STATION / 9995 W.FLORISSANT AVE
1:30 AM — DELLWOOD CITY HALL / 1415 CHAMBERS RD
12:40 AM — BOOST MOBILE / 10425 W.FLORISSANT AVE
12:40 AM — FAMILY DOLLAR / 9070 W.FLORISSANT AVE
12:30 AM — QUICK CASH / 10220 W.FLORISSANT AVE

SUNDAY, AUGUST 10

11:45 PM — FOOTLOCKER / 8023 W.FLORISSANT AVE
10:45 PM — POLICE RIOT LINE ESTABLISHED / W.FLORISSANT AVE & CHAMBERS RD
10:30 PM — ZISSER TIRE & AUTO SERVICE / 9990 W.FLORISSANT AVE
8:00 PM — QUIK-TRIP / 9420 W.FLORISSANT AVE

SATURDAY, AUGUST 9

12:02 PM — MURDER OF MICHAEL BROWN / CANFIELD GARDENS

See also   1.2.06   4.1.02

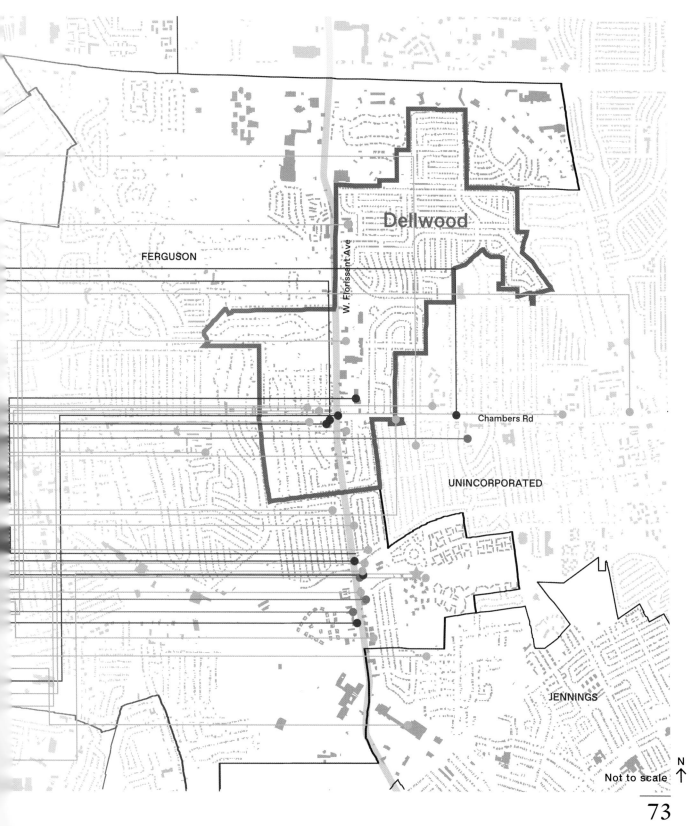

Public space

Photo by Kathleen Caulderwood, 2014
Sidewalks, despite their condition, are the front line in the battle for the democratic suburb.

In May 2021, the Missouri legislature passed a bill that made protests in the street a felony crime. Here, earlier in 2014, activists protested along the curb-less, undefined paved zone next to West Florissant Avenue, where it is unclear what is sidewalk and what is street. The edge condition is sometimes a traffic breakdown lane; other times a parking shoulder, a utility or drainage corridor. But this image reminds us that indeterminacy also allows for its reclaiming as public space.

75

2.M.01

Diagrammatic collages highlighting the indeterminate, blurred-edge condition between street, sidewalk and utility corridor (in orange) along West Florissant Avenue that passes through Ferguson and Dellwood, MO (2018).

Mobilize
The right-of-way

Along the first-ring suburban strip, it is not clear what is sidewalk and what is road or parking lot; where the utility corridor, bus stop or shoulder starts or stops. The blurred condition privileges cars, but this right-of-way is also presumably public and for pedestrians. During the 2014 Ferguson uprisings, the suburban right-of-way along West Florissant Avenue was claimed as public space.

Investments in pedestrian spaces like this will amplify social, democratizing impacts.

↳ Adding trees, healthy water catchment systems like rain gardens, and permeable surfaces will have exponential environmental benefits.

↳ Drawing by Ethan Miller, "The Strip: Improvised," Patty Heyda, *The Problem of the Suburb*, Washington University in St. Louis, 2016.

CAR HAS FREE-REIGN

BUS ST

6 INCH CURB SEPARATES PEDESTRIANS FROM 40-50 MPH TRAFFIC

AFRICAN
BEAUTY SUPPLIES
PHARMACY

RETAIL ADVERTISEMENT

See also   2.1.04   2.1.06

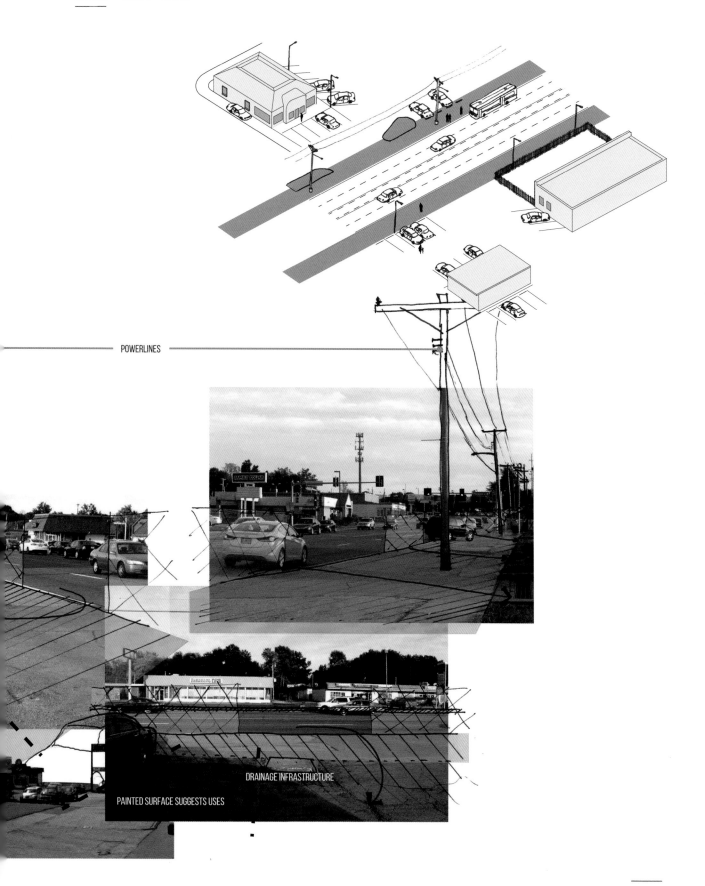

POWERLINES

DRAINAGE INFRASTRUCTURE

PAINTED SURFACE SUGGESTS USES

2.M.02

→

Plan drawing (right) and axonometric drawing (below) of a hypothetical wind-based zoning code for a site in St. Louis City (2021), imagining the kinds of passive energy-based infill buildings and urban blocks and spaces that might result.

Mobilize
Sustainable zoning

What if zoning regulations ensured that buildings and blocks were designed for healthy alternate energy systems and urban /suburban social life? The hypothetical plan shown here (for a site in St. Louis City, MO) explores the possibilities of a wind-based zoning code.

Not only does that suggest a porous, social, connected block that is pedestrian-friendly with circulation separated from cars but it also would ensure cleaner air and important reduction of emissions and energy costs in developments moving forward. The building envelope zoning in this proposal is designed to

accommodate solar panels on buildings when there is appropriate exposure. The project suggests ways the existing planned residential district (PRD) tool could be reclaimed to make urban or suburban developments with the public good in mind (over segregationist priorities of creating a private enclave).

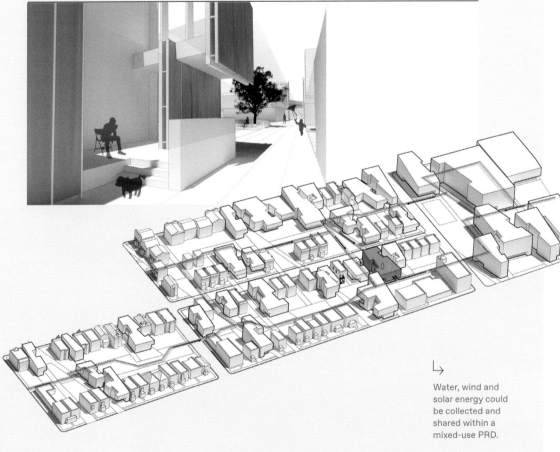

↳
Drawings by Connor Merritt, "A Wind-based Zoning Code," Patty Heyda, *Passive Aggressive: New Architectures for a Hot Planet*, Washington University in St. Louis, 2021.

↳
Water, wind and solar energy could be collected and shared within a mixed-use PRD.

See also   2.1.02   5.M.04

AREA COMMERCIAL
MAX HEIGHT: 8 STORIES OR 85FT

MULTI-FAMILY DWELLING
MAX HEIGHT: 3 STORIES OR 45FT

↰ Existing zoning plan

Hypothetical new wind-based zoning plan to guide new urban infill

Wind from the south in summer (St. Louis, MO)

Not to scale

N

2.M.03

Diagrams of some of the quirky local forms of architectural adaptation found in the first ring. Amidst intense efficiency and separation, these first-ring suburban aesthetics define place as they allow for flexibility and change.

Mobilize
Adaptation

Against the backdrop of single-use zoning, there are creative workarounds that governments and local businesses finagle to reuse and blend architectural typologies in tight financial circumstances. "Blending" is found all over the first ring. These practices signal sustainable approaches to building reuse and adaptation, just as they mark a distinctly local first-ring character.

"Generic-specific"

Embraces idiosyncratic but flexible interpretations of multiple architectural styles.

"Domestic"

Sustainable repurposing that subtly brings the center of government near neighborhoods it serves with approachable architecture—although not conducive to public gatherings and meetings.

"Blended"

Allows for expansion and opportunity while maintaining flexibility and reprogramming.

↳

Drawings by Casey Ryan, "Fragmentation Road," Patty Heyda, *The Problem of the Suburb*, Washington University, 2016.

See also   2.1.01   5.M.03

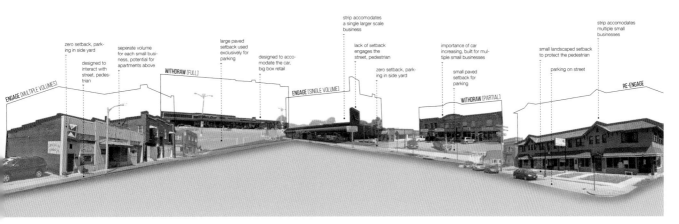

Strip

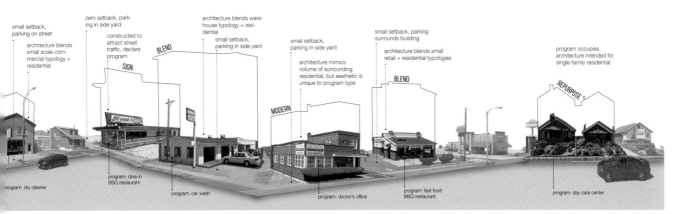

Commercial

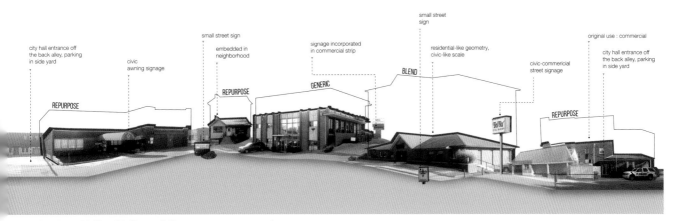

Institutional/ City Halls and Courts

03

Opportunity

Exclusion
Choice
Democracy
Empowerment

Access to property, housing and education

This chapter speaks to the common urban and suburban systems that maintain access to life opportunities for some and not others. The maps here further the themes in the first two chapters to highlight tools that have been weaponized to channel privilege or prevent access to property as access to opportunity.

The second section looks at access to opportunity through education, which, because of how public schools are funded, is an extension of access to property. Education funding in low-income, low-land-value areas is further bound by state austerity measures and privatization imaginaries, causing a host of complications. The neoliberal 'solutions' grow unrelated private capital and only make things harder for those trying to access education.

3.1.01

Below, the original 1937 Home Owner's Loan Corporation (HOLC) "Residential Security Map" of St. Louis.

At right, map of St. Louis City and County showing areas of highest and lowest median income (2016), against the HOLC map's rated zones (1937).

Redlining

The 1937 federal Home Owner's Loan Corporation (HOLC) "Residential Security Maps" gave power and legitimacy to private sector lenders to "redline" (deny federally backed loans) in neighborhoods designated as "declining" or "hazardous." In St. Louis, these were the predominantly African American areas.

The maps are clear examples of historic U.S. public policy that steered (white) wealth accumulation through property, in partnership with private-sector financial institutions. The HOLC "Residential Security Map" designations indexed white and Black neighborhoods with "A" and "B," or "Best" and "Desirable" (green and blue) for higher-income white areas; and "C," "Definitely declining," or "D," "Hazardous" (yellow and red) for Black communities. When compared to current-day wealth and poverty in the region, the former C- and D-rated designations are among those with the lowest median income, but so are some of the former B-rated areas. This finding speaks to the greater socioeconomic shifts that plagued the region since 1937 when manufacturing jobs left and those with means moved to the outer exurbs or back downtown.

Neighborhoods are still being rated to enable "informed investment decisions." See, for example, the algorithm-driven maps of Roofstock, a company that matches investors to lucrative single-family rental properties in U.S. cities. Like the HOLC, their map uses green for the highest-rated areas and red for the lowest. [1]

1 Jeff Rohde, "The St. Louis real estate market: Stats & trends for 2022," *Roofstock*, June 28. 2022.

HOLC St. Louis map: Robert K. Nelson, LaDale Winling, Richard Marciano, Nathan Connolly, et al., "Mapping Inequality," *American Panorama*, ed. Robert K. Nelson and Edward L. Ayers, accessed July 4, 2023.

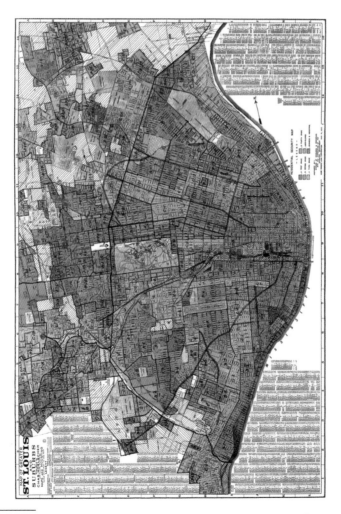

The term "redlining" refers to the ability of banks to strike a red rejection line through loan applications for houses within what were deemed "risky" areas.

See also   1.1.03   1.2.05   4.C.14

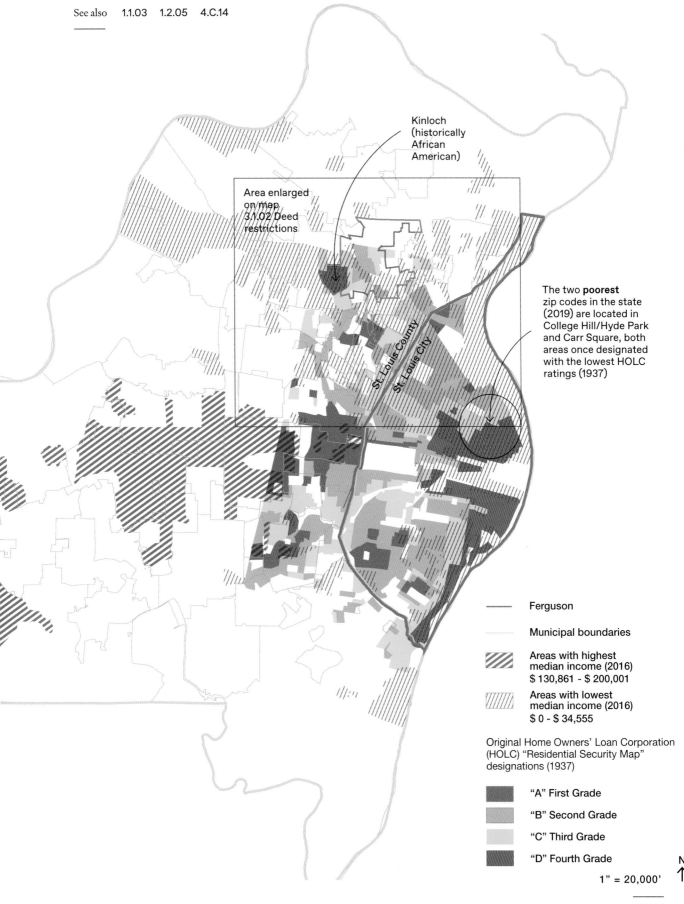

Kinloch
(historically
African
American)

Area enlarged
on map
3.1.02 Deed
restrictions

The two **poorest**
zip codes in the state
(2019) are located in
College Hill/Hyde Park
and Carr Square, both
areas once designated
with the lowest HOLC
ratings (1937)

St. Louis County
St. Louis City

——— Ferguson

——— Municipal boundaries

Areas with highest
median income (2016)
$ 130,861 - $ 200,001

Areas with lowest
median income (2016)
$ 0 - $ 34,555

Original Home Owners' Loan Corporation
(HOLC) "Residential Security Map"
designations (1937)

"A" First Grade

"B" Second Grade

"C" Third Grade

"D" Fourth Grade

1" = 20,000'

N
↑

85

3.1.02

Close-up map of the eastern portions of North St. Louis County and northwest St. Louis City, showing areas with properties that have or had a deed restriction in the historic chain of title (as of 2022), overlaid against an adaptation of the (1937) Home Owners' Loan Corporation "Residential Securities" map's rated properties that determined access to government-backed loans.

Deed restrictions

Financial institutions, white homeowners and developers were beneficiaries of the 1937 HOLC map that racially constructed the 'safest' places to invest. Later, real estate agents protected "A" and "B" grade neighborhoods by writing race-restrictive covenants directly into property deeds to prevent sales to Black buyers. The map reveals this practice of layered protective reinforcement between 'desirable' HOLC areas and where restrictive covenants were written into the property deeds.

In 1948 the U.S. Supreme Court Case Shelly vs Kramer in St. Louis City determined that deed restrictions were unenforceable by law. As real estate agents moved away from the practice, suburbs and neighborhoods were intentionally isolated in other ways, with tools like planned residential developments (PRDs) and Homeowners Associations (HOAs).

1 Loewen, James W. "Ferguson, Missouri as a Sundown Town." History and Social Justice, February 24, 2021.

Adaptation of HOLC St. Louis map: Robert K. Nelson, LaDale Winling, Richard Marciano, Nathan Connolly, et al., "Mapping Inequality," *American Panorama*, ed. Robert K. Nelson and Edward L. Ayers.

St. Louis County municipal boundaries (2022)

St. Louis City neighborhood boundaries (2022)

Properties with restrictive covenants by 1950

Approximate boundary and "grade ratings" of original Home Owners' Loan Corporation (HOLC) "Residential Security Map" designations (1937)

"A" grade

"B" grade

"C" grade

"D" grade

See also   2.1.02   2.1.03   3.1.01

70,000
properties in St. Louis County
have a racial covenant in their
historic chain of title (2022)

Ferguson

(Also likely a
"Sundown Town"
between the 1940s
and 1960s) 1

Kinloch

St. Louis County

St. Louis City

30,000
properties in St. Louis City
have a racial covenant in
their historic chain of title
(2022)

N

1" = 5,000'

3.1.03

Below, the 1937 Home Owner's Loan Corporation (HOLC) map of St. Louis showing the area of Ferguson, Kinloch, Missouri and North County today, enlarged in the map on the right.

Right, a close-up view of the 1937 HOLC map (below) overlaid onto Ferguson and Kinloch, MO, today.

Floodlining

The overlay shows that the low-income neighborhood along Canfield Drive where Michael Brown was killed was untouched by historic racial redlining because it was not residential. It was in a flood zone. 'Floodlining' is the more recent weaponization of the environment, where private developers inappropriately build affordable neighborhoods in flood zones to exploit access to cheap land and to extract returns. This continues today with commercial areas along the fragile Missouri River.

⌐→ If an apartment is damaged by flooding from an outside source like a stream overflow, the landlord is responsible for repairs. Tenants are nonetheless vulnerable because they must pay for temporary housing and other damages to personal items unless they have rental insurance, something increasingly difficult to obtain in flood-prone areas.

HOLC St. Louis map: Robert K. Nelson, LaDale Winling, Richard Marciano, Nathan Connolly, et al., "Mapping Inequality," *American Panorama*, ed. Robert K. Nelson and Edward L. Ayers, accessed July 4, 2023.

AREA ENLARGED

 Ferguson today

- - - - - Rail lines

 Stream and Floodway / Flood Hazard Area

(Underlay, from 1937) The original Home Owners' Loan Corporation (HOLC) map. From the legend:

 "A_FIRST GRADE"

 "B_SECOND GRADE"

 "C_THIRD GRADE"

 "D_FOURTH GRADE"

 "UNDEVELOPED"

As the late 1960s and 1970s public-private planning replaced ideas of direct public housing, the resulting developer-led projects shifted to cost-saving, exploitative shallow versions of 'housing provision.'

⌐→ Vegetated stream banks and flood areas are part of a healthy riparian ecosystem and should not be compromised by development.

See also   1.1.01   2.1.02   3.1.10-11   5.3.14

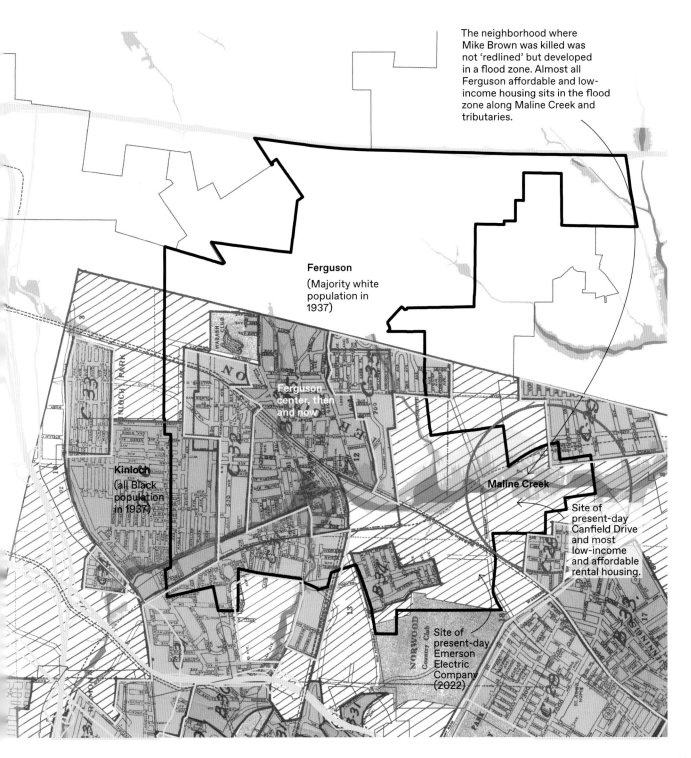

The neighborhood where Mike Brown was killed was not 'redlined' but developed in a flood zone. Almost all Ferguson affordable and low-income housing sits in the flood zone along Maline Creek and tributaries.

Ferguson
(Majority white population in 1937)

Ferguson center, then and now

Kinloch
(all Black population in 1937)

Maline Creek

Site of present-day Canfield Drive and most low-income and affordable rental housing.

Site of present-day Emerson Electric Company (2022)

N

1" = 3,750'

3.1.04

Map of St. Louis County and City showing the uneven pattern of 'minority' vs. 'white' homeowners who received a mortgage loan in 2018-2019. Data adapted from National Community and Reinvestment Coalition (2018).

Below, a chart showing the rates of mortgage denials by race for Black and white borrowers in the U.S. between 2000 and 2015.

Redlining 2.0

U.S. mortgage denial rates are down overall since 2000 (in 2015), but this map shows a persistence of contemporary forms of redlining, seen in the pattern of uneven access to mortgage loans between minority and white borrowers in the St. Louis region. 1

Exclusionary loan practices by some area banks are still being called out. Efforts by the Metropolitan St. Louis Equal Housing Opportunities Council are slowing changing the tide of available credit to minority borrowers. 2

Areas where median home values are less than $100,000 (2021) (National average: $264,000)

——— Ferguson

HOME PURCHASE LOANS (2018-2019) (1 symbol = 50 borrowers)

✛ Minority borrower

✚ White borrower

"Lending discrimination deprives communities of access to credit and leaves the residents of minority neighborhoods vulnerable to predatory lenders. This type of discrimination is part of the web of intolerable practices that stripped vast amounts of wealth from communities of color in the last decade." 2

1 Data adapted from *National Community and Reinvestment Coalition (NCRC) Report*, "Home Mortgage Lending in St. Louis, Milwaukee, Minneapolis and Surrounding Areas," July, 2016.

2 Quote by Thomas E. Perez, Assistant Attorney General for the Justice Department's Civil Rights Division: "Justice Department Reaches Settlement with Midwest BankCentre Regarding Alleged Lending Discrimination in St. Louis," Office of Public Affairs, U.S. Department of Justice, June 16, 2011.

Chart based on data and graph from the PEW Research Center, 2017.

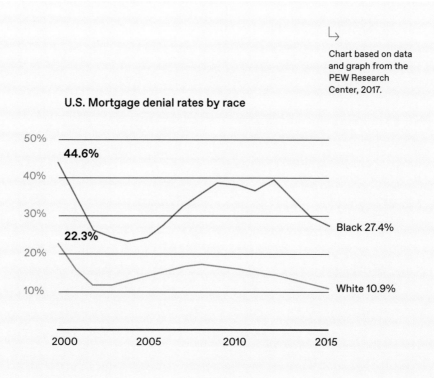

U.S. Mortgage denial rates by race

See also   3.1.01   3.1.06   3.2.12

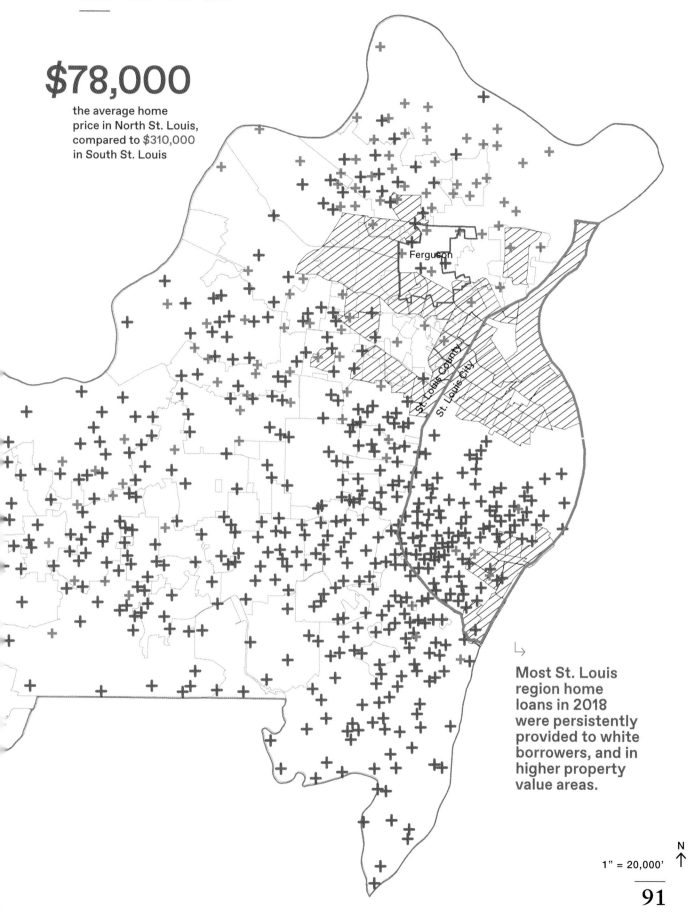

$78,000

the average home
price in North St. Louis,
compared to $310,000
in South St. Louis

Ferguson

St. Louis County

St. Louis City

Most St. Louis
region home
loans in 2018
were persistently
provided to white
borrowers, and in
higher property
value areas.

1" = 20,000'

N

3.1.05 | Municipal credit/debt

Map of St. Louis County and City showing which municipalities had debt (2014), as a reflection of access to credit markets. Tax Increment Financing (TIF) districts are overlaid (2006-2023).

Impoverished municipalities, like people, get shut out of traditional credit markets. Lack of capital impacts a city's ability to provide services and implement programs. 1

"We've long known that individuals in poor communities were shut out of traditional credit markets and are often forced to turn to alternate sources of capital. Go to any impoverished neighborhood in the area, and you will find an abundance of alternative 'financial institutions.' Places like payday loan stores, pawn shops, title loan stores or check-cashing shops—all of which charge exorbitant rates and fees to access much-needed capital. This is no secret. However, what we didn't realize was that it's not just individuals who are shut out of traditional markets. In many municipalities without debt, the entire community is also shut out of traditional markets, with even fewer places to turn for capital to reinvest." 1

↳

It's not necessarily good to owe debt. But in today's economic system, debt is access to capital that builds racialized power. 2 Lack of holding debt reveals who may have ample access to capital to pay it off, but also who is shut out of access to credit markets.

1 Quote by Jim Buford, former head, Urban League St. Louis, in Better Together, "Municipalities with and without debt," August 19, 2014.

2 John Robinson III, "Race, Poverty, and markets: urban inequality after the neoliberal turn." *Sociology Compass*, 2016.

ST. LOUIS CITY AND COUNTY MUNICIPALITIES

▨	With no municipal debt (2014)
▧	With municipal debt (2014)
≡	Unincorporated areas
☐	Tax Increment Financing (TIF) districts (2006-2023)

↳

Tax Increment Financing provides public subsidy to private redevelopment.

See also   4.2.10-11   4.3.21   4.3.25-26

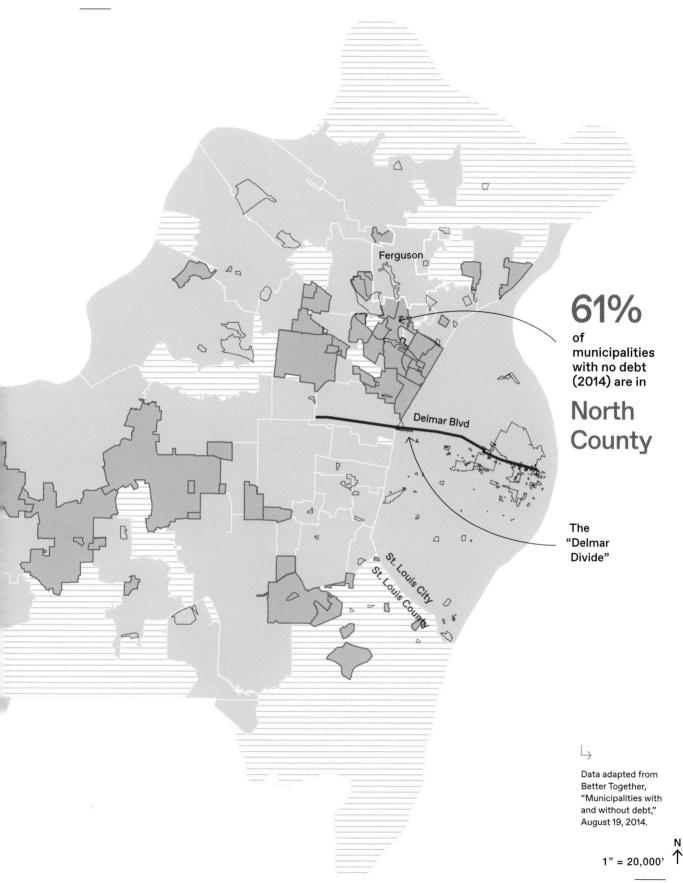

Ferguson

61%
of
**municipalities
with no debt
(2014) are in**

**North
County**

Delmar Blvd

The
"Delmar
Divide"

St. Louis City
St. Louis County

Data adapted from
Better Together,
"Municipalities with
and without debt,"
August 19, 2014.

1" = 20,000'

N

3.1.06

Charts showing comparative economics and demographics of home owning vs. renting in the U.S., with details about how the federal mortgage interest tax deduction program subsidizes property ownership. A comparison of two houses in the same census tract in Ferguson, MO—one rented, one owned—are shown alongside a house in wealthier Wildwood, MO. The more expensive house receives the lowest effective interest rate after the deduction.

Mortgage interest tax deduction (MID)

The federal mortgage interest tax deduction (called MID) is a public instrument for building property equity, designed to benefit wealthier homeowners the most. It builds what geographer Samuel Stein calls the "real estate state" 1 by subsidizing those with access to a mortgage in the first place (as it benefits financial institutions who charge mortgage interest). The incentive allows homeowners to deduct a percentage of the interest paid from their federal taxes.

On the one hand, the charts show how savings accrue over time for homeowners with the benefit vs. renters. On the other hand, the diagrams show the MID privileges wealthier buyers who earn more than $100,000 per year (see map 3.1.04 for the geography of these buyers in St. Louis). The benefit requires taxpayers to itemize deductions (something lower-income households don't typically do), and the deduction available is based on the percent-tax bracket of the household (note that bank loan interest rates are also lower for those who spend more money). The higher the tax bracket, the greater percentage deduction is available.

"The MID is a costly federal tax expenditure that disproportionately benefits higher-income households who do not need assistance to afford their homes. At the same time, nearly eight million extremely low-income renters spend more than half of their incomes on housing, forcing them to sacrifice other necessities. The federal revenue lost to the MID would be better spent on housing assistance for these lowest-income households who have the greatest need." 2

↳

Right, map of the St. Louis Region showing Ferguson and Wildwood, MO, in blue, where the comparative houses at right are located.

1 Samuel Stein, *Capital City, Gentrification and the Real Estate State*, (London: Verso, 2019).

2 Andrew Aurand, "The Mortgage Interest Deduction," *National Low Income Housing Coalition*, 2022 Advocates' Guide.

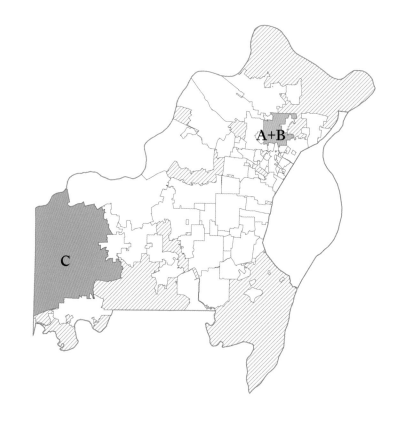

See also   2.1.03   3.1.04

↳

Savings for homeowners with a fixed mortgage and deduction accrue over time, compared to renters whose rent generally increases each year by 3-5%.

Chart and points above adapted from Dan Brassil, Renting vs Buying in St. Louis (2023).

Years	Rent Payment	Mortgage Payment	Monthly Difference	After Tax Savings	Yearly Difference	After Tax Savings
1	800	1000	-200	-50	-2400	-600
2	840	1000	-160	-10	-1920	-120
3	882	1000	-116	+32	-1416	+384
4	926	1000	-74	+76	-888	+912
5	972	1000	-28	+122	-336	+1464
6	1021	1000	+21	+171	+252	+2052
7	1072	1000	+72	+222	+864	+2664
8-30						

Annual savings increase every year for homeowners

A. Rented house

3 Bed / 1 Bath
960 Sq ft
Rent: $945/mo

Southwest Ferguson, MO

Savings

No real savings in long term

B. Owned house

2 Bed / 1 Bath
1,008 Sq ft
List: $100,000
Avg 30 year mortgage
(7.2% on $95,000):
$650/mo

Southwest Ferguson, MO

buyer in
12%
tax bracket

Savings

Difference in mortgage and rental over time

Tax savings in first year $1760

Effective interest rate after tax deductions

5.611%

↳ **Mortgage Interest Deduction is likely less than standard deduction, so benefit would not even apply**

C. Owned house

5 Bed /5 Bath
5590 Sq ft
List: $1,000,000
Avg 30 year mortgage
(6.46% on 800,000):
$5035/mo

Wildwood, MO

buyer in
32%
tax bracket

Savings

Tax savings in first year $31,134

Effective interest rate after tax deductions

3.075%

3.1.07

Map showing
foreclosures
in St. Louis
County and City
(2020) against
the backdrop
of areas where
subprime
loans were
most prevalent
(2004). The
map also shows
how the same
North County
areas with
concentrated
foreclosures
and a history of
subprime loans
are where more
than 40% of
mortgages were
"underwater,"
meaning more
was owned on
the mortgage
than the value of
the house (2014).

Foreclosure

Foreclosure reinforces ideas of housing as a market tool rather than a right.

Foreclosure is a profitable business: Lenders can deduct the amount of a non-performing loan from taxes, while "they are still allowed to pursue the debts and generate revenue from them." [1] Lenders can also sell the non-performing loans to secondary companies that purchase them in 'bundles' at discounted rates, then foreclose the properties and resell them. Foreclosure has been described as a way to keep property financially 'productive.' [2] Home foreclosures concentrate in North St. Louis, where predatory subprime loans were most prevalent in 2004.

●   Home foreclosures (2020)

SUBPRIME HOME LOANS (2004)
Percentage of subprime loans per census
tract in 2004, prior to the housing collapse
of 2008

	0-10%
	11-20%
	21-35%
	36-54%

UNDERWATER HOME MORTGAGES (2014)

Zip codes where 43% or more
home mortgages were
"underwater" (2014), meaning that
more was owned on the home
than the value of the home itself.

↳
1 Laura Greene,
"Why Do Banks
Write Off
Bad Debt?"
Investopedia,
June 30, 2021.

2 Kimberly
Manning, "What
happened
to Ferguson,
Missouri's
housing market
in the past year?"
Inman, August 17,
2015.

↳
Underwater
mortgage data
adapted from
Gallagher, Jim. "St.
Louis Is Hot Spot
for 'underwater'
Mortgages."
*St. Louis Post-
Dispatch*, May 9,
2014.

Subprime loan
data adapted from
Duncan, Michael.
"Snapshot: An
Ordinary Suburb,
an Extraordinary
Number of
Foreclosures." *Saint
Louis Fed Eagle*,
October 1, 2008.

73%

the increase
in Ferguson
foreclosures from
the first half of
2015 compared
to the last half of
2014

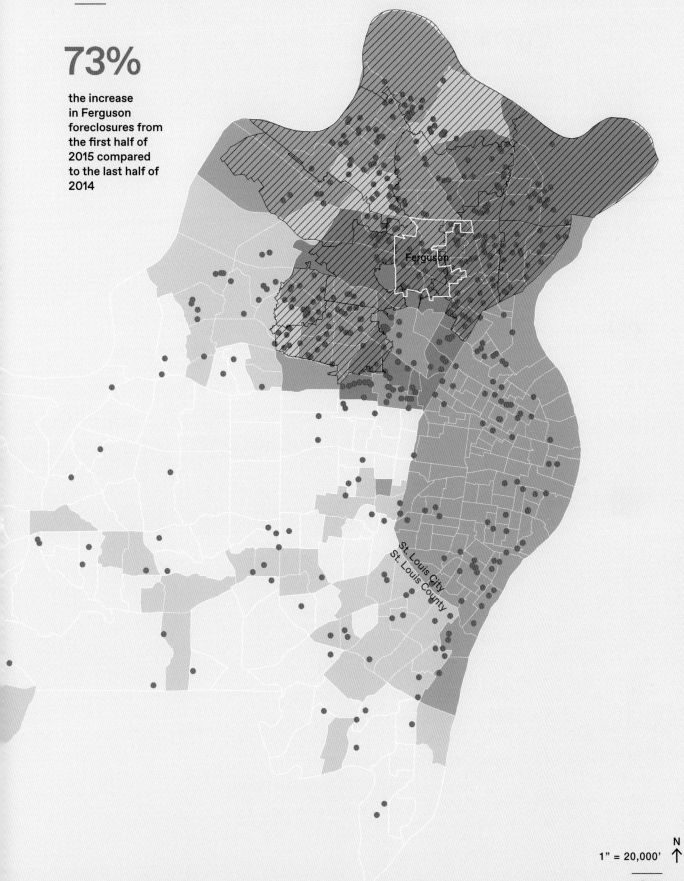

Ferguson

St. Louis City
St. Louis County

1" = 20,000'

N
↑

97

3.1.08

Map of St. Louis City and County showing "property crimes" as rates of property and vehicle theft, burglary and arson (2022) but also as areas of concentrated fraudulent subprime mortgage lending (2004, shown in the county only).

Property crime

Property crime rates are high in North St. Louis County, but so are predatory kinds of white-collar property crime committed by lending institutions. The map reminds us that these illegal activities by financial institutions are also crimes, yet rarely mapped as such.

The map shows the prevalence of predatory forms of 'property crime' via exploitative subprime mortgages that were issued in North St. Louis in 2004 leading up to the 2008 housing foreclosure crisis.

During that 2008 crisis, 80% of the home loan fraud cases were committed by "for-profit" brokers (i.e. not the home-buyers). These brokers were not necessarily major banks, but bank "affiliates" and "subsidiaries"— yet another hidden set of processes that underlie the property exchange and that happen often with no say or knowledge by homeowners.

—— Ferguson

PROPERTY CRIME (2022)

Property crime grades from CrimeGrade.org based on rates of property theft, vehicle theft, burglary and arson per 1,000 residents (2022):

Grade "C" (below the U.S. average metro area)

Grade "D" (higher than the U.S. average metro area)

Grade "F" (higher than the U.S. average metro area)

WHITE-COLLAR PROPERTY CRIME (2004)

Census tracts with the highest percentage (36-54%) of subprime loans (2004). When the 2008 housing loan crisis occurred in the U.S., 80% of the fraudulent loan cases were committed by for-profit brokers, not by homebuyers.

↳
Subprime loan data adapted from Duncan, Michael. "Snapshot: An Ordinary Suburb, an Extraordinary Number of Foreclosures." *Saint Louis Fed Eagle*, October 1, 2008.

See also   3.1.01-04   5.3.15

Ferguson

St. Louis County
St Louis City

Ferguson, MO, has
slightly lower rates of
traditionally defined
property crime but
substantial areas
where white-collar
crime occurred when
subprime loans were
issued.

1" = 20,000'   N

3.1.09

Map of North St. Louis County showing where federal Section 8 low-income housing vouchers are offered (scaled according to the number of voucher holders, by race).

Low-income housing "choice" vouchers

The public Section 8 "Housing Choice Voucher" program provides rent assistance for low-income families by contradictorily serving the private housing market instead.

"Vouchers" are given to qualifying residents to use towards the cost of rent. But the "Housing Choice Vouchers" do not actually provide choice of where to live for low-income renters, since the private market drives where and which apartment complexes offer voucher-accepting units. As a result, voucher holders are stuck in the same areas of compounded poverty and low educational opportunity.

The map shows the spatial distribution of Section 8 voucher rental units that concentrate in North St. Louis County and northern parts of St. Louis City. As seen on other maps, these are areas of low-performing schools and concentrated poverty. The federally funded voucher program is locally administered by the St. Louis County Housing Authority. Waiting lists to receive vouchers or units can take years if not decades.

↳

Landlord discretion

Section 8 low-income rental housing vouchers "often reinforce existing patterns of segregation" because private landlords decide whether they will offer them or not. 1

1 Quote by Margery Turner at the Urban Institute, from, Haeyoun Park, "Many Minority Families Stuck in Poor Neighborhoods Despite Housing Voucher Program," *New York Times*, August 8, 2015.

↳

Voucher location data adapted from Haeyoun Park, "Many Minority Families Stuck in Poor Neighborhoods Despite Housing Voucher Program," *New York Times*, August 8, 2015.

Adapted from Nakesha Newsome, "Race, Property and Housing opportunities," Patty Heyda, *Radical Mapping*, Washington University in St. Louis, 2021.

- - - - - Ferguson

▨ "Promise Zone" eligible areas

Areas accepting low-income housing vouchers (scaled to reflect relative amount of units available):

◯ (dashed) Voucher holders mostly white (2013)

◯ Voucher holders mostly minority (2013)

▨ Areas with 100% more than average eviction filings (July-August, 2022)

Racial demographics (1 dot = 66 people)

■ Black population

● White population

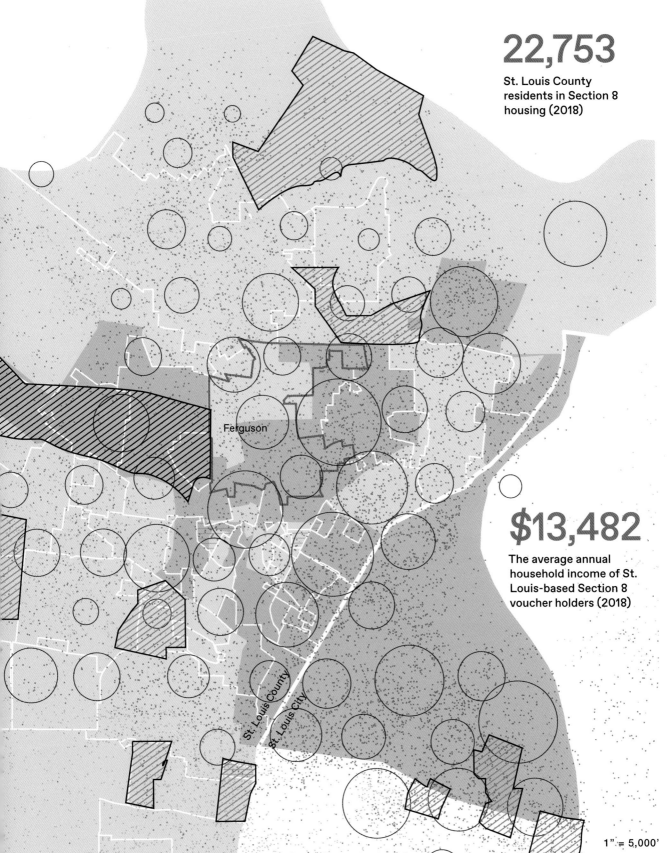

22,753

St. Louis County
residents in Section 8
housing (2018)

Ferguson

$13,482

The average annual
household income of St.
Louis-based Section 8
voucher holders (2018)

St. Louis County

St. Louis City

1" = 5,000'

N

3.1.10

Map of St. Louis County and City showing eviction filing rates against renters compared to the national average, for the four-week period from July to August 2020 (by census tract).

Eviction

Eviction is a tool that is frequently abused by large company landlords to expediently collect overdue rent. (As opposed to informal, personal communication methods between single-proprietor landlords and tenants). 1

Sometimes, if Section 8 landlords are cited for repairs by the government, their government funding will be withheld until repairs are made. Instead, landlords evict residents rather than complete the needed work. Accountability to uphold health and safety standards—rights to housing—is difficult or slow in the blurred space between public and private sectors, and can backfire for residents.

It appears that Ferguson has average eviction filing rates compared to the above average rates in North County. However, at a finer scale, eviction rates are higher in the southeast area of Ferguson, where most of the affordable apartment complexes are. Many of these are owned and run by large landlords.

"We hate to see you go!

We hate to lose you as a resident, but per county housing they will not allow Park Ridge Apartments to continue housing you any longer. November 14, 2018 has to be your last day with us. I know this is such short notice, but just know we have fought so hard to keep all our residents but unfortunately we can't." 2

Excerpt from an eviction letter to a resident from property owner TEH Realty in Ferguson, Missouri (November, 2018). The housing choice voucher isn't protected. Here, the government decided to withhold Section 8 funding due to poor conditions to encourage the landlord to make necessary fixes. But it resulted in unexpected evictions for innocent families.

2 Quote is from an image of the letter in Nassim Benchaabane, Rachel Rice, "Ferguson apartment complex tells some low-income tenants to leave, but housing authority says they can stay," *St. Louis Post-Dispatch*, November, 2018.

EVICTION FILING RATES

"The number of eviction filings divided by the number of renter households in the area—or compared to the typical number of filings in the average year." (Evictionlab.org)

% of filings compared to average (July, 2022)

-100%   average   100%

Ferguson

St. Louis County
St. Louis City

1 Research summary,
"Do Large Landlords'
Eviction Practices
Differ from Small
Landlords'?"
Housing Matters,
February 1, 2023.

↳

Eviction rate data
adapted from
Evictionlab.org. It
represents eviction
filings from four
weeks between July
2020 and August
2020, by census
tract.

1" = 20,000'

N
↑

3.1.11

Map of Ferguson, MO, highlighting some of the largest apartment complexes and their owner-companies, with locations of the companies as listed in public records (2023). The map also shows how almost all of the large affordable apartment complexes in Ferguson are exploitatively located in and along a flood zone.

Large/company & absentee landlords

The same system that generates returns for large-capital landlords generates insecurity for renters who live in the properties: Large/company landlords manage multiple complexes from a distance and use eviction as a coercive rent-collection tool.

Large landlords are defined as generally having more than 15 properties that are operated and managed as companies. The owners almost never live on or near the properties, and most own property through multiple companies, many under different names. [1]

Affordable rental housing supply

With the decline of government-sponsored housing over the last decades in the United States (and the rule of developers to follow high-return markets) a crisis of available affordable rental units has resulted, hitting the lowest-income renters the hardest. In Ferguson, low-income renters (including non-voucher holders) are limited to these same large-landlord-owned affordable apartment complexes.

In 2021 the St. Louis metro area had only:

34,324

available rental homes for

91,662

"extremely low income renter households." [2]

A market-based housing system, even when offering "affordable units," will only follow profitability, reproducing and exacerbating the need for accessible units.

One study showed that landlords that are companies or shell companies file eviction notices

186% more often

than small single-proprietor landlords do [1]

1 Research summary, "Do Large Landlords' Eviction Practices Differ from Small Landlords'?" *Housing Matters*, February 1, 2023.

2 National Low Income Housing Coalition, "National Shortage of Affordable Rental Housing," *The Gap: A Shortage of Affordable Rental Homes*; Gap Data for Missouri, 2021.

Legend:

— 'Large-landlord' / company owned multifamily rental complexes (apartments or townhomes, 2023)

— Ferguson municipal boundary

- - - Railroad tracks

▓ Flood hazard zones

▨ Area where 80% or more of the population identifies as Black (approx 2020-22)

See also   3.1.03   3.1.10

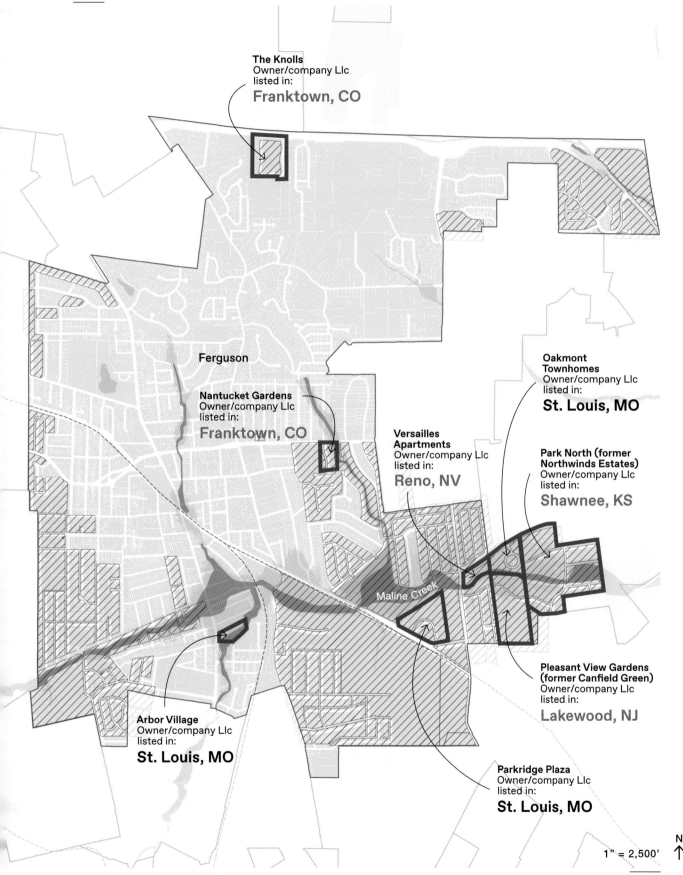

The Knolls
Owner/company Llc
listed in:
Franktown, CO

Ferguson

Nantucket Gardens
Owner/company Llc
listed in:
Franktown, CO

**Versailles
Apartments**
Owner/company Llc
listed in:
Reno, NV

**Oakmont
Townhomes**
Owner/company Llc
listed in:
St. Louis, MO

**Park North (former
Northwinds Estates)**
Owner/company Llc
listed in:
Shawnee, KS

Maline Creek

**Pleasant View Gardens
(former Canfield Green)**
Owner/company Llc
listed in:
Lakewood, NJ

Arbor Village
Owner/company Llc
listed in:
St. Louis, MO

Parkridge Plaza
Owner/company Llc
listed in:
St. Louis, MO

1" = 2,500'

N
↑

3.2.12

Map of St. Louis County and City showing median household income (2016) relative to school districts, with selected performance ratings and funding details highlighted. Lower-rated districts receive less funding from local sources while state sources have remained historically insufficient. 1

↳

2017 Missouri Assessment Program (MAP) scores reflecting the percent of students deemed proficient or advanced, by school district and subject.

↳

1 There is more to the story. For a detailed explanation of Missouri's inequitable allocation system of state school funding, see *Still Separate, Still Unequal* (2020); https://stillunequal.org/funding/

Public school funding

Public school districts are not funded in equal proportions of state and local sources because funding is tied to capital property markets. This limits access to opportunity through education.

School district performance correlates to higher local sources of funding where household income is higher. This reproduces a feedback loop of school district capacity based on the buying power of households—and on land values, which are in turn tightly protected by suburban systems of exclusion shown on other maps. Access to opportunity through education is access to the property market.

Ferguson-Florrisant district

K-12 Enrollment: 10,495 (2017)

Eng. Language Arts	41%
Mathematics	20.5%
Science	32%
Social Studies	54.5%

Normandy district

K-12 Enrollment: 3,083 (2017)

Eng. Language Arts	34%
Mathematics	19.2%
Science	11.1%
Social Studies	17.4%

Riverview Gardens district

K-12 Enrollment: 5,213 (2017)

Eng. Language Arts	29.5%
Mathematics	15%
Science	16.9%
Social Studies	46.2%

Brentwood district

K-12 Enrollment: 797 (2017)

Eng. Language Arts	77.1%
Mathematics	67.9%
Science	71%
Social Studies	76.5%

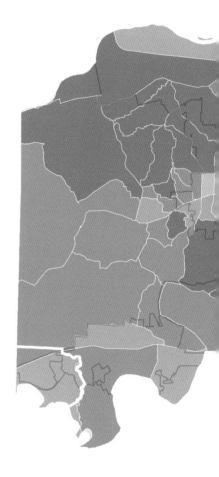

See also   3.1.06   3.2.15-17   3.M.01   4.3.25-26

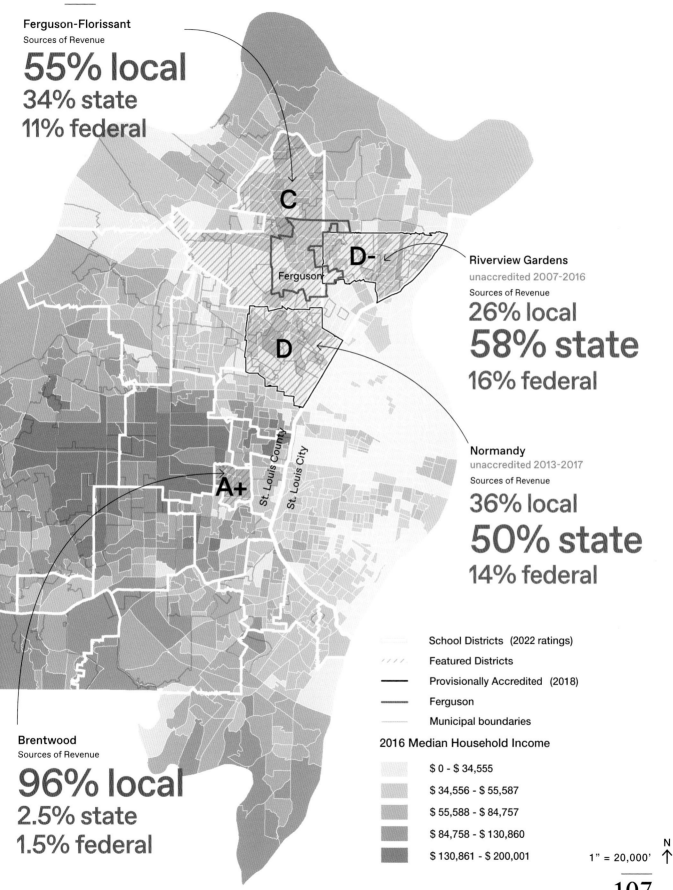

Ferguson-Florissant
Sources of Revenue

55% local
34% state
11% federal

Riverview Gardens
unaccredited 2007-2016

Sources of Revenue

26% local
58% state
16% federal

Normandy
unaccredited 2013-2017

Sources of Revenue

36% local
50% state
14% federal

St. Louis County
St. Louis City

Ferguson

Brentwood
Sources of Revenue

96% local
2.5% state
1.5% federal

School Districts   (2022 ratings)

//// Featured Districts

—— Provisionally Accredited   (2018)

—— Ferguson

—— Municipal boundaries

2016 Median Household Income

$ 0 - $ 34,555

$ 34,556 - $ 55,587

$ 55,588 - $ 84,757

$ 84,758 - $ 130,860

$ 130,861 - $ 200,001

1" = 20,000'

N

3.2.13

Map of St. Louis region school districts showing the chain of deaccreditation and provisional accreditation (2007-2018), and the assistance provided by accredited districts (2015), with other complexities of this system detailed below.

Deaccreditation

Deaccreditation and reaccreditation are politicized when the state removes and restores accreditation without notable improvements. [1] **Losing accreditation replaces the democratically elected school board with a state-appointed one that does not necessarily answer to the community. Deaccreditation often reduces federal /state funding and does not solve the problem of school disinvestment.**

Deaccreditation hurts students' abilities to be considered for college and requires them to retake classes to prove proficiency. For a time, it also involved the right of students to transfer to an accredited district, a solution that drained the unaccredited districts of future funding, with piecemeal limitations despite few benefits.

Ft. Zumwalt

Francis Howell

Rockwood

↳

Meanwhile, the Missouri state legislature attempts to "tweak the transfer law" with provisions for private-backed charter schools and other measures that ultimately undermine the public system altogether (as "solution" to the crisis). In 2014, this effort was vetoed by then Governor Nixon (D).

↳

On the one hand, the regional collaboration pooled support from across the region, saving unaccredited districts the (high) cost of transferring students; keeping kids in neighborhood-based schools. On the other hand, the collaboration allowed higher performing districts to avoid taking additional transfer students, limiting opportunities for students in unaccredited districts.

2 "School desegregation efforts in St. Louis," *St. Louis Post-Dispatch*, February 18, 2022.

Student transfer law

2013

A timeline of events: The Missouri Student Transfer Law is upheld by the Missouri Supreme Court. It allows that the 2,200 students from the unaccredited districts of Normandy and Riverview Gardens can transfer to accredited schools in neighboring districts.

Normandy and Riverview Gardens School Districts collectively spend nearly $23 million on transportation costs and tuition to accredited schools (up to $20,000 per transfer student).

2014

As the law is challenged, and when some districts announced they would no longer take transfers from unaccredited districts, the Normandy District is undemocratically taken over by the state and reorganized as a "new" Normandy Schools Collaborative, thus erasing its unaccredited status so that transfers can continue (while schools and the boundaries stay intact).

2015

24 higher performing school districts in the region partner with Normandy and Riverview Gardens to form the St. Louis Regional Collaborative for Educational Excellence.

2017 / 2018

Riverview Gardens School District and Normandy Schools Collaborative granted provisional accreditation status.

───────────

↳

In both the county and the city, bus transfer programs are ending. "New students will be accepted into the program for the last time in the 2023-2024 school year." [2]

Assisting districts:

- Opened training sessions and professional development programs to educators in unaccredited districts.

- Took on, or provided, staff or teachers.

- Placed voluntary caps on transfer tuition.

1 Brett Robertson, education policy analyst, in conversation with the author, July 14, 2023.

See also   3.2.14-15

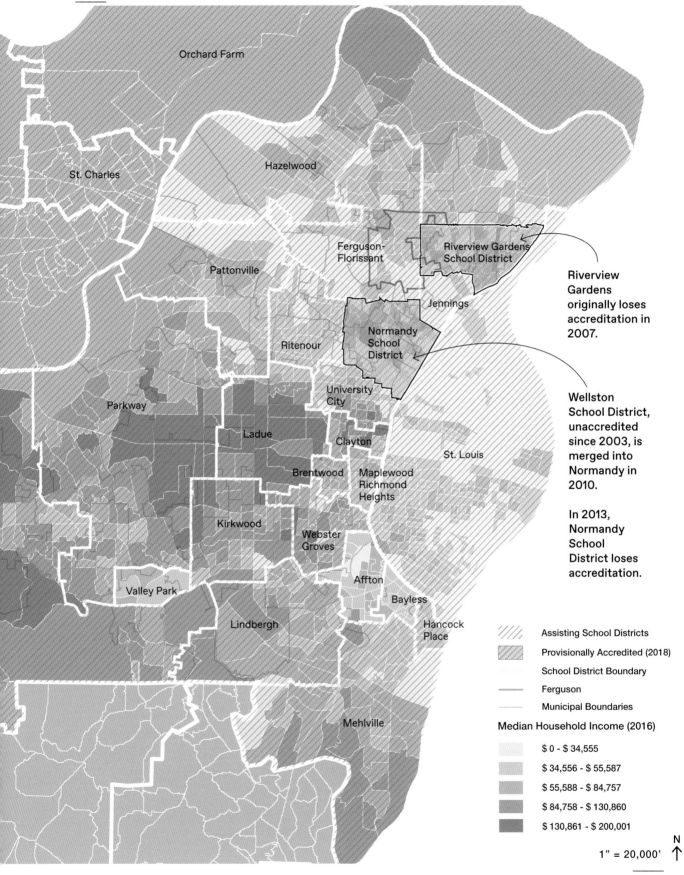

Orchard Farm

St. Charles

Hazelwood

Pattonville

Ferguson-
Florissant

Riverview Gardens
School District

Jennings

Riverview
Gardens
originally loses
accreditation in
2007.

Normandy
School
District

Wellston
School District,
unaccredited
since 2003, is
merged into
Normandy in
2010.

In 2013,
Normandy
School
District loses
accreditation.

Ritenour

University
City

Parkway

Ladue

Clayton

St. Louis

Brentwood

Maplewood
Richmond
Heights

Kirkwood

Webster
Groves

Valley Park

Affton

Bayless

Lindbergh

Hancock
Place

Mehlville

Assisting School Districts

Provisionally Accredited (2018)

School District Boundary

Ferguson

Municipal Boundaries

Median Household Income (2016)

$ 0 - $ 34,555

$ 34,556 - $ 55,587

$ 55,588 - $ 84,757

$ 84,758 - $ 130,860

$ 130,861 - $ 200,001

1" = 20,000'

N

3.2.14

These diagrams compare the daily experiences of three kids in the same grade with different access to educational opportunities.

The snapshot of John and Chris's school experiences compared to Mark's* shows underlying costs of being in an unaccredited district, even with the bus-transfer program option.

↳

1 Mark's school experience ideally would be walkable. But because he lives in a subdivision in the suburbs, his street is either cut off from the next neighborhood, or is defined by car-oriented commercial strips, making the commute longer and more convoluted than necessary. His experience ends up revealing the additional costs of suburban planning.

Student transfer programs

The transfer option signals an erosion of the commitment to neighborhood public schools as important community anchors.

While transfer programs provide access to education for students in underperforming districts, they also contribute to profound fragmentation of local and social neighborhood space. It would be better to support public school districts in the first place. The transfers provide access to accredited schools for those in unaccredited districts but at a burden to participants and families that travel greater distances with less flexibility.

Additional cost of the transfer program:

5.76

metric tons CO_2/year/ household

St. Louis County

Francis Howell School District

St. Charles County

35 minute commute via School Bus

♦ Mark's House
Bryan Middle School

John's House
Chris's House

St. Ann's of Normandy

Normandy Schools Collaborative (unaccredited 2014)

St. Louis City

Adaptation of Ryan Treacy, "Invisible Education." Patty Heyda, In\Visible Cities, Washington University in St. Louis, 2017.

90 minute commute via Metro Bus + 3 mile walk

John and Chris are middle school students who live near each other in an unaccredited school district. Mark is a middle school student who lives in a highly ranked, accredited district in St. Charles County. Chris travels by bus with the voluntary bussing program to Mark's district, and John pays to attend a local private Catholic school. In the end, Mark is best off because he can directly attend a high performing school in his own neighborhood—with kids who also live on his block. Mark's parents have the benefit of building community with other parents of kids at the school, a process reinforced by the fact that they are also neighbors.

	FRANCIS HOWELL SCHOOL DISTRICT Rated A+ (2022)	NORMANDY SCHOOLS COLLABORATIVE Rated D (2022)
DROPOUT RATE (2017)	0.7 %	11.2 %
FREE/REDUCED LUNCH (2017)	18.7 %	95.3 %
PROFESSIONAL STAFF WITH ADVANCED DEGREES (2017)	81.9 %	56.7 %

John

From Pasadena Hills
(Normandy District/ unaccredited)
Attends nearby Catholic School

$5,000

Approximate annual cost of tuition for 1 child, non-parishioner (2021-22)

Unpaid balances allow school to withhold transcripts to the next school;
Strict legal course of action is followed for unpaid tuition debts

WAKE UP

6:20 AM

Eats breakfast at home

Attends jazz program at school in AM

TRAVEL TIME: *SHORT*

5-20 min

Parents drive him to school on their way to work or walks/takes bus

AFTER SCHOOL

Joins science club, wins award

After school activities, serves on student council

Doesn't know kids on block as well to hang out with (they go to different schools)

Chris

From Northwoods (Normandy District)

Takes bus to Francis Howell, a high-ranked school district

Eats dinner with family when possible & does homework; sometimes distractions from neighborhood

Free school but commute costs in time and money and environment - tardiness - superior facilities - school friends live far away - family supports each other - less flexibility after school

52 miles/day each week for commuting the distance

WAKE UP

4:30 AM

Mom still at her second job
Fridge is sometimes empty
Eats breakfast at school

TRAVEL TIME: *LONG*

35 min

via school bus, or parents' car

9,048 miles per year
5.76+ metric tons CO2e /year

over 2 hours

via Metro bus + 3 mile walk

FREE school lunch

AFTER SCHOOL

Takes bus back to Northwoods

Unable to join any after-school activities

Doesn't know kids on the block as well to hang out with (they go to different schools)

Extended family nearby. Dinner with family when possible;
Sometimes family eats at different times because of work schedules

PACKS OR BUYS LUNCH

Sometimes hunger or neighborhood distracts from homework

Mark

From St. Charles (Francis Howell District/ fully accredited)

Lives in high-ranking district; carpools or walks to school

Free and potentially walkable - superior classes & facilities - school friends live nearby - parents have a network to support each other - flexibility after school

Free/healthy, minimal commute 1

WAKE UP

7:30 AM

Eats breakfast at home

Attends jazz program in AM

TRAVEL TIME: *SHORT*

5-15 min

via school bus, rides bike or walk

PACKS OR FREE school lunch

AFTER SCHOOL

Rides bike or walks home with friends who live nearby

Stays to meet teacher for help, or after-school activities

Joins science club, wins award

Hangs out with friends on the block

Dinner with family when possible, starts homework

3.2.15

At right, map of St. Louis City highlighting the (8) public schools closed in 2021, with locations of charter schools (2020).

This page, a timeline of intense charter school growth in St. Louis City since 2000. Each bar represents a charter school, represented according to when it opened and failed / closed.

SLPS: St. Louis Public Schools

1 Chad Davis, "Planned charter school in St. Louis County renews debate over public school funding," *St. Louis National Public Radio*, March 15, 2022,

2 Kurt Erickson, "Senate cuts funding for 'controversial' St. Louis school program," *St St. Louis Post-Dispatch*, April 19, 2021, accessed March, 2023.

3 Colin Gordon, "Closing Doors: Race and Opportunity in St. Louis Schools," *Dissent*, January 6, 2021.

Adaptation of Meredith Busch, "Mapping Education," Patty Heyda, *Climate Action Now*, Washington University in St. Louis, 2021.

Charter schools

Charter schools are a privatized model for addressing (and causing) structural disinvestment of "public education." They drain students and funding from state public sources, yet they operate independently and undemocratically from public districts. They are led by boards with no accountability to the community, and they are typically corporate-backed nonprofit entities.

In Missouri, charter schools, like magnet schools, were created (initially for St. Louis City and Kansas City districts only) as the desegregation bussing transfer programs were starting to wind down around 1999. Charter schools were said to solve inequities by drawing students from across districts, but this solution is not accountable to the democratically elected school board. It allows for autonomous curricular decisions and channels students and state public funding away from districts that need it most.

Charters are now allowed in St. Louis County—in unaccredited districts only. In 2022, the first county charter school opened in Pagedale, North St. Louis County, despite resistance and critiques from leaders in the provisionally reaccredited Normandy Schools Collaborative district it falls within. 1

Charter schools are "chartered," often by nonprofit institutions such as major universities. In addition to public sources, funding comes from organizations connected to the regional power elite with access to capital and government decision-making, such as banks and other corporate industries. St. Louis County's new charter "Leadership School," is sponsored by the Opportunity Trust—who receives funding from a national City Fund organization actively working to undermine democratic control of schools, "...whose strategy includes increasing the number of public schools that are run by private boards or nonprofits instead of elected school boards." 2

As charters were added, many others were notably still failing (indicated where red lines end).

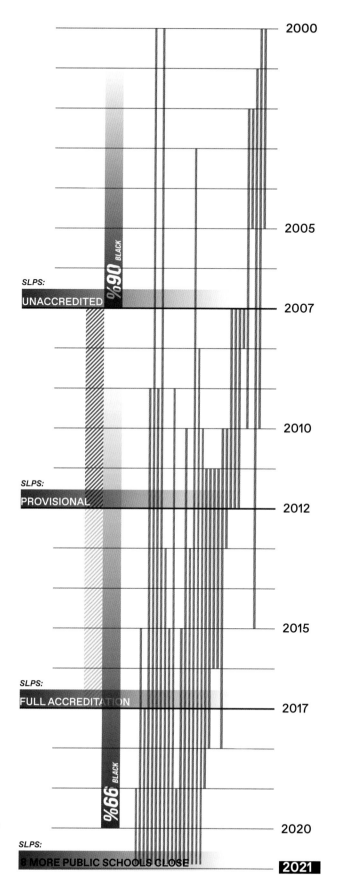

SLPS: **UNACCREDITED**

%90 BLACK

2000

2005

2007

SLPS: **PROVISIONAL**

2010

2012

SLPS: **FULL ACCREDITATION**

2015

%66 BLACK

2017

2020

SLPS: **8 MORE PUBLIC SCHOOLS CLOSE**

2021

See also   0.1.01   3.2.13-14

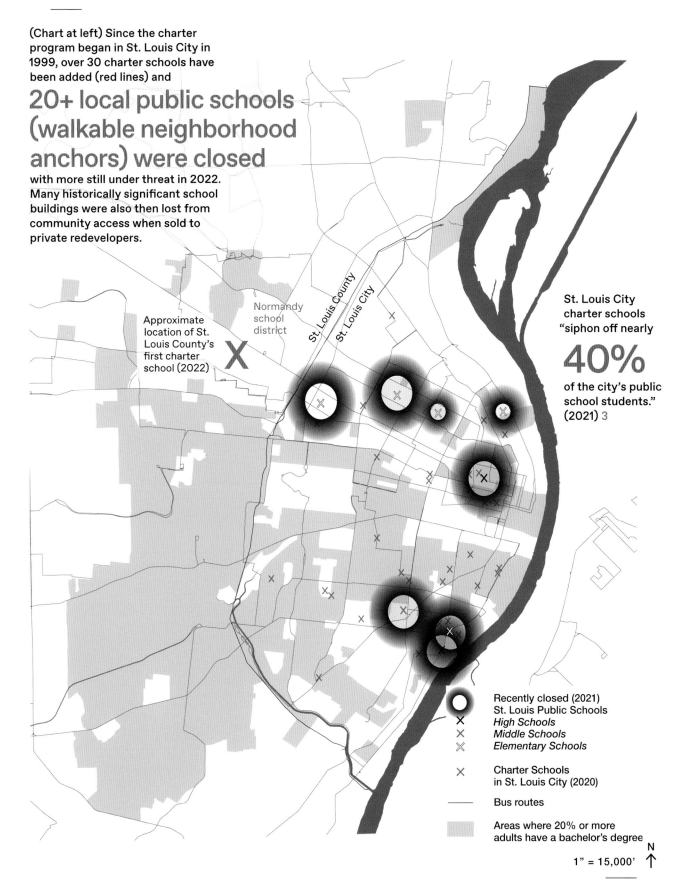

(Chart at left) Since the charter program began in St. Louis City in 1999, over 30 charter schools have been added (red lines) and

20+ local public schools (walkable neighborhood anchors) were closed

with more still under threat in 2022. Many historically significant school buildings were also then lost from community access when sold to private redevelopers.

Normandy school district

St. Louis County

St. Louis City

Approximate location of St. Louis County's first charter school (2022)

St. Louis City charter schools "siphon off nearly

40%

of the city's public school students." (2021) 3

Recently closed (2021) St. Louis Public Schools
X High Schools
× Middle Schools
✕ Elementary Schools

× Charter Schools in St. Louis City (2020)

— Bus routes

Areas where 20% or more adults have a bachelor's degree

N

1" = 15,000'

113

3.2.16

Map of St. Louis County and City population density, with St. Louis County school districts rated C+ or lower (2022), against an inventory of nonprofit organizations that have "youth," "empowerment" or "boys" in the name (2022, in St. Louis County only).

Empowerment centers

The concentration of nonprofit centers becomes a meter of structural educational underfunding in North County. The centers are valued community resources, but their presence is not guaranteed; the distribution of their locations is not necessarily equitable. Their programming is not vetted by an elected board. Youth and empowerment centers only mask the ongoing public disinvestment.

This is a mapping of supplemental nonprofit empowerment-type centers that appeared in Google map searches of the terms "youth," "empowerment," or "boys." Despite the fact that North St. Louis County shares a similar population density as areas of South St. Louis County, there are notably more youth empowerment centers in North County, where schools are under-supported.

○   Nonprofit organizations with "Youth," "Boys" or "Empowerment" in the name (St. Louis County only)

▭   School Districts (white borders)

▨   St. Louis County school districts with a rating of C+ or lower (2022-23)

——   Ferguson

——   Municipal boundaries

2021 Population Density (people per sq mile)

▨	3.5-2,070
▨	2,071-3,940
▨	3,941-5,950
▨	5,951-9,645
▨	9,646-25,500

Community Action Agency of St. Louis County, Inc

This is a supplemental "community" support organization that demonstrates the blurred public/private sectors characterized by the privatization (thus erosion) of U.S. public policy. CAASTLC is a nonprofit organization that administers Federal Community Service Block Grants to assist communities. 1

The board of directors is made up of:

"Democratically selected" representatives from low-income families/ communities the organization serves   **1/3**

Public elected officials   **1/3**

"Private 'Major Groups and Interests in the Community Served'"   **1/3**

↳

1 "2022-2023 Board of Directors (09/30/23)," CAASTLC website, 2021.

See also 3.2.12-15 3.M.01 4.1.08 4.3.27-33

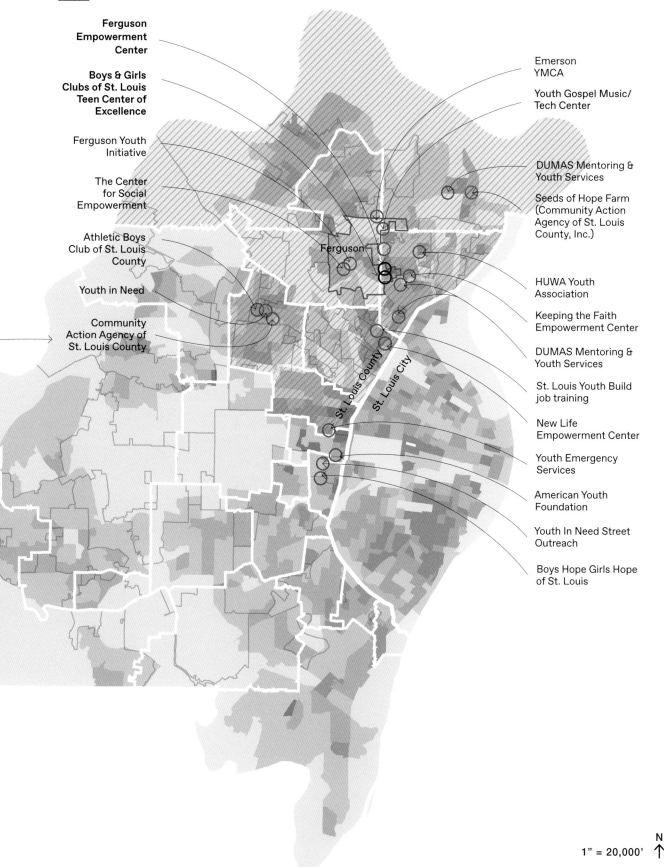

Ferguson
Empowerment
Center

Boys & Girls
Clubs of St. Louis
Teen Center of
Excellence

Ferguson Youth
Initiative

The Center
for Social
Empowerment

Athletic Boys
Club of St. Louis
County

Youth in Need

Community
Action Agency of
St. Louis County

Emerson
YMCA

Youth Gospel Music/
Tech Center

DUMAS Mentoring &
Youth Services

Seeds of Hope Farm
(Community Action
Agency of St. Louis
County, Inc.)

HUWA Youth
Association

Keeping the Faith
Empowerment Center

DUMAS Mentoring &
Youth Services

St. Louis Youth Build
job training

New Life
Empowerment Center

Youth Emergency
Services

American Youth
Foundation

Youth In Need Street
Outreach

Boys Hope Girls Hope
of St. Louis

Ferguson

St. Louis County

St. Louis City

1" = 20,000'

N

Beyond empowerment

Photo by author, 2023 In the first-ring suburb, crucial "empowerment," represented here by the Boys & Girls Clubs building, hits the ground in the same hostile built environment of tree-less asphalt, cars and fumes—and under-funded schools.

See also   2.1.06   3.2.16   4.3.29

3.2.17

Map of St. Louis County and City showing race by census tract, and educational attainment. Each dot represents 100 people with a bachelor's degree or higher (2020).

Higher education

Higher education un-attainment is a ripple effect of compromised access to opportunity at the K-12 school level (in addition to cost and other factors). Neighborhoods with predominantly Black residents in North St. Louis County have less residents with a bachelor's degree or higher, making them less qualified for many of the kinds of jobs offered at current North County industries.

Summer melt

The Ferguson-Florissant school district graduation rate is above the Missouri and U.S. national averages (2019-2021), but the level of college bachelor's degree attainment in North County remains lower than the rest of St. Louis County. Summer melt happens when students who have been accepted to college do not complete the enrollment process over the summer. It usually has to do with additional registration fees, "missed deadlines, difficulty navigating complicated enrollment paperwork and uncertainties over financial aid,"1 among changing circumstances for families—and other underlying structural determinants.

"First-generation college students and students from low-income backgrounds are the most susceptible, with as many as

40%

melting away" (at University of Missouri St. Louis). 1

1 (The quote at right is by Alan Byrd, dean of enrollment services at the University of Missouri-St. Louis), Koran Addo, "Summer is risky time for college-bound students," *The St. Louis Post-Dispatch*, June 15, 2015.

Educational Attainment

●   Bachelor's Degree or Higher
        1 Dot = 100 People

Percentage of Black Population (Census Tract)

	0-20%
	20-40%
	40-60%
	60-80%
	80-100%

See also   3.2.12   3.2.13   4.3.23

(Public) Saint Louis Community College:
Estimated in-district residents-tuition and living expenses:

$13,825

(2021/2022)

(Public) University of Missouri-St Louis:
Estimated Missouri in-state tuition and living expenses:

$28,514

(2021/2022)

1" = 20,000'

N

3.M.01

→

Map of St. Louis County and City showing population density and the relatively even distribution of public schools and library locations, although their funding is uneven. Private schools are also shown.

Mobilize
Public schools and libraries

Public schools and libraries are some of the last remaining local, public social institutions that support people, as they anchor neighborhoods around them. They should be well funded and protected from state censorship and privatization. Maintaining walkable, transit-based access to public institutions is also crucial.

If education is freedom 1 and knowledge is power, then anchor institutions provide access to empowerment for all community members. Historically these institutions were spaced throughout the city and suburb to be within walkable reach in every neighborhood. Over the years, schools have experienced closures and the historic buildings sold. This spreads out remaining buildings that residents can only access with a car or other transit. Accessibility to public anchor institutions impacts citizen's access to participate in government since many schools also serve as spaces for voting; libraries provide passport applications, Internet access, tax form support, community development and skills workshops and other crucial supports—in addition to free access to the world through books and media. Libraries and schools carry an oversized burden to support communities when so much of the American public sector has been otherwise 'value engineered' out.

1 Bell Hooks, *Teaching to Transgress: Education as the Practice of Freedom*, (New York: Routledge, 1994).

Radical Atlas of Ferguson, USA

See also   3.2.12   3.2.14-15

Ferguson

St. Louis County

St. Louis City

●   Public schools (K-12)

○   Private schools (K-12)

✚   Public libraries

▭   Public school districts (white lines)

2021 Population Density (people per sq mile)

3.5-2,070

2,071-3,940

3,941-5,950

5,951-9,645

9,646-25,500

1" = 20,000'

N
↑

Mobilize
Taxes directed at common wealth

Map of every public building and park in Ferguson, MO, with the Ferguson Public Library and St. Louis Community College—Florissant campus called out.

At left, a timeline diagram of sources of funding for the Ferguson Public Library and St. Louis Community College.

Mobilizing local and regional taxes may involve complicated processes, given legal restrictions on what cities are allowed to do with or without a referendum (and given voters' willingness to approve). But apart from ballot measures to raise revenues, corporations and nonprofits could contribute to the city as fair taxpayers, instead of contributing via discretionary philanthropy. The intensity of tax incentives that go to industry and corporate development should be reevaluated and those funds channeled to urgent public institutions and programs instead.

Adaptation of Madison Dugar, "Public Over Private: Creating Sustainable Community Investment Post-Uprising," Patty Heyda, Radical Mapping, Washington University in St. Louis, 2023.

As state funding cuts to public universities continue, the St. Louis Community College (STLCC) and the Ferguson Library both received funding boosts through local ballot propositions.

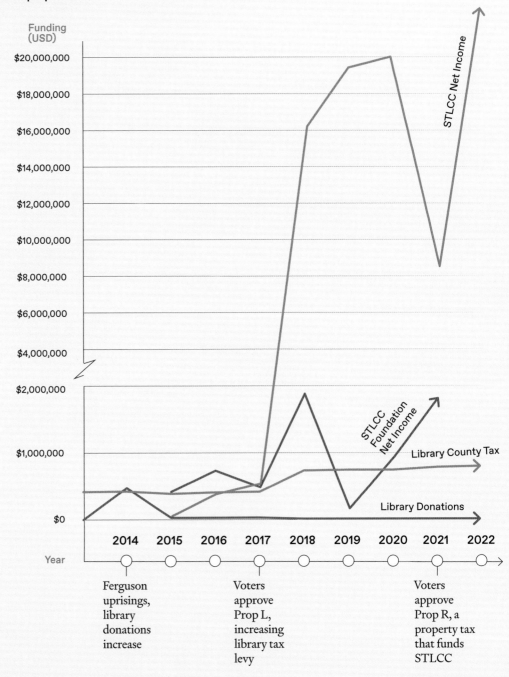

Funding (USD)

$20,000,000

$18,000,000

$16,000,000

$14,000,000

$12,000,000

$10,000,000

$8,000,000

$6,000,000

$4,000,000

$2,000,000

STLCC Net Income

STLCC Foundation Net Income

Library County Tax

Library Donations

$1,000,000

$0

Year   2014   2015   2016   2017   2018   2019   2020   2021   2022

Ferguson uprisings, library donations increase

Voters approve Prop L, increasing library tax levy

Voters approve Prop R, a property tax that funds STLCC

See also   3.2.12   4.1.07   4.3.27-33

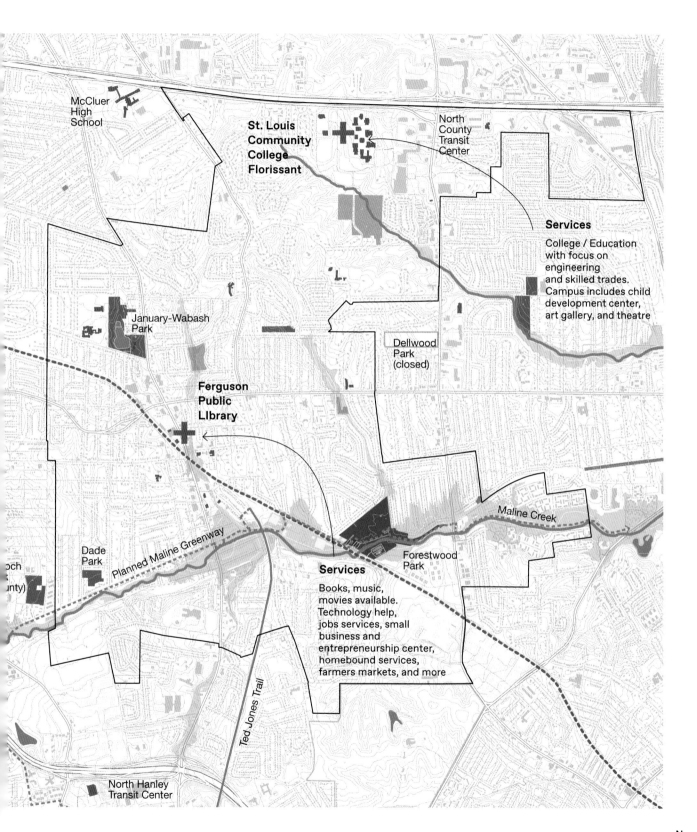

McCluer
High
School

St. Louis
Community
College
Florissant

North
County
Transit
Center

Services

College / Education
with focus on
engineering
and skilled trades.
Campus includes child
development center,
art gallery, and theatre

January-Wabash
Park

Dellwood
Park
(closed)

**Ferguson
Public
LIbrary**

Maline Creek

Dade
Park

Planned Maline Greenway

Forestwood
Park

Services

Books, music,
movies available.
Technology help,
jobs services, small
business and
entrepreneurship center,
homebound services,
farmers markets, and more

Ted Jones Trail

North Hanley
Transit Center

↳   All the public buildings and
parks of Ferguson, MO
(in red or blue)

1" = 2,500'

N
↑

123

3.M.03

Map of St. Louis County and City showing school districts and performance ratings alongside food insecure areas, defined as low-income areas with at least 33% population living more than 1/2 mile from a grocery store and at least 100 households with low or no access to a vehicle (2015).

Mobilize
School lunch

Mobilizing school lunch is a part of mobilizing public schools, who provide daily food access to students who may otherwise not have consistent or easy access to healthy food at home.

The St. Louis County area that experiences low food and low transportation access is also where there are underfunded, lower-performing school districts. Studies have shown correlations between food insecure children, increased weight, and social and academic performance. [1] Public schools and other anchors (like libraries in the summer) play a critical role in providing meals to kids— free or reduced breakfast and lunches—among other programs. They are some of the last public social support institutions left in these times of privatization and should be protected and funded.

Normandy High School (2014):

99.6%

students qualifying for free or reduced lunch

Missouri State average (2014):

44%

students qualifying for free or reduced lunch

Clayton High School (2014):

11%

students qualifying for free or reduced lunch

1 Diana F. Jyoti, Edward A. Frongillo, Sonya J. Jones, "Food Insecurity Affects School Children's Academic Performance, Weight Gain, and Social Skills," *Journal of Nutrition*, December 1, 2005.

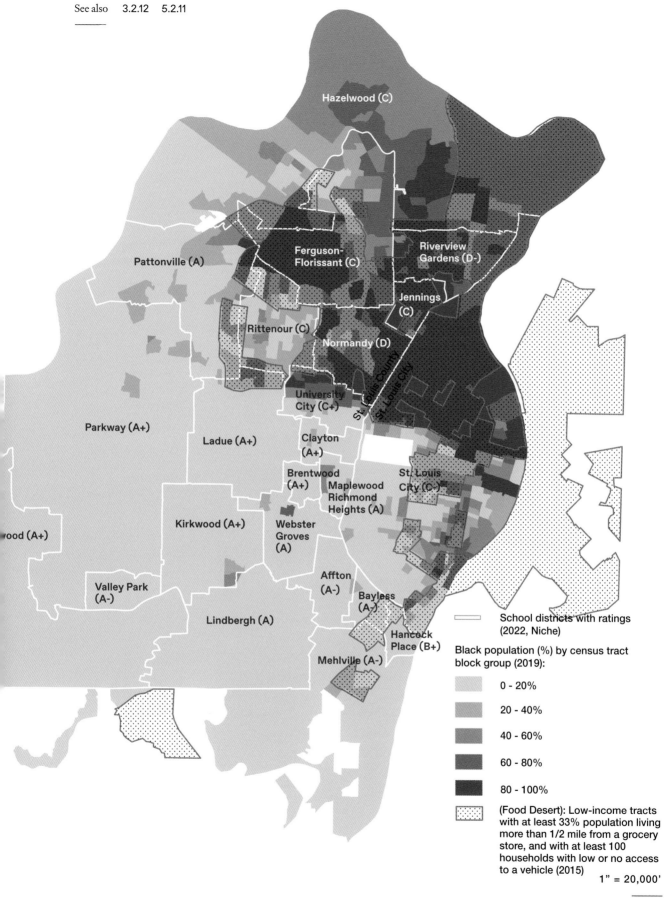

Hazelwood (C)

Ferguson-
Florissant (C)

Riverview
Gardens (D-)

Pattonville (A)

Jennings
(C)

Rittenour (C)

Normandy (D)

University
City (C+)

St. Louis County
St. Louis City

Parkway (A+)

Ladue (A+)

Clayton
(A+)

Brentwood
(A+)

Maplewood
Richmond
Heights (A)

St. Louis
City (C-)

Webster
Groves
(A)

...ood (A+)

Kirkwood (A+)

Affton
(A-)

Valley Park
(A-)

Bayless
(A-)

Lindbergh (A)

Hancock
Place (B+)

Mehlville (A-)

School districts with ratings
(2022, Niche)

Black population (%) by census tract
block group (2019):

0 - 20%

20 - 40%

40 - 60%

60 - 80%

80 - 100%

(Food Desert): Low-income tracts
with at least 33% population living
more than 1/2 mile from a grocery
store, and with at least 100
households with low or no access
to a vehicle (2015)

1" = 20,000'

N

04

Politics

Private-public sectors

The Politics chapter unpacks what government and governance look like in the American city-suburb, mapped through the lens of Ferguson and North County.

Maps highlight the three sectors of governance and how they are structured, from democratic to private: The elected public sector, the quasi-public-private civic sector of nonprofits and think tanks and the private corporate sector that 'governs' through influence, philanthropy or with embedded actors on public boards and commissions. The chapter ends with an examination of market-based public policies as seen in incentives and tax systems among North County Fortune-500 companies. These are subsidies that otherwise deplete funds for social services and programs for people.

The chapter includes a longitudinal case study of *erasure suburbanism* in the small municipality of Kinloch, MO, and Robertson and Carrollton, in Hazelwood and Bridgeton, MO, respectively. The case highlights years of airport-related redevelopment imaginaries that replaced all three communities with regional and global market priorities.

4.1.01

Map of the St. Louis Metropolitan Statistical Area (MSA) and its counties, showing the many separate governmental units that make up the MSA in Illinois and Missouri (2017). Ferguson, MO, is one of 88 other municipalities in St. Louis County alone. And St. Louis City is a separate entity from St. Louis County—see maps 1.2.04 and 1.2.05.

Governmental units

The St. Louis Metropolitan Statistical Area (MSA) has the fifth most governmental units in the United States (2020). If this region is highly politically fragmented, then it is also compounded. Since 'governmental units' refers to cities but also to special districts that overlay an area, the resulting system is characterized by both redundant micro-territories, and by scales of competing overlap between units.

ST. LOUIS COUNTY

ST. LOUIS CITY

↳

Above, St. Louis City and County are at the center of the St. Louis Metropolitan Statistical Area (MSA).

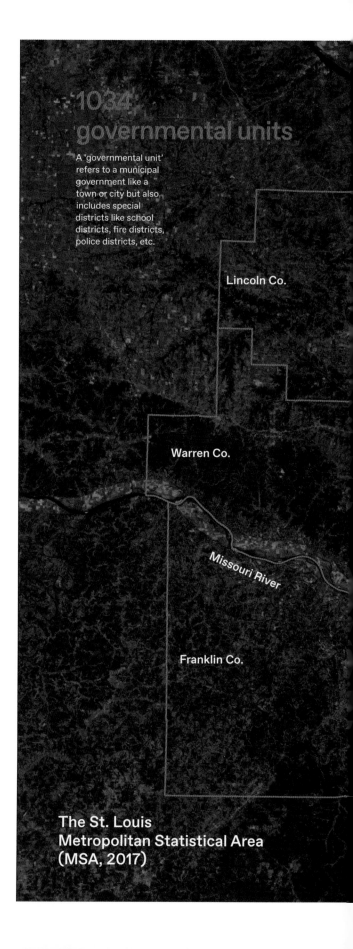

1034 governmental units

A 'governmental unit' refers to a municipal government like a town or city but also includes special districts like school districts, fire districts, police districts, etc.

Lincoln Co.

Warren Co.

Missouri River

Franklin Co.

The St. Louis Metropolitan Statistical Area (MSA, 2017)

Calhoun Co.

Mississippi River

Macoupin Co.

Jersey Co.

Bond Co.

St. Charles Co.

Madison Co.

Ferguson

Clinton Co.

St. Louis
City

St. Louis County

St. Clair Co.

Jefferson CO.

Monroe Co.

Mississippi River

4.1.02

Map of North St. Louis County and surrounding areas, showing its many small municipalities, each with its own mayor and separate government (2021).

Governmental multiplicity

As if cities were products, this concept represents the economic, market-based logic of having many separate municipalities in order to promote choice—capitalist competition—between them. In St. Louis, this ideology of multiplicity enabled racial segregation and redundant incorporations. Further, as multiplicity combined with economic austerity, it produced a staggering number of financially struggling small municipalities, each with exponentially eroded civic capacities, as seen throughout the maps in this atlas.

St. Louis County is comprised of a decentralized system of 88 municipal governments. These municipalities range in size from University City, which has over 30,000 residents, to Champ, which only has 12 residents (Champ has no mayor). Over 50 of these municipalities emerged between 1945 and 1952. Since then, some have merged or dissolved.

> "A multiplicity of governments promotes choice, a value exceedingly compatible with American individualism." 1

In St. Louis County

98 Municipalities in 1959
88 Municipalities in 2021

1 Terrence Jones, *Fragmented by Design* (Palmerston & Reed, 2000).

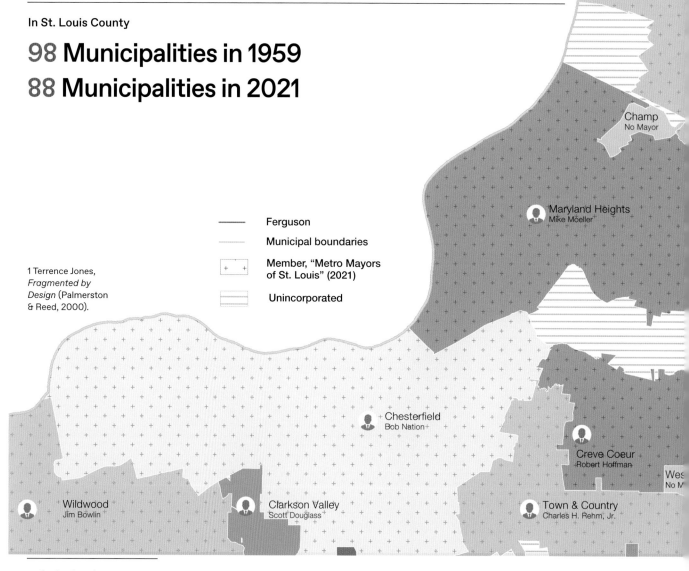

——— Ferguson

——— Municipal boundaries

[+ +] Member, "Metro Mayors of St. Louis" (2021)

[≡] Unincorporated

Champ
No Mayor

Maryland Heights
Mike Moeller

Chesterfield
Bob Nation

Creve Coeur
Robert Hoffman

Wes
No M

Wildwood
Jim Bowlin

Clarkson Valley
Scott Douglass

Town & Country
Charles H. Rehm, Jr.

54 Municipalities in North St. Louis County alone

Black Jack
Norman C. Mccourt

Florissant
Timothy J. Lowery

Hazelwood
Matthew G. Robinson

Bellefontaine Neighbors
Tommie Pierson, Sr.

Berkeley
Babatunde Deinbo

Dellwood
Reggie Jones

Bridgeton
Terry Briggs

Ferguson
Ella Jones

Moline Acres
Michele Deshay

Riverview
(No Mayor)

Kinloch
Evelyn Carter

Edmundson
John Gwaltney

St. Ann
Michael G. Corcoran

Woodson Terrace
Lawrence P. "Butch" Besmer

Jennings
Yolanda Austin

Country Club Hills
Bender Mckinney, Jr.

Cool Valley
Jayson Stewart

Flordell Hills
Joseph Noeth

St. John
Tom Halaska

Bellerive Acres
Nancy Hartman

Breckenridge Hills
Jack Shrewsberry

Pasadena Hills
Jason Quinlisk

Bel-Ridge
Willie "Lawn Mower Man" Fair

Northwoods
Sharon Pace

Beverly Hills
Brian Jackson

Bel-nor
Bill Hook

Overland
Michael Schneider

Normandy
Mark Beckmann

Pine Lawn
Terry Epps

Uplands Park
B.W. Shelton (Chairman)

Charlack
Mark Chamberlain

Vinita Park
James W. Mcgee

Velda City
Melda Bernard Collins

Sycamore Hills
Phillip Burke (Chairman)

Velda Village Hills
Patricia Ross

Pagedale
Ernest "E.G." Shields

Greendale
Tiffany Graham

Olivette
Sidney Clark

University City
Terry Crow

Wellston
Nathaniel Griffin

Hillsdale
Dorothy Moore (Chairwoman)

Hanley Hills
Jeffrey Walton (Chairman)

Ladue
Nancy Spewak

St. Louis City
Tishuara Jones

Frontenac
Kate Hatfield

Clayton
Michelle Harris

Richmond Heights
Jim Thomson

1" = 10,000'

N

131

4.1.03

Map of Ferguson, MO, and immediate surrounding municipalities indicating what kind of government they each have. A sampling of mayor salaries for Ferguson and Dellwood, MO, reflects the symbolism of the role that has varying levels of actual administrative power, depending on the government type.

Weak-mayor government

The global media celebrated the election of Ferguson's first Black woman mayor, Ella Jones, in 2020. The importance of this is noted for a city that had steadily shifted to a largely Black population after decades of being majority white. Representation matters. But the mayor of Ferguson actually has little administrative power because of the city's 'weak-mayor' form of government.

A government is considered a 'weak-mayor' form when the main city administrative positions are elected by the public or appointed by the city council or board of aldermen (vs. appointed by the mayor). The administrators are thus accountable to the public or to the council before they answer to the mayor.

Ferguson and Dellwood both have a mayor, city manager and council in their governments, but in Ferguson the city manager is hired/appointed by (and reports to) the city council. In Dellwood, the city manager is appointed by the mayor and serves both the mayor and council. A city manager is considered the chief executive and administrator of the local government, and they carry out most of the management of the city.

↳

Mayors who are technically also members of the city council are paid similarly to council members. Urban austerity means that in both weak- and strong-mayor governments, like in Ferguson and Dellwood, the annual salary of the mayor is more symbolic and necessitates that they continue other jobs on the side.

Municipal mayor salaries

Ferguson, MO
pop. 18,143 (2022)
Mayor Ella Jones

Dellwood, MO
pop. 4,882 (2021)
Mayor Reggie Jones

$4,200
Mayor of Ferguson annual salary (2016)

$8,400
Mayor of Dellwood annual salary (2016)

Mayor salaries: Better Together, *General Administration #3 Appendix*, January, 2016.

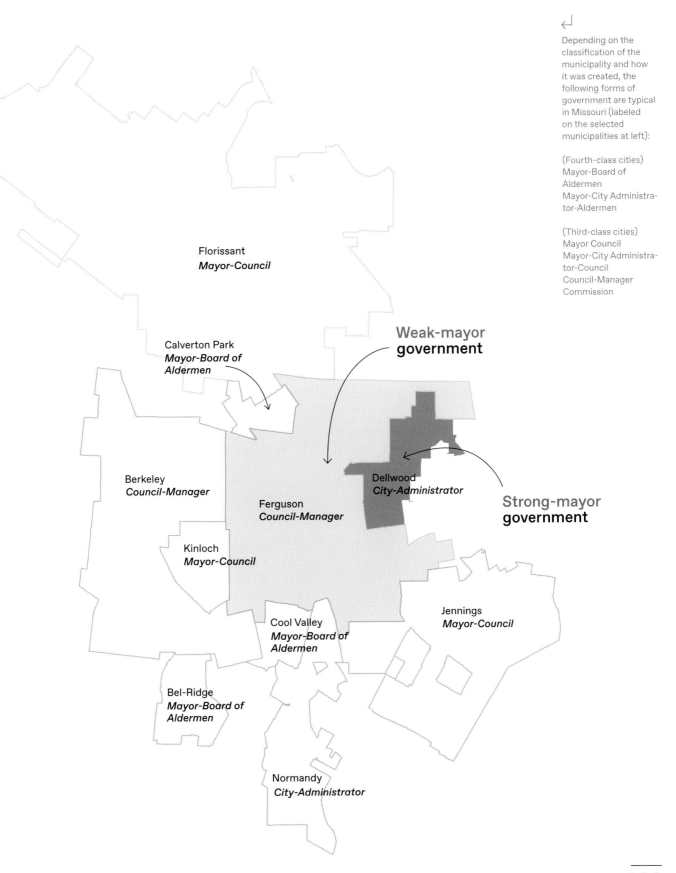

Depending on the classification of the municipality and how it was created, the following forms of government are typical in Missouri (labeled on the selected municipalities at left):

(Fourth-class cities)
Mayor-Board of Aldermen
Mayor-City Administrator-Aldermen

(Third-class cities)
Mayor Council
Mayor-City Administrator-Council
Council-Manager
Commission

Florissant
Mayor-Council

Calverton Park
Mayor-Board of Aldermen

Weak-mayor **government**

Berkeley
Council-Manager

Ferguson
Council-Manager

Dellwood
City-Administrator

Strong-mayor **government**

Kinloch
Mayor-Council

Jennings
Mayor-Council

Cool Valley
Mayor-Board of Aldermen

Bel-Ridge
Mayor-Board of Aldermen

Normandy
City-Administrator

133

4.1.04

Diagram of elected positions in Ferguson city government, with map of Ferguson, MO, below, showing municipal wards (2021).

City managers

Who really holds power?
The structure of Ferguson's city government is what is called a "weak-mayor" system that utilizes the city council for decision-making (not the mayor) alongside a city manager who is meant to run day-to-day operations. The city council members and mayor are elected, and the city manager is hired by the council.

Ferguson,
Missouri
pop. (2022)

18,143

↳

City department/ administration descriptions from the Ferguson, MO - Official Website (2021)

Annual pay: Better Together, *General Administration #3 Appendix*, January, 2016.

Ferguson City Administration (2021)

Mayor
Ward 1   Ward 1   Ward 2   Ward 2   Ward 3   Ward 3

The mayor is a "part-time public servant" and serves for a three-year term, with a three consecutive term limit.

↳ **Annual pay (2016)**

$4,200

Ward council members are elected and serve three-year overlapping terms with a three consecutive term limit. Responsibilities include setting policies and passing ordinances. They appoint and vote on the city manager position.

↳ **Annual pay (2016)** $3,000

City Clerk
Supports city council & city manager. Maintains official city records.

Assistant to the City Manager

City Manager
Appoints, supervises, and removes employees of the city. Directs and supervises the administration of all departments. Prepares the annual budget. Advises council on financial condition of the city.

↳ **Annual pay (2016)** $110,000

City Attorney
Advises and counsels the city to navigate federal oversight in compliance with Department of Justice Consent Decree (2014).

Municipal Court   Personnel

City Departments

Director of Planning & Development
Community development, economic development, planning and zoning, housing and block grants.

Chief of Fire Department
Fire suppression, fire prevention, emergency medical services operations, and emergency preparedness.

Assistant City Manager
Public relations and information technology.

Director of Parks & Recreation
General recreation, swimming pool, concessions, special events, senior citizens activities, community center.

Director of Public Works
Facility maintenance, street maintenance, municipal garage, engineering, park maintenance, code enforcement, permitting.

Director of Finance
Accounting, revenue collection, cash management, purchasing, payroll, reporting.

Chief of Police
Patrol, investigation, records, communications, juvenile, detention.

4.1.05

A timeline of Ferguson city leadership from 2005 to 2021 showing how actors shuffle positions interchangeably over time.

Muni maneuvers

In small governments, people can maintain administrative roles after term limits, by changing positions.

This is done through appointments or votes, internal political connections or unexpected vacancies. Opportunistic ventures also arise, where someone with less than 30 votes can gain a position if uncontested, like the case of Kynan Crecelius. The relationship between the council and city manager and others in a small government can have substantial influence on the implementation of day-to-day operations. 1

Muni maneuvering allows people to seek promotion or stay in power via different roles over multiple terms. After Jeffrey Blume, the "architect of the Black body ATM," and James Knowles III were called out in the Ferguson Commission report for their role in perpetuating the system of revenue from police tickets and fines, they both stayed on in power. 2

1 In January, 2023 the Ferguson City Manager Eric Osterberg quit after repeated difficulties with a council member.

1 Taylor Tiamoyo Harris, "Ferguson city manager resigns, this time permanently," *The St. Louis Post-Dispatch*, January 25, 2023.

2 (No author), Political Eye News, "Ferguson extends contract of Jeff Blume, a villain of DOJ report," *St. Louis American*, February 27, 2020.

↳ Adaptation of Max Posen, "Power Pipeline," Patty Heyda, *Radical Mapping*, Washington University in St. Louis, 2021.

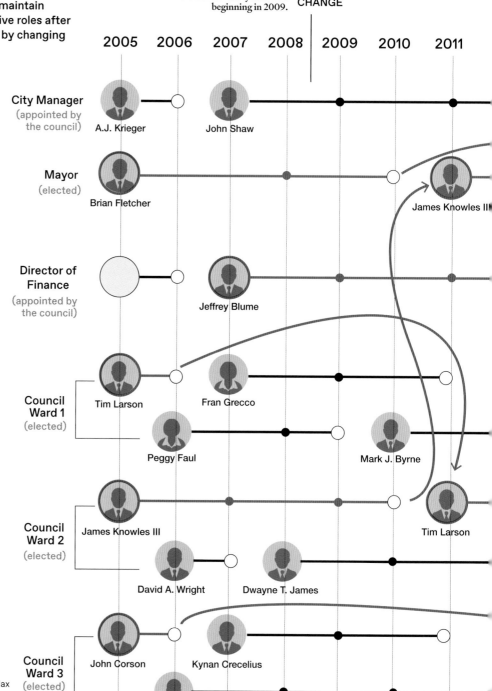

In 2008, voters passed reforms to the city council, including term limits and a change in term length for council members from 2- to 3-year terms beginning in 2009.

COUNCIL TERM RULE CHANGE

2005 2006 2007 2008 2009 2010 2011

City Manager (appointed by the council) — A.J. Krieger, John Shaw

Mayor (elected) — Brian Fletcher, James Knowles III

Director of Finance (appointed by the council) — Jeffrey Blume

Council Ward 1 (elected) — Tim Larson, Fran Grecco, Peggy Faul, Mark J. Byrne, Tim Larson

Council Ward 2 (elected) — James Knowles III, David A. Wright, Dwayne T. James

Council Ward 3 (elected) — John Corson, Kynan Crecelius, Michael Salant

See also   4.1.04   5.1.04-05

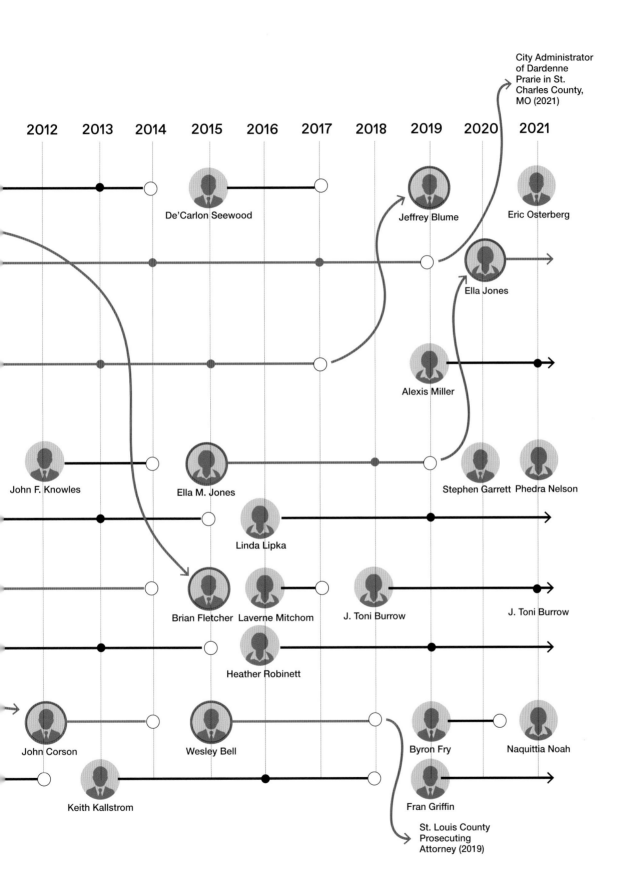

City Administrator of Dardenne Prarie in St. Charles County, MO (2021)

2012   2013   2014   2015   2016   2017   2018   2019   2020   2021

De'Carlon Seewood

Jeffrey Blume

Eric Osterberg

Ella Jones

Alexis Miller

John F. Knowles

Ella M. Jones

Stephen Garrett   Phedra Nelson

Linda Lipka

Brian Fletcher   Laverne Mitchom   J. Toni Burrow   J. Toni Burrow

Heather Robinett

John Corson   Wesley Bell   Byron Fry   Naquittia Noah

Keith Kallstrom   Fran Griffin

St. Louis County Prosecuting Attorney (2019)

4.1.06

Map of Ferguson, MO, showing polling places relative to bus lines and stops, and to pedestrian-friendly areas (in the downtown district) with wards and elected council representatives.

Adaptation of Celine Haddad, "Ferguson: Voting and Government; The convoluted path from Ward 3 to City Hall," Patty Heyda, *Suburban Publics*, Washington University in St. Louis, 2023.

Polling places

The most disenfranchised ward in Ferguson has the least access to participate in democracy and vote. There is no polling place in the Third Ward where Michael Brown was killed and where the protests demanding civil rights and social justice unfolded in the days after. The map depicts the elevated rail line as a wall because of how it physically divides the southeastern part of Ward 3 from the center of government and city hall, which are located in the (more walkable—more accessible) historic center. To get there from the Third Ward, one has to traverse both elevated track and the Maline Creek, among other infrastructures (like missing sidewalks along some of the roads).

——	Bus line
•	Bus stop
	DOWNTOWN CORE I-III DISTRICT "Focuses pedestrian-friendly retail and service uses on the ground story with residential and/or office uses in upper stories." (zoning code)
	DOWNTOWN CORE IV-V DISTRICTS "Zoned for larger commercial and residential structures." (zoning code)
	WARD 1
	WARD 2
	WARD 3
▨	Area where 80% or more of the population identifies as Black (approx 2020-22)
👤	Ferguson City Council Members by Ward (2023)
●	Voting locations (2023)

↳ Below, demographics of Ferguson, MO (2010), alongside the demographic of those who voted in municipal elections (from 2008-2014). 1

1 Adaptation of data from Amaris Montes and Zack Avre, "How Ferguson's Black Majority Can Take Control of Their City," *In These Times*, November 3, 2014.

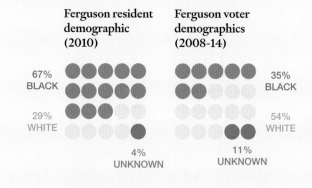

Ferguson resident demographic (2010)

67% BLACK
29% WHITE
4% UNKNOWN

Ferguson voter demographics (2008-14)

35% BLACK
54% WHITE
11% UNKNOWN

Ferguson precincts by number of ballots cast (2018)

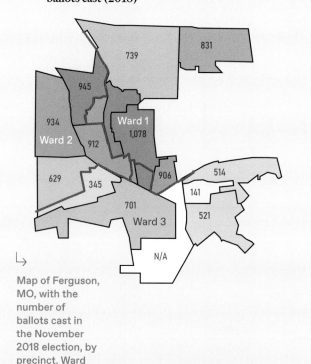

↳ Map of Ferguson, MO, with the number of ballots cast in the November 2018 election, by precinct. Ward divisions in red.

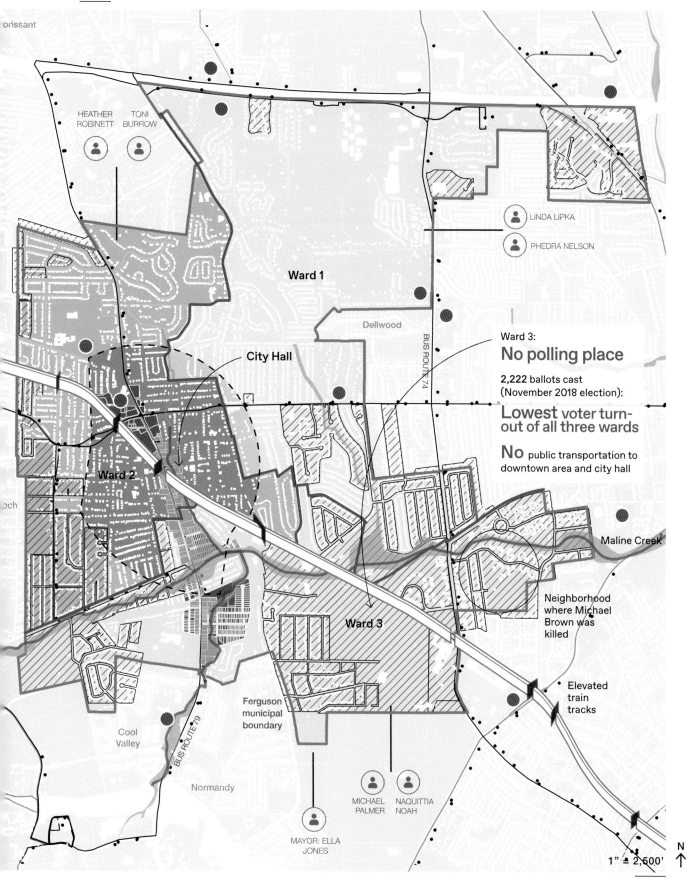

orissant

HEATHER ROBINETT

TONI BURROW

LINDA LIPKA

PHEDRA NELSON

Ward 1

Dellwood

BUS ROUTE 74

City Hall

Ward 3:

No polling place

2,222 ballots cast (November 2018 election):

Lowest voter turn-out of all three wards

No public transportation to downtown area and city hall

Ward 2

och

Maline Creek

Neighborhood where Michael Brown was killed

Ward 3

Elevated train tracks

Ferguson municipal boundary

Cool Valley

BUS ROUTE 79

Normandy

MICHAEL PALMER

NAQUITTIA NOAH

MAYOR: ELLA JONES

1" ≙ 2,500'

N

4.1.07

Map of St. Louis County and City shaded to show the percent of registered voters who cast ballots in municipal elections (2014). The map also outlines in red those municipalities that problematically included a polling place in a police station, with the number of outstanding warrants in that municipality called out in red.

Voter participation

Voter participation in municipal elections is also low due to the timing in April and in odd years from state and national elections. The timing compounds decreased turnout among lower-income and younger voters and for those who may have difficulty getting to a polling place –see map 4.1.06.

Even more striking, in some municipalities (outlined in red) polling places were in the same building as municipal police (2014), a major deterrent for residents with outstanding warrants for their arrest on unpaid fines. 1

The situation encapsulates the contradiction of "neoliberal democracy" in the suburbs, where fiscal austerity depletes city buildings, infrastructure and services that could otherwise uphold democratic processes like voting, while predatory systems of policing attempt to make up for the missed revenues by only further eroding access to democracy and ideas of freedom.

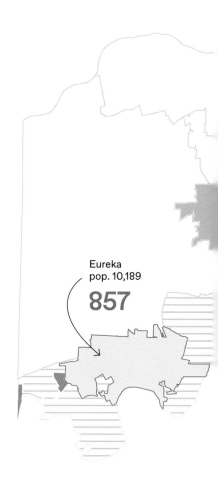

Eureka
pop. 10,189

857

% REGISTERED VOTERS WHO CAST BALLOTS in 2014 municipal elections.

(For comparison, an average of 40% participate in national elections.)

- 60% participation
- 48% participation
- 37% participation
- 25% participation
- 14% participation

- Municipalities that included a polling place in the same building as municipal police headquarters (2014) with the number of outstanding warrants in that municipality, as of June 30, 2014. 1

- Unincorporated areas

1 Better Together, *General Administration Study #4*, January, 2016.

Black Jack
pop. 6,929
1,606

Hazelwood
pop. 25,703
11,716

Calverton Park
pop. 1,293
10,832

Maryland
Heights
pop. 27,472
4,046

St. John
pop. 6,517
4,556

St. Louis
County

St. Louis
City

Maplewood
pop. 8,046
3,106

Fenton
pop. 4,022
2,698

Outstanding
arrest warrants
(red figures) in
each municipality
with a polling
station located
within in a police
station
(June, 2014)

Riverview
pop. 2,856   **10,407**

Country
Club Hills
pop. 1,274   **34,745**

Normandy
pop. 5,008   **12,540**

Beverly Hills
pop. 574   **n/a**

Pine Lawn
pop. 3,275   **20,525**

Bel-Nor
pop. 1,499   **2,111**

Bel-Ridge
pop. 2,737   **4,227**

Pagedale
pop. 3,304   **22,384**

Hanley Hills
pop. 2,101   **1,545**

Vinita Park
pop. 1,880   **1,419**

N

1" = 20,000'

141

4.1.08

Map of North St. Louis County showing a mix of public urban programs (2015) and the nonprofit civic sector agencies that support and implement them.

Mixed public-private civic sector

Private nonprofit organizations that coordinate with public sector initiatives constitute a third kind of quasi-public-private sector known as the civic sector.

On the one hand, this system lends supports where public sector capacity is low due to austerity. On the other hand, it becomes very hard to see the line between public and private governance, something that compromises the ability of citizens to hold decision-makers accountable (through the vote). Further, in some small municipalities, these overlaid, coordinated nonprofit arrangements mask or supplant the need for larger structural reforms. 1

Nonprofits

THE PROMISE ZONE STRATEGIC ALLIANCES (2015)

ARCH CITY DEFENDERS

FOR THE SAKE OF ALL / HEALTH EQUITY WORKS (WASHINGTON UNIVERSITY)

NEIGHBORHOOD LEADERSHIP FELLOWS (UMSL)

ST. LOUIS RECAST

BETTER FAMILY LIFE

GENERATE HEALTH STL

READY BY 21 STL

NORMANDY SCHOOLS COLLABORATIVE

GRACE HILL

Public, administered by nonprofit

Promise Zone (2015)

1 Jason Rosenbaum, "Is Smaller Better? Multitude of Municipalities Plays Into City-County Merger Debate," *St. Louis Public Radio*, April 23, 2014.

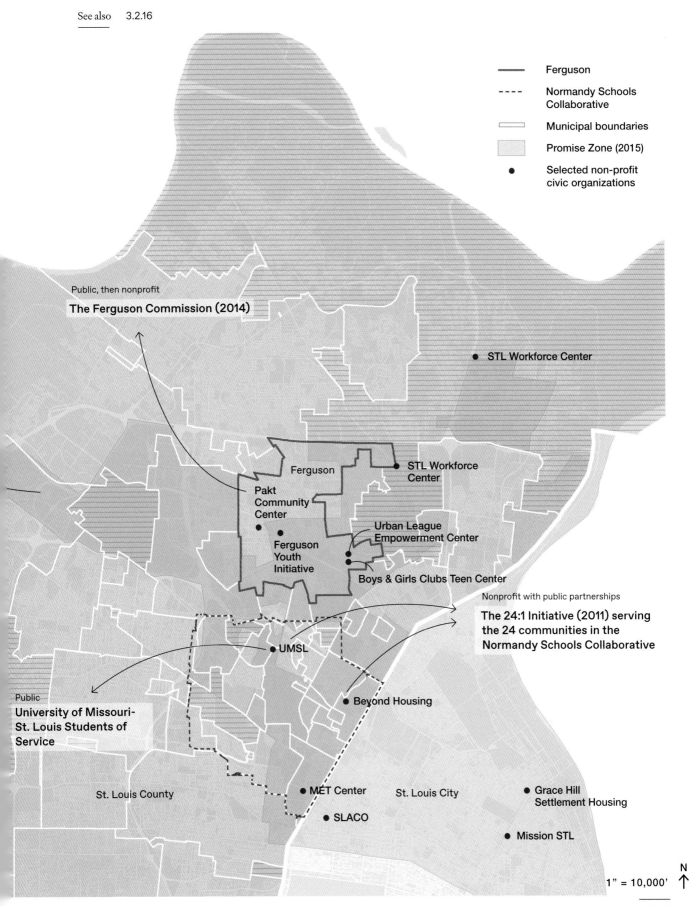

4.2.09

Map of St. Louis County and City showing state and federal development incentive programs that concentrate in North St. Louis County. The programs each began in different time periods but are ongoing, and most have been in effect for at least 10 years (as of 2023).

State & federal development incentives

State and (locally administered) federal programs concentrate in distressed North St. Louis County, where quality of life and opportunities have changed little for residents over the decades of the programs. Instead, incentives are captured for private industrial expansion.

The most vulnerable communities like Kinloch, Missouri, have become battleground sites for corporate access to low-cost land, enabled by incentives.

New Market Tax Credits

New Market Tax Credits are a federal program, administered locally by the Heartland Regional Investment Fund. There is also a national coalition of nonprofit, venture fund and bank leaders that steer the fund's various applications into new (secondary) markets that don't follow economic growth profiles. The credits are intended to help distressed communities in those markets—but the resulting projects contradictorily reproduce industry that destroys residential communities. The scale and character of massive industrial warehouse developments alone are an affront to lived community space and the environment.

Missouri Enhanced Enterprise Zone

These are special zones in "blighted" areas that offer tax abatements to industries that want to expand. The incentives are granted on the basis that their investments will bring promised job growth. The EEZs skip the neighborhood scale and augment global economies that don't (financially) articulate local space and jobs.

Targeted Employee Area

These are specially created enclaves where the rules for foreign investments are bent to privilege developing industries in high-unemployment areas or rural areas. The incentive lowers the required amount of foreign investment from $1 million to $500,000 in qualifying areas, with the idea that this will help bring employment. In North County, many industrial jobs are no longer manufacturing-based and don't match the educational attainment of the population. Or, if jobs exist, they have unsustainable contracts with wages far outpaced by inflation and the rising costs of living.

Promise Zone

The Promise Zone is a 10-year federal designation that was granted to the St. Louis region for most of North County in 2015. It is administered locally through nonprofit partners. The goal is to help seed programs to stabilize communities, grow the economy, and improve health and education outcomes.

Chapter 353 Redevelopment Corporations and Tax Abatement

Chapter 353 allows a mix of private and public actors to fund a Redevelopment Corporation (RC) for projects in large areas that are designated "blighted." They need to be approved by the local government—a process that effectively gives away to private enterprise the power to redevelop on the public's behalf. Until recently—after excessive abuses of the power—redevelopment corporations could leverage the law of eminent domain to take private property for redevelopment in Missouri. 1 Redevelopment Corporations still get special access to tax abatements and other incentives in addition to being able to skirt fair democratic processes required of fully public projects.

1 For more on redevelopment corporations and urban erasure, see Patty Heyda, "Façade of Redevelopment," *Common Reader: Material World of Modern Segregation* (St. Louis: Washington University, 2022).

The NorthPark Chapter 353
Redevelopment Corporation Tax
Abatement—along with other
incentives and land use changes—
enabled warehouse development
in Kinloch, Cool Valley and
Berkeley, MO, as it enabled the
erasure of communities who
lived there. Who benefits from
state corporatization of urban
"revitalization?"

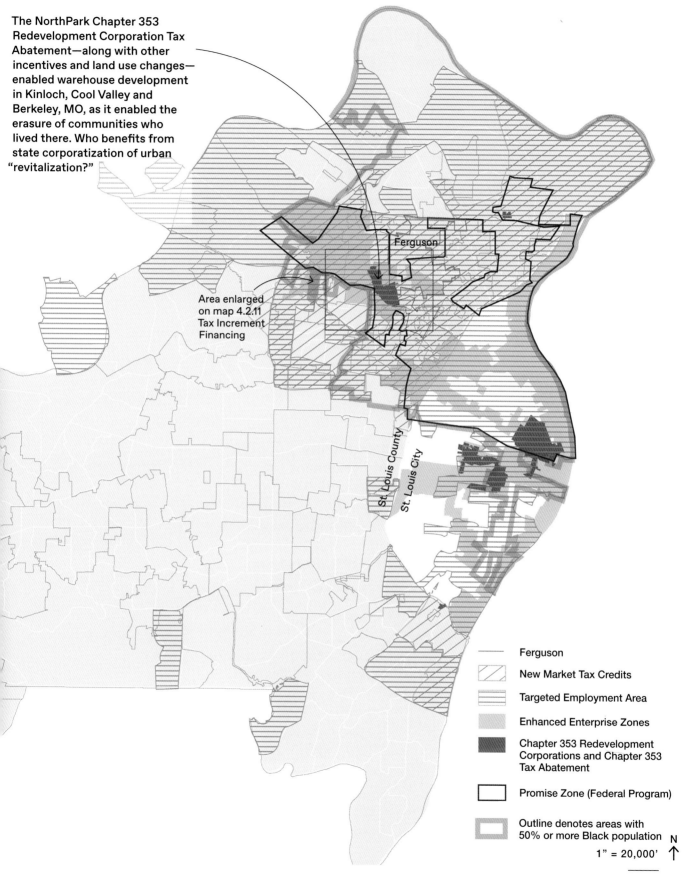

Area enlarged
on map 4.2.11
Tax Increment
Financing

Ferguson

St. Louis County
St. Louis City

	Ferguson
	New Market Tax Credits
	Targeted Employment Area
	Enhanced Enterprise Zones
	Chapter 353 Redevelopment Corporations and Chapter 353 Tax Abatement
	Promise Zone (Federal Program)
	Outline denotes areas with 50% or more Black population

1" = 20,000'

N

145

4.2.10

Map of St. Louis County and City showing areas where public local/regional tax incentives are available to aid economic development projects (shown for the period from approximately 2006-2023).

Local & regional development incentives

City and county economic development follows logics of investment returns instead of addressing community needs.

In North County, a majority of local development incentives enable large-scale industrial expansion that leverages the airport, or big box development that leverages the highway and regional markets. Or, they augment already stable commercial areas in white neighborhoods. In this map the various locally incentivized areas scatter across the St. Louis region, reflecting the fragmented reality of many local governments, each controlling their own development priorities. But the map also shows the larger incentive footprints in North St. Louis City and North County—historic Black neighborhoods aggressively reimagined as regional industrial hubs.

↳

"Public officials decided that the compact that government has concerning economic development is between the state and capitalist elites, not between the state and its entire population." 1

Local or District Tax Increment Financing (TIF)

Provides public (borrowed) funds to subsidize development infrastructure costs within designated districts on the assumption that the funding will be replenished by future taxes generated after the project's completion. But even if the project doesn't materialize the taxes (and jobs promised by the development), the city is obligated to pay back the borrowed funds.

Community Improvement District (CID)

Establishes a special tax district that unevenly privileges the businesses who pay into it. It is a tool that unevenly bolsters extra-localized enclaves. This benefits those in the bubble of the district, but increases disparities outside the CID's boundaries.

Transportation Development District (TDD)

Provides funding assistance for projects that involve highway or transportation-related features. The first-ring suburbs continue to suffer from a lack of efficient public transit. But planning for increased density—affordable housing—with access to public transit, not highways, should be the model for these types of incentives.

1 Michael Allen, "Never Mind McKee, Start Empowering Impacted Communities" *Next STL*, June 20, 2018.

See also   4.2.13   4.C.17-18

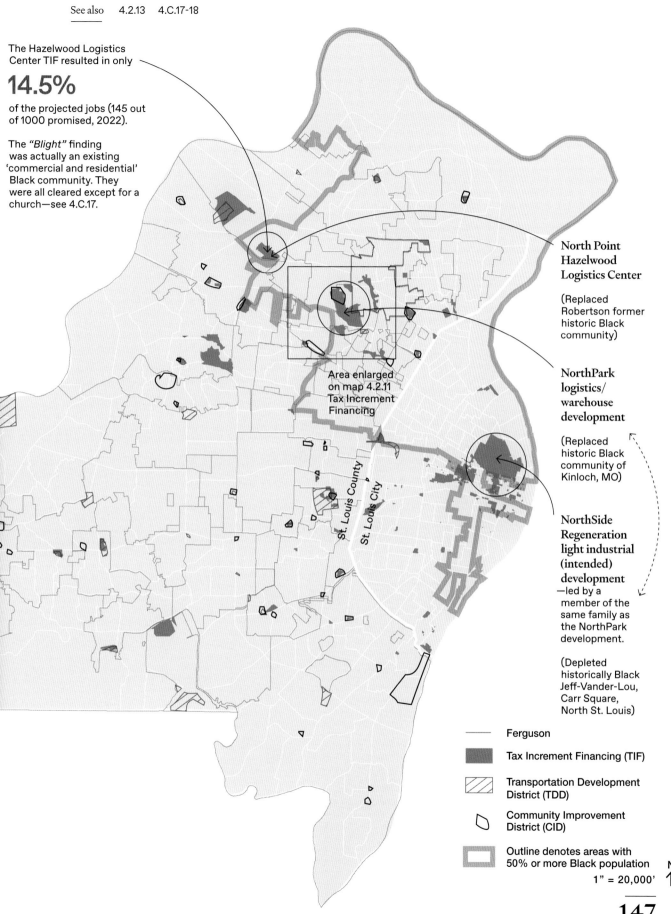

The Hazelwood Logistics Center TIF resulted in only

14.5%

of the projected jobs (145 out of 1000 promised, 2022).

The *"Blight"* finding was actually an existing 'commercial and residential' Black community. They were all cleared except for a church—see 4.C.17.

North Point Hazelwood Logistics Center

(Replaced Robertson former historic Black community)

NorthPark logistics/ warehouse development

(Replaced historic Black community of Kinloch, MO)

NorthSide Regeneration light industrial (intended) development —led by a member of the same family as the NorthPark development.

(Depleted historically Black Jeff-Vander-Lou, Carr Square, North St. Louis)

Area enlarged on map 4.2.11 Tax Increment Financing

St. Louis County

St. Louis City

Ferguson

Tax Increment Financing (TIF)

Transportation Development District (TDD)

Community Improvement District (CID)

Outline denotes areas with 50% or more Black population

1" = 20,000'

N

147

4.2.11

Close up map of Kinloch, MO, and surrounding municipalities in the state Enhanced Enterprise Zone, with local Tax Increment Financing (TIF) districts overlaid to show how the incentive zones are coordinated to grow industry capital in lieu of public—common—wealth.

1 Team TIF, "What is TIF?" https://teamtifstl.com/

2 Missouri Department of Revenue website, "Local Tax Increment Financing," n.d.

3 *Ferguson, MO Downtown Strategic Development Plan*, December, 2008.

See also: Walter Johnson, *Broken Heart of America*, (New York: Basic Books, 2020).

5 The shallow determination of "blight" itself is a weapon. Patty Heyda, "Façade of Redevelopment," *Common Reader: Material World of Modern Segregation* (St. Louis: Washington University, 2022).

See also Andrew Herscher, ""Blight," Spatial Racism, and the Demolition of the Housing Question in Detroit," *Housing After the Neoliberal Turn,* Stefan Aue, et al, eds., (Spector Books, 2016).

Tax Increment Financing (TIF)

"TIF is a tool where cities borrow against future tax revenue in order to finance or encourage development in the present day." 1 TIF was originally intended as a strategy for incentivizing private investment in weak market areas that developers would not otherwise take the risk in. Now, the tool is either used to subsidize development in areas that are relatively more stable already (like South Florissant Avenue in Ferguson), or, in the poorest areas where the TIF follows disinvestment and displacement, to fund entirely new industries in place of the community that needed investment (like in Kinloch, MO).

One critique of the misuse of TIF is that it inappropriately concentrates public assistance in areas that are relatively financially stable. In Missouri, "areas eligible for Local TIF must contain property classified as a 'Blighted,' 'Conservation' or an 'Economic Development' area, or any combination thereof..." 2 In Ferguson the more demographically middle-class downtown commercial district and the regional-attractor big-box North County Festival retail strip on northern West Florissant Avenue at I-270 received TIF assistance to build developments that cater to people from much farther outside of the area. 3 But TIF also concentrates in poor, historically Black neighborhoods, like in Kinloch, MO, by the airport. Except in that case, TIF was not leveraged for local development of needed amenities but was weaponized to channel externalized corporate growth. 4 As the layering of incentives like TIF denies revenue to local schools and services, it also actively creates "blight" in the poorest neighborhoods—"blight" that later justifies TIFs for projects that only further undermine disenfranchised communities. 5

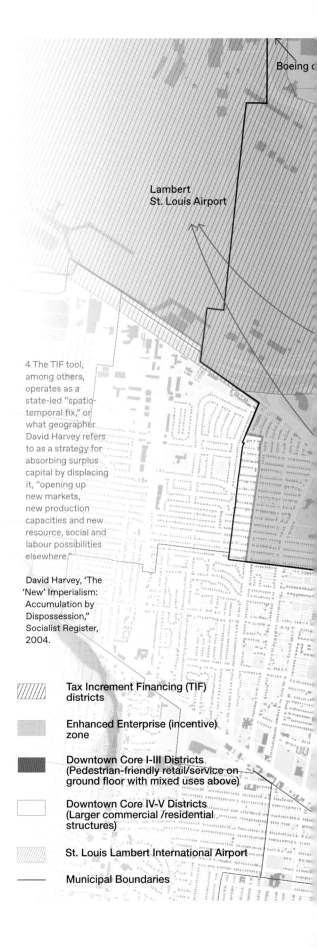

Boeing (

Lambert
St. Louis Airport

4 The TIF tool, among others, operates as a state-led "spatio-temporal fix," or what geographer David Harvey refers to as a strategy for absorbing surplus capital by displacing it, "opening up new markets, new production capacities and new resource, social and labour possibilities elsewhere."

David Harvey, 'The 'New' Imperialism: Accumulation by Dispossession," Socialist Register, 2004.

Tax Increment Financing (TIF) districts

Enhanced Enterprise (incentive) zone

Downtown Core I–III Districts (Pedestrian-friendly retail/service on ground floor with mixed uses above)

Downtown Core IV–V Districts (Larger commercial /residential structures)

St. Louis Lambert International Airport

Municipal Boundaries

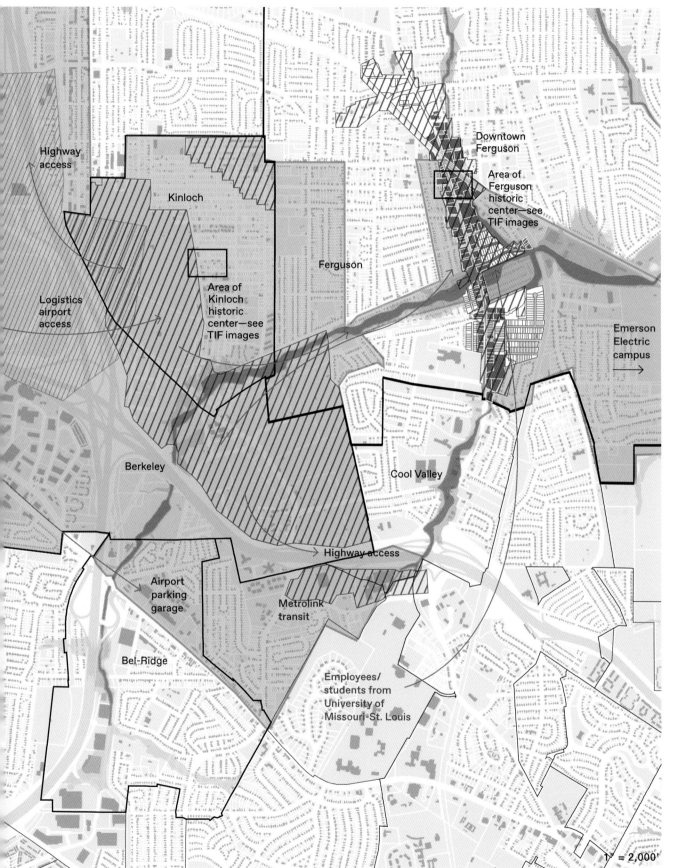

Highway
access

Kinloch

Logistics
airport
access

Area of
Kinloch
historic
center—see
TIF images

Ferguson

Downtown
Ferguson

Area of
Ferguson
historic
center—see
TIF images

Emerson
Electric
campus

Berkeley

Cool Valley

Highway access

Airport
parking
garage

Metrolink
transit

Bel-Ridge

Employees/
students from
University of
Missouri-St. Louis

N

1" = 2,000'

See also   4.2.11

Tax Increment Financing (TIF) district area, Ferguson, MO, historic center

Photo by author, 2024
View of South Florissant Avenue in the historic center of Ferguson, MO, an area with access to local Tax Increment Financing (TIF).

See also   4.2.11   4.C.19

Tax Increment Financing (TIF) district, Kinloch, MO, historic center

Photos by author, 2023, left; 2010, above Views from Martin Luther King (MLK) Avenue in the historic center of Kinloch, MO, an area with predominantly Black residents designated as a Tax Increment Financing (TIF) district. By 2023 the site of the historic building above (located a few feet outside the line of the district) was overgrown and vacant. A completely fenced and barbed wired distribution warehouse unrelated to the town, at left, was constructed there instead with the TIF incentives.

The writing on the wall on TIF policy

Photo by author, 2010
A local business in
Kinloch, MO, sends
a message to the
region about their
experience with the
TIF development
incentive created
for the NorthPark
industrial area.

See also   4.2.11

4.2.12

A timeline and map showing different attempts to gain advantage via economic development or annexation in the small municipality of Bel-Ridge, MO, located south of Ferguson in North County.

Annexation

After intensive patterns of city separation and incorporation, then political economic austerity, annexation is a tool for expansion to gain additional population to add to the tax base.

Other tax mechanisms like the "pool" county sales tax system allocate funding back to municipalities based on population. Bel-Ridge tried annexing its neighboring unincorporated areas several times in the last decades, alongside maneuvering to leverage public TIF and other incentives to compete for private development.

▬▬▬	Bel-Ridge Municipal Boundary
▬▬▬	MetroLink Line
▬▬▬	Natural Bridge Road
▬▬▬	Major Highways
▬▬▬	Neighboring Municipal Boundaries
	Unincorporated Land
	Enhanced Enterprise Zone
✚	TIF project

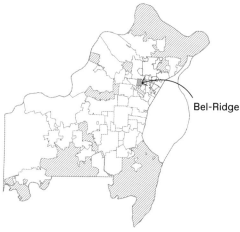

Bel-Ridge

Drawing by Casey Ryan, "Fragmentation Road" Patty Heyda, *The Problem of the Suburb*, Washington University in St. Louis, 2016.

1978
FAILED
Increased "Community Development (CD) funding" is sought by Bel-Ridge from the state to improve the "financially beleaguered community."

1993
FAILED
Motion to annex the neighboring unincorporated Carsonville fails.

2000
FAILED
Motion to annex Carsonville put to a vote for the second time in 10 years. The motion fails.

2006
PASSED
Bel-Ridge city council gains TIF funding for an 80-acre shopping center development along Natural Bridge road.

2006
Bel-Ridge Village trustees submit plan to Boundary Commission for potential annexation of adjacent unincorporated areas, including Carsonville.

2009
State of Missouri declares Bel-Ridge a "Distressed Municipality," opening up tax credits for development.

2012
State of Missouri declares the area of Bel-Ridge north of Natural Bridge Road an "Enhanced Enterprise Zone" to create tax incentives for development and investment in the area.

2012
FAILED
Shopping center project is put on hold due to extraordinary costs and infrastructure upgrades required for completion.

2012
FAILED OR SUCCESS?
Separate Natural Bridge Road TIF district project reaches completion. The funding was intended to redevelop the district into mixed-use commercial, retail, and governmental uses. A parking garage was constructed.

See also   1.2.05   4.1.02

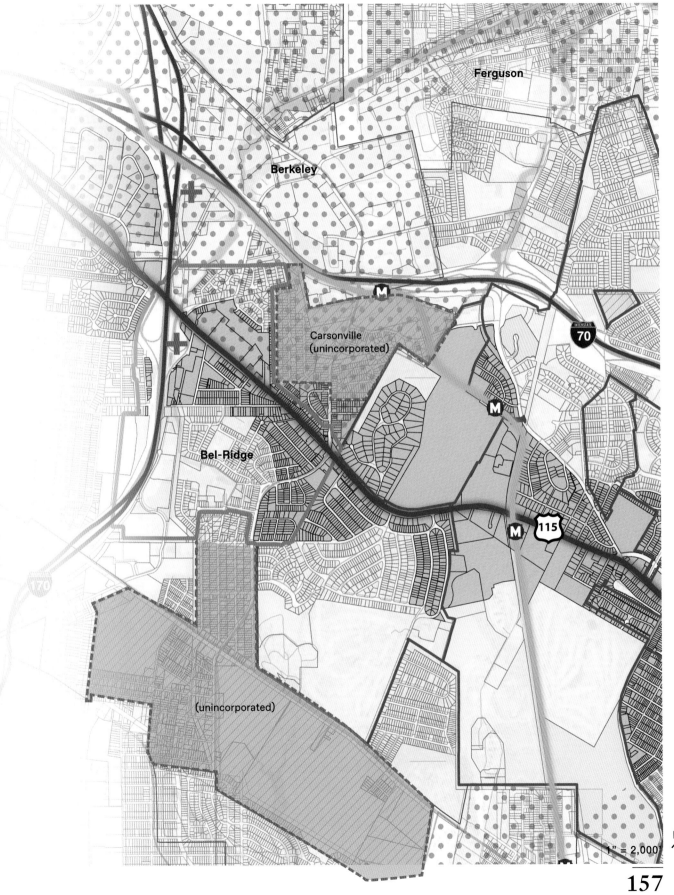

Ferguson

Berkeley

Carsonville
(unincorporated)

Bel-Ridge

(unincorporated)

1" = 2,000'

N

Public infrastructure 'improvements' provided by Tax Increment Financing (TIF)

Photo by Casey Ryan, 2016
Kids navigate a newly redeveloped but barren civic landscape that remains car-oriented, dangerous, treeless and sidewalkless. This is infrastructure funded by a TIF in Bel-Ridge. The TIF supported development that prioritized airport-related capital growth. How exactly does that improve civic space for current and future residents?

4.2.13

At right, diagram showing part of St. Louis City's elected government and appointed redevelopment commissions (2018).

The diagram reveals how the commissions were heavily populated with corporate industry elites (shown as circles), many who held positions on multiple related commissions at once.

Commission stacking

21st-century urban property steering happens deep within government commissions captured by the corporate elite. Shown here are St. Louis City redevelopment-related commission boards (2018) populated directly with real estate and business leaders.

The circles represent individuals on the public boards, color coded by the sector they work in (public sector in blue; private sector— corporate and power elites—in orange and warm tones).

The neoliberal approach that elevates private actors directly into public decision-making roles brings conflicts of development interest into matters of urban redevelopment that might otherwise address social, environmental and public concerns.

Real estate and corporate interests are directly embedded *in* government. These positions of power are hidden within the everyday commissions of contemporary governance.

Each dot represents a person on the "public" decision-making redevelopment board / commission, color coded by the sector and industry in which they work (2018) :

-
- Law
- Real Estate
- Financial
- Industry/Commercial

- Institutions (NON-PROFIT)

Many of the same people sit on different decision-making boards. (Vertical lines connect repeating people).

Inset diagram based on: Sherry Arnstein, "A Ladder of Citizen Participation," *Journal of the American Planning Association*, Volume 35; 1969. Her 'ladder' describes tiers of public engagement between residents and planning officials during the federal Model Cities program. This chart repositions her work, placing engagement farther from democratic processes, now within an embedded public-private milieu.

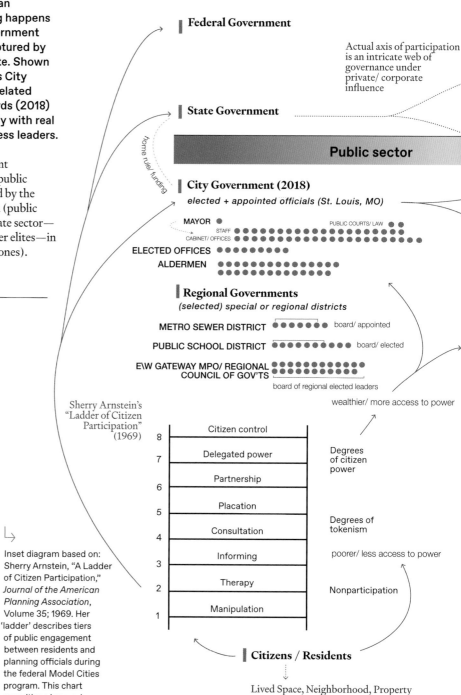

See also   4.2.10-11   4.C.17-19   4.3.27

The prevalence of orange and warm-colored circles shows how private interests have come to dominate what should be public redevelopment processes and decisions.

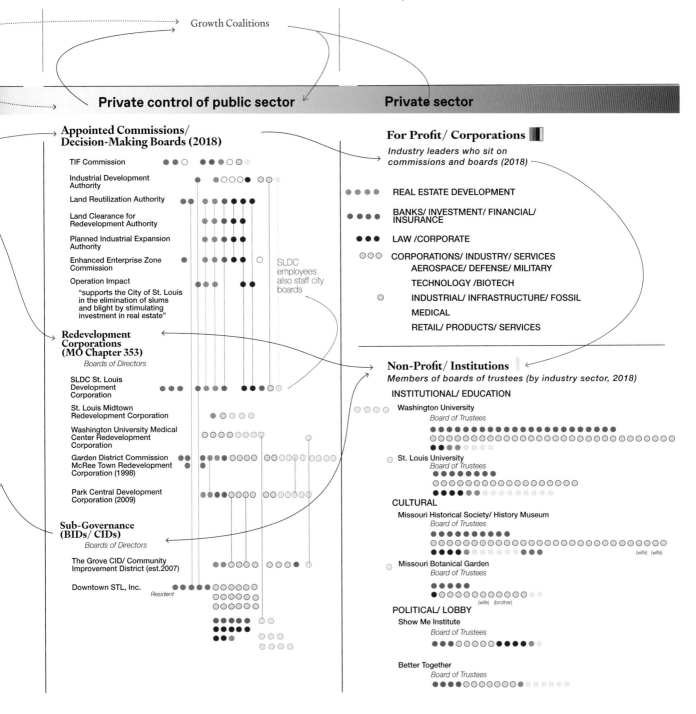

Growth Coalitions

Private control of public sector   **Private sector**

Appointed Commissions/ Decision-Making Boards (2018)

TIF Commission

Industrial Development Authority

Land Reutilization Authority

Land Clearance for Redevelopment Authority

Planned Industrial Expansion Authority

Enhanced Enterprise Zone Commission

Operation Impact
"supports the City of St. Louis in the elimination of slums and blight by stimulating investment in real estate"

SLDC employees also staff city boards

Redevelopment Corporations (MO Chapter 353)
Boards of Directors

SLDC St. Louis Development Corporation

St. Louis Midtown Redevelopment Corporation

Washington University Medical Center Redevelopment Corporation

Garden District Commission McRee Town Redevelopment Corporation (1998)

Park Central Development Corporation (2009)

Sub-Governance (BIDs/ CIDs)
Boards of Directors

The Grove CID/ Community Improvement District (est.2007)

Downtown STL, Inc.
Resident

For Profit/ Corporations
Industry leaders who sit on commissions and boards (2018)

REAL ESTATE DEVELOPMENT

BANKS/ INVESTMENT/ FINANCIAL/ INSURANCE

LAW /CORPORATE

CORPORATIONS/ INDUSTRY/ SERVICES
AEROSPACE/ DEFENSE/ MILITARY
TECHNOLOGY /BIOTECH
INDUSTRIAL/ INFRASTRUCTURE/ FOSSIL
MEDICAL
RETAIL/ PRODUCTS/ SERVICES

Non-Profit/ Institutions
Members of boards of trustees (by industry sector, 2018)

INSTITUTIONAL/ EDUCATION

Washington University
Board of Trustees

St. Louis University
Board of Trustees

CULTURAL

Missouri Historical Society/ History Museum
Board of Trustees
(wife) (wife)

Missouri Botanical Garden
Board of Trustees
(wife) (brother)

POLITICAL/ LOBBY

Show Me Institute
Board of Trustees

Better Together
Board of Trustees

Erasure suburbanism

A longitudinal case study of public-private redevelopment in Kinloch, MO, and the Robertson & Carrollton communities

Erasure Suburbanism builds on and updates prior case studies by the author on these North St. Louis County sites, all clear models of Harvey's "accumulation by dispossession" 1

Patty Heyda, "Erasure Urbanism," eds. Esther Choi and Marrikka Trotter, *Architecture is All Over* (New York: Columbia Books on Architecture and the City, 2017).

Patty Heyda, "Food Desert: Feeding the Regional Economic Imaginary," *Journal of Architectural Education* 77:2, fall, 2023.

Patty Heyda, "The City as Diagram Agency," eds. Terry Schwarz, Karen Lewis, *Urban Infill Diagrammatically* (Kent State, 2012).

1 David Harvey, "The New Imperialism: Accumulation by Dispossession," *The Socialist Register*, 2004.

Reference Guide

Kinloch
pages   164-167
         172-173
         176-185

Robertson
pages   166-167
         172-175

Carrollton
pages   166-171

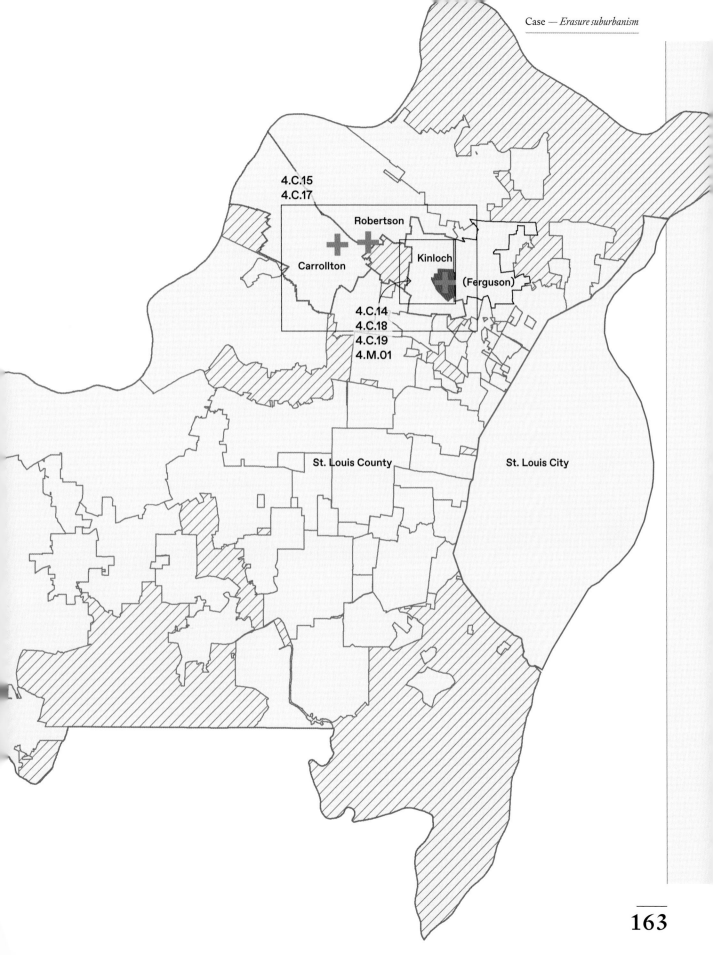

4.C.15
4.C.17

Robertson

Kinloch

Carrollton

(Ferguson)

4.C.14
4.C.18
4.C.19
4.M.01

St. Louis County

St. Louis City

4.C.14

Map of Kinloch, MO (outlined in red), with surrounding area showing the municipality's relationship to the St. Louis Lambert Airport.

Bottom graph shows the steep decline of Kinloch's population after its peak in 1960.

Missouri's "first Black city"

Next to Ferguson, MO, is Kinloch, the state's first 'all-Black' town to incorporate, in 1948. The historic community once had over 6,000 residents, notable schools and alumni, many churches and local businesses.

Over the decades, poverty in Kinloch compounded as racial exclusions and regional policy neglect—or targeting— systematically destabilized the community, staging it for future airport-related industrial imaginaries.

Mundane violence

In the 1980s, cable companies came through to establish lines for services. A Kinloch resident noted that they brought cable to all the surrounding neighborhoods but skipped Kinloch. He said, "I knew, at that time, that there were other plans for Kinloch." 1 An airport buy-out program started several years later.

↳ Kinloch was formed after it was isolated when the surrounding majority-white neighborhoods formed their own city (Berkeley, MO), to avoid integrating schools. (1937). 2

↳ While new subdivisions and infrastructures were built all around it, Kinloch still lacked a sewer system until the later 1960s. 2

↳ In 2006 the polling place was moved to neighboring Berkeley, MO, when St. Louis County eliminated polling places in towns with less than 700 residents. 3

1 As told to Alana Fields by an anonymous resident in an interview. Patty Heyda, "Erasure Urbanism," eds. Choi and Trotter, *Architecture is All Over* (New York: Columbia Books on Architecture and the City, 2017).

2 John A. Wright Sr., *Kinloch Missouri's First Black City* (Charleston: Arcadia, 2000).

3 Norm Parish, "Kinloch Protests Polling Site in Berkeley," *The St. Louis Post-Dispatch*, Metro Section, March 2, 2006, B1.

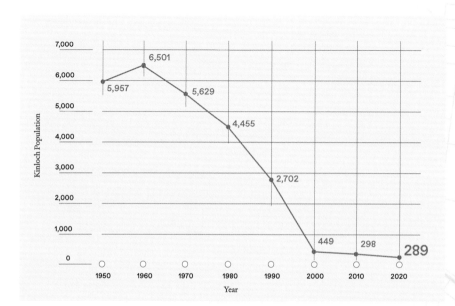

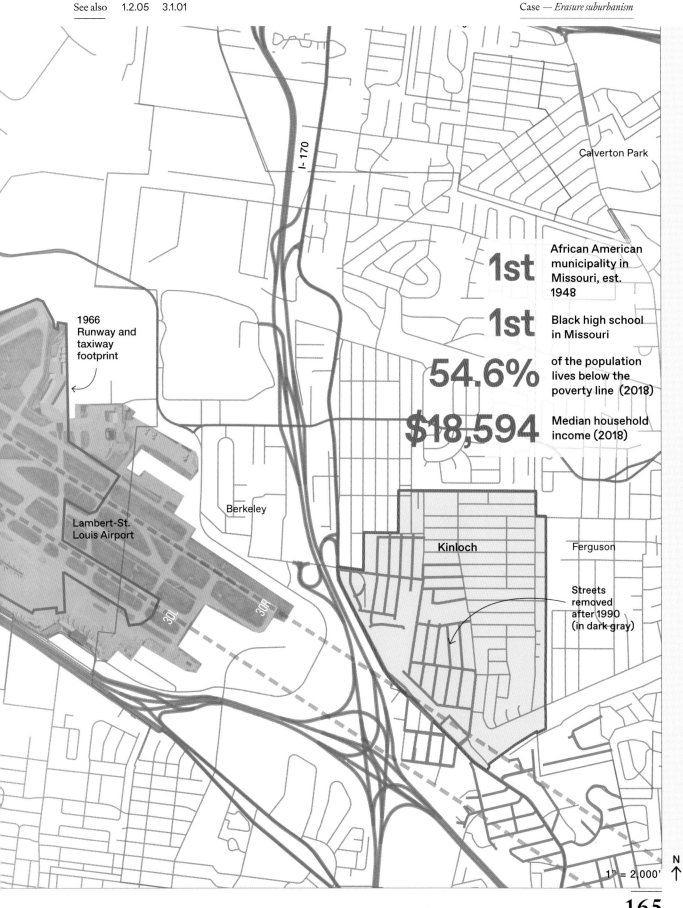

1966
Runway and
taxiway
footprint

Lambert-St.
Louis Airport

Berkeley

I-170

Calverton Park

1st African American
municipality in
Missouri, est.
1948

1st Black high school
in Missouri

54.6% of the population
lives below the
poverty line (2018)

$18,594 Median household
income (2018)

Kinloch

Ferguson

Streets
removed
after 1990
(in dark gray)

3OL   3OR

N
↑

1" = 2,000'

4.C.15

Aerial photograph (1995) showing the St. Louis Lambert International Airport and surrounding suburban neighborhood fabrics of Robertson and Kinloch, MO, historic Black communities (outlined in red), and the Carrollton subdivision of Bridgeton, MO, a mostly white middle-class suburb (also outlined in red). The airport's 1999 "eligible sound mitigation areas" are highlighted in blue.

1 David Harvey, "The New Imperialism: Accumulation by Dispossession," *The Socialist Register*, 2004.

2 Ishmael Ahmad, lawyer for the Kinloch community, quoted in "Kinloch Sues St. Louis to Halt Home Buyouts near Lambert; Redevelopment Deal Was Broken, Community Says," The St. Louis American, March 9–15, 2000.

Airport expansion

The map shows three communities erased by airport and regional planning policies weaponized for targeted economic growth.

Noise mitigation

One of these policies was the airport sound mitigation insulation program (in blue, initiated in 1999) that was offered to residential areas near the flight path but that deliberately skipped over Kinloch. Instead, Kinloch residents were offered a buy-out program to sell their homes and leave (and have the houses leveled). Later, the airport authority reduced the boundary of allowable decibel levels for departing and arriving planes, as newer aircraft became quieter and the number of flights decreased.

The buy-outs exemplify what geographer David Harvey calls "accumulation by dispossession." 1 Private family property was transferred into public (St. Louis Airport Authority) possession for 'public' airport-related purposes. But several years later, the land was conveyed back to private—this time corporate—hands, to the NorthPark development consortium. The neighborhood-scaled suburban block patterns were leveled and parcels aggregated for massive warehouses.

Runways

Around the same time, planning began for a new airport runway. Even though industrial-zoned sites were available to the airport's north, the decision was made to buy out and level 2,000 homes and additional schools and churches in Carrollton, to the west.

↳

"A massive federally financed land grab which had the effect to ruin a Black community." 2

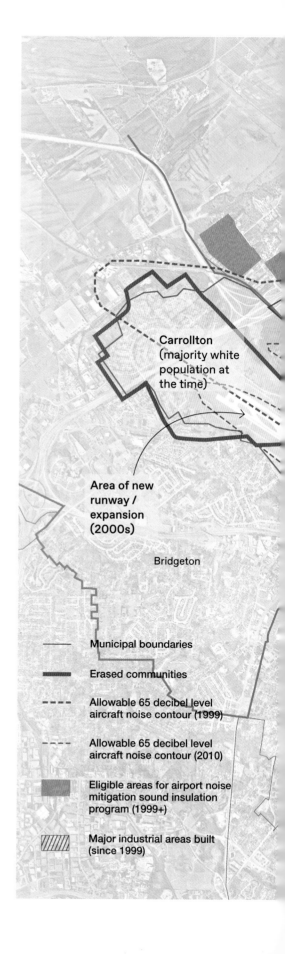

Carrollton (majority white population at the time)

Area of new runway / expansion (2000s)

Bridgeton

— Municipal boundaries

▬ Erased communities

---- Allowable 65 decibel level aircraft noise contour (1999)

---- Allowable 65 decibel level aircraft noise contour (2010)

■ Eligible areas for airport noise mitigation sound insulation program (1999+)

▨ Major industrial areas built (since 1999)

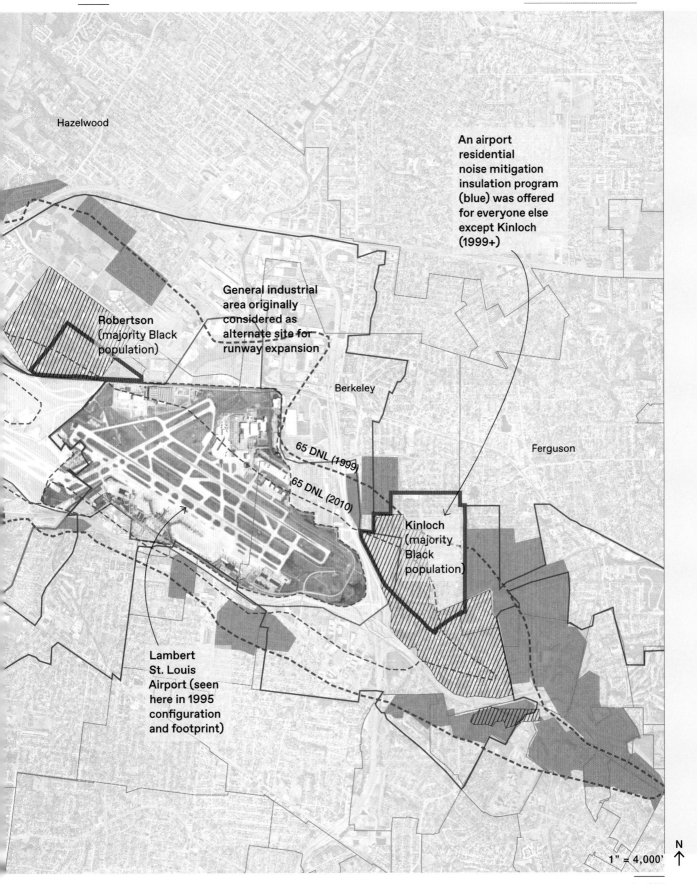

Hazelwood

An airport
residential
noise mitigation
insulation program
(blue) was offered
for everyone else
except Kinloch
(1999+)

General industrial
area originally
considered as
alternate site for
runway expansion

Robertson
(majority Black
population)

Berkeley

Ferguson

65 DNL (1999)

65 DNL (2010)

Kinloch
(majority
Black
population)

Lambert
St. Louis
Airport (seen
here in 1995
configuration
and footprint)

1" = 4,000'

N

4.C.16

A timeline showing the number of flight operations at Lambert St. Louis International Airport, alongside federal and state legislative bills that paved the way for the clearing of Kinloch, and Carrollton, in Bridgeton, MO, for the new runway west of the airport. The aerial images above show snapshots of the long haphazard pattern of home buy-outs and demolition, correlated by year, highlighting the last house to be demolished. The bottom aerials correlate snapshots of the noise impact areas and a new runway that was eventually constructed over the neighborhood.

1 See Jami Desy Schoenweis, *56 Houses Left* weblog, 2015.

2 Amber Victoria Woodburn, *Pushback in the Jet Age: Investigating Neighborhood Change, Environmental Justice, and Planning Process in Airport-Adjacent Communities*, Penn Dissertation (2016).

Aerial imagery, Google Earth Pro, 2011.

Airline hub

A timeline of the public-private St. Louis Airport growth imaginary that claimed 2000 homes in the Carrollton neighborhood of Bridgeton, MO, for a new runway—despite the fact that there was available industrial land to the north. That land would prove to be more lucrative for further industrial redevelopment.

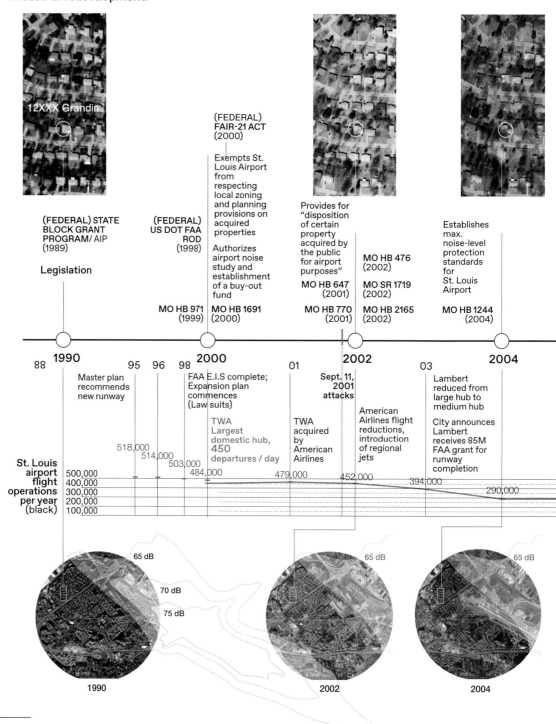

(FEDERAL) STATE BLOCK GRANT PROGRAM/ AIP (1989)

(FEDERAL) US DOT FAA ROD (1998)

(FEDERAL) FAIR-21 ACT (2000)

Exempts St. Louis Airport from respecting local zoning and planning provisions on acquired properties

Authorizes airport noise study and establishment of a buy-out fund

Provides for "disposition of certain property acquired by the public for airport purposes"

Establishes max. noise-level protection standards for St. Louis Airport

MO HB 476 (2002)

MO HB 647 (2001)

MO SR 1719 (2002)

MO HB 971 (1999)

MO HB 1691 (2000)

MO HB 770 (2001)

MO HB 2165 (2002)

MO HB 1244 (2004)

Legislation

88 **1990** 95 96 98 **2000** 01 **2002** 03 **2004**

Master plan recommends new runway

FAA E.I.S complete; Expansion plan commences (Law suits)

Sept. 11, 2001 attacks

Lambert reduced from large hub to medium hub

TWA Largest domestic hub, 450 departures / day

TWA acquired by American Airlines

American Airlines flight reductions, introduction of regional jets

City announces Lambert receives 85M FAA grant for runway completion

St. Louis airport flight operations per year (black)

518,000
514,000
503,000
484,000
479,000
452,000
394,000
290,000

500,000
400,000
300,000
200,000
100,000

65 dB
70 dB
75 dB

65 dB

65 dB

1990 2002 2004

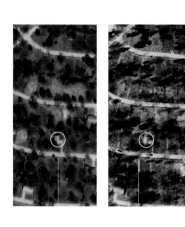

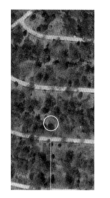

The house shown here on Grandin Avenue was the last to be demolished after 9 years of waiting out the buy-out process. 1

Studies have shown that most airport-adjacent communities remain below the median income after airport expansion. 2

MO HB 840 (2011) Aerotropolis trade incentive /tax credits

Economic + Aerotropolis trade incentives, data center support, tax credits (reduced neighborhood assistance, low income tax credits, neighborhood preservation tax credits)

MO SB 100 (2011)

Allows transportation authority to enter public-private partnerships (tax credits)

MO HB 354 (2009)

MO HB 2058 (2008) Business development tax incentives

MO HB 2393 (2008) Enhanced enterprise zone mega-project tax credits

2006 07 **2008** 09 **2010** 11 **2012**

05

Pending closure of Lambert Military Base announced

Runway 11-29 is operational

American Airlines announces flight cuts

St. Louis-China hub idea announced

297,000 282,000 257,000 248,000

AA hub reduced 1/3 of daily departures

450 350 250 150

TWA/ AA Daily Departures (red line)

St. Louis city passes Board Bill 72, allowing airport to selectively relieve passenger fees as incentive for attracting airlines; passes as emergency measure "being an ordinance for the preservation of public peace, health or safety, it is hereby declared an emergency measure..."

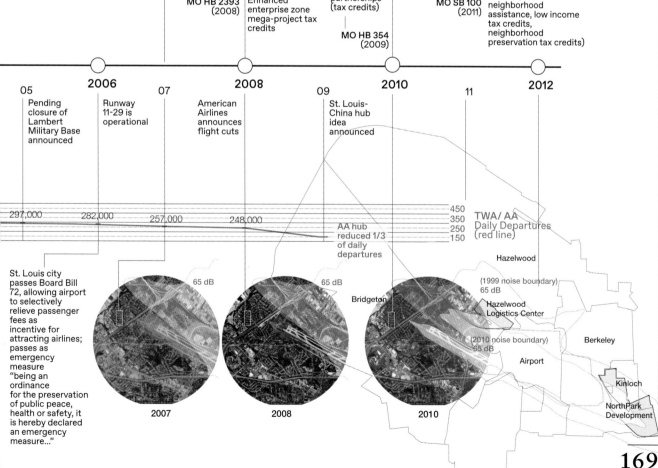

65 dB 65 dB

2007 2008 2010

Hazelwood

(1999 noise boundary) 65 dB

Bridgeton

Hazelwood Logistics Center

(2010 noise boundary) 65 dB

Berkeley

Airport

Kinloch

NorthPark Development

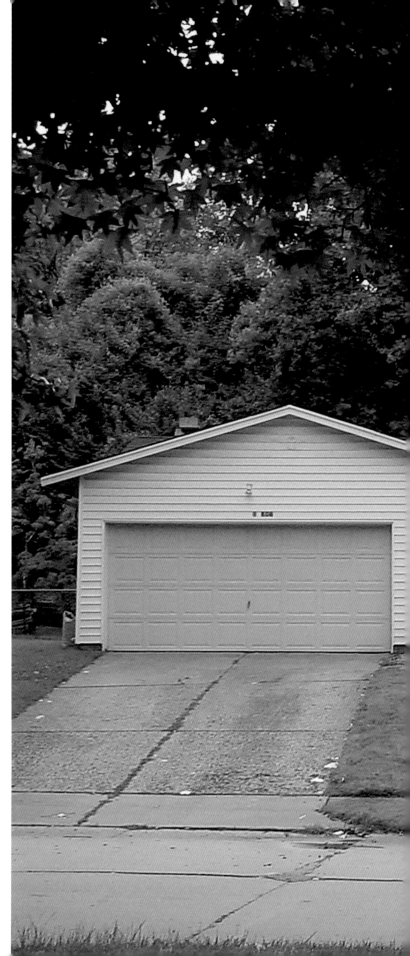

Suburban subtraction

Photo
Jami Desy Schoenweis,
2007
A typical suburban
ranch house in
the Carrollton
neighborhood of
Bridgeton, MO, just
before its demolition
for capital airport
expansion—Cookie
cutter suburban
economies are now
refinancialized into
global industrial
imaginaries. 1

Jami Desy Schoenweis, *56 Houses Left* weblog, 2007.

1 A nod here to Keller Easterling's operative potentials of "subtraction" as productive growth. In the absence of design's critical engagement, suburban subtraction forges on as capital accumulation in service of the corporate imaginary. Keller Easterling, *Subtraction* (London: Sternberg Press, 2014).

4.C.17

Close-up map of North St. Louis County showing the St. Louis Lambert International Airport with the Enterprise Zone incentive area overlaid, and major logistics center investments called out. The historic Black communities of Robertson and Kinloch, MO, that were slowly erased to enable economic development are outlined in red.

1 See quote by St. Louis County Executive, 2015, in map 4.C.19.

Regional investment

Two historically significant neighborhoods, Kinloch and Robertson, with majority Black residents get major investments to "revitalize the community."1 The investments skip the neighborhoods themselves and maneuver their erasure. Colonialism 2.0 takes the form of public policy—steered by a powerful urban business elite—to exploit weak market sites for corporate growth.

The combined public funding programs for the two large projects on the map are listed below. The Enterprise Zone overlay stretches like a thin bridge east of Kinloch to minimally thread between neighborhoods on its way to downtown and industrial parts of Ferguson. There, it overlays with a local TIF to attract visitors to the city—see map 4.2.11. Some argue that industry is a necessary component of a region's global economic positioning. But it shouldn't absorb such public funding that strips people and the environment of basic social infrastructure. And it shouldn't exploit low-income neighborhoods and citizens' rights to have and call a place home.

Combined, the Hazelwood Logistics Center and NorthPark had access to and used the following public-aid programs:

Tax Increment Financing (TIF)

Super TIF

Chapter 100 and Chapter 99 Bond Financing - Real or Personal Tax Abatement

New Market Tax Credits

Foreign Trade Zone Status

Missouri BUILD

Quality Jobs

Missouri State Tax Credit Programs

Enterprise Zone (blue overlay on map)

Significant erased areas where Black residents were displaced

Municipal boundaries

Allowable noise contour for 65 decibels (1999)

Enterprise Zone (incentive area)

Major industrial parks

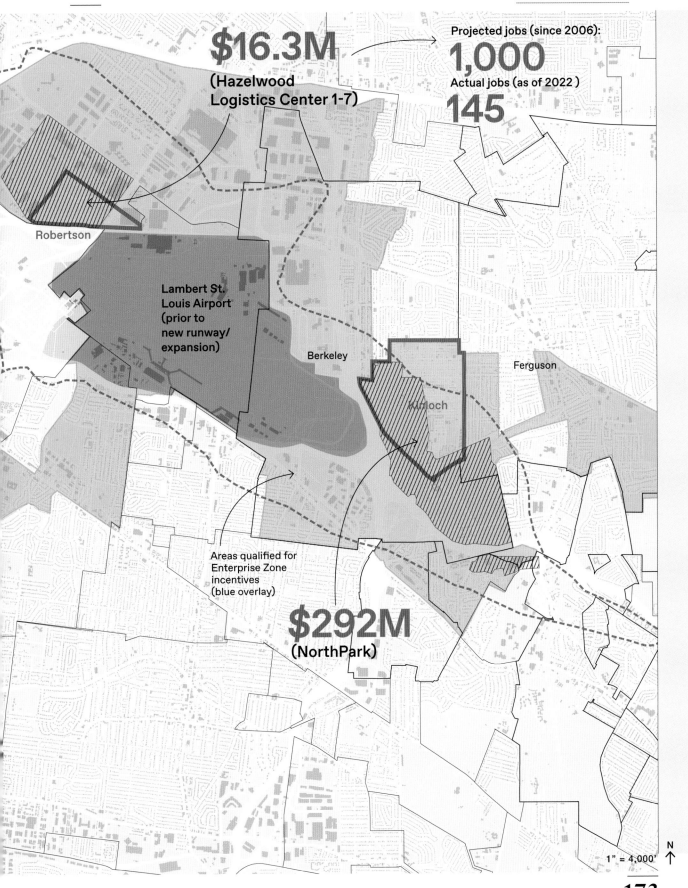

$16.3M
(Hazelwood
Logistics Center 1-7)

Projected jobs (since 2006):
1,000
Actual jobs (as of 2022)
145

Robertson

Lambert St.
Louis Airport
(prior to
new runway/
expansion)

Berkeley

Ferguson

Kinloch

Areas qualified for
Enterprise Zone
incentives
(blue overlay)

$292M
(NorthPark)

1" = 4,000'

N

1 This refers to a
phrase American
Studies scholar
George Lipsitz uses to
describe marginalized
communities' social
congregation as
resistance, or resource,
in the face of capital
accumulation.

George Lipsitz, "The
Racialization of Space,
and the Spatialization
of Race," *Landscape
Journal* 26:1, 2007.

Accumulation vs Congregation 1

Photos by author, 2023
At right, the First
Missionary Baptist
Church of Robertson,
MO, stands alone,
surrounded by out-
of-scale warehouse
buildings and parking
lots where the
rest of the historic
community used to
be, just outside the
photo frame (and
seen in the distance
in photo above, with
broader context). The
St. Louis Airport is
visible beyond. Signs
in the parking lot of
the Berlin packaging
company warehouse
across from the church
unabashedly champion
the development
violence of this
'progress' over people.

4.C.18

Map of the NorthPark industrial redevelopment area in Kinloch and part of Berkeley, MO, with warehouse buildings highlighted to show the difference in scale of the industrial vs residential buildings and blocks that were there before.

Big box / basements

The spatial mismatch of corporate capital and community is legible in the literal scale of the megaparcels, megablocks and buildings that were built over Kinloch, MO. The violence of "redevelopment" is also legible in the associated environmental harms caused by this type of truck based, impermeable condition that leveled a hilly, wooded terrain.

Economic development accumulates on top of peoples' former basements in starkly contrasting urban scales and patterns. [2] While these big box constructions are often critiqued as 'generic' standardized architecture, it is important to realize that processes that shape the production of these spaces are highly specific, generated by cultivated relationships and deals between powerful actors and government leaders. In other words, what architects call "site specificity" is not lost here as it seems, but dangerously manifested as political procedure that takes place before and after clearing. [3]

The aerial underlay of the NorthPark site is from 2002, showing traces of the old suburban streets prior to the final acquisition and clearing for redevelopment around 2006 and onwards.

⌐

"Opportunities to improve the bottom line for your real estate needs are available at NorthPark" [1]

1 Quote from NorthPark website, dated 2017.

2 Patty Heyda, "Food Desert: Feeding the Regional Economic Imaginary," *Journal of Architectural Education* 77:2, fall, 2023.

3 Patty Heyda, "Erasure Urbanism," eds. Esther Choi and Marrikka Trotter, *Architecture is All Over* (New York: Columbia Books on Architecture and the City, 2017).

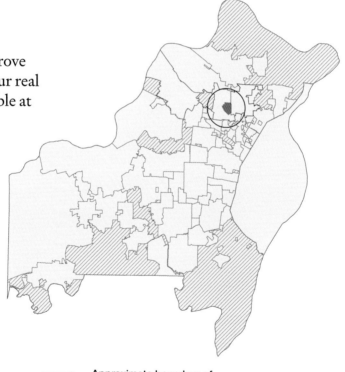

Approximate boundary of NorthPark industrial area (2017)

Municipal boundaries

 NorthPark industrial/commercial building footprints (2021)

(White lines): Trace of Kinloch neighborhood streets (2002)

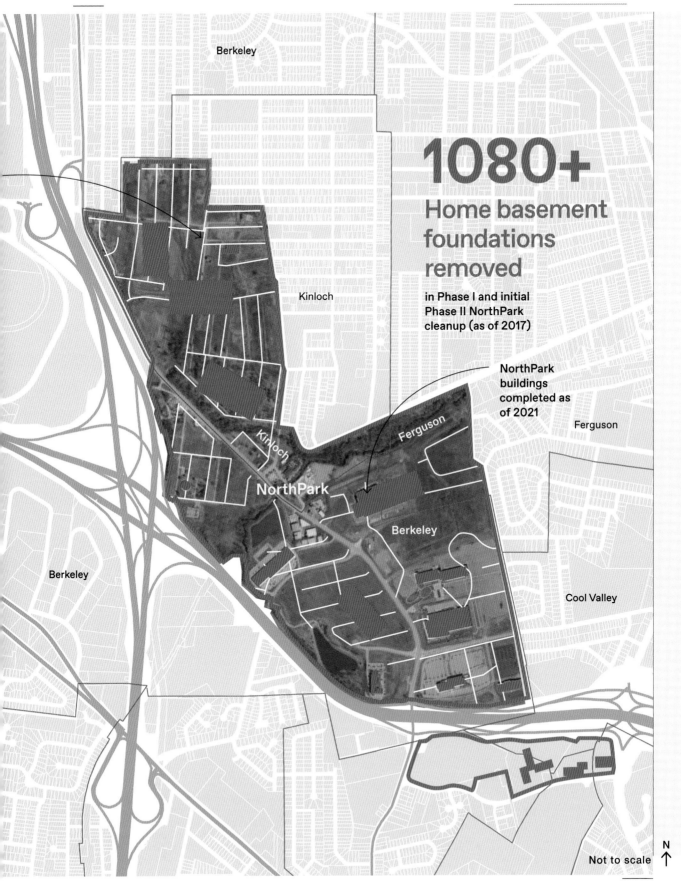

Berkeley

Kinloch

1080+

Home basement foundations removed

in Phase I and initial Phase II NorthPark cleanup (as of 2017)

NorthPark buildings completed as of 2021

Ferguson

Ferguson

Kinloch

NorthPark

Berkeley

Berkeley

Cool Valley

Not to scale

N
↑

4.C.19

Close-up aerial perspective drawing of the Schnucks grocery chain's regional distribution center built in the NorthPark industrial area of Kinloch, MO (2023). The map below shows Kinloch, highlighted, in the St. Louis region, with areas considered a 'food desert,' or, with low access to healthy food and transportation (2015).

Food desert

A 915,000 square foot, $100 million Schnucks grocery chain food distribution center is built, paradoxically, in the center of Kinloch, a community in a 'food desert.' 1

Food and revenue flow across this space but do not touch down to improve conditions for residents. 2 The productive "both/and" contradiction that defined Missouri in the early days of imperial expansion still undergird economic development today. As the growth paradigm brings food, literally, to this place, Kinloch remains in a food desert. See image page 152.

"I commend Schnucks' commitment to building this facility in Kinloch. It's projects like this that will help revitalize our community." 3

Steve Stenger, St. Louis County Executive (2015)

1 The grocery chain paved a few parking lots for the city and supported a clean-up activity in the community. These are helpful surface level, not structural, changes.

Vince Brennan, "Schnucks keeps the community in mind with Kinloch distribution center," St. Louis Business Journal, Sep 21, 2017.

2 Patty Heyda, "Food Desert: Feeding the Regional Economic Imaginary," *Journal of Architectural Education* 77:2, fall, 2023.

3 Kristen Cloud, "Schnucks Building New DC In Kinloch, Missouri," *The Shelby Report*, May 28, 2015.

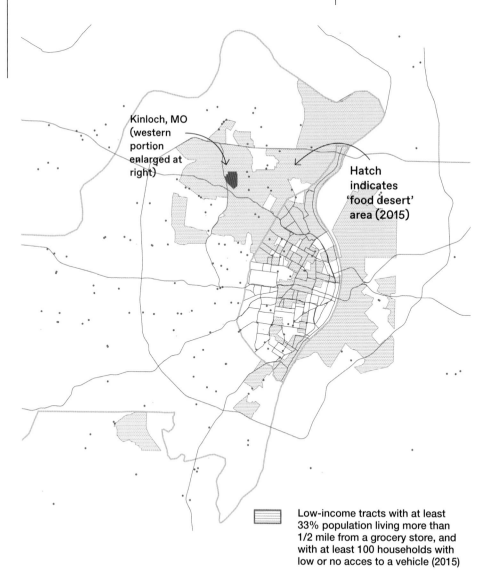

Kinloch, MO (western portion enlarged at right)

Hatch indicates 'food desert' area (2015)

Low-income tracts with at least 33% population living more than 1/2 mile from a grocery store, and with at least 100 households with low or no acces to a vehicle (2015)

1,200 sf
(square feet) average single-family home

Kinloch

I-170

915,000 sf
(square feet) distribution center

Cultivation

Photo by Christian Gooden, 2012
St. Louis Post-Dispatch, Polaris.
Two friends talk after picking mustard greens and sweet potatoes at the community farm Mr. Walton (right) took care of in Kinloch, MO.1 The farm brought fresh produce to an area of low food and low transit access, an area under the flight path of nearby St. Louis Lambert International Airport. Thus, it was an area in the path of economic development. Just a few years after this photo was taken, the farm was relocated to make space for a massive grocery food distribution logistics center on the site that has nothing to do with the people who live there. See page 152.

1 Paul Hampel, "Urban farmers working vacant Kinloch property get surprise when land's rightful owner shows up," *St. Louis Post-Dispatch*, February 9, 2015.

See also   5.2.11

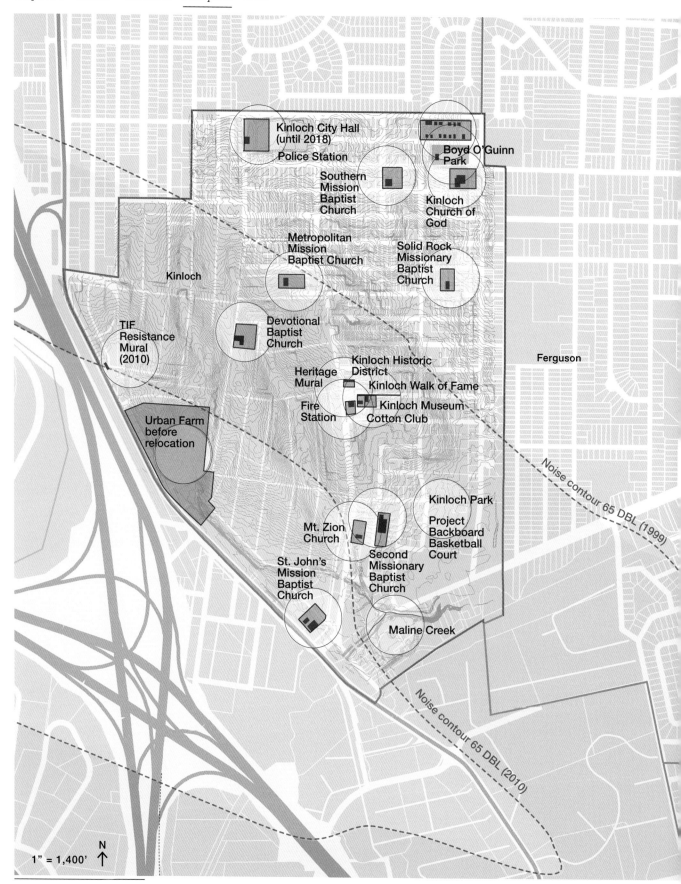

Kinloch City Hall
(until 2018)

Police Station

Boyd O'Guinn
Park

Southern
Mission
Baptist
Church

Kinloch
Church of
God

Metropolitan
Mission
Baptist Church

Solid Rock
Missionary
Baptist
Church

Kinloch

TIF
Resistance
Mural
(2010)

Devotional
Baptist
Church

Kinloch Historic
District

Heritage
Mural

Kinloch Walk of Fame

Fire
Station

Kinloch Museum

Cotton Club

Ferguson

Urban Farm
before
relocation

Kinloch Park

Project
Backboard
Basketball
Court

Mt. Zion
Church

Second
Missionary
Baptist
Church

St. John's
Mission
Baptist
Church

Maline Creek

Noise contour 65 DBL (1999)

Noise contour 65 DBL (2010)

1" = 1,400'

N

Radical Atlas of Ferguson, USA

Mobilize Fellowship

Local institutions anchor Kinloch, MO, as global capital imaginaries erode it.

In 2011, a density of churches still stood amidst the landscape of empty parcels. These historically strong institutions continue to mobilize fellowship and community for displaced churchgoers who return from afar for services.

Local planning

In the early 2000s, Kinloch residents and leaders created a small historic district and museum along Scott Avenue in the town's center. Measures like this signal subtle ways communities can reclaim the instruments of planning from within the system itself.

4.M.01

Map of Kinloch, MO, showing the remaining churches and community-oriented institutions still standing after the town's airport-related buy-outs and initial clearings (2011). The original topography is shown, since that too was leveled by development on the western edge.

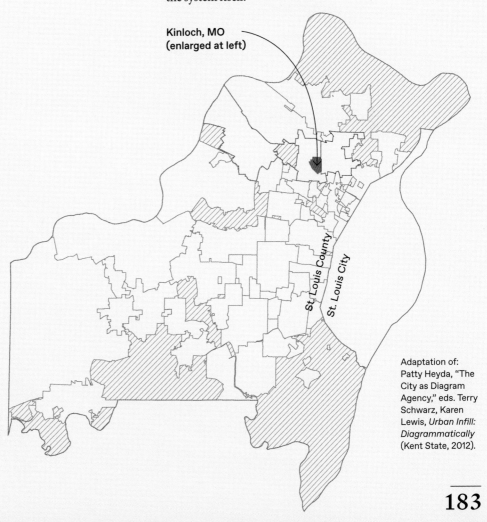

Kinloch, MO
(enlarged at left)

St. Louis County

St. Louis City

Adaptation of: Patty Heyda, "The City as Diagram Agency," eds. Terry Schwarz, Karen Lewis, *Urban Infill: Diagrammatically* (Kent State, 2012).

183

Radical Atlas of Ferguson, USA

Reclaiming Space

Photo by Daniel Peterson, Project Backboard, 2017 Vibrantly painted basketball courts reclaim public space in Kinloch Park in Kinloch, MO(2017). This simple move demonstrates the power of design to reinscribe local territorial histories in the struggle for suburban lived space.

Court graphic design by artist William LaChance, with Project Backboard.

On territorial histories, see Delores Hayden, *The Power of Place: Urban Landscapes as Public History* (Boston: MIT Press, 1997).

185

4.3.20

Map of the St. Louis County and City region showing Fortune 500 companies, with incentive areas (2018).

Fortune 500

Three of St. Louis's top ten-ranking Fortune 500 companies are in North County (2018) while the rest concentrate along the region's central east-west "power corridor" with other major companies and institutions.

Boeing Industries and Emerson Electric in North County are historic manufacturing campuses that relocated to Ferguson and Berkeley during or between the wars, as industry grew outside the city and around the airport. Workers lived in Ferguson, Berkeley, Kinloch and surrounding areas.

COMPANY/RANK (2018)	REVENUE/PRIMARY INDUSTRY
Express Scripts Holding (#25)	**$100,064 Million** Health Care: Pharmacy & other services
Boeing [HQ in Chicago] **(#27)**	**$93,392 Million** Aerospace and Defense
Centene Corporation (#61)	**$48,572 Million** Health Care: Insurance & Care
Emerson Electric (#178)	**$16,301 Million** Electrical, Industrial Machinery
Monsanto (#199)	**$14,640 Million** Chemicals
Reinsurance Group of America (#234)	**$12,516 Million** Health & Life Insurance
Edward Jones Investments (#329)	**$7,597 Million** Finance - Securities
Graybar Electric (#426)	**$6,631 Million** Wholesale
Olin Corporation (#448)	**$6,268 Million** Chemicals
Ameren (#453)	**$6,177 Million** Electric
Peabody Energy (#491)	**$5,579 Million** Energy, Coal

See also   4.3.28   4.3.32-33

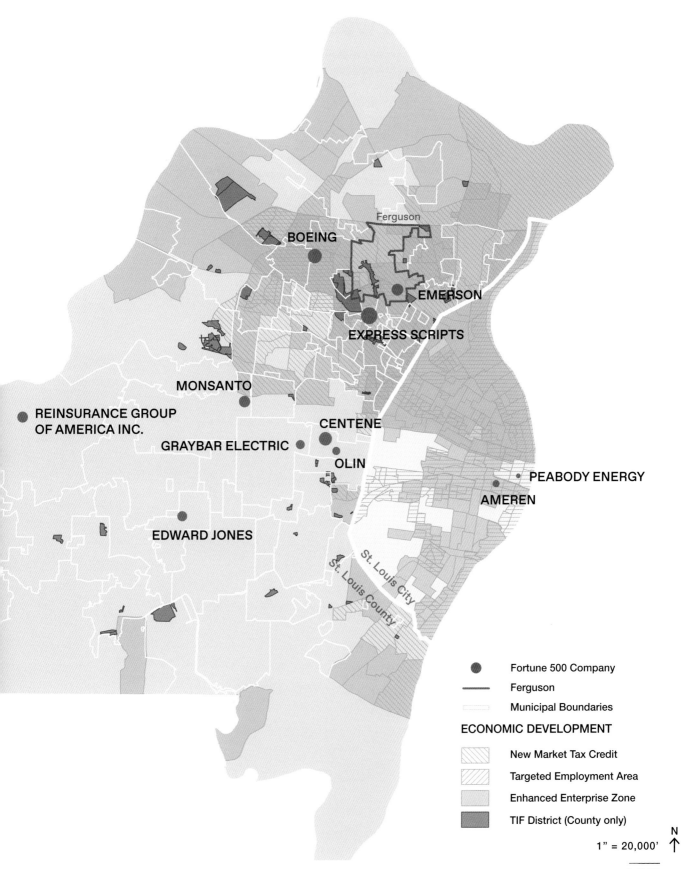

BOEING

EMERSON

EXPRESS SCRIPTS

Ferguson

MONSANTO

REINSURANCE GROUP
OF AMERICA INC.

CENTENE

GRAYBAR ELECTRIC

OLIN

PEABODY ENERGY

AMEREN

EDWARD JONES

St. Louis City

St. Louis County

● Fortune 500 Company

── Ferguson

▭ Municipal Boundaries

ECONOMIC DEVELOPMENT

▨ New Market Tax Credit

▨ Targeted Employment Area

▨ Enhanced Enterprise Zone

▨ TIF District (County only)

1" = 20,000'

N

187

4.3.21

Close-up map of Ferguson, Berkeley and Cool Valley, MO, in North St. Louis County, highlighting the Fortune 500 companies located there alongside (this page) comparative metrics of the three municipalities, with Missouri state averages (2016-2018).

Concentrated wealth

Where Fortune 500 wealth concentrates in North County, there is concentrated poverty. 1

Missouri state avg	Ferguson	Berkeley	Cool Valley
Median Age			
38.3	35.9	32.8	45.8
Unemployment			
4.1%	7.1%	9.3%	4.7%
Median Hh income			
$51,542	$41,369	$32,589	$49,780
Median Home Value			
$151,400	$93,682	$65,900	$81,205
H.S. Degree or Higher			
89.2%	89.4%	85.4%	85.6%
B.A. Degree or Higher			
28.2%	18.5%	13.9%	17.6%
Home Ownership			
66.8%	56.9%	51.1%	70.1%
Below Poverty Level			
13.4%	22.5%	26.9%	11.4%
Air Quality Index (2013) (101-150 = Unhealthy for sensitive groups)			
143	114	114	114
Violent Crime (2014) per 10,000 Residents			
44.29	54.53	47.29	181.8
No Health Insurance (<65)			
10.8%	13.1%	15.6%	8.09%

1 Historian Walter Johnson asks, "Why is the city government filling out its budget with municipal court fines when Emerson Electric is doing $24 billion a year in business out of its headquarters on West Florissant Avenue?" 2

This map and those that follow are elaborations of this question that points to contradictions of privatized and corporatized public policy.

2 Walter Johnson, "Ferguson's Fortune 500 Company," *The Atlantic*, April 26, 2015.

See also 4.3.24-26

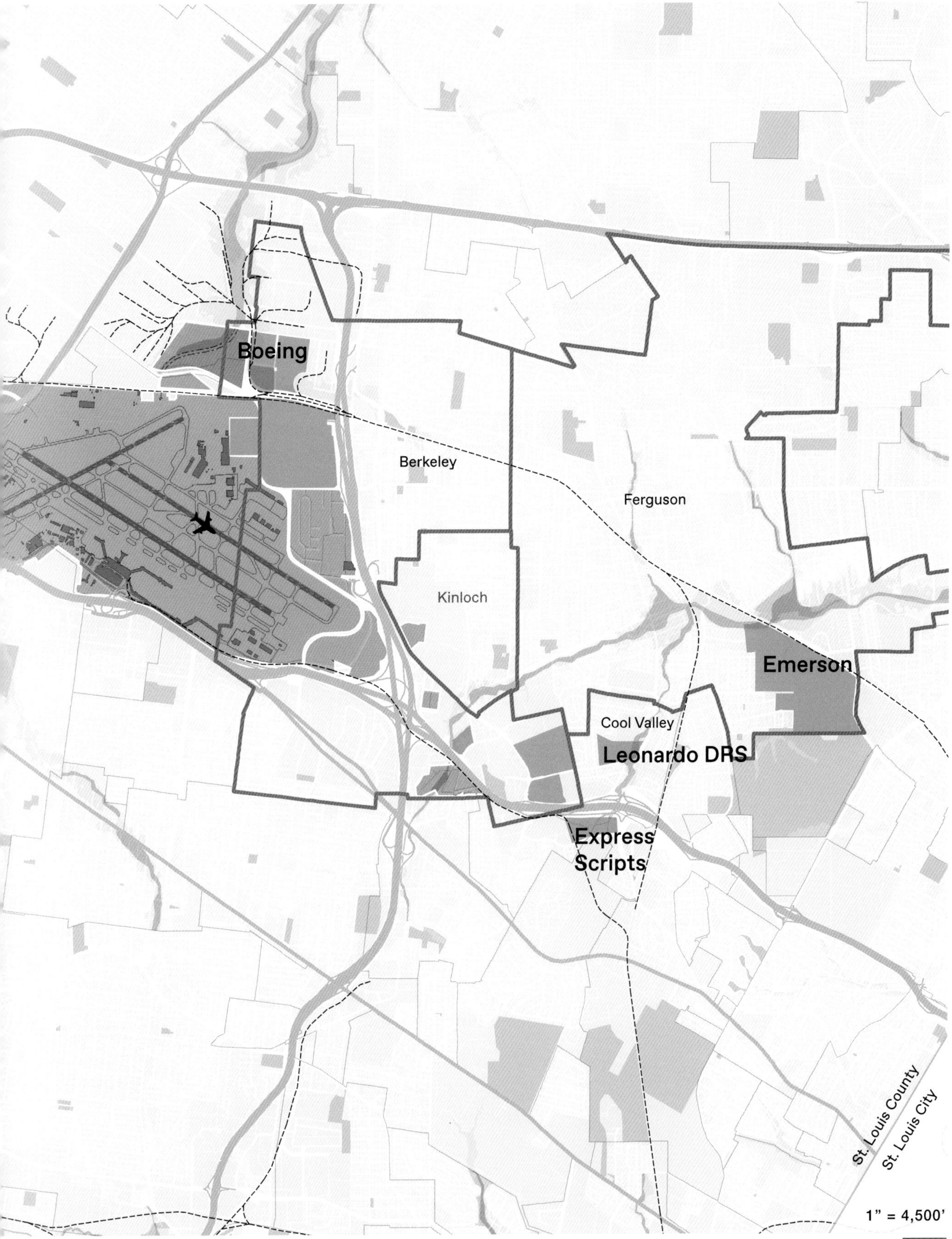

Boeing

Berkeley

Ferguson

Kinloch

Emerson

Cool Valley

Leonardo DRS

Express
Scripts

St. Louis County
St. Louis City

1" = 4,500'

N

4.3.22

Map of Ferguson showing land use and location of the Fortune 500 company Emerson Electric, just blocks from Canfield Drive, where Michael Brown was killed by police.

Company town

Ferguson was once like a company town to (now Fortune 500) company Emerson Electric, which was founded in 1890 and moved to Ferguson in 1940.

The historical concept of a paternalistic, walkable company town designed for workers who live alongside the industry campus, for better or for worse, is no longer. As companies are more global, their footprints encompass an expanded operational financial territory beyond local space. 1 The major companies in Ferguson are now walled-off enclaves to the communities around them. They hire from the greater region (not their immediate surroundings). The maps show the mismatch of median household incomes in Ferguson, and average yearly salaries of Emerson employees.

Emerson Co.

Approx. 76,500 Employees worldwide
155 Manufacturing locations worldwide

CEO Income (2017)

$12.5 M

Headquarter Average Yearly Salary

$100,000

Annual Revenue (2017)

$15.26 B

1,300

Employees in St. Louis (2014)
1.7% of total employees

$81,506

Average yearly salary at Emerson Co. (2018)

"Now hiring"
Headquarter Work: Highly Skilled
Financial and/or Management Work
No Manufacturing

>/= HS
HIGH SCHOOL DIPLOMA

- Valve Technician
- Engineering Lab Technician
- Test Technician
- Production Technician
- Operations Specialist

</= BS BACHELOR'S DEGREE

- Welding Engineer
- Commodity Engineer Actives
- Process Automation System Engineer
- Digital Customer Experience Director
- Electrical and Instrumentation Engineer
- Technical Training Specialist - HVAC
- Cyber Security Risk Management Specialist
- Product Development Engineer

30+ job openings in St. Louis
1700+ job openings worldwide

1 See Saskia Sassen,
The Global City
(Princeton University
Press, 2001).

See also   2.1.05   4.3.23   4.3.27

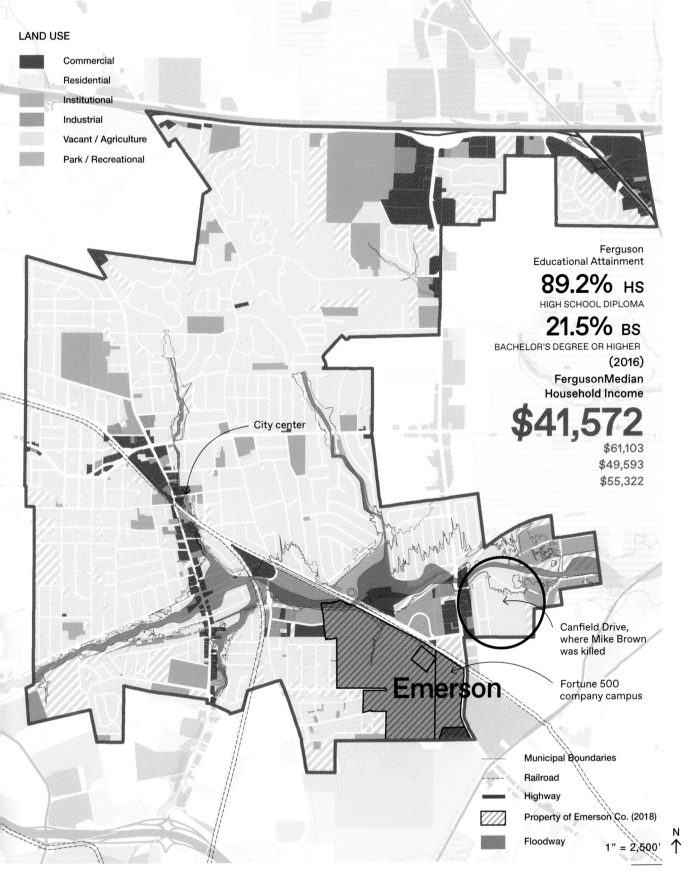

LAND USE

- Commercial
- Residential
- Institutional
- Industrial
- Vacant / Agriculture
- Park / Recreational

Ferguson
Educational Attainment

89.2% HS
HIGH SCHOOL DIPLOMA

21.5% BS
BACHELOR'S DEGREE OR HIGHER
(2016)

FergusonMedian
Household Income

$41,572
$61,103
$49,593
$55,322

City center

Canfield Drive,
where Mike Brown
was killed

Emerson

Fortune 500
company campus

Municipal Boundaries
Railroad
Highway
Property of Emerson Co. (2018)
Floodway

1" = 2,500'

N

4.3.23

Map of Berkeley, MO, showing its two Fortune 500 companies and their employer profiles, compared to average resident salaries and education levels.

Boeing Industries' campus in North County dates back to 1939. The company grew in tandem with its municipality Berkeley (incorporated in 1937).

Express Scripts arrived in the early 2000s, in the first phase of the NorthPark development. The nature of manufacturing today means that there is a disjoint between what used to be an ecosystem of jobs, a company and the town. Industry jobs don't match the educational training of local residents, if those jobs materialize at all.

1 Nathan Rubbelke, "Emerson's Monser on bolstering the region's STEM education," *St. Louis Business Journal*, June 21, 2018.

Adaptation of Lige Tan, "Berkeley: Two Cities" Patty Heyda, *The Problem of the Suburb*, Washington University in St. Louis, 2016.

Jobs

Economic development of industry does not build access to jobs as commonly claimed. There is a persistent mismatch of jobs, education and income in Berkeley, MO, despite it being home to two major Fortune 500 companies.

Boeing

Employs approximately 160,000 people across the U.S. and in more than 65 countries.

Boeing Median Salaries

Mechanical Engineer
$71,478

Software Engineer
$70,566

Financial Analyst
$64,396

Procurement Agent
$59,665

Express Scripts

Over 30,000 employees worldwide.

Express Scripts Median Salaries

Pharmacist
$123,000

Senior Business Analyst
$70,000

Associate Business Analyst
$45,738

Customer Service Supervisor
$41,000

"The amount of STEM jobs in St. Louis will grow 12 percent by 2022, but there's a shortage of skilled workers in the region." 1

Ed Monser, Emerson Electric President

15,000

Employees in St. Louis

$76,100

Median yearly salary at Boeing St. Louis (2018)

"Now hiring" (fall 2016)

>/= HS HIGH SCHOOL DIPLOMA

- Repair Mechanics
- Procurement Agent
- Assembly Mechanics

</= BS BACHELOR'S DEGREE

- Manufacturing Engineer
- Contracts & Pricing Representative
- Global Sales & Marketing Air Capture Manager
- Project Management Specialist
- Flight Engineering Manager
- Information Technology Manager
...110+ jobs

3,858

Employees in St. Louis

$74,132

Average yearly salary at Express Scripts

"Now hiring" (2016 fall)

>/= HS HIGH SCHOOL DIPLOMA

- Pharmacy Production Clerk
- Warehouse Assistant
- Accounting Assistant

</= BS BACHELOR'S DEGREE

- Manager, Litigation Services
- Business Analyst
- Staff Client Auditor
- Cyber Ark Subject Matter Expert (SME)
...200+ jobs

See also   3.2.17   4.C.17

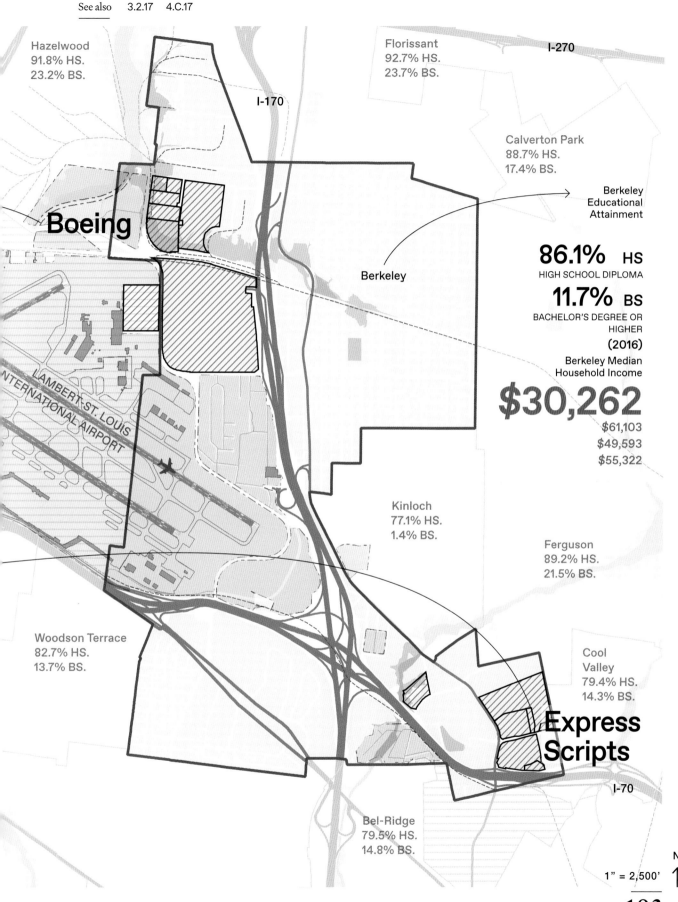

Hazelwood
91.8% HS.
23.2% BS.

Florissant
92.7% HS.
23.7% BS.

I-270

I-170

Calverton Park
88.7% HS.
17.4% BS.

Boeing

Berkeley
Educational
Attainment

Berkeley

86.1% HS
HIGH SCHOOL DIPLOMA

11.7% BS
BACHELOR'S DEGREE OR
HIGHER
(2016)

Berkeley Median
Household Income

$30,262

$61,103
$49,593
$55,322

LAMBERT ST. LOUIS INTERNATIONAL AIRPORT

Kinloch
77.1% HS.
1.4% BS.

Ferguson
89.2% HS.
21.5% BS.

Woodson Terrace
82.7% HS.
13.7% BS.

Cool
Valley
79.4% HS.
14.3% BS.

Express
Scripts

I-70

Bel-Ridge
79.5% HS.
14.8% BS.

N

1" = 2,500'

4.3.24

Map of Berkeley, MO, in relation to the Lambert St. Louis International Airport. The map shows land use and the locations of the Boeing and Express Scripts company campuses. Diagrams below show many layers of public subsidies that benefit industry in Berkeley.

Corporate land use

Berkeley, MO, appears evenly split between industrial and residential uses. But the overlay of economic development incentives (below) makes access to extra financing much more uneven. Excessive public funding for the industrial side of Berkeley ensures underfunding for the residential side.

In 2021 St. Louis County endorsed

$45 M

in bonds to aid construction of Boeing's new operations facility on their Berkeley campus. 1 Boeing revenues that year were

$62.3 B

The project was estimated to produce

...30 jobs

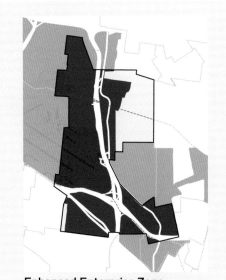

Enhanced Enterprise Zone

TIF District

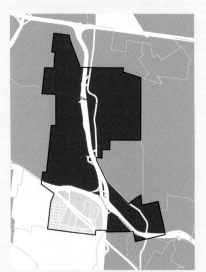

Targeted Employment Area

Chapter 353 Redevelopment Area

1 Jacob Barker, "Boeing Eyes Expansion at North St. Louis County Campus," *Aviation Pros*, January 27, 2021.

Adaptation of Lige Tan, "Berkeley: Two Cities" Patty Heyda, *The Problem of the Suburb*, Washington University in St. Louis, 2016.

See also   3.2.12   4.3.23   4.3.32   5.3.12

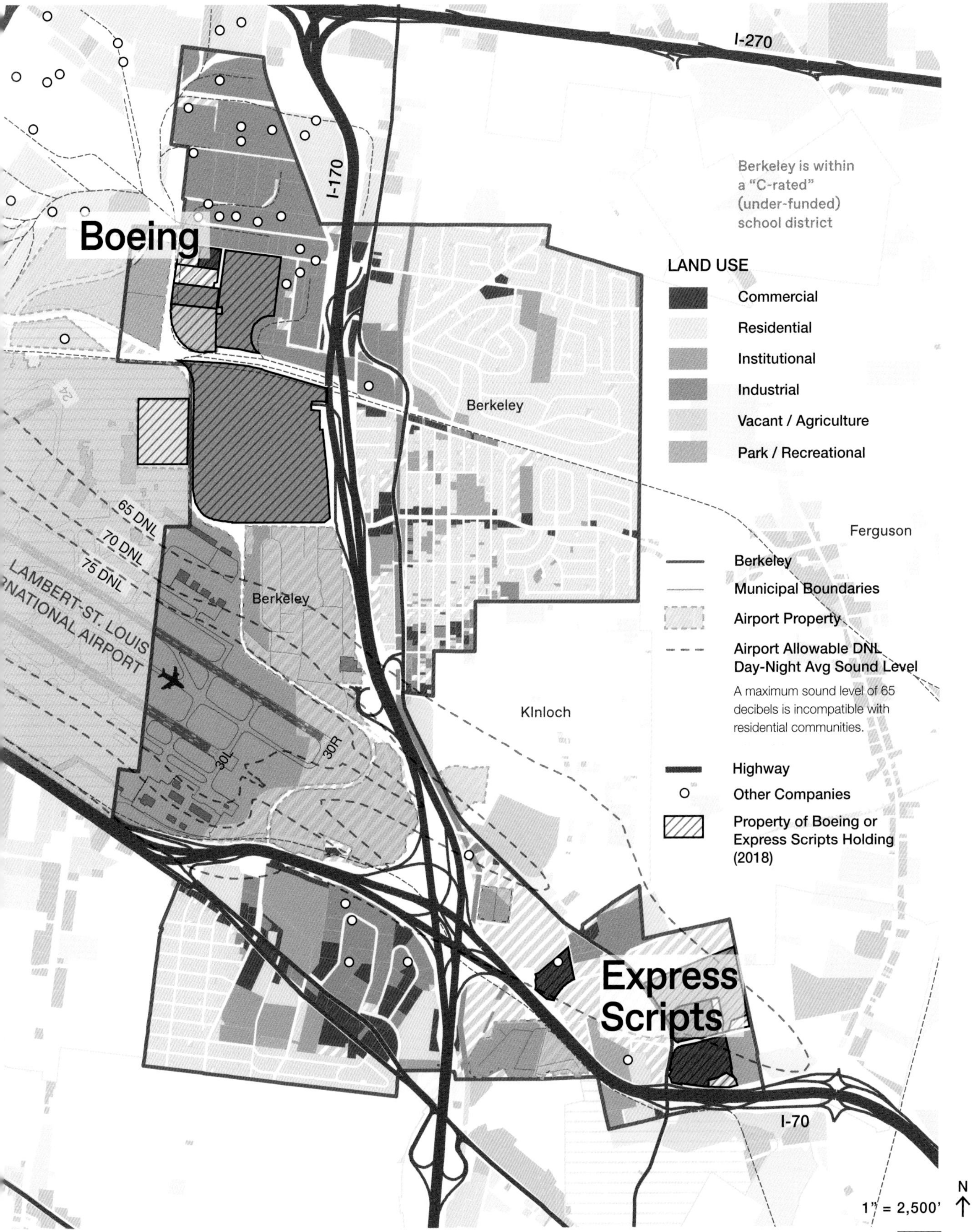

I-270

Boeing

Berkeley is within
a "C-rated"
(under-funded)
school district

LAND USE

Commercial

Residential

Institutional

Industrial

Vacant / Agriculture

Park / Recreational

Berkeley

65 DNL

70 DNL

75 DNL

LAMBERT-ST. LOUIS
INTERNATIONAL AIRPORT

Berkeley

Ferguson

Kinloch

Berkeley

Municipal Boundaries

Airport Property

Airport Allowable DNL
Day-Night Avg Sound Level

A maximum sound level of 65
decibels is incompatible with
residential communities.

Highway

Other Companies

Property of Boeing or
Express Scripts Holding
(2018)

Express
Scripts

I-70

1" = 2,500'

N

4.3.25

Map of Berkeley, MO, and highlights below showing the wide differences of value in low property tax assessments vs. appraisals. The difference between the amounts results in missed revenue for the city.

Property tax assessment

 Boeing and Express Scripts corporate campuses, Berkeley, MO

Low-assessed property value is another form of corporate subsidy that costs cities revenue that otherwise could fund services.

Properties are appraised high for resale and bank loans, and then they are separately assessed for government taxation. When cities make low tax assessments on exceptionally wealthy companies' properties (in addition to granting tax abatements and incentives) they feed the perpetual problem of government revenue shortfalls. This missing revenue could, for example, provide tax abatement for the community's lowest-income homeowners. If urban austerity refers to federal funding cuts to cities for public programs, it can also be characterized as the willful corporate welfare that strips cities of their own capacity.

Berkeley 2017 Revenue

NO. 1 - SALES TAX	$3,278,423
NO. 2 - UTILITY TAX	$2,578,498
NO. 3 - LICENSE/PERMITS/FINES	$2,324,963
NO. 4 - PROPERTY TAX	$1,872,812

Boeing

5 parcels in Berkeley + Airport:

(2017) Appraised value

$145.29 M

vs.
(2017) Assessed value

$42.96 M

<29.6% of appraised value

PROPERTY TAX

$ 5.13 M

<4% of appraised value

<12% of Assessed value

Express Scripts

4 parcels in Berkeley

(2017) Appraised value

$63.49 M

vs.
(2017) Assessed value

$5.69 M

9% of appraised values

PROPERTY TAX

$ 634,237.88

<1% of appraised value

<12% of Assessed value

↳ Express Scripts is located in the NorthPark Redevelopment area. See Map 4.C.18.

Adaptation of Lige Tan, "Berkeley: Two Cities" Patty Heyda, *The Problem of the Suburb*, Washington University in St. Louis, 2016.

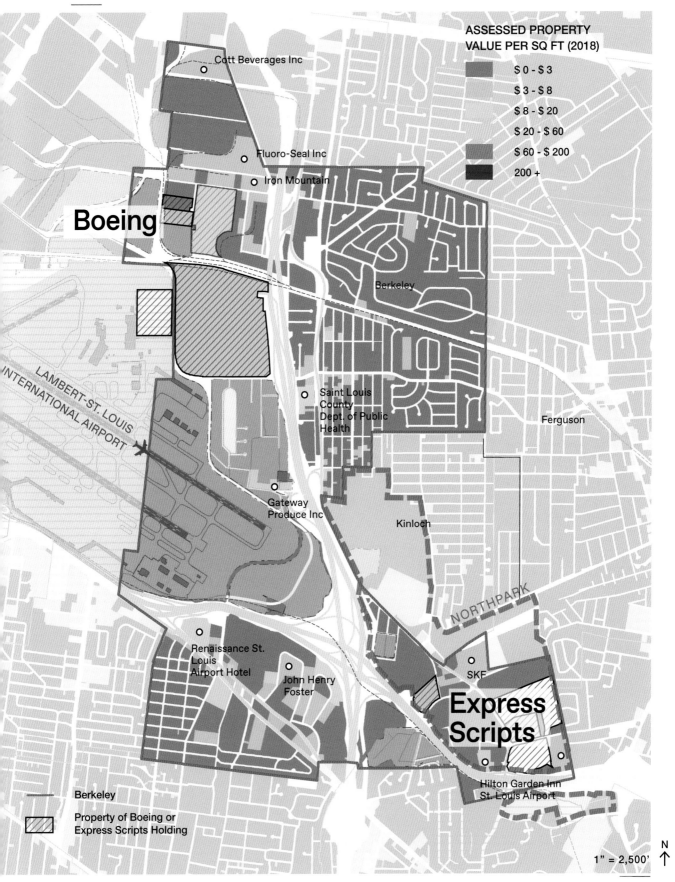

ASSESSED PROPERTY
VALUE PER SQ FT (2018)

$ 0 - $ 3
$ 3 - $ 8
$ 8 - $ 20
$ 20 - $ 60
$ 60 - $ 200
200 +

Cott Beverages Inc

Fluoro-Seal Inc

Iron Mountain

Boeing

LAMBERT-ST. LOUIS
INTERNATIONAL AIRPORT

Berkeley

Ferguson

Saint Louis
County
Dept. of Public
Health

Gateway
Produce Inc

Kinloch

NORTHPARK

Renaissance St.
Louis
Airport Hotel

John Henry
Foster

SKF

**Express
Scripts**

Hilton Garden Inn
St. Louis Airport

Berkeley

Property of Boeing or
Express Scripts Holding

1" = 2,500'

N

197

4.3.26

Map of Ferguson, MO, showing assessed property value per square foot relative to appraised values shown for the Fortune 500 company Emerson Electric's campus below.

Property tax assessment

Property tax assessments are hidden incentives for Ferguson's major corporations.

"The vast wealth of the city is locked up in property owned by major corporations, and is scarcely taxed at all." 1

Emerson
Corporate campus,
Ferguson, MO

Ferguson 2017 Revenue

NO. 1 - SALES TAX	$7,968,300
NO. 2 - UTILITY TAX	$2,732,867
NO. 3 - LICENSE/PERMITS/FINES	$824,929
NO. 4 - PROPERTY TAX	$2,234,406

Emerson

3 Parcels/152 acres in Ferguson

Total Appraised value

$19.5 M

vs.
(2017) Assessed value

$6.2 M

32% of Appraised value

**PROPERTY TAX PAID
TO FERGUSON**

$413,972

~2% of Appraised value

<7% of Assessed value

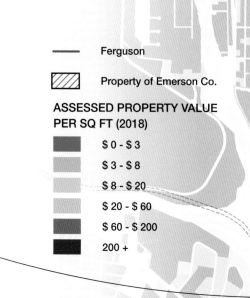

——	Ferguson
▨	Property of Emerson Co.

**ASSESSED PROPERTY VALUE
PER SQ FT (2018)**

■	$ 0 - $ 3
■	$ 3 - $ 8
■	$ 8 - $ 20
■	$ 20 - $ 60
■	$ 60 - $ 200
■	200 +

1 Walter Johnson, Ferguson's Fortune 500 Company, *The Atlantic*, 2015.

See also   3.2.12   4.3.27

Ferguson

Emerson

1" = 2,500'

N

4.3.27

Map of Ferguson, MO, showing the location of the Emerson Company campus in relation to racial demographics of the area and protests in 2014. The map calls out Emerson's assistance to the community after those pivotal events.

Philanthropy

The 2014 protests were effective in calling attention to needs in Ferguson, and the *Ferguson Commission* is one example of a robust publicly led response. But with privatization and austerity, many of the calls were otherwise answered by the private sector. Emerson Electric in Ferguson recruited philanthropic support to specific area programs. This support was worth close to fifteen times more than the amount the company paid in taxes to Ferguson and St. Louis County in 2014. In this arrangement, the company and its advisors and partners determine where and on what to focus funding. While assistance may be needed, the model is undemocratic. Why does a Fortune 500 corporation set the priorities and sites of urban reform?

Emerson Electric

"In the three years since Brown's death on Aug. 9, 2014, the company has given and pledged

$15.4 million

to 80 organizations and initiatives devoted to assisting the residents of Ferguson and the north St. Louis County region." 1

$2.3 M Various early childhood and high school programs

Such as the Head Start Program at Ferguson-Florissant School District and Challenger Learning Center St. Louis at McCluer South-Berkeley High School

$1.65 M STL Youth Jobs

which provides employment opportunities in North County Communities to at-risk youth

~ $2 M Community Organizations

such as Beyond Housing, St. Louis County Library Foundation and Urban League of Metropolitan St. Louis

1 Steph Kukuljan, "Emerson CEO on Ferguson: 'This was a wake-up call'" *St. Louis Business Journal,* August 9, 2017.

Emerson Company Campus (2018)

Ferguson

Stream Floodway / Flood Hazard Area

RACE AND ETHNICITY (2018)
(1 dot = 1 person)

- White
- Black
- Other

AUGUST, 2014 PROTEST LOCATIONS & SIZE
(no. of people)

<50

50-100

100-150

150-200

>200

See also   2.1.08   4.2.13   4.3.22   4.3.33

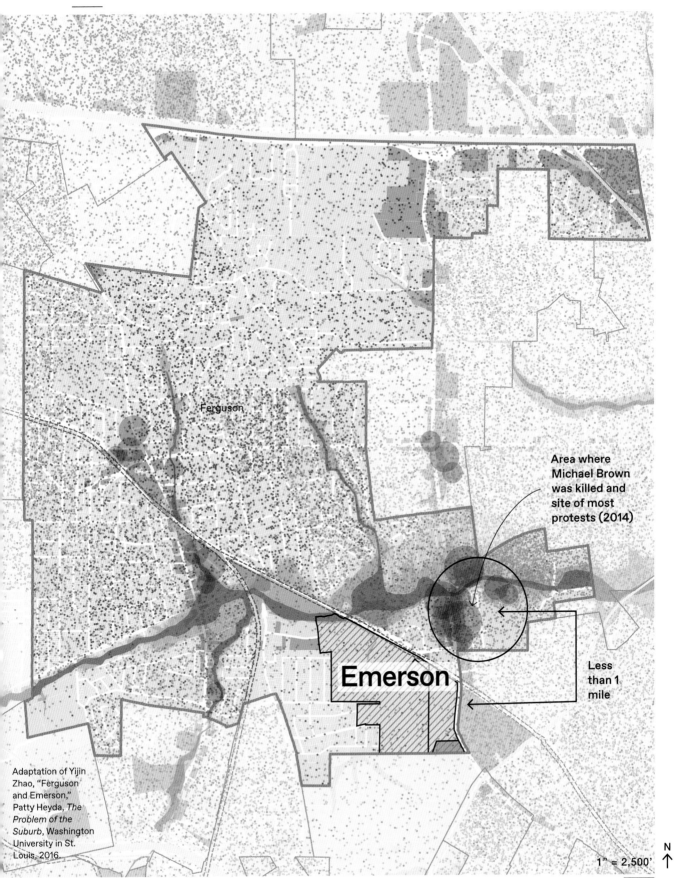

Ferguson

Area where
Michael Brown
was killed and
site of most
protests (2014)

Less
than 1
mile

Emerson

Adaptation of Yijin
Zhao, "Ferguson
and Emerson,"
Patty Heyda, *The
Problem of the
Suburb*, Washington
University in St.
Louis, 2016.

1" = 2,500'

N

4.3.28

Map of the St. Louis region indexing the territories of influence and board members (listed and grouped by the company they represent, and sector) of the nonprofit organization Better Together. The numbers on the map locate each board members' affiliated company or nonprofit in the region (2021).

↳

The red bar is a meter of private, for-profit industries (vs. nonprofit or public), by sector and interests.

* Indicates companies or organizations that are also on boards of other nonprofit organizations in this series.

Nonprofit index: Better Together (2021)

Who else steers the production of suburban space? The region's nonprofit organizations are major non-democratic entities influencing public policy.[1] This index provides a snapshot of leading St. Louis region nonprofit organizations, their agendas, and the boards that steer them. The boards are listed according to the company or organization each board member affiliates with (grouped by sector, with red bar indicating for-profit-oriented entities, 2021). The index illuminates who leads, and according to what priorities and motivations, in the public-private system.

Founded in 2013, Better Together is a nonprofit organization that researched St. Louis city and county "finances, economic development, public health and safety to form a proposal for a city/county merger." [2]

Board (by members' affiliated companies)

Fossil Fuel/ Energy / Utility
1. Patriot Coal Corporation
2. Spire*
3. Premcor Oil Refinery
4. Peabody Energy

Finance / Banking
5. Adven Capital Partners
6. Stifel
7. CIBC US

Business / Consulting
8. Pelopidas LLC*
9. Brassavola Group
10. Ernst & Young
11. The Wilkinson Group

Consulting
12. Director of Intergovernmental Affairs
13. Rainford and Associates

Real estate
14. Gundaker Commercial Group

Manufacturing
15. Flowserve Corporation
16. Emerson Electric*

Education /Institutions
17. St. Louis University*
18. Webster University*
19. Washington University in St. Louis*

Nonprofit
20. Urban League of Metropolitan St. Louis
21. United Way of Greater St. Louis
22. Civic Progress
23. St. Louis Regional Business Council*
24. St. Louis Building Trades Council

1 Nonprofit organizations also don't pay taxes.

2 Better Together, https://www.bettertogetherstl.com/

See also   4.3.21-22   4.3.26-27

Works towards reunifying a
fragmented region to create
economic development

Joe Adorjan
George Herbert Walker III
Nancy Rice

Chairman of the Board
Chairman Emeritus
Executive Director

Ferguson
16
14
10
23
5
19
1
8
7
11   20
17
21   6
12
24
9
18
4
2
22

Primary area of impact
is regional-political. The
organization studies impacts
of regional fragmentation,
the county/city divide, and
generates studies for how to
reunify the region.

4.3.29

Map of the St. Louis region indexing the territories of influence and boards of the nonprofit Forward Through Ferguson organization that followed the state-led Ferguson Commission. The numbers on the map locate each board members' affiliated company or nonprofit in the region (2021).

↳

The red bar is a meter of private, for-profit industries (vs. nonprofit or public), by sector and interests.

* Indicates companies or organizations that are also on boards of other nonprofit organizations in this series.

Nonprofit index:

A snapshot of the nonprofit Forward Through Ferguson's board, by company or organization each member affiliates with (grouped by sector, with red bar indicating for-profit entities, 2021). This index provides a view of who leads, and according to what priorities, in the public-private system.

Forward Through Ferguson (2022)

Forward Through Ferguson is a nonprofit organization formed in December 2015, in order to see through the initiatives proposed by the governor-appointed 2014 Ferguson Commission in their final report, called Forward Through Ferguson. [1]

Board (by members' affiliated companies)

Finance / Banking / Venture Capital
1. U.S. Bancorp (Community Development Corporation)
2. Cultivation Capital/ ImageMoverMD
3. Algrthm Technology Venture Capital

Consultancy
4. Independent / Nonprofit/Philanthrophic Leadership consultants

Education / Institutions
5. Washington University in St. Louis, Brown School*

Nonprofit
6. St. Louis Community Foundation
7. We Stories
8. Missouri Historical Society
9. Missouri Jobs for Justice
10. University of Missouri Extension
11. Cortex Innovation Community
12. Legal Services of Eastern Missouri
13. St. Louis Regional Health Commission

Public Sector/ Boards
14. St. Louis Regional Health Commission
15. St. Louis Schools / Ferguson Personnel Board
16. St. Louis County Prosecutor's Office

1 Forward through Ferguson, https://forwardthroughferguson.org/

Melanie Powell-Robinson   Co-Chair
Josina Greene   Co-Chair
Adelaide Lancaster   Vice Chair
Gary Parker   Treasurer
David Dwight IV   Executive Director, Lead Strategy

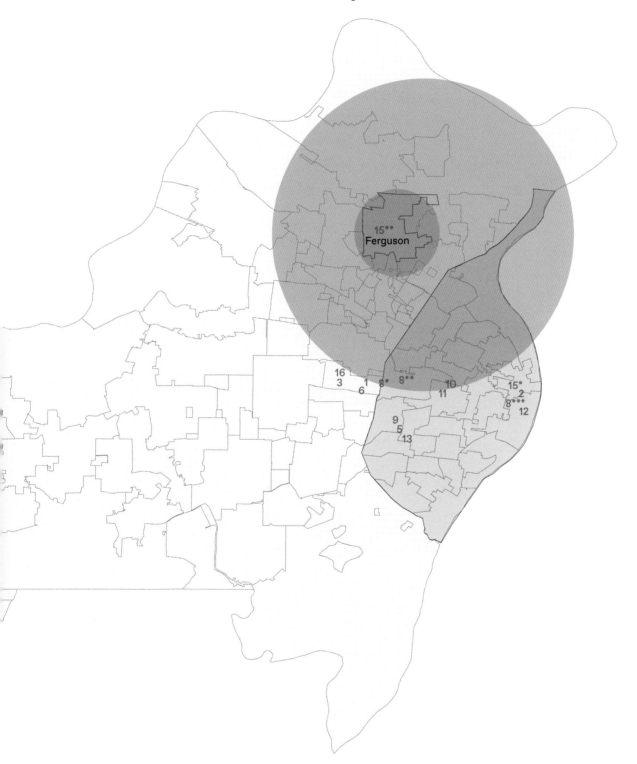

4.3.30

Map of the St. Louis region indexing the territories of influence and board of the nonprofit Greater St. Louis Inc. The numbers on the map locate each board members' affiliated company or nonprofit in the region (2021).

The red bar is a meter of private, for-profit industries (vs. nonprofit or public), by sector and interests.

* Indicates companies or organizations that are also on boards of other nonprofit organizations in this series.

Nonprofit index:

A snapshot of the nonprofit Greater St. Louis Inc.'s board, by company or organization each member affiliates with (grouped by sector, with red bar indicating for-profit entities, 2021). This index provides a view of who leads, and according to what priorities, in the public-private system.

Greater St. Louis Inc. (2021)

Founded in 2021, Greater St. Louis Inc. is a combination of five regional organizations: AllianceSTL, Arch to Park, Civic Progress, Downtown STL Inc., and the St. Louis Regional Chamber. The leaders of these groups "came together with the goal of bringing together business and civic leaders to create jobs, expanding inclusive economic growth and improving St. Louis' global competitiveness." 1

Board (by members' affiliated companies)

Finance / Banking
1. Commerce Bancshares
2. McKinsey & Company

Media
3. The St. Louis American*
4. STL Made

Law
5. Thompson Coburn LLP

Construction
6. Tarlton Corporation

Market / Services / Other
7. Enterprise Holdings*
8. Focus St. Louis*
9. Less Annoying CRM
17. St. Louis City SC

Medical / Healthcare
10. SSM Health*
11. Anthem

Education / Institutions
12. Washington University in St. Louis*
13. Harris Stowe State University
14. St. Louis Community College*
15. Claim Academy

Nonprofit
16. United Way of Greater St. Louis

1 Greater St. Louis, Inc., https://www.greaterstlinc.com

Focused on building growth
downtown, to benefit
business

Andrew C. Taylor
Valerie E. Patton
Jason R. Hall

Founding Chairman
President
CEO

Ferguson

14

10

9
8
5

2
7
12

6
13
15 16

11
17
3

Primary areas of
impact are along
the central "power"
corridor and
downtown St. Louis
City.

4.3.31

Map of the St. Louis region indexing the territories of influence and board of the think tank Show Me Institute (SMI). The numbers on the map locate each board members' affiliated company or nonprofit in the region (2021).

↳

The red bar is a meter of private, for-profit industries (vs. nonprofit or public), by sector and interests.

* Indicates companies or organizations that are also on boards of other nonprofit organizations in this series.

Nonprofit index:

A snapshot of the nonprofit Show Me Institute's board, by company or organization each member affiliates with (grouped by sector, with red bar indicating for-profit entities, 2021). This index provides a view of who leads, and according to what priorities, in the public-private system.

Show Me Institute (2021)

The SMI was founded in 2005 to focus on "promoting public policies that advance free market principles; usually in support of minimized government intervention." In 2020 the SMI annual report promoted "freedom from government" taxation but acknowledged the need for public infrastructures that help businesses run—that board member firms rely on, particularly in the fossil fuel industry.

Board (by members' affiliated companies)

Fossil Fuel/ Energy / Gas
1. Moto, Inc
2. Forsyth Carterville Coal Company

Finance / Banking
3. Dimensional Fund Advisors
4. Commerce Bank of Saint Louis*
5. UMB Bank
6. Clayton Capital Partners

Business / Consulting
7. Pelopidas LLC*
8. Atlas Strategy Group

Government / Lobbying
9. Missouri State Senate
10. American Conservative Union
11. Faith & Freedom Coalition

Law
12. Shock Law
13. Bukowsky Law Firm
14. Jennifer Bukowsky Show
15. Missouri State Public Defender
16. Shannon County Circuit Court

Real Estate
17. Janet McAfee Inc
18. Missouri Real Estate

Manufacturing / Storage
19. Forshaw
20. Springfield Underground

Education / Institutions
21. Saint Louis University*
22. University of Missouri Columbia

Medical / Arts / Faith-based
23. St. Vincent Home for Children in St. Louis
24. St. Louis Symphony - Botanical Garden - St. Louis
25. Art Museum - Contemporary Art Museum St. Louis
26. St. Luke's Hospital
27. Archdiocese of Saint Louis

Show Me Institute, https://showmeinstitute.org

Pursues access to private wealth
accumulation as "liberty"

Rex Sinquefield   President
Joseph Forshaw   Chairman and Treasurer
Megan Holekamp   Vice Chairman
W. Bevis Schock   Secretary

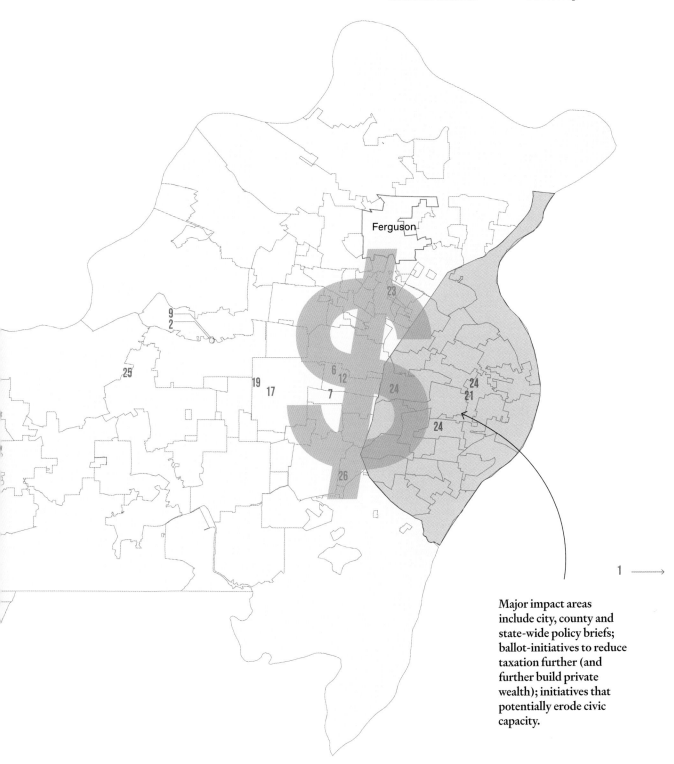

Ferguson

23

9
2

25

19   17

6
12

7

24

24
21

24

26

1 ⟶

Major impact areas
include city, county and
state-wide policy briefs;
ballot-initiatives to reduce
taxation further (and
further build private
wealth); initiatives that
potentially erode civic
capacity.

4.3.32

Map of the St. Louis region indexing the territories of influence and board of the local United Way of Greater St. Louis organization. The numbers on the map locate each board members' affiliated company or nonprofit in the region (2021).

↳

The red bar is a meter of private, for-profit industries (vs. nonprofit or public), by sector and interests.

* Indicates companies or organizations that are also on boards of other nonprofit organizations in this series.

Nonprofit index:

A snapshot of the nonprofit United Way of Greater St Louis' board, by company or organization each member affiliates with (grouped by sector, with red bar indicating for-profit entities, 2021). This index provides a view of who leads, and according to what priorities, in the public-private system.

United Way of Greater St. Louis (2021)

Founded in 1922, United Way of Greater STL is an affiliate of United Way Worldwide, and it focuses on "mobilizing volunteers, organizations, and companies to raise funds for charities within the region." [1]

Board (by members' affiliated companies)

Fossil Fuel/ Energy / Utility
1.   Ameren*
2.   Spire*

Finance / Banking
3.   Edward Jones*
4.   Schmersahl Treloar & Company
5.   The Federal Reserve Bank of St. Louis
6.   Associated Bank
7.   Commerce Bank*

Business / Consulting
8.   BEATTY
9.   HBM Holdings
10.   Maritz Inc.

Media / PR
11.   The St. Louis American*
12.   Fleishman Hillard

Market / Service / Medical
13.   Hunter Engineering Company
14.   UniGroup
15.   Bayer*
16.   Holland Construction Services
17.   Schnuck Markets*
18.   Kelly Mitchell Group, Inc.
19.   Mercy Hospital St. Louis
20.   Express scripts*

Education / Institutions
21.   Southern Illinois University Edwardsville
22.   Southwestern Illinois College
23.   University of Missouri*
24.   Washington University in St. Louis*

Nonprofit
25.   Show Me Institute
26.   Greater St. Louis Labor Council
27.   Greater St. Louis, Inc.
28.   LaunchCode
29.   Regional Business Council*
30.   SEIU Local 1 MO Benefit Trust

1 United Way, https://helpingpeople.org

See also   4.3.20-21   4.3.24   5.3.19

Supplements the (revenue-deficient) public
sector by helping people.

Supported largely by private corporate and
nonprofit beneficiaries of public austerity.

Primary impact areas
include support of 160
nonprofits located across the
region (represented by blue
dots).

211

4.3.33

Map of the St. Louis region indexing the territories of influence and board of the Urban League of Metropolitan St. Louis. The numbers on the map locate each board members' affiliated company or nonprofit in the region. (2021).

↳

The red bar is a meter of private, for-profit industries (vs nonprofit or public), by sector and interests.

* Indicates companies or organizations that are also on boards of other nonprofit organizations in this series.

Nonprofit index:

A snapshot of the nonprofit Urban League's board, by company or organization each member affiliates with (grouped by sector, with red bar indicating for-profit entities, 2021). This index provides a view of who leads, and according to what priorities, in the public-private system.

Urban League of Metropolitan St. Louis (2021)

Founded in 1918, the Urban League of Metropolitan St. Louis is an affiliate of the National Urban League, and it focuses on "empowering African Americans and others in the region by pursuing educational excellence, economic opportunity, community empowerment, and civil rights." 1

Board (by members' affiliated companies)

Fossil Fuel/ Energy/Utility
1. AT&T
2. Spire*
3. Ameren*

Finance / Banking
4. Edward Jones*
5. U.S. Bank
6. Simmons Bank
7. Wells Fargo*
8. Merrill Lynch
9. Build-A-Bear Foundation
10. Regions Bank
11. First Bank
12. CitiGroup
13. Mastercard

Media
14. The St. Louis American*
15. Fleishman Hillard

Government / Consult.
16. Ascension
17. House of Representatives

Law
18. Lashly & Baer, PC
19. Thompson Coburn LLP
20. Lewis Rice
21. Lowenhaupt & Chasnoff, LLC
22. Bryan Cave Leighton Paisner

Real Estate
23. Laura McCarthy Realtors

Construction / Industry
24. Clayco
25. Emerson*
26. Boeing

Market / Services
27. D&D Concessions, LLC
28. United Correctional Food Service

30. Schnucks*
31. Drury Hotels
32. World Wide Technology
33. Anheuser-Busch
34. Bayer*
35. Centene Corporation
36. Panera Bread
37. Enterprise Holdings*

Medicine / Healthcare
38. Barnes Jewish hospital
39. Home State Health Plan
40. Valitas Health Services, Inc.
41. SSM HEALTH*
42. Express Scripts*

Education / Institutions
43. University of Missouri-St. Louis*
44. Webster University*
45. University of Health Sciences and Pharmacy in St. Louis
46. St. Louis Community College*

Nonprofit
47. Regional Business council*
48. Greater Stl Inc.
49. Heat Up St. Louis
29. Focus St. Louis*

13

12

1 Urban League of Metropolitan St. Louis, https://www.ulstl.com

See also   4.C.19   4.3.20-21   4.3.24-27   5.3.19

Mark Levison   Chairman
Darryl T. Jones   Vice Chairman
Robert Wallace   Treasurer
Arvetta Powell   Assistant Treasurer
Emily Pitts   Secretary
Sonette Magnus   General Counsel

Ferguson

11
46
26
25
32
42
39 30
40
9, 24
47
16
34
8
37
6
23
41   35   10   1
38   49
45   3
44   33

5
18
19, 20
29
48
22
15
21
2, 4
14
7

31
36

Primary impact areas are via
programs provided by Urban
League offices and centers,
shown here (with 1-mile
radius around each, in blue).

4.M.02

Map of the St. Louis region indexing the territories of influence and board of the nonprofit Action STL. The numbers on the map locate each board members' affiliated company or nonprofit in the region. (2021).

↳

Founded in response to the 2014 Ferguson Uprisings, Action STL is "a grassroots racial justice organization that seeks to build political power for Black communities in the St. Louis region."

↳

The red bar is a meter of private, for-profit industries (vs nonprofit or public), by sector and interests.

* Indicates companies or organizations that are also on boards of other nonprofit organizations in this series.

Mobilize
Nonprofits that rebuild root systems of democracy
Action STL (2021)

A snapshot of Action STL's board, by company or organization each member affiliates with (grouped by sector, with red bar indicating for-profit entities, 2021). This index provides a view of who leads, and according to what priorities, in the public-private system. Action STL advocates for people's power.

Board (by members' affiliated companies)

Law
1. Armstrong Teasdale

Services / Other
2. Honorable Film LLC
3. Purpose in Everything LLC
4. Music Freedom Dreams LLC

Education / Institutional
5. University of South Carolina

Nonprofit
6. Freedom Community Center
7. The Bail Project
8. ArchCity Defenders
9. Children's Defense Fund

Faith-based
10. St. John's United Church of Christ
11. SBFGBC

Action STL, https://actionstl.org/

Works to build political power and access to democratic processes for marginalized communities in the region.

Rev. Michelle Higgins
Kayla Reed

Chair
Executive Director

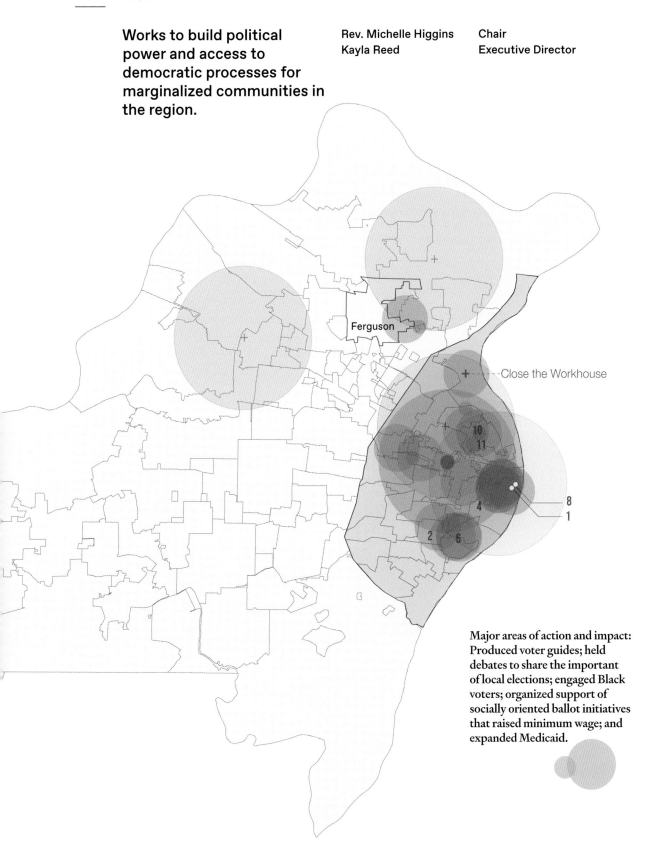

Ferguson

——— Close the Workhouse

10
11

8
1

4

2   6

Major areas of action and impact: Produced voter guides; held debates to share the important of local elections; engaged Black voters; organized support of socially oriented ballot initiatives that raised minimum wage; and expanded Medicaid.

4.M.03

Map of the St. Louis region indexing the territories of influence and board of the legal advocacy group Arch City Defenders. The numbers on the map locate each board members' affiliated company or nonprofit in the region. (2021).

↳

Founded in 2009, Arch City Defenders is a nonprofit public defender that "addresses the gap in St. Louis-area legal services by providing free and holistic legal representation to individuals who would otherwise not have access to a public defender or legal aid attorney." 1

↳

The red bar is a meter of private, for-profit industries (vs nonprofit or public), by sector and interests.

* Indicates companies or organizations that are also on boards of other nonprofit organizations in this series.

1 Arch City Defenders, https://www. archcitydefenders. org/about-us/board- of-directors/

Mobilize
Nonprofits that hold power accountable
Arch City Defenders (2021)

A snapshot of Arch City Defenders' board, by company or organization each member affiliates with (grouped by sector, with red bar indicating for-profit entities, 2021). This index provides a view of who leads, and according to what priorities, in the public-private system.

Board (by members' affiliated companies)

Finance / Banking
1. US Bancorp

Law
2. Attorney

Services / Other
3. Werner Associates, LLC
7. St. Louis Cardinals, LLC

Medical / Insurance
4. Reinsurance Group of America

Education / Institutional
5. Washington University in St. Louis*

Nonprofit
6. Action STL

Areas of impact include challenges to debtor's prison systems, municipal revenue collection from excessive fines, fees and jails. Efforts have lowered the percentage of racially targeted revenue-based policing by 70% to 100%. In Ferguson, "warrants have dropped from 33,000 issued annually to 1,500." 1

Works to hold accountable those in power, to stop the criminalization and profit off of poverty in the region.

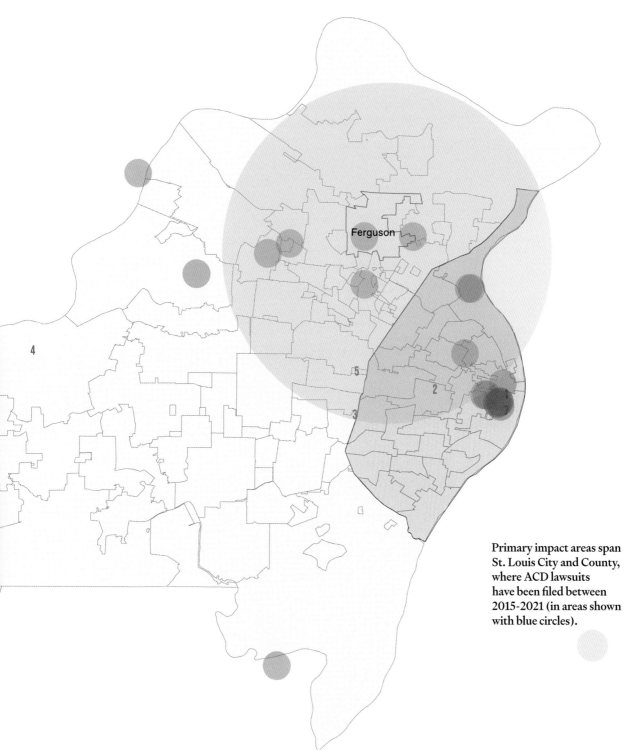

Primary impact areas span St. Louis City and County, where ACD lawsuits have been filed between 2015-2021 (in areas shown with blue circles).

05

Justice

Social and human rights

This chapter covers the erosion of rights to freedom and health under market-based policy and 'efficiency.' It starts with an overview of the predatory criminal justice system, where police and courts in North St. Louis County profit off of poverty as a mechanism for making up austere municipal revenue shortfalls.

It follows social justice with human justice to track the state of privatized health and the degrees of environmental exploitation for commercial and industrial growth. These routine protocols compromise collective access to clean air, water and soil for human's and all species' health. Ultimately, corporate externalizations by the Malinckrodt Company, who disposed of radioactive waste in North County years ago, compound citizens' access to health in the suburb, with cloudy accountability for the cleanup.

5.1.01

Map of North St. Louis County and surrounding areas, showing police jurisdictions and overlaps (2018).

Police patrols

When municipalities are small, the economies of scale for policing do not always follow municipal lines. Some areas share police resources, and others have overlapping patrols, making the system and jurisdictions opaque.

Some municipalities have independent police departments while others rely on county police. Not shown here are private police and security overlays that undermine the public sector system by creating uneven access to added 'safety' for those with means—without the same levels of public accountability.

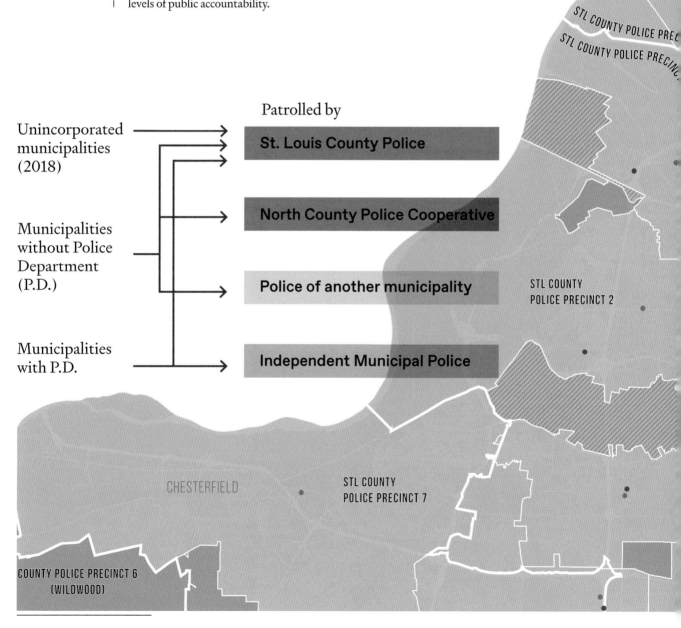

Patrolled by

Unincorporated municipalities (2018)

St. Louis County Police

Municipalities without Police Department (P.D.)

North County Police Cooperative

Police of another municipality

Municipalities with P.D.

Independent Municipal Police

STL COUNTY POLICE PREC

STL COUNTY POLICE PRECINC

STL COUNTY POLICE PRECINCT 2

CHESTERFIELD

STL COUNTY POLICE PRECINCT 7

COUNTY POLICE PRECINCT 6 (WILDWOOD)

See also   5.1.02

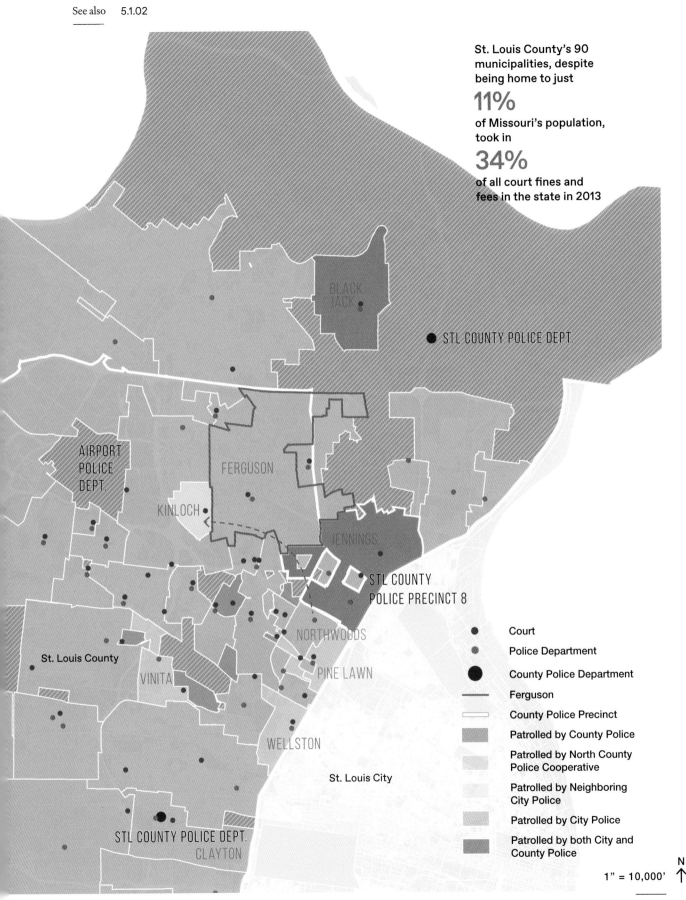

St. Louis County's 90 municipalities, despite being home to just

11%

of Missouri's population, took in

34%

of all court fines and fees in the state in 2013

STL COUNTY POLICE DEPT.

BLACK JACK

AIRPORT POLICE DEPT.

FERGUSON

KINLOCH

JENNINGS

STL COUNTY POLICE PRECINCT 8

NORTHWOODS

St. Louis County

PINE LAWN

VINITA

WELLSTON

St. Louis City

STL COUNTY POLICE DEPT.
CLAYTON

● Court
● Police Department
● County Police Department
—— Ferguson
☐ County Police Precinct
▨ Patrolled by County Police
▨ Patrolled by North County Police Cooperative
▨ Patrolled by Neighboring City Police
▨ Patrolled by City Police
▨ Patrolled by both City and County Police

1" = 10,000'

N
↑

5.1.02

Map of the St. Louis County region showing the even distribution of population against an uneven number of municipalities and courts in North St. Louis.

Municipal courts

The population is fairly evenly distributed in St. Louis's northern and southern first-ring suburbs. The distribution of municipalities and courts, however, is not.

Self-rule with many separate municipalities becomes over-rule in North County, where, as a result, there are more courts per person than anywhere else in the county. This hyper-fragmentation of tiny cities, police and courts enables the exponential system of tickets and fines, bail and warrants between municipalities known as the debtors' prison.

↳

A comparison of the number of municipalities in Jackson County, MO, that includes Kansas City, with St. Louis County, MO, that does not include St. Louis City.

Jackson County

St. Louis County

88 municipalities in St. Louis County, not including St. Louis City

19 municipalities in Jackson County, including Kansas City

Missouri

Casey Ryan, "Fragmentation Road," Patty Heyda, *The Problem of the Suburb*, Washington University in St. Louis, 2016.

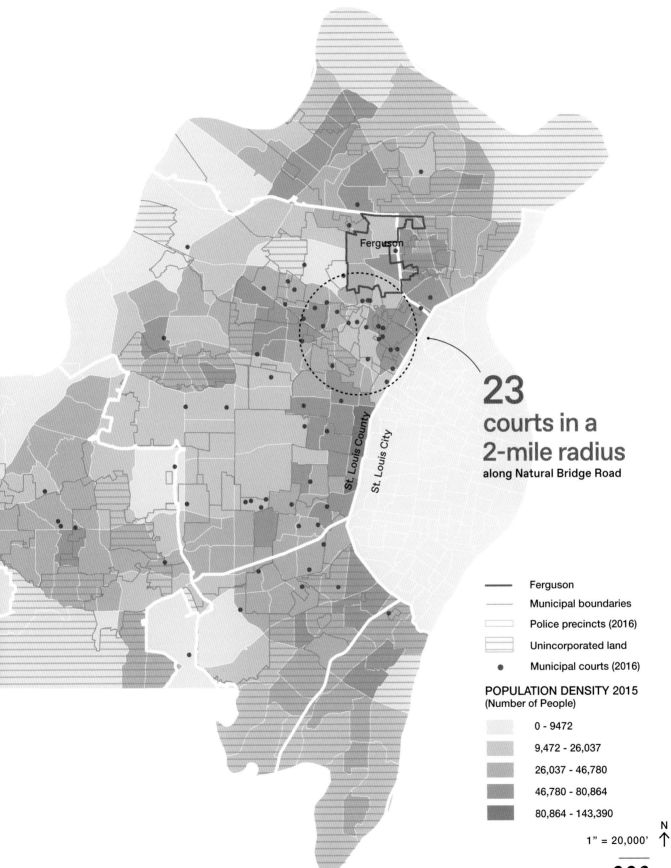

23
courts in a
2-mile radius
along Natural Bridge Road

Ferguson

St. Louis County

St. Louis City

——— Ferguson

——— Municipal boundaries

▨ Police precincts (2016)

▨ Unincorporated land

● Municipal courts (2016)

POPULATION DENSITY 2015
(Number of People)

0 - 9472

9,472 - 26,037

26,037 - 46,780

46,780 - 80,864

80,864 - 143,390

1" = 20,000'

N

223

5.1.03 | Municipal borders

Close-up map of a five-mile section of Natural Bridge Road in North St. Louis County, highlighting the number of municipalities the road traverses in that short distance, each with a separate court and police station, called out.

In five miles: eleven jurisdictions. The physical-legal geography of redundancy is made up of borders, police stations and courts. An extreme view of this is along Natural Bridge Road, where successive jurisdictions set up conditions for the racialized revenue traps called the 'debtors' prison' and 'muni shuffle.'

Minor traffic violations absurdly put people in jail when they cannot pay the fines or the bail. If someone has outstanding warrants in more than one municipality, they are not freed when they produce the bail but are instead sent to the next municipal jail.

'We haven't changed from wanting to punish poor people for being poor ... if you are charged in a municipal court you are by definition not a threat to the community, so why would this ever end in jail? We're talking about traffic tickets. These aren't crimes.' 1

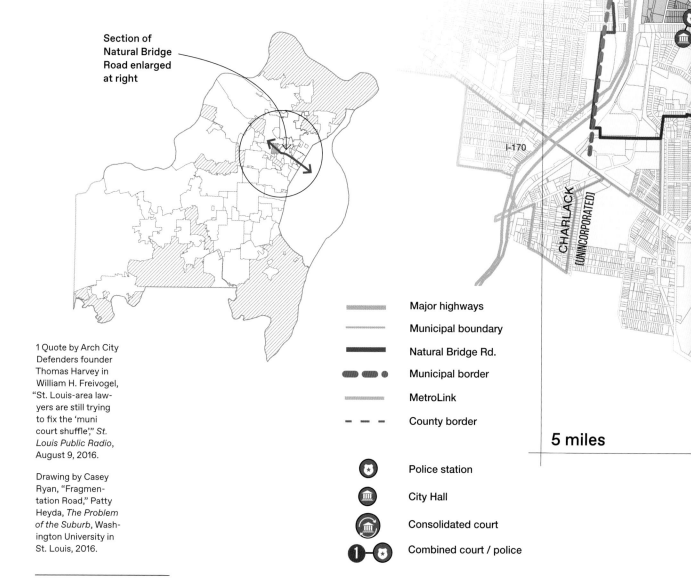

Section of Natural Bridge Road enlarged at right

1 Quote by Arch City Defenders founder Thomas Harvey in William H. Freivogel, "St. Louis-area lawyers are still trying to fix the 'muni court shuffle'," *St. Louis Public Radio*, August 9, 2016.

Drawing by Casey Ryan, "Fragmentation Road," Patty Heyda, *The Problem of the Suburb*, Washington University in St. Louis, 2016.

	Major highways
	Municipal boundary
	Natural Bridge Rd.
	Municipal border
	MetroLink
	County border
Police station	
City Hall	
Consolidated court	
Combined court / police	

5 miles

See also   4.1.02   5.1.02   5.1.05

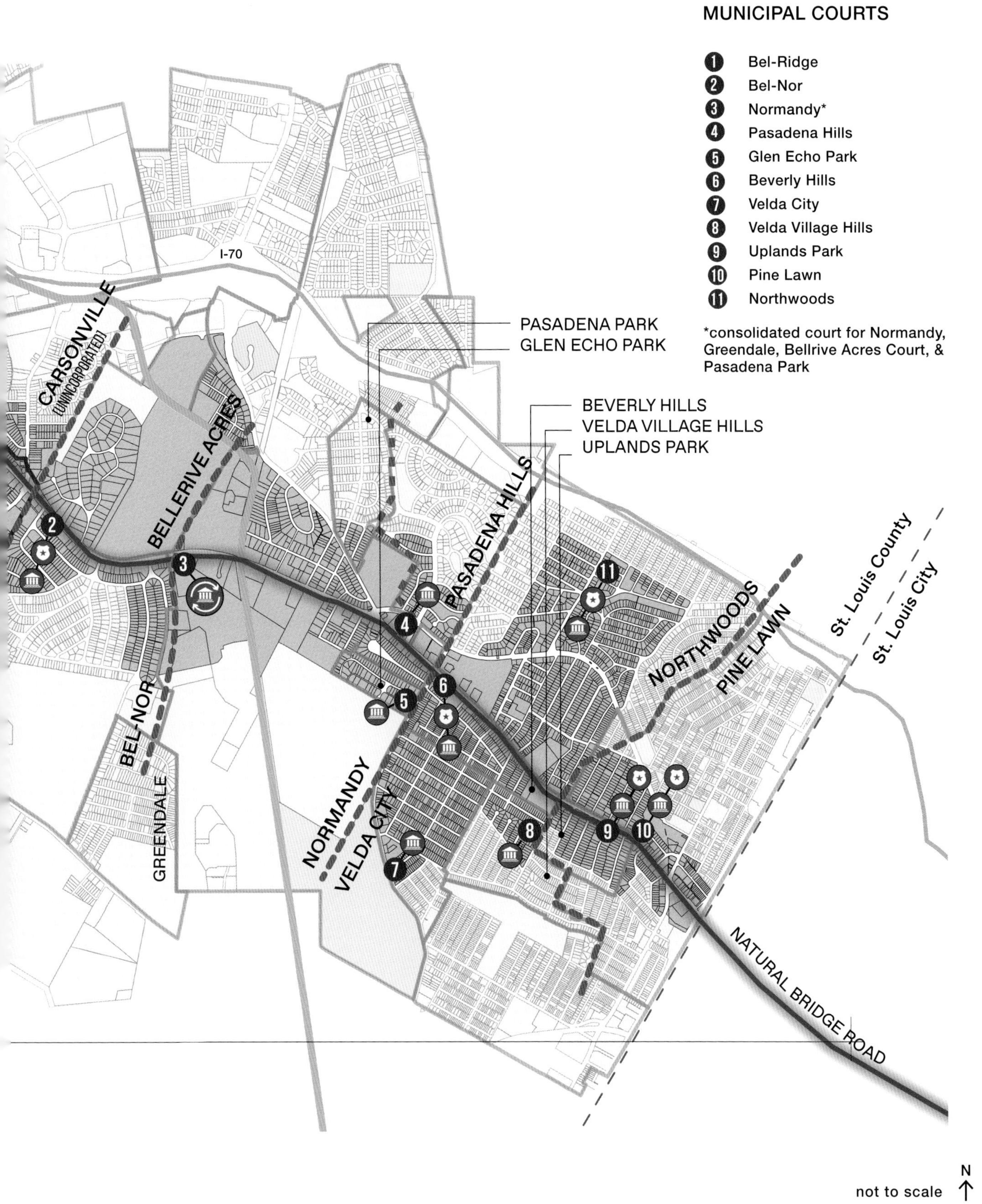

MUNICIPAL COURTS

1 Bel-Ridge
2 Bel-Nor
3 Normandy*
4 Pasadena Hills
5 Glen Echo Park
6 Beverly Hills
7 Velda City
8 Velda Village Hills
9 Uplands Park
10 Pine Lawn
11 Northwoods

*consolidated court for Normandy, Greendale, Bellrive Acres Court, & Pasadena Park

PASADENA PARK
GLEN ECHO PARK

BEVERLY HILLS
VELDA VILLAGE HILLS
UPLANDS PARK

I-70

CARSONVILLE
(UNINCORPORATED)

BELLERIVE ACRES

BEL-NOR

GREENDALE

NORMANDY

VELDA CITY

PASADENA HILLS

NORTHWOODS

PINE LAWN

St. Louis County
St. Louis City

NATURAL BRIDGE ROAD

not to scale

N
↑

5.1.04

Close-up
map (below)
of the many
municipalities
that Natural
Bridge Road
(in dark blue)
crosses in North
County, St. Louis.

At right, a chart
showing the
lawyers and
judges who
served in the
courts along
Natural Bridge
Road (2018).
The chart shows
how many
of these tiny
municipalities
relied on the
same people
to fill different
court roles
between nearby
jurisdictions.

Lawyer doubling

In North County, where there are so many tiny municipalities, lawyers and judges serve different roles across city lines. Legal representation by the same lawyers creates redundancy and conflicts of interest that compromise people's access to a fair hearing when they are shuffled between courts and municipalities.

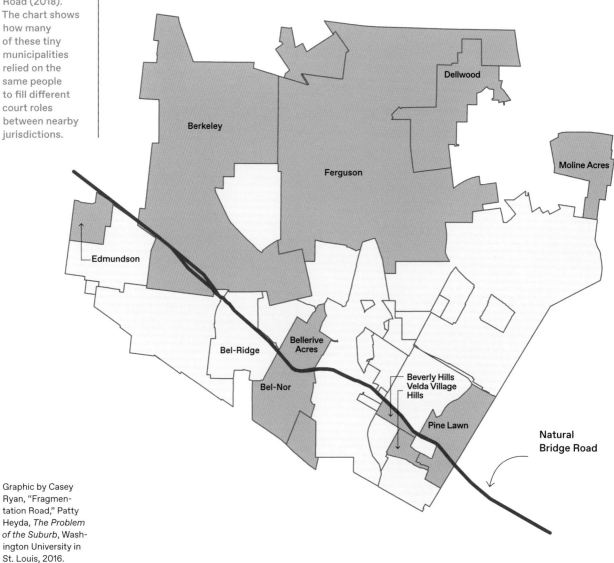

Graphic by Casey
Ryan, "Fragmentation Road," Patty
Heyda, *The Problem
of the Suburb*, Washington University in
St. Louis, 2016.

See also   5.1.02

Lawyer service overlaps along Natural Bridge Road (2018)

Private Practice	Total Municipalities Served #	OFFICIAL	ROLE		
			JUDGE	PROSECTUOR	CITY ATTORNEY
PRIVATE PRACTICE: MORRIS FIRM	2	RAPHAEL MORRIS	NORTHWOODS		
			PAGEDALE		
PRIVATE PRACTICE: CURTIS, HEINZ, GARRETT, & O'KEEFE (CHGO)	7	STEPHANIE KARR		FERGUSON	FERGUSON
				BEL-NOR	EDMUNDSON
				HAZELWOOD	CALVERTON PARK
					BELLERIVE ACRES
PRIVATE PRACTICE: CURTIS, HEINZ, GARRETT, & O'KEEFE (CHGO)	6	KEVIN O'KEEFE			BEL-NOR
					CLAYTON
					COOL VALLEY
					DES PERES
					FRONTENAC
					HAZELWOOD
PRIVATE PRACTICE: GENERAL	2	CHARLES KIRKSEY	NORMANDY		
			WELLSTON		
			BELLERIVE ACRES		
PRIVATE PRACTICE: CURTIS, HEINZ, GARRETT, & O'KEEFE (CHGO)	5	KEITH CHEUNG	LADUE	NORMANDY	
				FRONTENAC	
				ST. ANN	
				CRYSTAL LAKE PARK	
PRIVATE PRACTICE: SMITH & ASSOCIATES	7	DONNELL SMITH	DELLWOOD	BERKELEY	BERKELEY
			GREENDALE	MOLINE ACRES	BEVERLY HILLS
					MOLINE ACRES
					PINE LAWN
					VELDA VILLAGE HILLS
PRIVATE PRACTICE: DUNLOP & MCCARTER	2	BRIAN DUNLOP	GLEN ECHO PARK		
			BEVERLY HILLS		
PRIVATE PRACTICE: CLARK, CONNON, PISARKIEWICZ, TOLIN & WINES	4	STEVEN CLARK	HANLEY HILLS	VELDA VILLAGE HILLS	
			VALLEY PARK	COUNTRY CLUB HILLS	
PRIVATE PRACTICE: GENERAL	4	PHILIP AYERS	CALVERTON PARK	GREENDALE	GREENDALE
			UPLANDS PARK		

Municipality

1 Thomas Harvey and Brendan Roediger, "St. Louis County Municipal Courts, For-Profit Policing, and the Road to Reforms," in Kim Norwood, ed. *Ferguson's Fault Lines*, (ABA, 2016).

#UnWarranted

Photo by Mariah Stewart, 2014, Huffington Post, PARS International
A woman in Pine Lawn, MO, near Ferguson in 2014 calls out the unfair number of outstanding arrest warrants per capita there.

For reference, in 2016 ArchCity Defenders reported that the entire St. Louis County (population less than 1 million people) had 450,000 outstanding arrest warrants among residents, compared to Cook County, IL (an area with over 5 million people that includes the city of Chicago), where only 40,000 arrest warrants were outstanding. 1

St. Louis County, MO, pop < 1 million
Not including the City of St. Louis

450,000

outstanding arrest warrants (2016)

Cook County, IL, pop > 5 million
Including the City of Chicago

40,000

outstanding arrest warrants

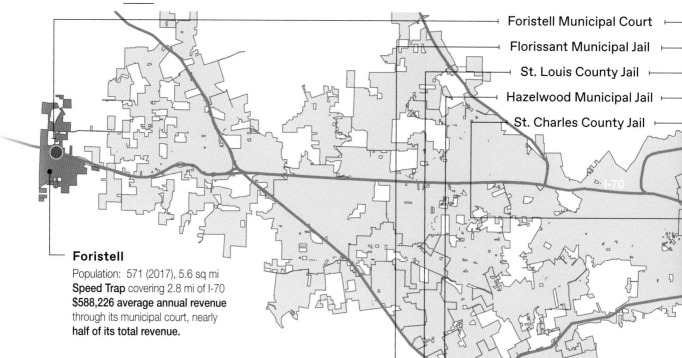

Foristell Municipal Court

Florissant Municipal Jail

St. Louis County Jail

Hazelwood Municipal Jail

St. Charles County Jail

I-70

St. Charles County

MISSOURI RIV

Foristell

Population: 571 (2017), 5.6 sq mi
Speed Trap covering 2.8 mi of I-70
$588,226 average annual revenue
through its municipal court, nearly
half of its total revenue.

5.1.05

Map detail
and timeline
highlighting
St. Louis area
resident Nicole
Bolden's personal
experiences and
costs from being
subjected to the
muni shuffle,
the coordinated
system that
extracts fines and
fees from people
because of their
poverty (2014).

↳

Based on the story
by Radley Balko,
"How municipalities in
St. Louis County, Mo.,
profit from poverty,"
The Washington Post,
September 3, 2014.

Author conversation
with Nicole Bolden,
April 2023.

Graphic by Casey Ryan,
"Fragmentation Road,"
Patty Heyda, *The
Problem of the Suburb*,
Washington University
in St. Louis, 2016.

The muni shuffle

Nicole Bolden's experience with law
enforcement after a traffic incident
that was not her fault imprisoned her
in multiple municipalities across many
miles and impacted her life across
many days, with consequences that
lasted many years—in addition to the
fees and fines.

↳

The "muni shuffle"
has also referred
to the system that
allows 'disgraced'
police officers
expelled from a
municipal police
force to freely
move and still work
in a neighboring
municipality.

Day 1   March 20, 2014

Someone makes an illegal U-turn in
front of Nicole Bolden, who is
driving with two of her children. She
cannot avoid a collison. Police are
called to the scene.

Bolden is arrested, not for the
accident but for **4 outstanding
warrents for prior traffic violations,**
which she was unable to pay.

+ 22 hours

After being held in horrible conditions,
**Bolden is released from Florissant
Jail** when her mother pays her bond.

– $400

Day 2

Bolden is transferred to Hazelwood,
where she is **required to pay another
bond.** She is forced to use her child
support money in order to pay.

– $120

+ 20 hours

Dellwood police hold Bolden at **St.
Louis County Jail** in Clayton until her
cousin pays her bond.

– $150

See also   4.1.01   4.M.03   5.1.03

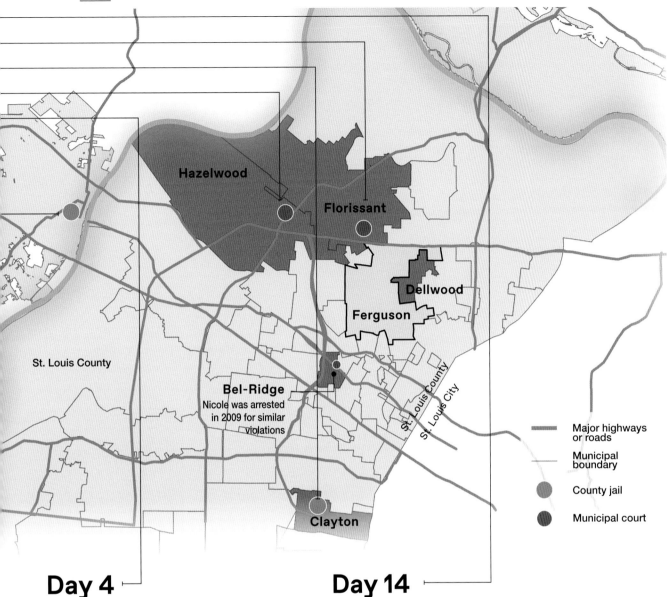

Major highways or roads

Municipal boundary

County jail

Municipal court

St. Louis County

Hazelwood

Florissant

Dellwood

Ferguson

Bel-Ridge
Nicole was arrested in 2009 for similar violations

St. Louis County

St. Louis City

Clayton

Day 4

At 4am, Foristell police pick up Bolden and she is transferred to St. Charles County Jail because Foristell is too small for its own holding cell.

Her bond is set at $1,700. She cannot pay and is forced to remain in jail for another 2 weeks until Foristell's next court hearing.

Bolden did not recieve medical attention following the crash. St. Charles Police charge $1/pill for Tylenol, so she can't afford to manage her pain.

Meanwhile, with no one to drive them, her children miss a week of school and are traumatized by her absence. Her financial situation is worse than it was before, as she will now spend months paying her family members back.

Day 14

At her hearing, with the help of Arch City Defenders, the bond is reduced to $700, which she still cannot afford. Bolden had scheduled a job interview for the day that she was arrested. Her detention deprived her of any opportunity to work and earn income. She is granted an indigency hearing but not for another 2 weeks.

Day 15

Bolden's disabled mother borrows against her life insurance so that Nicole can pay her bond.

−$700

Nicole is released from Jail

not to scale

N
↑

5.1.06

Map of North St. Louis County showing the number of vehicle stops by police in 2014, with three municipalities highlighted where the number of stops was drastically reduced in 2015.

Traffic stops

A reduction in the number of vehicle stops by police since 2014 is not the full picture.

The system of excessive and predatory traffic stops to issue tickets and fines to generate lost revenue for North County cities was called out in 2014. Details of the three municipalities below show that as overall traffic stops were reduced from 2014 to 2015, the underlying practices of disproportionately stopping Black drivers over white drivers has not improved but worsened.

 Ratio of Black drivers stopped in 2014

Increase in racial disparity from 2014-2015

Berkeley

Vehicle stops in 2014

Black	74%
White	18%

Vehicle stops in 2015

Black	80%
White	17%

Ferguson

Vehicle stops in 2014

Black	90%
White	9.5%

Vehicle stops in 2015

Black	92%
White	7.5%

Bellefontaine Neighbors

Vehicle stops in 2014

Black	84%
White	14.5%

Vehicle stops in 2015

Black	91%
White	7.5%

Adaptation of Boya Wang, "Mapping tickets and fines," Patty Heyda, *Radical Mapping*, Washington University in St. Louis, 2021.

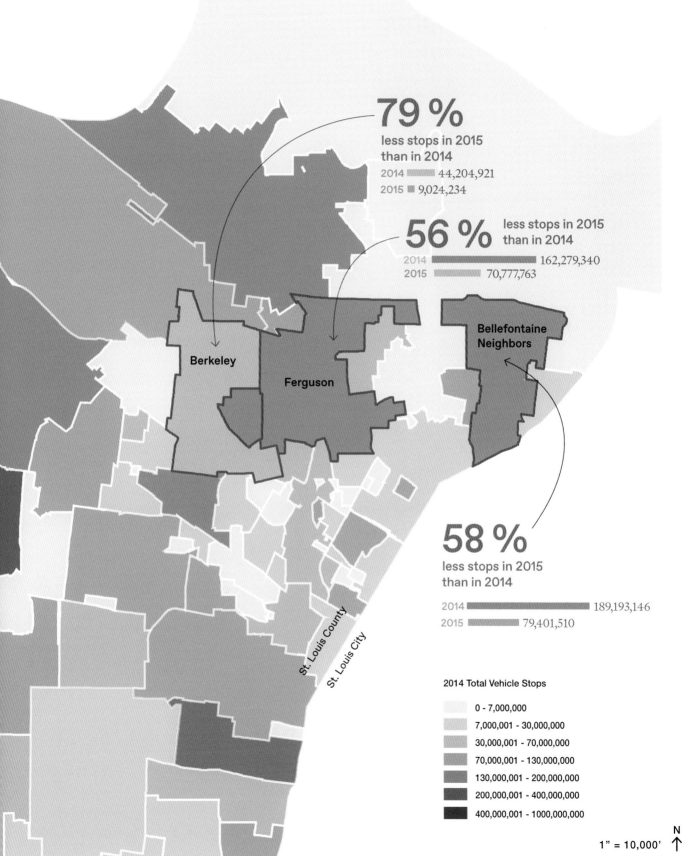

79 %

less stops in 2015
than in 2014

2014 ▬▬▬▬▬ 44,204,921
2015 ▬ 9,024,234

56 % less stops in 2015
than in 2014

2014 ▬▬▬▬▬▬▬▬▬ 162,279,340
2015 ▬▬▬▬ 70,777,763

Berkeley

Ferguson

Bellefontaine
Neighbors

58 %

less stops in 2015
than in 2014

2014 ▬▬▬▬▬▬▬▬▬▬ 189,193,146
2015 ▬▬▬▬ 79,401,510

St. Louis County

St. Louis City

2014 Total Vehicle Stops

0 - 7,000,000

7,000,001 - 30,000,000

30,000,001 - 70,000,000

70,000,001 - 130,000,000

130,000,001 - 200,000,000

200,000,001 - 400,000,000

400,000,001 - 1000,000,000

1" = 10,000'

N
↑

5.1.07

A chart illustrating the expected pretrial hearing process and rights of someone who has been arrested, with breaches in the protocol (in red) as experienced by St. Louis County resident Jocelyn Garner (2018).

Pretrial rights

There are anticipated steps in the criminal justice system before and after an arrest and leading up to an initial hearing (pretrial). Jocelyn Garner's experience in 2018 reveals breaches in the austere system meant to protect her rights.

01 ARREST

The beginning of the criminal justice process

Can occur 3 ways:
1) ~~Police observe a crime~~
2) ~~Police have probable cause~~
3) ~~Warrant issued~~

01 Incorrect police report filed; Arrested with no cause

02 BOOKING

Administrative tasks and information recorded on the defendant

- Contact information
- Nature of the crime
- Mug shot
- Personal property confiscated
- Fingerprinting
- Full-body search
- Check for warrants
- Health check
- Incarceration/Awaiting trial

For arrests without a warrant the defendant can only be held for 48 hours before the INITIAL APPEARANCE

02 During booking: Holding in inhumane conditions

03 INITIAL APPEARANCE

Either same day or day after arrest, at the initial hearing:

- Charge is read to defendant
- Penalties explained
- Defendant advised of right to preliminary hearing
- Right to counsel is explained
- Judge appoints lawyer if requested

In deciding to set bail, the judge considers:
- Risk of fleeing
- Type of crime
- Danger level of defendant
- Safety of community

The judge must hold a hearing to find out about life of defendant including:
- Length of residence in the community
- Family ties
- Prior criminal record
- Relevant threats
- Physical and mental condition
- History of drug and alcohol abuse
- Appearance at previous court proceedings
- FINANCIAL RESOURCES

03 Lawyers sometimes do not confer with defendants in hearings

A judge should release defendants from jail with only a promise to attend their next court date, unless the judge thinks that they are a risk to public safety or that they won't come back to court

ABILITY TO PAY

When a St. Louis Municipal court judge issues a fine for traffic violations or other minor offenses, they must take into account the defendant's ability to pay

The Court cannot put someone in jail for failing to pay a fee they cannot afford.

If these items are available and accessible, defendants should bring them to the pre-trial hearing:
- Documents showing financial situation
- Pay stubs
- Public benefit documents
- Bills
- A filled out "Affidavit of Indigency"

If someone is unable to pay the bond set for them, they are entitled to a hearing before a judge to have the bond reduced. In order to have one of these hearings, a written application must be filed to the Pre-trial Release Commissioner. The hearing will be conducted within 24 hours of the application's filing, or at the next regular court session.

Graphic by Carmen Chee, Avni Joshi, *Invisible St. Louis: People, Place and Power*, David Cunningham, Caity Collins, Patty Heyda, Washington University in St. Louis, 2020.

Based on interviews with Jocelyn Garner, 2019.

04 HEARING RESULTS

RELEASED ON OWN RECOGNIZANCE

It is believed the defendant does not pose a flight risk and will appear for their next court date. They are released after affirming in writing to appear in court.

PRETRIAL RELEASE

The defendant is free to go until their hearing. In the cash-bail system, freedom is predicated on the ability to pay and disciminates against low-income defendants.

06 Jocelyn is not really 'released' since she must wear an EMASS ankle bracelet & pay its mandatory monthly fees. Her freedoms of movement and social life are restricted.

BAIL SET

A bail amount is set if the judge believes the defendant poses a risk of not appearing in court.

This cash amount to be paid to the court will be returned to the defendant on appearing at their trial.

04 Bail set at $100,000, well above what Jocelyn could pay

A judge MUST INQUIRE about one's ability to pay - but this does not happen in many St. Louis cases

PAY BAIL/BOND

The defendant can pay the full amount of bail or secure their release through a bondsmen.

EMASS

In addition to bail, the defendant is sentenced to pretrial GPS monitoring by the private company Eastern Missouri Alternative Sentencing Services (EMASS). The cost of these services is paid by the defendant and not returned.

FULFILL PAYMENTS

CAN'T AFFORD PAYMENTS

BAIL PROJECT ASSISTANCE

Bail amounts are regularly altered to qualify for Bail Project support- to profit off of the nonprofit.

CAN'T AFFORD BOND

If the defendant cannot afford to pay the bond, they can apply to the Bail Project, a nonprofit that provides free bail assitance to low-income defendants for bail amounts below $5,000.

PRE-TRIAL INCARCERATION

The defendant, "presumed innocent," is detained pretrial before being proven innocent or guilty. Detainment is often in inhumane conditions, at St. Louis City's medium security institution, known as the Workhouse.

DENIED BAIL

It is deemed that there is a risk the defendant will not appear in court or is a danger to the community and is detained while awaiting trial.

05 She appeals the bail amount but must wait months at the Workhouse for a hearing

5.1.08

A timeline and map of St. Louis County and City depicting resident Jocelyn Garner's ordeal in the criminal justice system. Not only does the state extract exorbitant bail amounts (despite, or because of, the aid of nonprofit activist groups like the Bail Project), but there are for-profit services involved, with even less oversight and accountability.

↳

The national nonprofit Bail Project has helped thousands of nonviolent detainees pay the disproportionately high bail amounts set by courts for their pretrial release. It becomes complicated—extractive—when some courts intentionally set the bail extra high because they know the Bail Project will cover portions of it, effectively exploiting the nonprofit aid system too.

Graphic adapted from interview transcripts with Jocelyn Garner and Haley Eagle, Ellie Zimmerman and Ethan Chiang, *Invisible St. Louis: People, Place and Power*, David Cunningham, Caity Collins, Patty Heyda, Washington University in St. Louis, 2019.

Public safety

Jocelyn Garner was the victim of an attempted robbery. This is the story of her further victimization by the criminal justice system even as she sought help.

After she calls police for help, they arrest her and put her in the Workhouse medium security institution, a jail noted for its extremely inhumane conditions. She spends months waiting for a bail reduction hearing. Being away so long causes her to lose her job and home. After the bail hearing she is set "free" until trial, but required to make payments to Eastern Missouri Alternative Sentencing Services (EMASS), a private monitoring company with little public oversight. This takes hours and money she doesn't have, to travel by bus one to three times a month to report in-person. She spends three years of her life waiting for continually postponed court dates. When the trial finally goes to court, the case is dismissed.

1 Jocelyn is the victim of a crime

March 26, 2018

Jocelyn is attacked by strangers attempting to rob her. She, along with several witnesses, call 911 thirteen times over the course of two hours.

She is informed by the dispatcher, who eventually hangs up on her, that the police are very busy, despite being in a neighborhood frequently patrolled by police. Terrified, Jocelyn uses self-defense to protect herself and her belongings.

2 Police "investigation"

Two hours later, police arrive at the scene. They treat the robbers as victims, ignoring protests from several witnesses and Jocelyn's attempts to explain.

The police officer who wrote the police report fabricated details, including that Jocelyn fled the scene of the crime, despite evidence proving otherwise. This officer later goes on trial herself for covering up an act of police brutality against an undercover Black officer.

3 Jocelyn is arrested

Jocelyn is arrested and brought to a police department in North County, less than a five-minute drive from the incident. She is later transferred to St. Louis City Justice Center and booked.

Jocelyn is shoved into a cold cell with no shower, blanket or food.

4 Arraignment

Jocelyn is charged with two counts of aggravated assault, both of which are ruled as a Class A Felony. At her arraignment the next morning, she pleads not guilty to both charges.

Based on the fabricated police report, the Judge sets her bail at $100,000. She cannot afford her bail, much less an attorney, so she files for a public defender.

5 A month in jail

Jocelyn is incarcerated pretrial at St. Louis's infamous medium security institution, known as the Workhouse.

She watches as guards instigate violence between inmates (89% of whom are Black), mentally ill women are terrorized, and her cellmate's asthma attacks go untreated. Her first week there, she loses nearly 10 lbs. Guards threaten to place her on suicide watch if she continues to refuse her meals, which are contaminated with mold and rat feces.

6 Appeals bail

After a month at the Workhouse, Jocelyn is finally assigned a public defender. By the time they meet, Jocelyn barely feels human.

While Jocelyn remains locked up, her public defender repeatedly files for bail reduction, citing evidence of the 911 dispatcher's negligence and the arresting officer's lack of credibility. Meanwhile, Jocelyn meets with 'Bail Disrupters' from the Bail Project, who can cover up to $5,000 of her bail.

See also   4.M.02-03   5.1.02   5.1.07

For more
information see:
ClosetheWorkhouse.org

Arch City Defenders
helped Jocelyn get back on
her feet after her release
from the Workhouse, and
as the case proceeded.
See: https://www.archci-
tydefenders.org/

Courts (2016)

Greater North St. Louis County

Jocelyn is
the victim
of a robbery
in North
County

Ferguson

The
Workhouse
Prison

St. Louis County

St. Louis City

St. Louis City
Justice Center

(private)
Eastern
Missouri
Alternative
Sentencing
Services
(EMASS)

Bail is set at absurd amount of

$100,000

7 Court bail hearing

Six months after she was robbed, Jocelyn
attends court for yet another bail reduction
hearing. Her attorney's motion is finally approved, and her bail is reduced to $10,000.

Bail is reduced to

$10,000

8 Awaits trial "presumed innocent" but confined to for-profit "e-carceration"

September 13, 2018

Upon her release, Jocelyn is court-ordered
to sign up within 24-hours with EMASS, a
for-profit monitoring service. She pleads
her case to a "counselor," who explains
that she won't need an ankle monitor but
will still have to abide by EMASS's strict
stipulations and pay $30/month for bond
supervision check-ins.

9 Then after **3 years** of waiting for trial dates that were set and reset,

the case is dismissed.

She calls 9-1-1

13 times in 2 hours

before police arrive.

She spends

1 month

in the Workhouse jail
before she is assigned a
public defender

She spends overall

6 months

in the jail and horrible
conditions waiting for a
bail reduction hearing at
the City Justice Center

Although presumed
innocent, Jocelyn is
released, yet confined
via a private

for-profit

electronic-carceration
company
that collects fees each
month and requires long
commutes to report
in-person.

1" = 20,000'   N ↑

5.2.09

Map of St. Louis County and region showing the relative age of life expectancy by zip code (county only, 2015) with areas where more than 20% of the population lacks access to health insurance.

Health insurance

Human health and life expectancy depend on access to insurance and primary care—both systems that are heavily privatized and thus largely inaccessible to those with low incomes, part-time jobs or lower access to "quality jobs" that pay "80% or more of the national median salary" ($40,000 in 2021), since those typically include health insurance benefits or earnings are enough for employees to purchase separate insurance. 1

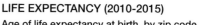

Chart:
St. Louis County
Department of
Public Health (2020)

1 St. Louis
Community College
Workforce Solutions
Group. 2021 State
of the St. Louis
Workforce.

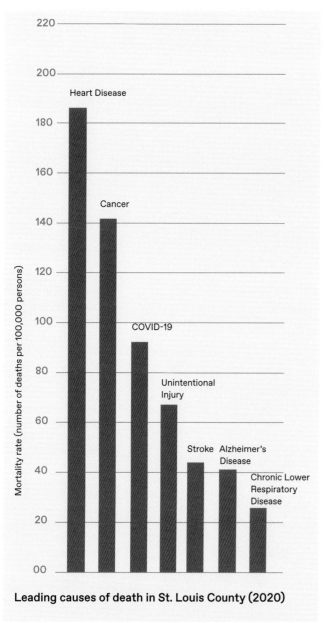

Mortality rate (number of deaths per 100,000 persons)

Heart Disease
Cancer
COVID-19
Unintentional Injury
Stroke
Alzheimer's Disease
Chronic Lower Respiratory Disease

Leading causes of death in St. Louis County (2020)

LIFE EXPECTANCY (2010-2015)

Age of life expectancy at birth, by zip code

- 66.0 - 72.3 years old
- 72.4 - 74.7 years old
- 74.8 - 77.2 years old
- 77.3 - 81.0 years old
- 81.1 - 85.6 years old
- (Unpopulated or 'unstable' data)

- Area (per zip code) where the most people regionally (more than 20% population) lack health insurance (2020)

- Area (per zip code) where 17-19% population lacks health insurance (2020) (The national average is 14.3%)

- Outline denotes areas with 50% or more Black population

- Ferguson

80.3

74.3

72.3

73.8

73.4

70.9

67

74.5

66

70.2
Ferguson

66.6

69.1

71

75.4

72.3

71.4

68.5

78.4

Wellston,
Pagedale,
Hanley Hills

66.1

79.8

76.6

Less
than
2 miles

85.6

78.9

75.7

80.3

Clayton

78.4

82.4

82.2

76

79.6

80

St. Louis City
St. Louis County

8.9

78.2

79.7

6.4

73

81

77.2

77.9

82.3

78.4

74.7

76.1

Note:
Data is not
available on
private employer-
provided health
benefits 1

1" = 20,000'

N

5.2.10

Map of St. Louis County and region showing COVID-19 death rates (2020). Below, a breakdown of these rates by race for St. Louis County (2020).

Public trust

The COVID-19 pandemic disproportionately impacted North County residents, but it also impacted wealthier areas in West County.

In North County, the rates point to lower access to health insurance, health care and other social determinants. But the rates also reveal the accumulated harm of years of marketized government policy that systematically disenfranchised residents. This is perceived in current levels of mistrust of government, the vaccine program specifically, in North County—and perhaps also by the "small government" champions in other parts of the region where people seek even more individualism and autonomy out from under the state. 1

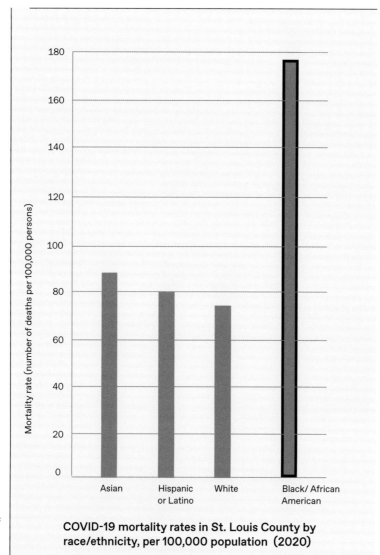

COVID-19 mortality rates in St. Louis County by race/ethnicity, per 100,000 population (2020)

↳

1 See, for example, Maritza Vasques Reyes, "The Disproportional Impact of COVID-19 on African Americans," in *Health and Human Rights Journal*, 2020 Dec; 22(2): 299–307.

St. Louis County Department of Public Health *Leading Causes of Death Profile*, October 4, 2021.

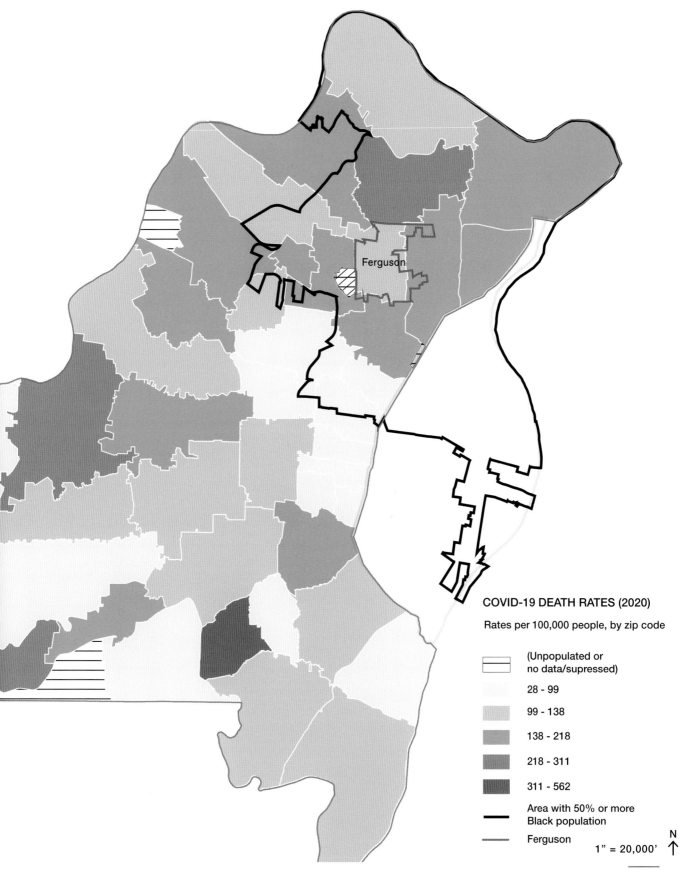

Ferguson

COVID-19 DEATH RATES (2020)

Rates per 100,000 people, by zip code

	(Unpopulated or no data/supressed)
	28 - 99
	99 - 138
	138 - 218
	218 - 311
	311 - 562
	Area with 50% or more Black population
	Ferguson

1" = 20,000'

N

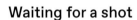

Waiting for a shot

Photo by author, 2020
People in line in the parking lot of St. Louis Community College in Ferguson, MO, waiting to receive the free COVID-19 vaccine from the St. Louis County Department of Health. While public trust in North St. Louis County was low, the public health vaccination program was significant.
In austerity, the parking lots of public institutions double as some of the few remaining 'civic' spaces left for large gatherings and public clinics like this.

5.2.11

Map of North St. Louis County and surrounding areas, showing the locations of fast food restaurants, grocery stores and fresh food markets against the median household income and areas with the highest regional rates of diabetes and obesity (2020).

Health / food

Among other things, public health is a product of people's access to affordable, fresh healthy food. The map correlates wealth with food access and lower rates of diabetes and obesity.

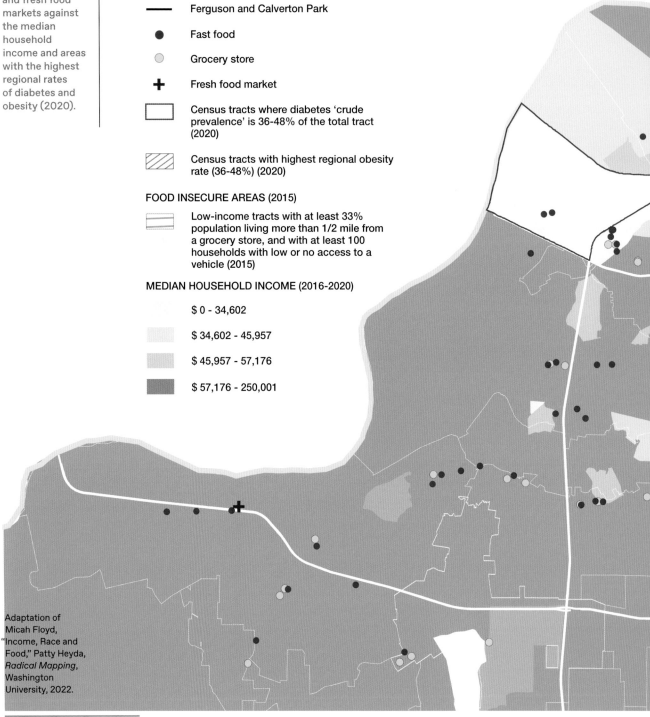

— Ferguson and Calverton Park

● Fast food

○ Grocery store

＋ Fresh food market

□ Census tracts where diabetes 'crude prevalence' is 36-48% of the total tract (2020)

▨ Census tracts with highest regional obesity rate (36-48%) (2020)

FOOD INSECURE AREAS (2015)

Low-income tracts with at least 33% population living more than 1/2 mile from a grocery store, and with at least 100 households with low or no access to a vehicle (2015)

MEDIAN HOUSEHOLD INCOME (2016-2020)

$ 0 - 34,602

$ 34,602 - 45,957

$ 45,957 - 57,176

$ 57,176 - 250,001

Adaptation of Micah Floyd, "Income, Race and Food," Patty Heyda, *Radical Mapping*, Washington University, 2022.

See also   2.1.05   2.1.07   3.M.03   4.C.19

Calverton Park

Ferguson

St. Louis County

St. Louis City

1" = 10,000'

N

5.3.12

A map of the 'lungs' of St. Louis County and City compares tree canopy coverage with areas of dangerously high levels of particulate matter (PM 2.5) from highway, airport and industry pollution; with asthma rates, per census tract (2020).

Land use

<u>Land use and tree policy is air quality.</u> Despite a high percentage of trees that clean the air in parts of North St. Louis County, asthma rates are persistently high. This is from exposures to the harmful microscopic particulates called PM 2.5 caused by pollution from highways, the airport, industries and coal-based power plants.

Federal clean-air standards are largely left to the states to regulate and enforce. Missouri is behind in reporting and addressing non-attainment of air quality. There is a breakdown of accountability between offending industries who evade responsibility and the public sector who enforces pro-growth deregulation, even as it is contradictorily called on to repair damages.

↳

Particulate Matter 2.5 (PM 2.5) refers to the most dangerous microscopic chemical particles in the air that are smaller than 2.5 micrometers in size, meaning they can be inhaled and get into the lungs and bloodstream. "Most particles form in the atmosphere as a result of complex reactions of chemicals such as sulfur dioxide and nitrogen oxides, which are pollutants emitted from power plants, industries and automobiles." 1

1 United States Environmental Protection Agency, *Particulate Matter (PM) Basics*, July, 2022.

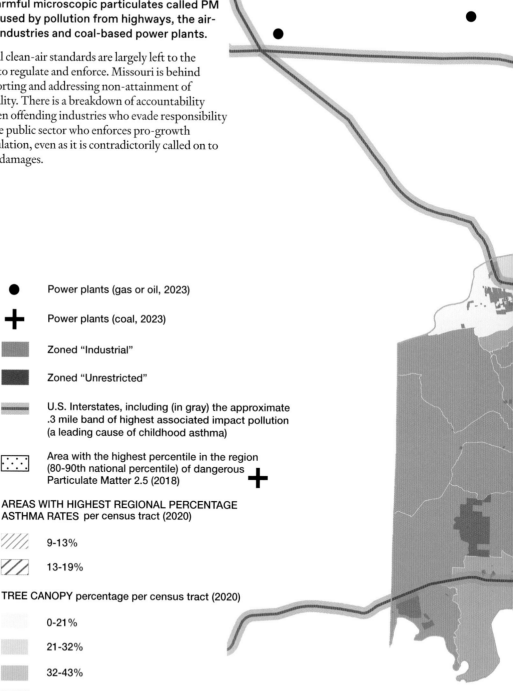

● Power plants (gas or oil, 2023)

✚ Power plants (coal, 2023)

▬ Zoned "Industrial"

▬ Zoned "Unrestricted"

▬ U.S. Interstates, including (in gray) the approximate .3 mile band of highest associated impact pollution (a leading cause of childhood asthma)

⬚ Area with the highest percentile in the region (80-90th national percentile) of dangerous Particulate Matter 2.5 (2018)

AREAS WITH HIGHEST REGIONAL PERCENTAGE ASTHMA RATES per census tract (2020)

⬚ 9-13%

⬚ 13-19%

TREE CANOPY percentage per census tract (2020)

⬚ 0-21%

⬚ 21-32%

⬚ 32-43%

⬚ 43-54%

⬚ 54-85%

See also   4.3.24   5.2.09   5.3.15-16   5.3.19   5.M.01   5.M.04

The area with the most
PM 2.5 has the highest rates of
asthma and the least access to
health insurance and primary
health care

Ferguson

1" = 20,000'

N

5.3.13

Map of North
St. Louis County
highlighting the
flight patterns of
planes arriving
and departing
from the St.
Louis Lambert
International
Airport with
areas designed
residential land
use (2022).

Air use

Air use is land control. St.
Louis Lambert International
Airport is technically public
and owned by the City of St.
Louis. It has been in North
County since before the suburban fabric encircled it. On
the one hand, communities
near the airport have long
been subjected to noise and
pollution from planes. On
the other hand, the "public
health-oriented" policies to
mitigate adverse impacts of
the noise on residents were
weaponized against them for
redevelopment advantage.

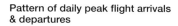

Pattern of daily peak flight arrivals
& departures

Noise contours

St. Louis Lambert International Airport

Single-family residential

Two-family duplex / town homes

Multi-family residential

River

See also   4.C.15-16   5.3.12   5.M.01

Robertson

Kinloch

Ferguson

geton

St. Louis
Lambert
International
Airport

St. Louis County

St. Louis City

1" = 10,000'

N
↑

5.3.14

Topographic map of St. Louis County and City region showing extents of the Great Flood of 1993, with the extent of man-made levees and new commercial projects built in the floodplain since then.

Commercialized floodplain

Controlling the river's tendency to flood with levees represents the reckless capture, literally and figuratively, of sensitive ecological zones for industrial and commercial use (abuse.)

For riverside municipalities, development in (what should be restricted) floodplains exploits new land markets that were otherwise not available. Chesterfield Commons, a massive one-and-a-half-mile-long suburban strip mall of impermeable pavement, was built in the floodplain behind new levees, with public flood recovery money—after the destructive 1993 flood. Meanwhile, this part of the Missouri River is compromised to the extent that is has become the second-most endangered river in the nation.

Levees continue to be upgraded or built since the Great Flood of 1993 to spur commercial development. When a river loses the ability to naturally flood within its meander banks, the water quality, the wildlife it supports, the sediment balance and erosion control are all compromised. Levees are instruments for exploiting the environment and passing off the risks of flooding further downstream.

The lower Missouri River is now the

no. 2 most endangered

river in the entire U.S. (2021)

It is also the source of 80% of the drinking water for St. Louis and St. Charles Counties

○ Commercial developments built in the flood plain since the Great Flood of 1993

— Ferguson

— County boundaries

Extent of 1993 flood

500-year levees or other system

100-year levees

25-year or less levees

New levee projects or upgrades constructed or approved since 1993

New levees or upgrades under consideration since 2005

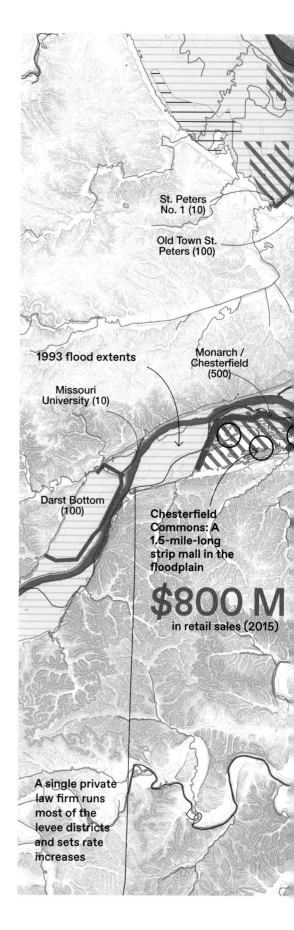

St. Peters No. 1 (10)

Old Town St. Peters (100)

1993 flood extents

Monarch / Chesterfield (500)

Missouri University (10)

Darst Bottom (100)

Chesterfield Commons: A 1.5-mile-long strip mall in the floodplain

$800 M

in retail sales (2015)

A single private law firm runs most of the levee districts and sets rate increases

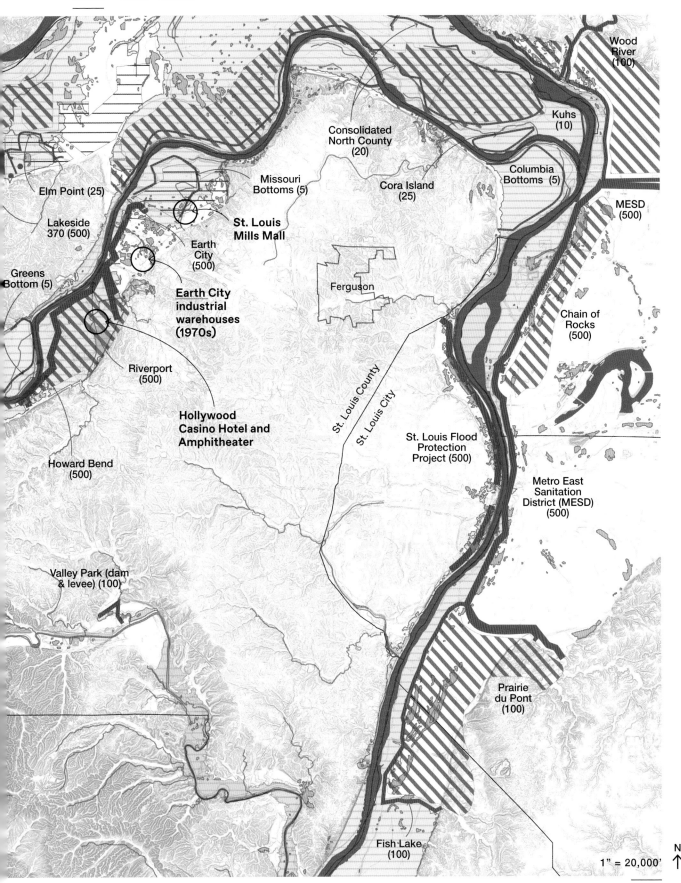

Wood River (100)

Kuhs (10)

Consolidated North County (20)

Columbia Bottoms (5)

Cora Island (25)

MESD (500)

Elm Point (25)

Missouri Bottoms (5)

St. Louis Mills Mall

Lakeside 370 (500)

Earth City (500)

Greens Bottom (5)

Earth City industrial warehouses (1970s)

Ferguson

Chain of Rocks (500)

Riverport (500)

Hollywood Casino Hotel and Amphitheater

St. Louis County

St. Louis City

St. Louis Flood Protection Project (500)

Howard Bend (500)

Metro East Sanitation District (MESD) (500)

Valley Park (dam & levee) (100)

Prairie du Pont (100)

Fish Lake (100)

1" = 20,000'

N
↑

5.3.15

Map of St. Louis County and City region showing the interconnected systems of impaired rivers that provide water supply, streams, and areas of combined sewer systems and industry (2020).

Deregulation

Deregulation of agricultural and industrial runoff has polluted shared waterways. As a result, there is a crisis of impaired streams and rivers in the St. Louis region. Impairment is exacerbated by overflows of combined sanitary sewers into the rivers, the same rivers that provide the region's drinking water. Overflows happen in excessive rain events in areas without adequate permeable surfaces to absorb the water. This is caused in built-up areas with expanses of buildings and impermeable parking lots, much like the Chesterfield strip mall described in 5.3.14.

Combined wastewater and rainwater sewers, together with agricultural chemical runoff, are the largest sources of local water degradation. In addition to bacterial and chemical contamination, waterways are also polluted from industry. Coal ash by-products pollute nearby rivers at deregulated coal burning power plants. Radioactive industrial waste seeps into North County aquifers and soil. See map 05.3.16.

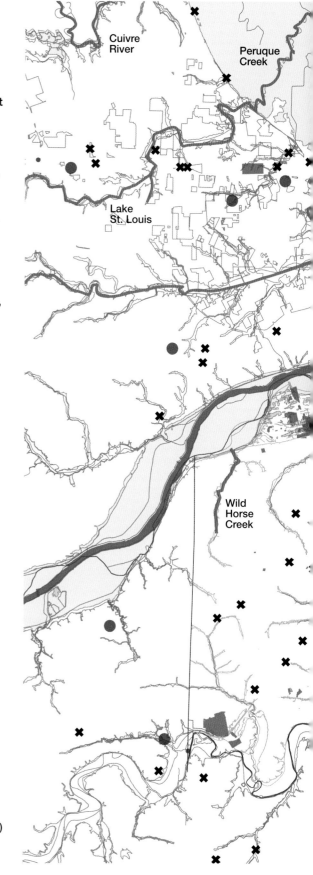

Legend:

—— Ferguson

—— Small rivers/creeks

Floodzones

Extents of 1993 flood

Area with a combined sanitary and storm sewer system

✖ Factories

Areas designated industrial land use

● EPA designated brownfield sites (contaminated)

MISSOURI DEPARTMENT OF NATURAL RESOURCES-LISTED IMPAIRED WATERS (2020)
Reported under the "303d" EPA Clean Water Act:

▬▬ High Priority impared waters (2020)

—— Medium and Low Priority impared waters (2020)

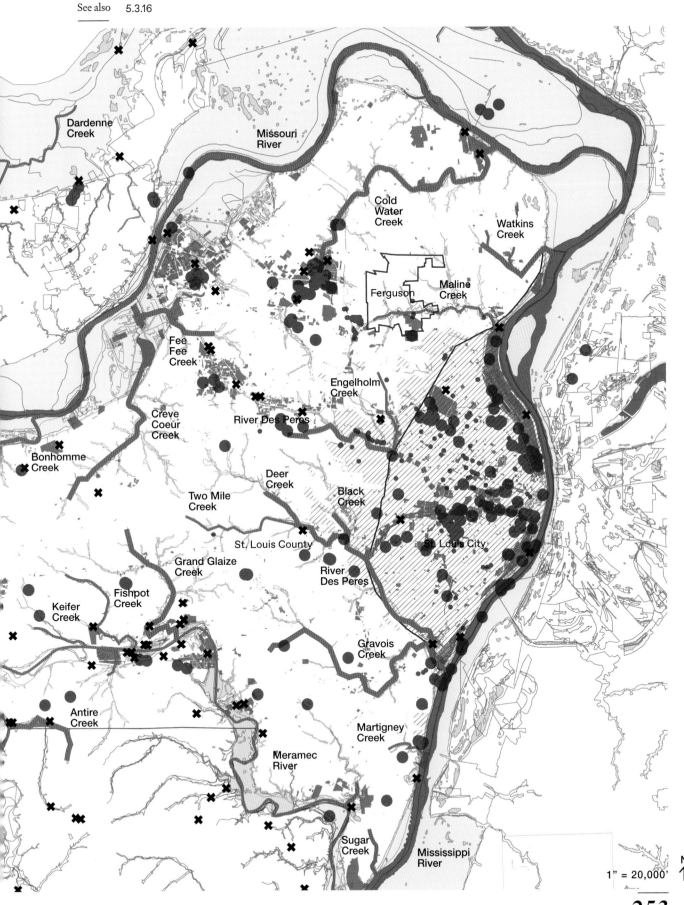

Dardenne
Creek

Missouri
River

Cold
Water
Creek

Watkins
Creek

Ferguson

Maline
Creek

Fee
Fee
Creek

Engelholm
Creek

Creve
Coeur
Creek

River Des Peres

Bonhomme
Creek

Deer
Creek

Two Mile
Creek

Black
Creek

St. Louis County

St. Louis City

Grand Glaize
Creek

River
Des Peres

Fishpot
Creek

Keifer
Creek

Gravois
Creek

Antire
Creek

Martigney
Creek

Meramec
River

Sugar
Creek

Mississippi
River

1" = 20,000'

N
↑

253

See also   2.M.01-02

Public Health

Photo by author, 2023
A view from the entrance of the John C. Murphy County Health Center in Berkeley, MO, highlights the neoliberal contradiction of providing health services without the capacity to maintain a healthy underlying built environment. The image shows the extent that ideas of collective environmental and civic well-being have been degraded in the austere first-ring suburb.

255

5.3.16

Map of North St. Louis County and surrounding areas, showing the different storage sites where the Mallinckrodt Company moved and improperly stored 1940s-era uranium-production waste, with a radius shown of the extents of radioactive dust that can spread from sites like this. The map highlights eight zip codes around Coldwater Creek where significantly high rates of some cancers were documented between 1996-2004 by the Missouri Department of Health and Senior Services (2014). 1

Externalized costs

Externalizations refer to the passing off of costs or responsibilities onto others, including onto future generations.

From the 1940s to the 1960s, St. Louis-based Mallinckrodt Chemical (later Pharmaceutical) Company externalized, or transferred, radioactive waste from their government-contracted WWII-era Manhattan Project uranium production project downtown to sites around Coldwater Creek in North County, without taking accountability for overseeing its safe storage or cleanup. The area rapidly developed after that into a middle-class suburb. Decades later, the community that grew up near those sites continues to get disproportionately ill, while the toxic sites have yet to be cleaned up—a situation that has taken decades to establish accountability for and action on. This crisis is not a racialized one but part of the broader mundane violence of externalizations allowed by private companies (and in this case a public-private arrangement) that impact everyone's collective rights to clean air, water and soil. 2

Coldwater Creek is

radioactively contaminated.

It connects to additional tributaries and to the underground water table.

The radioactive material is at West Lake Landfill (as of 2024), where it was dumped illegally in 1976 and contaminated another

46 acres

of land. The landfill has a smoldering underground fire that, if it reaches the radioactive material, will have catastrophic effects.

7 mile radius

reach of radioactive dust from original storage sites.

1 Missouri Department of Health and Senior Services (DHSS), *Analysis of Cancer Incidence Data in Coldwater Creek Area, Missouri, 1996-2004* Report, 2014. Map cancer rates are adapted from data in this report.

2 Allison Kite, "Records reveal 75 years of government downplaying, ignoring risks of St. Louis radioactive waste," Missouri Independent, July 12, 2023.

3 Coldwater Creek Factsheet, 2015.

─────── Ferguson

─────── Area of moderately high runoff soil

▬▬▬▬▬▬ Area of high runoff soil

Average cancer rates by zip code (1996-2004) DHSS Report, 2014

Significantly high cancer rates by zip code (1996-2004) DHSS Report, 2014

Denotes 7-mile possible radius reach of radioactive dust

See also   2.1.06-07   5.3.12   5.3.15

One online survey revealed

2700 documented reports

"of multi-generational illnesses, including rare cancers, thyroid problems, infertility, auto-immune diseases and genetic mutations in children" in people who used to live or still live near Coldwater Creek. 3

63034

Coldwater Creek

63031

63138

63033

2 Latty

1 SLAPS

63134

63135 Ferguson

63136

63137

63074

63140

63121

Radioactive waste transfers 1942-1960s

63114

↳
SLAPS:
St. Louis Airport
Storage Site

Adapted from
Elaina Echevarria,
"Health impacts
surrounding
Coldwater Creek,"
Patty Heyda,
Radical Mapping,
Washington
University in St.
Louis, 2021.

63133

St. Louis County

St. Louis City

Mallinckrodt
Chemical
Works

63105

1" = 10,000'

N
↑

5.3.17

Map of North St. Louis County and North St. Louis City showing industrial areas, and the various locations of the Mallinckrodt Chemical Company's headquarters over time, alongside the movements and locations of their 1940s-era government-contracted project's industrial waste. Population density is included to show where people live in the region relative to encroaching industry or lasting legacies of past maneuvers.

Spatial maneuvers

As an industry's activities concentrate impacts locally, law allows the industry's financial ties and responsibilities to diffuse outward. The Mallinckrodt Chemical/Pharmaceutical company maneuvers geographically, legally and financially to move away from any localized responsibilities.

The company was founded in St. Louis City in 1882. It later moved its headquarters to North St. Louis County by the airport, along with other industries. Eventually, it took the headquarters to Ireland for a "tax inversion." In 2022, the company filed for bankruptcy to avoid payouts of a legal settlement involving its damaging role in the U.S. opioid epidemic. Yet as the company maneuvers, its radioactive waste harms those from North County for decades to come. The map shows the contested first-ring suburbs where people live (population density), and where industry exploits space, even as those industries technically "locate" elsewhere.

Meanwhile, the philanthropic arms of these companies fund leading local institutions such as the Mallinckrodt radiation center at St. Louis's Barnes Jewish Hospital, Washington University, Harvard University chemistry endowments, and others. These seem to be unspoken contracts of deregulation that overlook environmental and financial exploitation in one place, in exchange for philanthropic donations in other places (among allied power interests).[1]

Waste moved to landfill

— Interstate highways

— Ferguson

(White lines) Municipal boundaries (county)

Industrial land use

St. Louis Lambert International Airport

POPULATION DENSITY (COUNTY)
(people per square mile, by census tract)

0- 9,472

9,472 - 26,037

26,037 - 46,780

46,780 - 80,864

80,864 - 143,390

1 William M. Kutik, "Mallinckrodt Gift Funds Six Chairs," *Harvard Crimson*, March 16, 1968.

See also   2.1.07   5.3.16

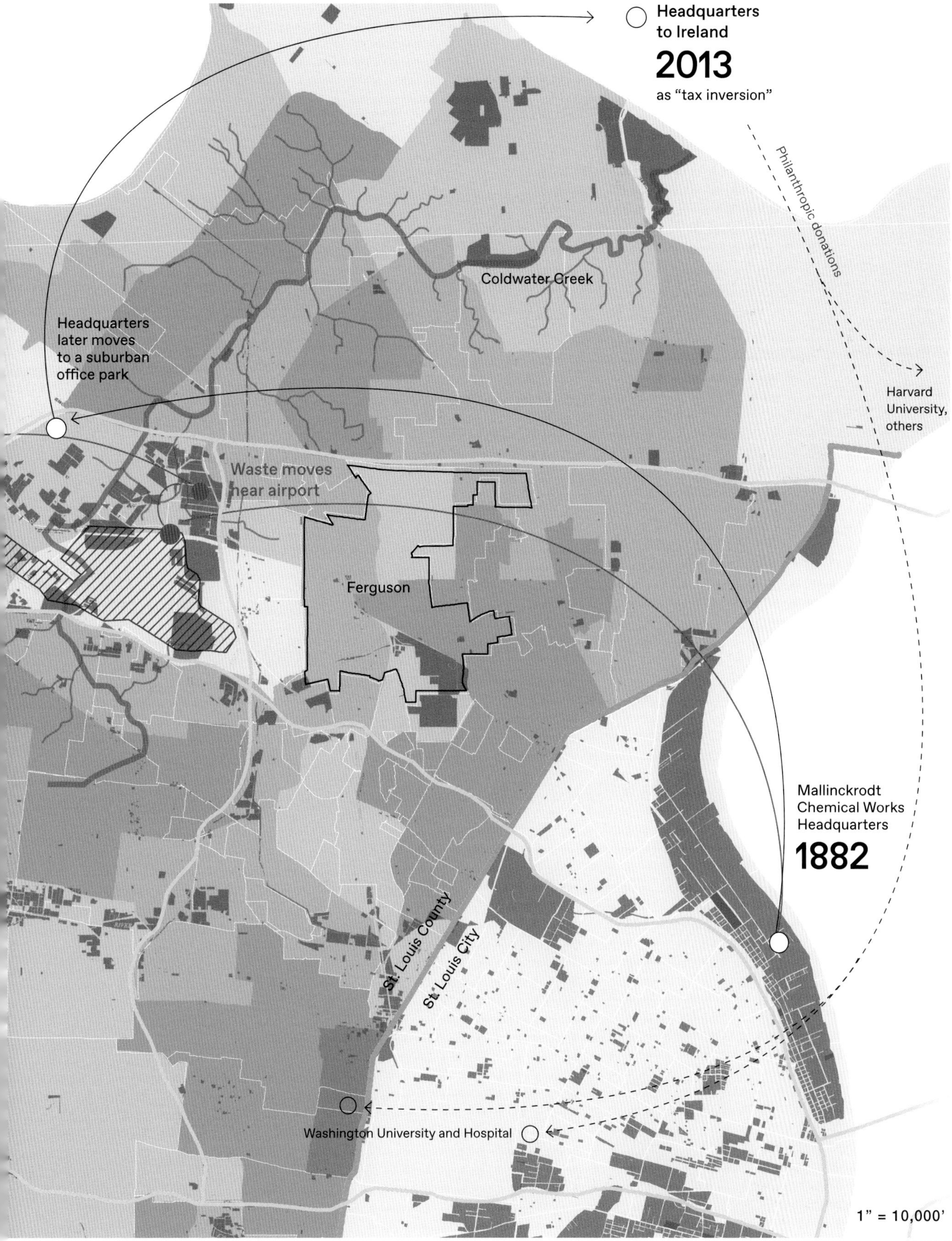

Headquarters
to Ireland
2013
as "tax inversion"

Philanthropic donations

Coldwater Creek

Headquarters
later moves
to a suburban
office park

Harvard
University,
others

Waste moves
near airport

Ferguson

Mallinckrodt
Chemical Works
Headquarters
1882

St. Louis County

St. Louis City

Washington University and Hospital

1" = 10,000'

N

5.3.18

A timeline of the production, movement and neglect of radioactive waste from the Mallinckrodt Company's 1940s-era production to sites in North St. Louis County. The funds allocated for cleanup vs. the Mallinckrodt Company's current annual revenues are shown in relation to timeline events.

Cleanup

The public sector shoulders burdens of cleaning up crises created by private industry. In this case, the Mallinckrodt Company, who produced radioactive waste years ago, did not dispose of it legally in sites in North St. Louis County. In 2021, as efforts to remediate the sites continue, the company posted revenues that exponentially exceed current allocations for cleanup of the waste—by thousands of times the amount. Meanwhile, people in North County are still waiting for answers and action.

↳

Key to acronyms:

SLAPS:
St. Louis Airport Storage Site

EPA: Environmental Protection Agency

FUSRAP:
U.S. Army Corps of Engineers' Formerly Utilized Sites Remedial Action Program

DHSS: Missouri Department of Health and Senior Services

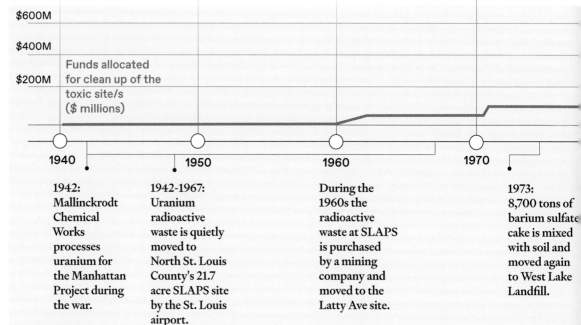

1942: Mallinckrodt Chemical Works processes uranium for the Manhattan Project during the war.

1942-1967: Uranium radioactive waste is quietly moved to North St. Louis County's 21.7 acre SLAPS site by the St. Louis airport.

During the 1960s the radioactive waste at SLAPS is purchased by a mining company and moved to the Latty Ave site.

1973: 8,700 tons of barium sulfate cake is mixed with soil and moved again to West Lake Landfill.

Time of the greatest growth of the suburbs around the sites

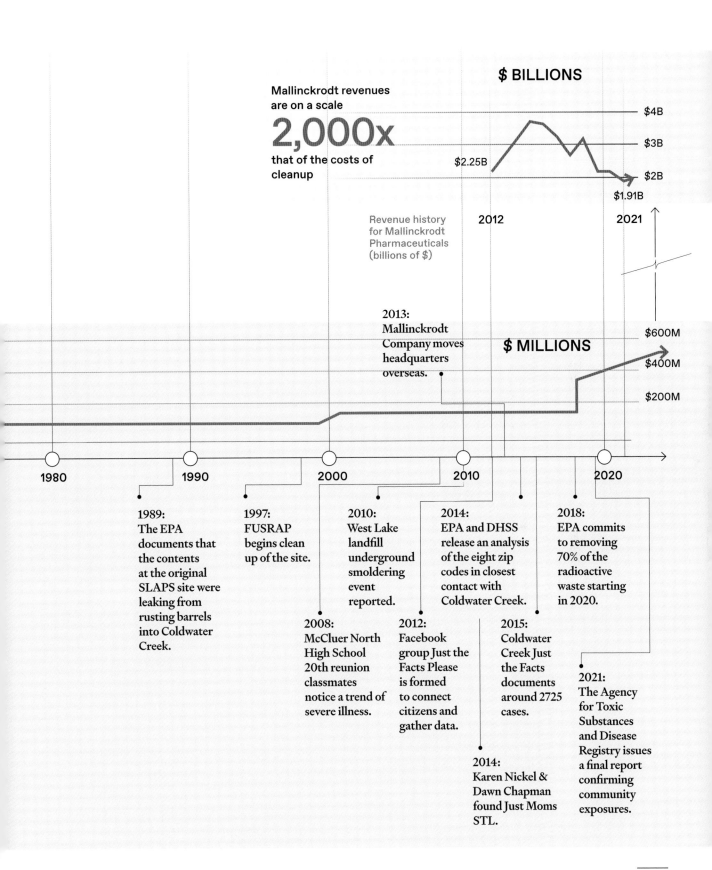

$ BILLIONS

Mallinckrodt revenues
are on a scale

2,000x

that of the costs of
cleanup

$4B
$3B
$2.25B
$2B
$1.91B

2012

2021

Revenue history
for Mallinckrodt
Pharmaceuticals
(billions of $)

2013:
Mallinckrodt
Company moves
headquarters
overseas.

$ MILLIONS

$600M
$400M
$200M

1980

1990

2000

2010

2020

1989:
The EPA
documents that
the contents
at the original
SLAPS site were
leaking from
rusting barrels
into Coldwater
Creek.

1997:
FUSRAP
begins clean
up of the site.

2010:
West Lake
landfill
underground
smoldering
event
reported.

2014:
EPA and DHSS
release an analysis
of the eight zip
codes in closest
contact with
Coldwater Creek.

2018:
EPA commits
to removing
70% of the
radioactive
waste starting
in 2020.

2008:
McCluer North
High School
20th reunion
classmates
notice a trend of
severe illness.

2012:
Facebook
group Just the
Facts Please
is formed
to connect
citizens and
gather data.

2015:
Coldwater
Creek Just
the Facts
documents
around 2725
cases.

2021:
The Agency
for Toxic
Substances
and Disease
Registry issues
a final report
confirming
community
exposures.

2014:
Karen Nickel &
Dawn Chapman
found Just Moms
STL.

261

5.3.19

Annotated map of the St. Louis region at right, with supporting list and U.S. map below, showing the Ameren electric company's extensive charitable giving in the region and nation. The chart below shows the multifaceted cycle of Ameren's political influence via the charitable trust and POWER-forward campaign that lobbies government, and how it generates revenue through infrastructure projects.

For-profit public utility

Energy politics is not just a North County issue but region-wide, and it is one that affects everyone and future generations. The public-private set up of the Ameren electric company exemplifies the extents and existential risks of privatized government.

Technically Ameren is a public utility, which means customers are protected from company rate increases that require the Public Service Commission's (PSC) approval. But the company expands infrastructure to charge customers special fees and generate profits.

Ameren's St. Louis service area is still 73% reliant on coal-based energy (2018). With the urgency of global climate crisis demanding immediate transition off of fossil fuels, and without a truly public utility, the St. Louis region is stuck with a profitable company that has no financial incentive to transition. The Ameren charitable trust maintains favor among local leaders by extending generously into the city. Without strong leadership in the true public interest, how will we transition from deadly fossil fuels to renewable sources before catastrophic global overheating? Experts say there is less than a five-year window to prevent 1.5°F of irreversible, catastrophic warming by 2027. But in our privatized system, Ameren gets to set the net-zero goal, currently at 2045—a predatory delay that is too late.

At right: Diagram of Ameren electric company's 2050 "integrated resource plan" timeline, showing very slow phased retirements of fossil fuel-based power plants (and no retirements of gas plants).

Ameren Charitable Trust contribution recipients, scaled on map by relative size of funding received (2018)

- POWER*forward* coalition
- Other organizations
- Ameren Co. headquarters
- Wood River oil refineries
- Coal power plants (Ameren owned)
- Gas or oil power plants
- Transmission lines
- BNSF Railway (carries coal)
- Gas pipelines

2020

MERAMAC - 2022
591 MW
2.6M tons coal
10,847,200,000 lb CO_2

SIOUX - 2028
972 MW
4.2M tons coal
17,522,400,000 lb CO2

coal-based power

(LABADIE - 2036)

RUSH ISLAND - 2039
1178 MW
5.1M tons coal
21,277,200,000 lb CO2

LABADIE - 2042
2372 MW
10.4M tons coal
43,388,800,000 lb CO_2

CALLAWAY - 2044
1194 MW
27 tons uranium

Renewable sources (brought on too late)

Adapted from Andrew Tsuei, "Politics of Energy," Patty Heyda, *Climate Action Now: Design and Energy for the Cities we Need*, Washington University in St. Louis, 2021.

CO_2 emissions have not been curbed despite passing the threshold for healthy levels (350 ppm).

CO_2 EMISSIONS

CO_2 CONCENTRATION

1750 year

2020

350ppm (1989)

Fossil-based electricity production is the second largest contributor to carbon emissions in the U.S. (2021).

Missouri relies 88% on fossil fuels (2021) with 66% from coal (2022).

See also   4.3.32-33   5.3.12   5.M.04

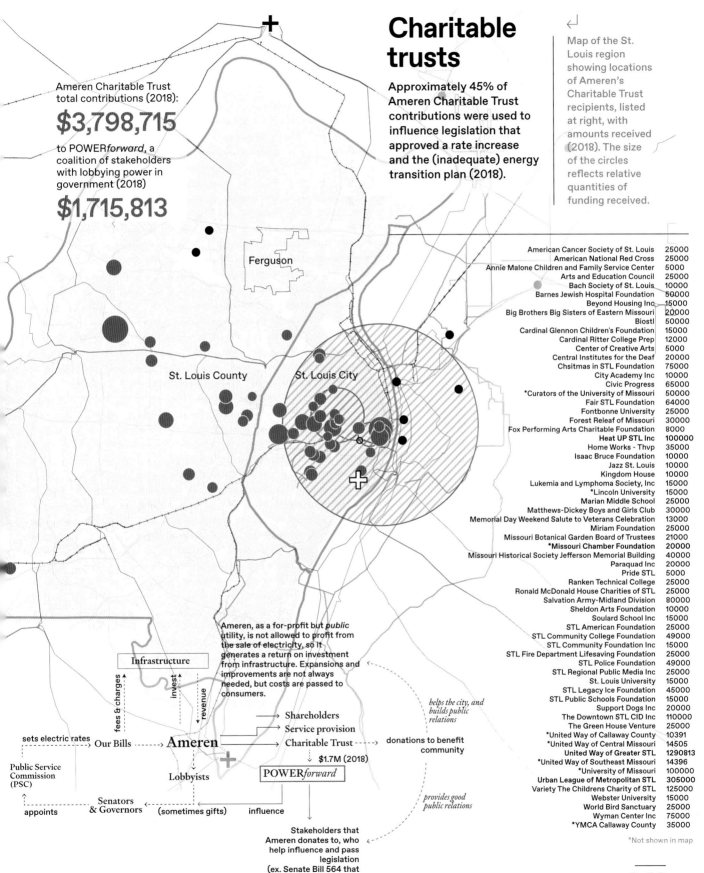

Charitable trusts

Ameren Charitable Trust total contributions (2018):

$3,798,715

to POWER*forward*, a coalition of stakeholders with lobbying power in government (2018)

$1,715,813

Approximately 45% of Ameren Charitable Trust contributions were used to influence legislation that approved a rate increase and the (inadequate) energy transition plan (2018).

Map of the St. Louis region showing locations of Ameren's Charitable Trust recipients, listed at right, with amounts received (2018). The size of the circles reflects relative quantities of funding received.

Ferguson

St. Louis County

St. Louis City

American Cancer Society of St. Louis	25000
American National Red Cross	25000
Annie Malone Children and Family Service Center	5000
Arts and Education Council	25000
Bach Society of St. Louis	10000
Barnes Jewish Hospital Foundation	50000
Beyond Housing Inc	15000
Big Brothers Big Sisters of Eastern Missouri	20000
Biostl	50000
Cardinal Glennon Children's Foundation	15000
Cardinal Ritter College Prep	12000
Center of Creative Arts	5000
Central Institutes for the Deaf	20000
Chsitmas in STL Foundation	75000
City Academy Inc	10000
Civic Progress	65000
*Curators of the University of Missouri	50000
Fair STL Foundation	64000
Fontbonne University	25000
Forest Releaf of Missouri	30000
Fox Performing Arts Charitable Foundation	8000
Heat UP STL Inc	**100000**
Home Works - Thvp	35000
Isaac Bruce Foundation	10000
Jazz St. Louis	10000
Kingdom House	10000
Lukemia and Lymphoma Society, Inc	15000
*Lincoln University	15000
Marian Middle School	25000
Matthews-Dickey Boys and Girls Club	30000
Memorial Day Weekend Salute to Veterans Celebration	13000
Miriam Foundation	25000
Missouri Botanical Garden Board of Trustees	21000
*Missouri Chamber Foundation	20000
Missouri Historical Society Jefferson Memorial Building	40000
Paraquad Inc	20000
Pride STL	5000
Ranken Technical College	25000
Ronald McDonald House Charities of STL	25000
Salvation Army-Midland Division	80000
Sheldon Arts Foundation	10000
Soulard School Inc	15000
STL American Foundation	25000
STL Community College Foundation	49000
STL Community Foundation Inc	15000
STL Fire Department Lifesaving Foundation	25000
STL Police Foundation	49000
STL Regional Public Media Inc	25000
St. Louis University	25000
STL Legacy Ice Foundation	45000
STL Public Schools Foundation	15000
Support Dogs Inc	20000
The Downtown STL CID Inc	110000
The Green House Venture	25000
*United Way of Callaway County	10391
*United Way of Central Missouri	14505
United Way of Greater STL	1290813
*United Way of Southeast Missouri	14396
*University of Missouri	100000
Urban League of Metropolitan STL	305000
Variety The Childrens Charity of STL	125000
Webster University	15000
World Bird Sanctuary	25000
Wyman Center Inc	75000
*YMCA Callaway County	35000

*Not shown in map

Ameren, as a for-profit but *public* utility, is not allowed to profit from the sale of electricity, so it generates a return on investment from infrastructure. Expansions and improvements are not always needed, but costs are passed to consumers.

Infrastructure

fees & charges

invest

revenue

sets electric rates → Our Bills ---→ **Ameren**

Public Service Commission (PSC)

appoints

Senators & Governors

Lobbyists

(sometimes gifts)   influence

→ Shareholders
→ Service provision
→ Charitable Trust ---→ donations to benefit community

↓ $1.7M (2018)

POWER*forward*

helps the city, and builds public relations

provides good public relations

Stakeholders that Ameren donates to, who help influence and pass legislation (ex. Senate Bill 564 that did not benefit the community)

5.M.01

→

Map of the St. Louis bistate region showing 'urbanized areas' and transit access (existing and future Metrolink corridors) with the region's rail lines, main roadways, bus lines and airports.

Mobilize
Public transit

Capital growth spurs uneven and unsustainable geographic expansion with environmental and human consequences. If highway building and the personal car helped construct America's sprawling suburbs, then new paradigms of public transit can remake the suburb of the future.

The North-South Metrolink light-rail extension has the possibility of reaching the north Ferguson transit center via West Florissant Road. This alignment could finally catalyze urgent public realm improvements along the corridor. Public transit should be electrified, powered by renewable sources. The St. Louis Airport might become an accountable partner if it remains in public ownership and decouples from expanding industrial priorities. Inter-city and high-speed rail, meanwhile, should become the next political priority as highly polluting air travel is increasingly unsustainable.

St. Charles County

I-64/40

Adapted from Fatimah Alsaggaf, "Regional transportation infrastructure," Patty Heyda, *Radical Mapping*, Washington University in St. Louis, 2022.

Radical Atlas of Ferguson, USA

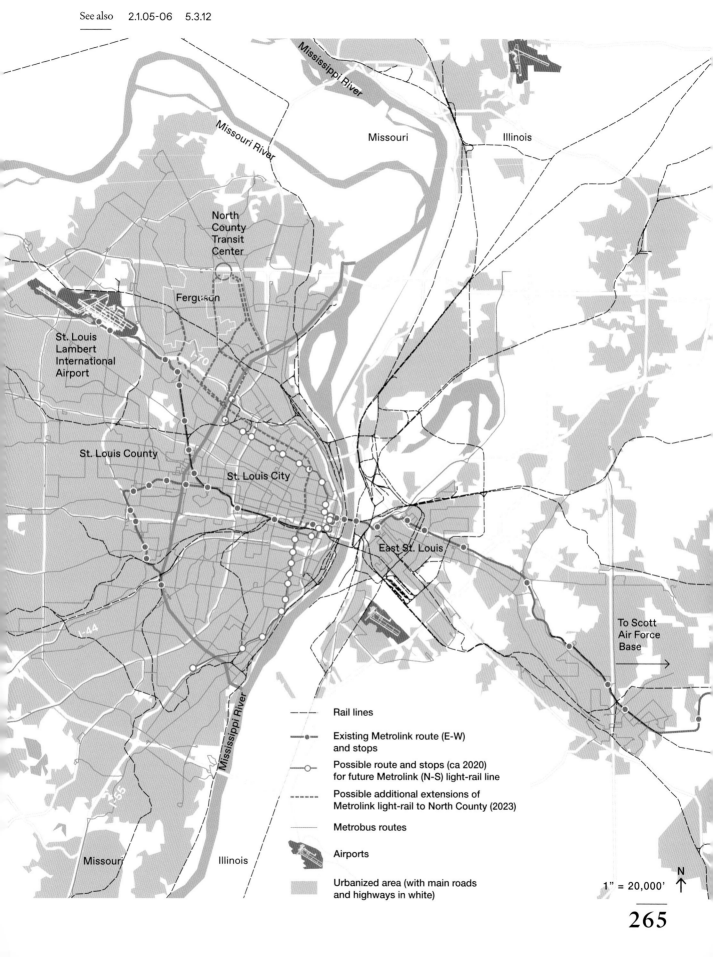

Mississippi River

Missouri River

Missouri

Illinois

North
County
Transit
Center

Ferguson

St. Louis
Lambert
International
Airport

I-70

St. Louis County

St. Louis City

East St. Louis

To Scott
Air Force
Base

I-44

I-55

Mississippi River

Missouri

Illinois

- - - -   Rail lines

●−●−●   Existing Metrolink route (E-W)
and stops

○−○−○   Possible route and stops (ca 2020)
for future Metrolink (N-S) light-rail line

- - - -   Possible additional extensions of
Metrolink light-rail to North County (2023)

────   Metrobus routes

▓▓▓   Airports

▓▓▓   Urbanized area (with main roads
and highways in white)

1" = 20,000'

N
↑

265

5.M.02

Map of St. Louis County and City showing public greenways (existing and planned), with parks and conservation lands with critical areas where threatened or endangered species are found (2018).

Mobilize
Public open space

Democratize open space: The region has a variety of parks and open space systems under state, city and county jurisdiction (although access to maintenance funding is uneven). Great Rivers Greenway has been a model public program for the development of trails and greenways to connect the region. It was formed in 2000 after a vote in St. Louis City, St. Louis County and St. Charles County that supported a new tax to fund it. Initiatives like this might be a reference point for an eco-social regional public planning authority with capacity to center people over profit.

The St. Louis metro region has

51,281

square feet of green space per person (2019) 1

- - - - - Existing or future greenways

———— Other trails

——— Ferguson

········· Municipalities

St. Louis County parks

Other parks or conservation areas

Approximate areas where 6-15 threatened or endangered species are found (2018)

Approximate areas where 15 or more threatened or endangered species are found (2018)

↳

1 The St. Louis region is ranked #7 in the U.S. for the most square feet of green space per capita. Kansas City, Missouri was #2 (2019).

See also   2.1.04   2.1.06

Ferguson

128 miles

of public
greenways
completed
since 2000 by
Great Rivers
Greenways
(2022)

1" = 20,000'

N

5.M.03

Map of North
St. Louis
County showing
"government
recognized
contaminated
areas" against
the area around
radioactively
contaminated
Coldwater
Creek, where
significantly
higher cancer
rates were found
in a separate
government
study (2014).
This study was
conducted after
a (voluntary)
citizen group
formed and led
their own effort
collecting and
sharing data
(2012-ongoing).

↳

1 See the foreword for
this book, by Teddy
Cruz and Fonna
Forman.

2 Allison Kite,
"Records reveal 75
years of government
downplaying, ignoring
risks of St. Louis
radioactive waste,"
Missouri Independent,
July 12, 2023.

For more information
see Coldwater Creek
Facts website: www.
coldwatercreekfacts.
com.

After the radioactive
waste was moved
again to the Bridgeton
West Lake landfill,
another group was
formed to continue
and expand advocacy.
See Just Moms STL
website:
www.stlradwastelega-
cy.com.

Mobilize
Local knowledge

Local knowledge enables *critical proximity*.1 In this case, citizen-led data collection and ground-up advocacy provided a means to discover and confront systems of injustice and the legacies of cloud-ed accountability between private industry and the public sector.

When a group of citizens realized that people who live or used to live by the long-contaminated Coldwater Creek in North County had gotten sick at high rates, they collected data on their own and started an advocacy campaign to get the area formally tested and get answers and action. The citizen-led efforts have brought local and national attention to the issue and did lead to government testing of the area. Additional groups have formed since to mobilize calls for remediation and assistance on additional sites and areas tied to this contamination.

The efforts demonstrate what is possible when citizens mobilize to share their experiences and elevate their voice. The map overlays the area of significant cancer rates measured by a Missouri Department of Health and Senior Services report (2014) that was finally done after residents called for answers. An overlay showing the area of 50% or more Black population (2016-2020) is included in this map so that we understand the crisis is not a racialized one but part of the broader mundane violence of public-private externaliza-tions and lack of oversight that impact everyone's collective rights to clean air, water and soil. 2

Missouri Depart-
ment of Health and
Senior Services
(DHSS), *Analysis of
Cancer Incidence
Data in Coldwater
Creek Area, Mis-
souri, 1996-2004*
Report, 2014. Map
of cancer rate area is
adapted from data
in this report.

Coldwater Creek

Latty
Ave
Storage
Site

St. Louis
Airport
Storage
Site
(SLAPS)

Ferguson

St. Louis County —— St. Louis City

Coldwater Creek and tributaries
(extremely impaired, considered radioactive)

Ferguson

Area with 50% or more
Black population (2016-2020)

Area with significantly high cancer rates,
by zip code (1996-2004) DHSS Report,
conducted after citizens pushed for more
answers and studies, 2014

● Government-mapped hazardous waste /
Petroleum sites

Government-recognized contamination
areas

1" = 10,000'

N
↑

5.M.04

Map of St. Louis County and City showing potential for solar-powered energy, against the uneven distribution of renewable infrastructure, including: schools that currently have solar panels; locations of electric vehicle (EV) charging stations and LEED (Leadership in Energy and Environmental Design) rated buildings.

Mobilize
The just transition

The St. Louis region has an abundance of renewable energy potential but most green projects still concentrate along the central 'power corridor,' where major companies and institutions align.

A just transition away from coal-based energy, to wind and solar and geothermal sources, must be led by the public sector that is free of corporate influence if it is to serve everyone. Instruments like building codes and standards, responsible infrastructure planning and incentives to benefit communities can lay new groundwork for a sustainable city. New systems of renewable energy should distribute access and benefits across the region, prioritizing North St. Louis and North St. Louis City and those most burdened by conventional energy costs and related asthma rates.

"Capitalism won't deliver the energy transition fast enough.... The sheer scale of the physical infrastructure that must be revamped, demolished or replaced is almost beyond comprehension. Governments, not BlackRock, will have to lead this Marshall Plan." 2

At right:
A. Missouri zones of solar potential. Lightest areas have most potential (2017).

B. Missouri zones of highest wind energy potential (50 m height). Darkest regions have the best wind (2017).

C. Missouri zones of highest geothermal energy potential. Darkest areas have the best potential (2017).

1 East-West Gateway, *Environmental Racism in St. Louis Report*, 2021.

2 Derek Brower, "An energy editor's farewell reflections; The energy transition will be volatile," *Financial Times*, June 29, 2023.

A

B

C

+ Electric Vehicle Charging Stations (2018)

▨ Areas with lowest median income $ 0 - $ 34,555 (2016)

Public or private schools with solar panels, by size of system / KW (2018)

○ less than or equal to 1 KW

○ less than or equal to 10 KW

○ less than or equal to 25 KW

○ less than or equal to 100 KW

Leadership in Energy and Environmental Design (LEED) Certified Buildings, by the U.S. Green Building Council; by rating standard (2018)

▮ LEED Platinum

▮ LEED Gold

▮ LEED Silver

▮ LEED Certified

Solar Potential as Direct Normal Irradiance (DNI) value (2018)

☐ <4.80 (better)

☐ <4.70 (good)

☐ <4.60 (moderate)

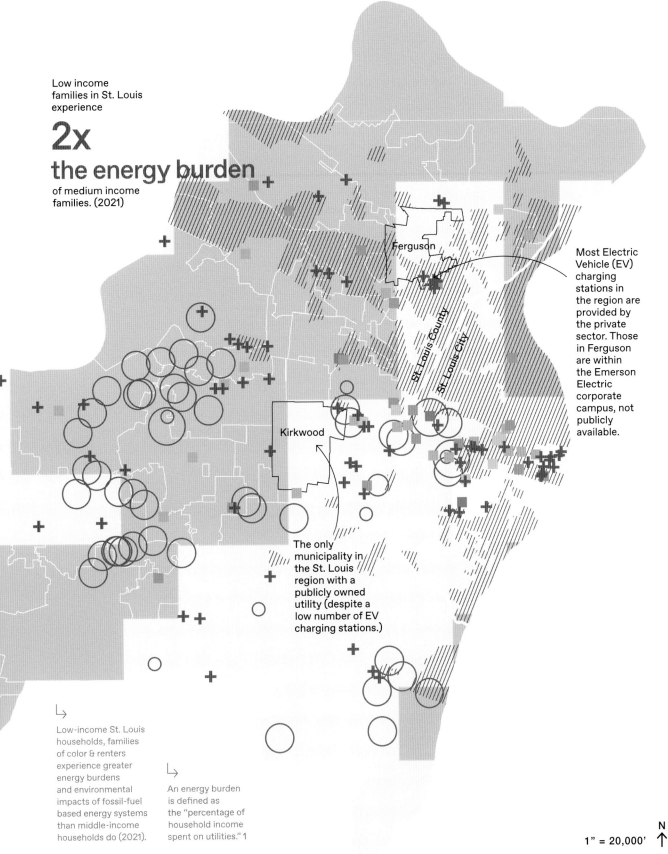

Low income
families in St. Louis
experience

2x

the energy burden

of medium income
families. (2021)

Ferguson

Most Electric
Vehicle (EV)
charging
stations in
the region are
provided by
the private
sector. Those
in Ferguson
are within
the Emerson
Electric
corporate
campus, not
publicly
available.

St. Louis County

St. Louis City

Kirkwood

The only
municipality in
the St. Louis
region with a
publicly owned
utility (despite a
low number of EV
charging stations.)

↳
Low-income St. Louis
households, families
of color & renters
experience greater
energy burdens
and environmental
impacts of fossil-fuel
based energy systems
than middle-income
households do (2021).

↳
An energy burden
is defined as
the "percentage of
household income
spent on utilities." 1

1" = 20,000'

N
↑

Sources

A note on the maps, graphics and credits

This atlas was not commissioned by any group or organization. It was built over several years with original drawings by Patty Heyda with Washington University students and research assistants. Every attempt has been made to maintain the accuracy of the facts being shown and to provide full credit to all data sources. The author has made every effort to contact all known copyright holders and give credit. If a copyright was missed, please inform the author and adjustments will be made in subsequent editions, and in any online content.

A note on sources

The maps of the atlas span geographies and time frames, but they primarily include data from 2014 to 2023. Many of the maps overlay more than one theme and combine data from different sources to highlight correlations and intersections between topics, or between seemingly unrelated topics. A few maps were generated by less conventional methods—through onsite observation, digital search engines, media interviews, news accounts, reports, scholarly research, or by transcribing historical or nondigitized information from other sources. Any spatial data that was adapted or spatialized from news articles or public or nonprofit reports is fully cited on the map and also listed here. Sources for all statistics in the maps are also listed here, by map and chapter. Every effort was made to use open, publicly available sources, to maintain the full accuracy of what is being shown, include correct dates and give full credit to the original source of the data.

General sources

Unless otherwise noted, base-layer data for the maps in the atlas was drawn from the following open data sources (with years noted within each map):

East-West Gateway Council of Governments GIS and Maps; and Data Center

Environmental Protection Agency, Environmental Justice Screen (EJ Screen mapper)

ESRI, GIS

Google Earth Pro, Google Maps

Social Explorer, American Community Survey various dates (5-Year Estimates)

St. Louis County Open data GIS

St. Louis City data

Washington University Libraries Geospatial Data Collection

U.S. Census Bureau; U.S. Census QuickFacts, various years as noted in the maps

U.S. Center for Disease Control, Places Local Data for Better Health, ArcGIS mapper

U.S. Energy Administration Information Maps

U.S. General Services Administration Data.gov: Missouri

00 Introduction

0.1.01 | Privatization of public policy

Cruz, Teddy, and Fonna Forman. *Spatializing Justice: Building Blocks*. Cambridge: MIT Press, 2022.

Fainstein, Susan, Todd Swanstrom, and Clarissa Hayward. "Redevelopment Planning and Distributive Justice in the American Metropolis." *SSRN Electronic Journal*, 2010. Accessed July 2, 2023. https://doi.org/10.2139/ssrn.1657723.

McBride, W. Scott. "The Use of Eminent Domain Under Missouri's Urban Redevelopment Corporations Law." *Journal of Urban and Contemporary Law* 37 (January 1990).

Rothstein, Richard. *The Making of Ferguson: Public Policies at the Root of Its Troubles*. Washington, DC: Economic Policy Institute, 2014.

Tranel, Mark. Essay. In *St. Louis Plans: The Ideal and the Real St. Louis*, 366. Saint Louis: Missouri Historical Soc. Press, 2007.

0.1.02/03 | Timeline: Civil rights & policy reactions

Brenner, Neil. *Implosions - Explosions: Towards a Study of Planetary Urbanization*. Berlin: Jovis Verlag GmbH, 2014.

Freixas, Catalina, and Mark Abbott. *Segregation by Design Conversations and Calls for Action in St. Louis*. Cham: Springer, 2019.

Horowitz, Juliana, Ruth Igielnik, and Rakesh Kochhar. "Trends in Income and Wealth Inequality." Pew Research Center, January 9, 2020. Accessed July 2, 2023. https://www.pewresearch.org/social-trends/2020/01/09/trends-in-income-and-wealth-inequality/.

Kent, Ana H., and Lowell R. Ricketts. "Wealth Inequality in America over Time: Key Statistics." Federal Reserve Bank of St. Louis, December 2, 2020. Accessed July 2, 2023. https://www.stlouisfed.org/open-vault/2020/december/has-wealth-inequality-changed-over-time-key-statistics.

Historic percentages of Black or white population

St. Louis MO Government Cultural Resources Office, "A Preservation Plan for St. Louis Part I: Historic Contexts, 8 - The African-American Experience." Accessed December 31, 2023. https://www.stlouis-mo.gov/government/departments/planning/cultural-resources/preservation-plan/Part-I-African-American-Experience.cfm.

U.S. Department of Commerce Bureau of the Census. "General Demographic Trends for Metropolitan Areas, 1960 to 1970." PHC (2)-27 Missouri. 1971.

01 Territory

1.1.01 | Confluence

"Ecoregions of North America." EPA, July 26, 2022. Accessed July 2, 2023. https://www.epa.gov/eco-research/ecoregions-north-america.

Gleick, Peter, and Matthew Heberger. "American Rivers: A Graphic." Pacific Institute, June 26, 2013. Accessed July 2, 2023. https://pacinst.org/american-rivers-a-graphic/.

Thompson, Shelby. "What Is the Frost Line and How Deep Does It Typically Go?" Powerblanket, November 3, 2022. Accessed July 2, 2023. https://www.powerblanket.com/blog/what-is-the-frost-line-and-how-deep-does-it-typically-go/.

1.1.02 | Contradiction

Johnson, Walter. *The Broken Heart of America: St. Louis and the Violent History of the United States*. New York: Basic Books, 2021. Pg. 163.

Johnston, Robert D. *The Making of America: The History of the United States from 1492 to the Present*. Washington: National Geographic, 2010.

"Louisiana Purchase - Definition, Facts & Importance." History, June 6, 2009. Accessed July 2, 2023. https://www.history.com/topics/westward-expansion/louisiana-purchase.

Nirazul. "WorldMap Generator - Generate Your Own Vector World Map." Worldmapgenerator. Accessed July 9, 2023. https://www.worldmapgenerator.com/en/.

1.1.03 | Manifest destiny

Eustis, David, Ed Weilbacher, Laura Lyon, Megan Reichmann, Sarah Vogt, Mark Lynott, John Kelly, et al. "The Mounds - America's First Cities. A Feasibility Study." *Heartlands Conservatory*, March 14, 2014. Accessed July 2, 2023. https://doi.org/https://heartlandsconservancy.org/wp-content/uploads/2021/05/the-mounds-america-s-first-cities-exec-sum-final-draft-for-web.pdf.

N.d. Native Land Digital. https://native-land.ca. 2023. Accessed October 2022.

"Osage." National Parks Service, May 25, 2022. Accessed July 2, 2023. https://www.nps.gov/fosc/learn/historyculture/osage.htm.

Royce, Charles C, and Cyrus Thomas. *Indian Land Cessions in the United States*. 1899. Pdf. Accessed July 2, 2023. https://www.loc.gov/item/13023487/.

1.2.04 | Urban divorce / Politicized court / Home rule

Bott, Celeste. "Repeated Efforts to Rejoin the City and County Have Been Rebuffed by Voters." *St. Louis Post-Dispatch*, January 5, 2019. Accessed July 2, 2023. https://www.stltoday.com/news/local/govt-and-politics/repeated-efforts-to-rejoin-the-city-and-county-have-been-rebuffed-by-voters/article_0450f139-6418-597b-abf8-2684a8d08d50.html.

Population figures

"Population History of St. Louis from 1830–1990." Boston University Arts & Sciences. Accessed July 16, 2023. http://physics.bu.edu/~redner/projects/population/cities/stlouis.html.

U.S. Census Bureau QuickFacts, St. Louis City. Accessed December 31, 2023. https://www.census.gov/quickfacts/fact/dashboard/stlouiscitymissouri#.

U.S. Census Bureau QuickFacts, St. Louis County. Accessed December 31, 2023. https://www.census.gov/quickfacts/fact/dashboard/stlouiscountymissouri.

Historic percentages of African-descendants

Rosabal, Kenya. "Taxation Led to Original St. Louis City and County Divide." *Webster Journal*, April 3, 2019. Accessed July 2, 2023. https://websterjournal.com/2019/04/03/taxation-led-to-original-st-louis-city-and-county-divide/.

Schmandt, Henry J. Municipal Home Rule in Missouri, 1953 WASH. U. L. Q. 385 (1953). Available at: https://openscholarship.wustl.edu/law_lawreview/vol1953/iss4/2.

St. Louis MO Government Cultural Resources Office, "A Preservation Plan for St. Louis Part I: Historic Contexts, 8 - The African-American Experience." Accessed December 31, 2023. https://www.stlouis-mo.gov/government/departments/planning/cultural-resources/preservation-plan/Part-I-African-American-Experience.cfm.

Historic maps

"Cities, Towns & Counties." Maps of Missouri. Accessed July 2, 2023. http://maps.slpl.org/ctc.html.

"Ferguson, Missouri." Wikipedia. Accessed July 2, 2023. https://en.wikipedia.org/wiki/Ferguson,_Missouri#cite_note-11.

1.2.05 | Municipal incorporation

Rosabal, Kenya. "Taxation Led to Original St. Louis City and County Divide." *Webster Journal*, April 3, 2019. Accessed July 2, 2023. https://websterjournal.com/2019/04/03/taxation-led-to-original-st-louis-city-and-county-divide/.

Wright Sr., John A. *Kinloch: Missouri's First Black City*. Charleston: Arcadia, 2000.

Wildwood's incorporation

Conversation with Dan Vogel, Patty Heyda, *Metropolitan Development,* Washington University in St. Louis, February 2011.

1.2.06 | Community of choice / Civic hub

"About Ferguson." City of Ferguson. Accessed July 16, 2023. https://www.fergusoncity.com/141/About-Ferguson.

Leonard, Mary Delach. "Ferguson's Yesterdays Offer Clues to the Troubled City of Today." STLPR, August 4, 2015. Accessed July 2, 2023. http://news.stlpublicradio.org/post/fergusons-yesterdays-offer-clues-troubled-city-today#stream/0.

Seal of Ferguson, Missouri. Wikipedia. Wikimedia Commons, n.d. Accessed July 2, 2023. https://commons.wikimedia.org/wiki/File:Seal_of_Ferguson,_Missouri.png.

1.2.07 | Division

N. A. "Crossing a St Louis street that divides communities." *BBC Magazine*, March 14, 2012. Accessed December 31, 2023. https://www.bbc.com/news/av/magazine-17361995.

Onwuachi-Willig, Angela. "Race and Racial Identity Are Social Constructs." *New York Times*, September 6, 2016. Accessed December 31, 2023. https://www.nytimes.com/roomfordebate/2015/06/16/how-fluid-is-racial-identity/race-and-racial-identity-are-social-constructs.

02 Space

2.1.01 | Minimum lot sizes / Single-use zoning

Ferguson Department of Zoning, Ch. 49-Zoning Ferguson, MO § (May 21, 2021). Accessed July 6, 2023. https://library.municode.com/mo/ferguson/codes/zoning?nodeId=CH49ZO.

Wildwood Department of Zoning. Ch. 415 - Zoning Regulations § (September 2022). Accessed September 2022. https://ecode360.com/27726435.

Zoning Map - Ferguson. n.d. St. Louis County Department of Planning: City of Ferguson. Accessed 2021. https://www.fergusoncity.com/DocumentCenter/View/603/Ferguson-Zoning-Map.

2.1.02 | Residential zoning / PRDs

"Apartments for Rent in Canfield Green Apartments." Nestoria. Accessed July 1, 2023. https://www.nestoria.us/canfield-green-apartments/apartment/rent.

Ferguson Department of Zoning, Ch. 49-Zoning Ferguson, MO § (May 21, 2021). Accessed July 6, 2023. https://library.municode.com/mo/ferguson/codes/zoning?nodeId=CH49ZO.

West Colony source: Zillow 11/2022.

"1XXXXX Williamsfield Dr, Saint Louis, MO 63135." Zillow. Accessed July 1, 2023.

"XX Lake Pembroke Dr, Saint Louis, MO 63135." Zillow. Accessed July 1, 2023.

Bertha source: Zillow 11/2022.

IMAGE R-4 Zoning: Planned Residential District

IMAGE R-4 Zoning: Planned Residential District

2.1.03 | Subdivision / HOAs

Ruff, Corinne. "80% of St. Louis County Homes Built by 1950 Have Racial Covenants, Researcher Finds." STLPR, January 31, 2022. Accessed July 6, 2023. https://news.stlpublicradio.org/culture-history/2022-01-26/80-of-st-louis-county-homes-built-by-1950-have-racial-covenants-researcher-finds.

Ruff, Corinne. "30,000 St. Louis Properties Have Racial Covenants in Their Deeds. Your Home Could Be One." STLPR, Nov 18, 2021. Accessed July 6, 2023. https://news.stlpublicradio.org/culture-history/2021-11-18/30-000-st-louis-properties-have-racial-covenants-in-their-deeds-your-home-could-be-one.

HOAs

"HOA Ferguson, MO." HOA Resource. Accessed July 1, 2023. https://hoa-resource.com/location/mo/ferguson-mo/.

"Subdivision Trustee Resource Guidebook." St. Louis: St. Louis County Department of Planning, March 2016. Accessed July 2, 2023. https://stlouiscountymo.gov/st-louis-county-departments/planning/subdivision-trustee-resources/subdivision-trustee-resource-guidebook1/.

IMAGE From covenants to cut-offs: Isolating wealth

IMAGE Isolating affordability

Moore, Sandra M. "Transformation Opportunity in Canfield Green." *St. Louis American*, July 14, 2016. Accessed July 6, 2023. https://www.stlamerican.com/business/business_news/transformation-opportunity-in-canfield-green/article_93399158-4959-11e6-b62a-a709bedc1f7c.html.

2.1.04 | Adequate landscaping

Ferguson Department of Zoning, Ch. 49-Zoning Ferguson, MO. Section 11.10 Landscaping (Ord. No. 2009-3416, 12-8-09) § (May 2021). Accessed July 2, 2023. https://library.municode.com/mo/ferguson/codes/zoning?nodeId=CH49ZO_11.0PLREDI_11.10LA.

"Satellite Map of Ferguson." Google Earth Pro. Accessed 2022.

Zoning Map - Ferguson. n.d. City of Ferguson. https://www.fergusoncity.com/DocumentCenter/View/603/Ferguson-Zoning-Map.

2.1.05 | Walkability

Median incomes

Data USA: Wildwood, Missouri, 2021. Accessed September 2023. https://datausa.io/profile/geo/wildwood-mo.
Data USA: Calverton Park, Missouri, 2021. Accessed September 2023. https://datausa.io/profile/geo/calverton-park-mo/.

"1XXX North Elizabeth Avenue." Walk Score. Accessed July 1, 2023.

"3X Grether Ave, Saint Louis, MO 63135: MLS #23035891." Zillow. Accessed July 1, 2023.

"1XXX North Elizabeth Avenue." Walk Score. Accessed July 1, 2023.

"5X Young Drive." Walk Score. Accessed July 1, 2023.

"Car-Dependent: A Location in Calverton Park." Walk Score. Accessed July 1, 2023. https://www.walkscore.com/score/calverton-park-mo.

2.1.06 | Parking requirements / Heat islands

Ferguson Department of Zoning, Ch. 26- Required Off-Street Parking Spaces, MO § (May 2021). Accessed July 6, 2023. https://library.municode.com/mo/ferguson/codes/zoning?nodeId=CH49ZO.

Heat islands

"Heat Island Effect." United States Environmental Protection Agency. Accessed July 1, 2023. https://www.epa.gov/heatislands.

Giegerich, Steve. "'Great Streets' Plan Advances for West Florissant." *St. Louis Post-Dispatch*, June 22, 2015. Accessed July 2, 2023. https://www.stltoday.com/news/local/metro/great-streets-plan-advances-for-west-florissant/article_42510093-4fbf-5636-9ef9-3f3cbd6b4aa0.html.

Biodiversity value

Davis, Amélie Y., Pijanowski, Bryan C., Robinson, Kimberly, Engel, Bernard. "The environmental and economic costs of sprawling parking lots in the United States." *Land Use Policy*, Volume 27, Issue 2, 2010, 255-261. Accessed December 2023. https://doi.org/10.1016/j.landusepol.2009.03.002.

IMAGE Public space

Giegerich, Steve. "'Great Streets' Plan Advances for West Florissant." *St. Louis Post-Dispatch*, June 22, 2015. Accessed July 6, 2023. https://www.stltoday.com/news/local/metro/great-streets-plan-advances-for-west-florissant/article_42510093-4fbf-5636-9ef9-3f3cbd6b4aa0.html.

2.1.07 | Fast food / Franchise / Supersize

Cutolo, Morgan. "Here's Why All Sizes of McDonald's Soft Drinks Are Only $1." *Reader's Digest,* July 16, 2021. Accessed July 16, 2023. https://www.rd.com/article/mcdonalds-dollar-soft-drinks/.

"Downtown Strategic Development Plan." City of Ferguson, December 2008. Accessed July 11, 2023. https://www.fergusoncity.com/DocumentCenter/View/387/Downtown-Strategic-Development-Plan-2008?bidId=.

Heyda, Patty. "Food Desert: Feeding the Regional Economic Imaginary." *Journal of Architectural Education* 77: 2 (fall, 2023).

"How Do Franchises Make Money." Why Franchise, November 2, 2021. Accessed July 2, 2023. https://www.whyfranchise.com/how-do-franchises-make-money/#mcdonalds.

Jones, David R. "Supersized Sugary Drinks Target the Poor." Community Service Society of New York, July 26, 2012. Accessed July 6, 2023. https://www.cssny.org/news/entry/supersized-sugary-drinks-target-the-poor.

Kaufman, Alexander C., and Hunter Stuart. "How One McDonald's Became the Epicenter of the Ferguson Conflict." *HuffPost*, December 7, 2017. Accessed July 6, 2023. https://www.huffpost.com/entry/ferguson-mcdonalds_n_5689428.

Koslosky, John-Erik. "3 Obvious and 4 Not So Obvious Ways Buffets Make Money." *The Motley Fool*, October 15, 2018. Accessed July 16, 2023. https://www.fool.com/investing/general/2013/12/12/how-buffets-make-money.aspx?awc=12195_1670383754_968283a9c7c046f55ea2e1b-793f82e06&utm_campaign=78888&utm_source=aw.

Nowak, Claire. "The Real Way McDonald's Makes Their Money-It's Not Their Food." *Reader's Digest*, July 19, 2021. Accessed July 2, 2023. https://www.rd.com/article/real-way-mcdonalds-makes-money/.

2.1.08 | Ferguson protest

Twitter search: #FergusonRiots

Twitter volume

Vogt, Nancy. "Cable, Twitter Picked up Ferguson Story at a Similar Clip." Pew Research Center, August 20, 2014. Accessed July 2, 2023. https://www.pewresearch.org/short-reads/2014/08/20/cable-twitter-picked-up-ferguson-story-at-a-similar-clip/.

IMAGE Public space

Rosenbaum, Jason. "Missouri House Passes Bill That Makes Street Protests a Felony Crime, Bans Police Chokeholds." St. Louis Public Radio, May 5, 2021. Accessed July 6, 2023. https://news.stlpublicradio.org/government-politics-issues/2021-05-05/missouri-house-passes-expansive-crime-bill-including-crackdown-on-street-protests.

2.M.01 | *Mobilize* The right-of-way

2.M.02 | *Mobilize* Sustainable zoning

2.M.03 | *Mobilize* Adaptation

03 Opportunity

3.1.01 | Redlining

"Federal Housing Administration." U.S. Department of Housing and Urban Development (HUD). Accessed July 1, 2023. https://www.hud.gov/program_offices/housing/fhahistory.

Lipsitz, G. "The Racialization of Space and the Spatialization of Race: Theorizing the Hidden Architecture of Landscape." *Landscape Journal* 26, no. 1 (2007): 10–23. https://doi.org/10.3368/lj.26.1.10.

"Map of Greater St. Louis." St. Louis: Chas Hoelscher Maps and Mounting, 1937.

Nelson, Robert K., LaDale Winling, Richard Marciano, Nathan Connolly, et al., "Mapping Inequality," *American Panorama*, ed. Robert K. Nelson and Edward L. Ayers, accessed July 4, 2023, https://dsl.richmond.edu/panorama/redlining/#loc=3/41.245/-105.469&text=downloads.

Rohde, Jeff. "The St. Louis Real Estate Market: Stats & Trends for 2022." Learn Real Estate Investing, June 28, 2022. https://learn.roofstock.com/blog/st-louis-real-estate-market.

Missouri's wealthiest and poorest municipalities, 2019

Konczal, Lea. "St. Louis' Wealthiest and Poorest Zip Codes." ksdk.com, November 6, 2019. Accessed July 2, 2023. https://www.ksdk.com/article/news/local/business-journal/st-louis-zip-codes-wealthiest-poorest/63-b1eb6b1a-fdf4-4057-95ec-4cbd49c76c51.

3.1.02 | Deed restrictions

Gordon, Colin. "Mapping Decline: St. Louis and the Fate of the American City." University of Iowa Libraries. Accessed July 9, 2023. http://mappingdecline.lib.uiowa.edu/map/.

Loewen, James W. "Ferguson, Missouri as a Sundown Town." History and Social Justice, February 24, 2021. Accessed July 9, 2023. https://justice.tougaloo.edu/sundown-towns/research-teach-sundown-towns/ferguson-sdt-map/.

"Redlining in St. Louis, MO." MySidewalk. Accessed July 9, 2023. https://reports.mysidewalk.com/59cc324517.

Ruff, Corinne. "80% of St. Louis County Homes Built by 1950 Have Racial Covenants, Researcher Finds." STLPR, January 31, 2022. Accessed July 6, 2023. https://news.stlpublicradio.org/culture-history/2022-01-26/80-of-st-louis-county-homes-built-by-1950-have-racial-covenants-researcher-finds.

3.1.03 | Floodlining

"Map of Greater St. Louis." St. Louis: Chas Hoelscher Maps and Mounting, 1937.

Nelson, Robert K., LaDale Winling, Richard Marciano, Nathan Connolly, et al., "Mapping Inequality," *American Panorama*, ed. Robert K. Nelson and Edward L. Ayers, accessed July 4, 2023, https://dsl.richmond.edu/panorama/redlining/#loc=3/41.245/-105.469&text=downloads.

"Renters Insurance Information." Missouri Department of Insurance Website. Accessed July 9, 2023. https://insurance.mo.gov/consumers/renters.php.

3.1.04 | Redlining 2.0

DeSilver, Drew, and Kristen Bialik. "Blacks and Hispanics Face Extra Challenges in Getting Home Loans." Pew Research Center, January 10, 2017. Accessed July 6, 2023. https://www.pewresearch.org/short-reads/2017/01/10/blacks-and-hispanics-face-extra-challenges-in-getting-home-loans/.

Eavis, Peter. "Race Strongly Influences Mortgage Lending in St. Louis, Study Finds." *The New York Times*, July 19, 2016. Accessed July 6, 2023. https://www.nytimes.com/2016/07/19/business/dealbook/race-strongly-influences-mortgage-lending-in-st-louis-study-finds.html.

"Justice Department Reaches Settlement with Midwest Bankcentre Regarding Alleged Lending Discrimination in St. Louis." Office of Public Affairs | United States Department of Justice, June 16, 2011. Accessed July 16, 2023. https://www.justice.gov/opa/pr/justice-department-reaches-settlement-midwest-bankcentre-regarding-alleged-lending#:~:text=Settlement%20Provides%20%241.45%20Million%20to,American%20areas%20of%20the%20St.

Lane, Ben. "Study: Race Still a Major Factor in Mortgage Lending." *HousingWire*, July 20, 2016. Accessed July 2, 2023. https://www.housingwire.com/articles/37576-study-race-still-a-major-factor-in-mortgage-lending/.

Mukherjee, Sy. "Blacks Are Still Significantly Less Likely to Get Approved for a Mortgage than Whites." *Fortune*, April 25, 2021. Accessed July 5, 2023. https://fortune.com/2016/07/19/mortgage-lending-racial-disparities/.

Richardson, Jason, Bruce Mitchell, and Nicole West. Home Mortgage Lending in St. Louis, Milwaukee, Minneapolis, and Surrounding Areas, July 2016. Accessed July 5, 2023. https://ncrc.org/wp-content/uploads/2018/01/Home-Mortgage-Lending2.pdf.

Rivas, Rebecca. "New Study Finds Significant Disparities in Region's Mortgage Lending." STLPR, July 21, 2016. Accessed July 4, 2023. https://news.stlpublicradio.org/government-politics-issues/2016-07-20/new-study-finds-significant-disparities-in-regions-mortgage-lending.

Additional sources for maps 3.1.01 to 3.1.04:

Housing discrimination, lending

Gordon, Colin. "Mapping Decline: St. Louis and the Fate of the American City." University of Iowa Libraries. Accessed July 9, 2023. http://mappingdecline.lib.uiowa.edu/map/.

Gordon, Colin. *St. Louis racial housing covenants time-lapse 1900–1950. Youtube.* University of Iowa, 2022. Accessed July 5, 2023. https://www.youtube.com/watch?v=B2yD2wAZuuQ.

National Community Reinvestment Coalition, "No Loans, No Growth: Mortgage Discrimination Still Happening in St. Louis Metro "NCRC." NCRC, January 7, 2022. Accessed July 2, 2023. https://ncrc.org/no-loans-no-growth-mortgage-discrimination-still-happening-in-st-louis-metro/?utm_source=rss&utm_medium=rss&utm_campaign=no-loans-no-growth-mortgage-discrimination-still-happening-in-st-louis-metro.

St. Louis Public Radio

Farzan, Shahla. "Black Borrowers in St. Louis Face Lending Discrimination, High Mortgage Rejection Rates." STLPR, August 3, 2020. Accessed July 2, 2023. https://news.stlpublicradio.org/government-politics-issues/2020-07-30/black-borrowers-in-st-louis-face-lending-discrimination-high-mortgage-rejection-rates.

Hemphill, Evie. "Advocates See Red Flags as First Mid Seeks to Acquire Jefferson Bank & Trust." STLPR, October 26, 2021. Accessed July 6, 2023. https://news.stlpublicradio.org/show/st-louis-on-the-air/2021-10-26/proposed-merger-of-first-mid-and-jefferson-banks-draws-ire.

Hemphill, Evie. "Advocates Drop Opposition to Jefferson Bank Merger after First Mid Inks a Community Benefits Agreement." STLPR, January 18, 2022. Accessed July 4, 2023. https://news.stlpublicradio.org/show/st-louis-on-the-air/2022-01-18/advocates-drop-opposition-to-jefferson-bank-merger.

Rivas, Rebecca. "New Study Finds Significant Disparities in Region's Mortgage Lending." STLPR, July 21, 2016. Accessed July 4, 2023. https://news.stlpublicradio.org/government-politics-issues/2016-07-20/new-study-finds-significant-disparities-in-regions-mortgage-lending.

Ruff, Corinne. "80% of St. Louis County Homes Built by 1950 Have Racial Covenants, Researcher Finds." STLPR, January 31, 2022. Accessed July 6, 2023. https://news.stlpublicradio.org/culture-history/2022-01-26/80-of-st-louis-county-homes-built-by-1950-have-racial-covenants-researcher-finds.

Ruff, Corinne. "30,000 St. Louis Properties Have Racial Covenants in Their Deeds. Your Home Could Be One." STLPR, November 18, 2021. Accessed July 6, 2023. https://news.stlpublicradio.org/culture-history/2021-11-18/30-000-st-louis-properties-have-racial-covenants-in-their-deeds-your-home-could-be-one.

St. Louis Post-Dispatch

Barker, Jacob. "Midwest BankCentre Opens New North St. Louis Branch." *St. Louis Post-Dispatch*, April 6, 2017. Accessed July 6, 2023. https://www.stltoday.com/business/local/midwest-bank-centre-opens-new-north-st-louis-branch/article_6d35ca17-2288-54b2-94d4-4f0891903d74.html.

Brown, Lisa. "One Year after Opening, Pagedale Bank Branch Fills Unmet Need." *St. Louis Post-Dispatch*, November 29, 2013. Accessed July 2, 2023. https://www.stltoday.com/business/local/one-year-after-opening-pagedale-bank-branch-fills-unmet-need/article_2ce0f560-200f-58da-9965-16c74470aea5.html.

Brown, Lisa. "Midwest BankCentre Settles with DOJ." *St. Louis Post-Dispatch*, June 16, 2021. Accessed July 2, 2023. https://www.stltoday.com/business/local/midwest-bankcentre-settles-with-doj/article_38f3d4fe-985d-11e0-8343-0019bb30f31a.html.

Cambria, Nancy. "A Tale of a House, a Pastor and One of Ferguson's First Black Families." *St. Louis Post-Dispatch*, October 26, 2014. Accessed July 4, 2023. https://www.stltoday.com/news/local/metro/a-tale-of-a-house-a-pastor-and-one-of-fergusons-first-black-families/article_db89b266-e5eb-56ea-a73a-a2c06756d769.html.

O'Neil, Tim. "June 17, 1968: A St. Louis Couple Win a Landmark Housing-Rights Case, but They Never Get Their Dream House." *St. Louis Post-Dispatch*, June 17, 2023. Accessed July 6, 2023. https://www.stltoday.com/news/archives/june-17-1968-a-st-lou-is-couple-win-a-landmark-housing-rights-case-but-they/article_08928410-2a54-5da6-b749-243ac259a83f.html.

O'Neil, Tim. "1963: Protests at Jefferson Bank Lead to Major Changes in Hiring Practices in St. Louis." *St. Louis Post-Dispatch*, August 31, 2022. Accessed July 4, 2023. https://www.stltoday.com/news/archives/1963-protests-at-jefferson-bank-lead-to-major-changes-in-hiring-practices-in-st-louis/article_d6be4178-cc1f-527a-a0d0-fd78a720456e.html.

St. Louis American

Robinson-Jacobs, Karen. "Midwest BankCentre Pledges More than $100 Million in Loans in St. Louis." *St. Louis American*, December 25, 2020. Accessed July 6, 2023. https://www.stlamerican.com/business/business_news/midwest-bankcentre-pledges-more-than-100-million-in-loans-in-st-louis/article_2da6b072-4676-11eb-9546-bbc1c01701ab.html.

St. Louis Magazine

Cooperman, Jeannette. "A Conversation with Clarence Harmon." *St. Louis Magazine*, November 29, 2012. Accessed July 9, 2023. https://www.stlmag.com/A-Conversation-with-Clarence-Harmon/.

Cooperman, Jeannette. "The Story of Segregation in St. Louis." *St. Louis Magazine*, October 17, 2014. Accessed July 9, 2023. https://www.stlmag.com/news/the-color-line-race-in-st.-louis/.

Stefene, Russell. "A Field Trip to a New Subdivision, circa 1966." *St. Louis Magazine*, June 15, 2017. Accessed July 9, 2023. https://www.stlmag.com/design/a-field-trip-to-a-new-subdivision-circa-1966/.

KSDK

Miller, Greg, PJ Kandhawa, and Erin Richey. "No Loans, No Growth: Mortgage Discrimination Still Happening in St. Louis Metro." KSDK 5 On Your Side, November 10, 2021. Accessed July 9, 2023. https://www.ksdk.com/article/news/investigations/mortgage-discrimination-still-happening-st-louis-metro/63-ffc-2de0a-2680-4866-a983-f1dc609d5e78.

US Department of Justice

"Justice Department Reaches Settlement with Midwest Bankcentre Regarding Alleged Lending Discrimination in St. Louis." Office of Public Affairs | United States Department of Justice, June 16, 2011. Accessed July 16, 2023. https://www.justice.gov/opa/pr/justice-department-reaches-settlement-midwest-bankcentre-regarding-alleged-lending#:~:text=Settlement%20Provides%20%241.45%20Million%20to,American%20areas%20of%20the%20St.

3.1.05 | Municipal credit / debt

Better Together. *St. Louis City and St. Louis County: Municipalities with and without debt* (seen in "For Anything to Change, Missouri Should Consolidate St. Louis" by Kriston Capps). August 19, 2014. *Bloomberg*. https://www.bloomberg.com/news/articles/2014-08-19/for-anything-to-change-missouri-should-consolidate-st-louis.

Robinson, John N. "Race, Poverty, and Markets: Urban Inequality after the Neoliberal Turn." *Sociology Compass* 10, no. 12 (December 2016): 1090–1101. https://doi.org/10.1111/soc4.12433.

Rosenbaum, Jason. "Is Smaller Better? Multitude of Municipalities Plays into City-County Merger Debate." STLPR, April 23, 2014. Accessed July 16, 2023. https://news.stlpublicradio.org/government-politics-issues/2014-04-23/is-smaller-better-multitude-of-municipalities-plays-into-city-county-merger-debate.

3.1.06 | Mortgage interest tax deduction (MID)

Aurand, Andrew. "The Mortgage Interest Deduction ." National Low Income Housing Coalition, 2022. Accessed July 16, 2023. https://nlihc.org/sites/default/files/2022-03/2022AG_6-09_Mortgage-Interest-Deduction.pdf.

DuPlessis, Jim. "Recovery Is Little, Late for African American Homeownership." Credit Union Times, April 26, 2019. Accessed July 6, 2023. https://www.cutimes.com/2019/04/26/recovery-is-little-late-for-african-american-homeownership/?slreturn=20230522182300.

Stein, Samuel M. *Capital City Gentrification and the Real Estate State*. London: Verso Books, 2019.

Renting vs owning chart

Brassil, Dan. "Renting vs. Buying in St. Louis." Dan Brassil, August 14, 2013. Accessed July 9, 2023. https://www.danbrassil.com/renting-vs-buying-in-st-louis/.

"3XX Louisa Ave, Saint Louis, MO 63135." Zillow. Accessed July 9, 2023.

"4XX Jean Ave, Saint Louis, MO 63135." Zillow. Accessed July 9, 2023.

Durway, Andrea. "Rent vs. Buy Examples in St. Louis." Dawn Griffin Real Estate Group, March 2016. Accessed July 9, 2023. https://dawngriffin.com/blog/2016/03/14/rent-vs-buy-examples-in-st-louis/.

3.1.07 | Foreclosure

Underwater mortgages

Gallagher, Jim. "St. Louis Is Hot Spot for 'Underwater' Mortgages." *St. Louis Post-Dispatch*, May 9, 2014. Accessed July 9, 2023. https://www.stltoday.com/business/local/st-louis-is-hot-spot-for-underwater-mortgages/article_1a9b46b5-38f4-5b93-b4b4-e895f8e0bab5.html.

Kouichi Shirayanagi. "Mortgage Crisis Still Persists in North St. Louis City, County." *St. Louis Post-Dispatch*, July 4, 2015. Accessed July 9, 2023. https://www.stltoday.com/business/local/mortgage-crisis-still-persists-in-north-st-louis-city-county/article_ac-751ca5-7b3d-5095-ac35-619ab760153f.html.

Subprime loans

Duncan, Michael. "Snapshot: An Ordinary Suburb, an Extraordinary Number of Foreclosures." *Saint Louis Fed Eagle*, October 1, 2008. Accessed July 9, 2023. https://www.stlouisfed.org/publications/bridges/fall-2008/snapshot-an-ordinary-suburb-an-extraordinary-number-of-foreclosures.

Foreclosures

"Foreclosures 2020." Saint Louis County Open Government, October 4, 2021. Accessed July 2, 2023. https://data.stlouisco.com/datasets/foreclosures-2020/explore.

Splitrock, Joe. "Do Banks Want to Profit from Foreclosures?" BiggerPockets, 2016. Accessed July 9, 2023. https://www.biggerpockets.com/forums/311/topics/267786-do-banks-want-to-profit-from-foreclosures.

Uptick quote

Manning, Kimberly. "What Happened to Ferguson, Missouri's Housing Market in the Past Year?" Inman, August 18, 2015. Accessed July 3, 2023. https://www.inman.com/2015/08/17/what-happened-to-the-housing-market-in-ferguson-missouri-in-the-past-year/.

Non-performing loan write-off quote

Green, Laura. "Why Do Banks Write off Bad Debt?" *Investopedia*, June 30, 2021. Accessed July 8, 2023. https://www.investopedia.com/ask/answers/070815/why-do-banks-write-bad-debt.asp.

3.1.08 | Property crime

"Crime Data Licensing Contact Form." CrimeGrade. Accessed July 9, 2023. https://crimegrade.org/crime-data-licensing/.

Herbert, Christopher E., and William C. Apgar. "Report to Congress on the Root Causes of the Foreclosure Crisis." Office of Policy Development and Research, January 2010. Accessed July 9, 2023. https://www.huduser.gov/portal/publications/Foreclosure_09.pdf.

"Race Must Never Be a Barrier to Opportunity." The Greenlining Institute, May 19, 2023. Accessed July 6, 2023. https://greenlining.org/press/news/2008/misplaced-blame/.

"The Safest and Most Dangerous Places in St. Louis, MO." CrimeGrade. Accessed July 10, 2023. Accessed July 5, 2023. https://crimegrade.org/safest-places-in-st-louis-mo/.

"St. Louis City, MO Theft Rates and Theft Maps." CrimeGrade. Accessed July 9, 2023. https://crimegrade.org/theft-st-louis-city-area-mo/.

White collar property crime / Subprime loans interpreted from

Duncan, Michael. "Snapshot: An Ordinary Suburb, an Extraordinary Number of Foreclosures." *Saint Louis Fed Eagle,* October 1, 2008. Accessed July 9, 2023. https://www.stlouisfed.org/publications/bridges/fall-2008/snapshot-an-ordinary-suburb-an-extraordinary-number-of-foreclosures.

3.1.09 | Low-income housing "choice" vouchers / Landlord discretion

Beachum, Lateshia. "St. Louis' Poorest Residents Ask: Why Can't Our Houses Be Homes?" STLPR, October 17, 2018. Accessed July 8, 2023. https://news.stlpublicradio.org/politics-issues/2018-10-17/st-louis-poorest-residents-ask-why-cant-our-houses-be-homes.

Byron, Aubrey. "Four Years Later, Ferguson Still Relies on the Poor to Pay Its Debt." Strong Towns, August 2, 2018. Accessed July 9, 2023. https://www.strongtowns.org/journal/four-years-later-ferguson.

Connelly-Bowen, Jenny. "De Facto or de Jure Housing Inequities: The Outcomes Are the Same." Community Builders Network, January 6, 2021. Accessed July 9, 2023. https://www.communitybuildersstl.org/stories-and-news/de-facto-or-de-jure-housing-inequities-the-outcomes-are-the-same.

Eligon, John. "A Year after Ferguson, Housing Segregation Defies Tools to Erase It." *The New York Times,* August 8, 2015. Accessed July 8, 2023. https://www.nytimes.com/2015/08/09/us/a-year-after-ferguson-housing-segregation-defies-tools-to-erase-it.html.

Gordon, Colin, and Clarissa Rile Hayward. "The Murder of Michael Brown." *Jacobin*, September 8, 2016. Accessed July 8, 2023. https://www.jacobinmag.com/2016/08/michael-brown-ferguson-darren-wilson-policing/.

Gordon, Tracy, and Sarah Gault. "Ferguson City Finances: Not The New Normal." Urban Institute, April 8, 2015. Accessed July 8, 2023. https://www.urban.org/urban-wire/ferguson-city-finances-not-new-normal.

Hertz, Daniel. "Make Housing Vouchers an Entitlement-We Can Afford It." City Observatory, May 1, 2016. Accessed July 8, 2023. https://cityobservatory.org/make-housing-vouchers-an-entitlement-we-can-afford-it/.

"Housing Choice Voucher Program." St. Louis Housing Authority. Accessed June 26, 2023. https://www.slha.org/for-residents/section-8/.

Kneebone, Elizabeth. "Ferguson, Mo.. Emblematic of Growing Suburban Poverty." Brookings, August 15, 2014. Accessed July 9, 2023. https://www.brookings.edu/blog/the-avenue/2014/08/15/ferguson-mo-emblematic-of-growing-suburban-poverty/.

Manning, Kimberly. "What Happened to Ferguson, Missouri's Housing Market in the Past Year?" Inman, August 18, 2015. Accessed July 9, 2023. https://www.inman.com/2015/08/17/what-happened-to-the-housing-market-in-ferguson-missouri-in-the-past-year/.

Meisenhelter, Jesse. "How 1930s Discrimination Shaped Inequality in Today's Cities." NCRC, March 27, 2018. Accessed July 8, 2023. https://ncrc.org/how-1930s-discrimination-shaped-inequality-in-todays-cities/.

Mitchell, Bruce, and Jason Richardson. *HOLC "redlining" maps: The persistent structure of segregation and economic inequality,* May 2018. https://doi.org/10.13140/RG.2.2.21841.48486. Accessed June 8, 2023. https://www.researchgate.net/publication/328954154_HOLC_redlining_maps_The_persistent_structure_of_segregation_and_economic_inequality.

Moskop, Walker, and Jesse Bogan. "As Low-Income Housing Boomed, Ferguson Pushed Back." *St. Louis Post-Dispatch*, October 19, 2014. Accessed July 8, 2023. https://www.stltoday.com/news/local/metro/as-low-income-housing-boomed-ferguson-pushed-back/article_fcb97a3c-8bb7-54a5-9565-255301753142.html.

"Not Even Past: Social Vulnerability and the Legacy of Redlining." Digital Scholarship Lab. Accessed July 9, 2023 https://dsl.richmond.edu/socialvulnerability/map/#loc=14/38.736/-90.31&city=st.-louis-mo&tract=29189212500.

"Property Lookup." St. Louis County GIS Service Center. Accessed July 9, 2023. https://stlcogis.maps.arcgis.com/apps/webappviewer/index.html?id=e70f8f1814a34cd7bf8f6766bd-950c68%2F.

"Real Estate Information." Saint Louis County Missouri. Accessed July 9, 2023. https://revenue.stlouisco.com/IAS/.

"Redlining and Neighborhood Health." NCRC, Accessed July 28, 2023. https://ncrc.org/holc-health/.

Rothstein, Richard. "The Making of Ferguson: Public Policies at the Root of Its Troubles." Economic Policy Institute, October 15, 2014. Accessed July 9, 2023. https://www.epi.org/publication/making-ferguson/.

Stanley, Kameel. "Housing Council Says Local Landlord Discriminated against Section 8 Voucher-Holders in St. Louis." STLPR, July 18, 2016. Accessed July 9, 2023. https://news.stlpublicradio.org/economy-business/2016-07-17/housing-council-says-local-landlord-discriminated-against-section-8-voucher-holders-in-st-louis.

Turner, Margery and Park, Haeyoun. "Many Minority Families Stuck in Poor Neighborhoods despite Housing Voucher Program." *The New York Times*, August 8, 2015. Accessed July 9, 2023. https://www.nytimes.com/interactive/2015/08/03/us/housing-choice-vouchers.html.

Walsh, Randall, Sijie Li, Allison Shertzer, and Prottoy A. Akbar. "Segregated Housing Markets and the Erosion of Black Wealth: New Evidence from Pre-War Cities." CEPR, August 31, 2019. Accessed July 9, 2023. https://voxeu.org/article/how-segregated-housing-eroded-wealth-black-families.

"Zoning Administration." Zoning Administration | Ferguson, MO - Official Website. Accessed July 9, 2023. https://www.fergusoncity.com/313/Zoning-Administration.

3.1.10 | Eviction

Duncan, Michael. "Snapshot: An Ordinary Suburb, an Extraordinary Number of Foreclosures." St. Louis Federal Reserve, October 1, 2008. Accessed July 2021. https://www.stlouisfed.org/publications/bridges/fall-2008/snapshot-an-ordinary-suburb-an-extraordinary-number-of-foreclosures.

Foreclosures 2020: St. Louis County Department of Planning, St. Louis County Open Government.

"St. Louis, Missouri: Eviction Tracking System." Eviction Lab. Accessed July 9, 2023. https://evictionlab.org/eviction-tracking/st-louis-mo/. Average eviction filings taken from Eviction Lab data for 2012, 2013, 2015, and 2016.

Eviction letter image

Rice, Rachel, and Nassim Benchaabane. "Ferguson Apartment Complex Tells Some Low-Income Tenants to Leave, but Housing Authority Says They Can Stay." *St. Louis Post-Dispatch*, November 11, 2018. Accessed July 9, 2023. https://www.stltoday.com/business/local/ferguson-apartment-complex-tells-some-low-income-tenants-to-leave-but-housing-authority-says-they/article_6e0e8526-5158-548b-b787-c3bd9050558d.html.

3.1.11 | Large / company & absentee landlords / Affordable rental housing supply

Aurand, Andrew, Dan Emmanuel, Emma Foley, Matt Clarke, Ikra Rafi, and Diane Yentel. "National Shortage of Affordable Rental Housing" from rep. *The Gap: Shortage of Affordable Homes.* National Low Income Housing Coalition, 2021. Accessed July 2023. https://nlihc.org/gap.

"Do Large Landlords' Eviction Practices Differ from Small Landlords'?" Housing Matters, February 1, 2023. Accessed July 9, 2023. https://housingmatters.urban.org/research-summary/do-large-landlords-eviction-practices-differ-small-landlords.

3.2.12 | Public school funding

Moskop, Walker. "Database: 2016 Missouri Map Scores by School." *St. Louis Post-Dispatch*, September 29, 2016. Accessed July 9, 2023. https://www.stltoday.com/news/local/education/database-2016-missouri-map-scores-by-school/html_35b780ed-aaa1-5f21-bf32-ea144a68e40e.html. (database no longer linked).

"St. Louis-Area MAP Scores by District." *St. Louis Post-Dispatch* - School Guide. Accessed 2016, 2018. https://graphics.stltoday.com/apps/education/schools/district-map-scores/.

Still Separate, Still Unequal (2020); "The St. Louis Region's Education Funding Landscape Is Highly Uneven and It's Not an Accident." Still Separate, Still Unequal - A Project of Forward Through Ferguson. Accessed July 9, 2023. https://stillunequal.org/funding/.

3.2.13 | Deaccreditation / Student transfer law

Bock, Jessica. "22 School Districts Offer Help to Normandy and Riverview Gardens Schools." *St. Louis Post-Dispatch,* June 23, 2015. Accessed July 9, 2023. https://www.stltoday.com/news/local/education/22-school-districts-offer-help-to-normandy-and-riverview-gardens-schools/article_e01a8007-6e76-59bd-9790-d3df-36cf80b1.html.

Cohen, Robert, and Christian Gooden. "School Desegregation Efforts in St. Louis." *St. Louis Post-Dispatch*, February 18, 2022. Accessed July 9, 2023. https://www.stltoday.com/school-desegregation-efforts-in-st-louis/collection_2ab47852-910e-11ec-909e-b7b9976bc1b2.html#1.

Crouch, Elisa. "TAB for Student Transfers Almost $23 Million for Normandy, Riverview Gardens." *St. Louis Post-Dispatch*, July 26, 2013. Accessed July 9, 2023. https://www.stltoday.com/news/local/education/tab-for-student-transfers-almost-million-for-normandy-riverview-gardens/article_58a24377-1dcb-5cee-805f-4b77135fdace.html."

Group of St. Louis-Area Schools Pledge to Assist Two Failing Districts." KBIA, June 23, 2015. Accessed July 9, 2023. https://www.kbia.org/post/group-st-louis-area-schools-pledge-assist-two-failing-districts.

Lee, Trymaine. "White School District Sends Black Kids Back to Failed Schools." MSNBC, June 14, 2014. Accessed July 9, 2023. http://www.msnbc.com/msnbc/white-district-sends-black-kids-back-failed-schools.

Lloyd, Tim. "Ferguson-Florissant Will Now Accept Normandy Transfers." STLPR, August 29, 2014. Accessed July 9, 2023. https://news.stlpublicradio.org/2014-08-28/ferguson-florissant-will-now-accept-normandy-transfers.

"Normandy Schools Granted Provisional Accreditation." *St. Louis American*, December 7, 2017. Accessed July 9, 2023. http://www.stlamerican.com/news/local_news/normandy-schools-granted-provisional-accreditation/article_35d156ec-daec-11e7-a7b0-3749f80d2a12.html.

"Riverview Gardens Loses Accreditation." *St. Louis American*, June 22, 2007. Accessed July 9, 2023. https://www.stlamerican.com/news/local_news/riverview-gardens-loses-accreditation/article_fb88e055-da9b-529c-ad39-710757ec0fe9.html.

Robertson, Brett, education policy analyst, in conversation with the author, July 14, 2023.

"Schools in Danger of Losing Their Accreditation, but What Does That Mean?" WRDW-TV/WAGT-TV, March 1, 2017. Accessed July 9, 2023. https://www.wrdw.com/content/news/Schools-in-danger-of-losing-their-accreditation-but-what-does-that-mean-415113673.html.

Shuls, James V. "Interdistrict Choice for Students in Failing Schools: Burden or Boon?" Show Me Institute, April 2015. Accessed July 9, 2023. https://showmeinstitute.org/sites/default/files/Interdistrict%20Choice%20-%20Shuls_0.pdf.

Singer, Dale. "Joint Effort to Help Normandy, Riverview Gardens Impresses Nixon." STLPR, August 4, 2015. Accessed July 9, 2023. https://news.stlpublicradio.org/post/joint-effort-help-normandy-riverview-gardens-impresses-nixon#stream/0.

Singer, Dale. "Missouri School Board Votes to Merge Wellston School District into Normandy." STLPR, December 17, 2009. Accessed July 9, 2023. https://news.stlpublicradio.org/education/2009-12-17/missouri-school-board-votes-to-merge-wellston-school-district-into-normandy.

Singer, Dale. "Missouri, Other Districts Will Aid Normandy and Riverview Gardens." STLPR, June 23, 2015. Accessed July 9, 2023. https://news.stlpublicradio.org/post/missouri-other-districts-will-aid-normandy-and-riverview-gardens#stream/0.

Social Explorer 2016 Median Household Income.

The St. Louis Regional Collaborative for Educational Excellence Update to the Governor.

Superville, Denisa R. "Missouri's Normandy District Sheds Its Unaccredited Status." *Education Week*, December 1, 2017. Accessed July 9, 2023. https://www.edweek.org/leadership/missouris-normandy-district-sheds-its-unaccredited-status/2017/12.

Tate, William F., Christopher Hamilton, William Brett Robertson, et al., "Who is my Neighbor? Turner v. Clayton: A Watershed Moment in Regional Education," *The Journal of Negro Education*, Volume 83 No. 3, Summer, 2014. Accessed July 14, 2023. https://doi.org/10.7709/jnegroeducation.83.3.0216.

Wax-Thibodeaux, Emily. "At Brown's Impoverished High School, Students Try to Make Gains against Odds." *The Washington Post*, April 15, 2023. Accessed July 9, 2023. https://www.washingtonpost.com/politics/at-browns-impoverished-high-school-students-try-to-make-gains-against-odds/2014/08/25/d8a33842-2b98-11e4-994d-202962a9150c_story.html?noredirect=on&utm_term=.abba89d42564.

3.2.14 | Student transfer programs

Glass, Ira, and Nikole Hannah Jones. 562: The Problem We All Live With - Part One. Other. *This American Life*, July 31, 2015. Accessed March 23, 2017. https://www.thisamericanlife.org/562/transcript.

Tuition policy 2021-22. St. Ann Catholic School, 2021. https://sacs-stl.org/wp-content/uploads/2021/11/Tuition-Policy-2021-22.pdf.

Chris from Northwoods' story

"2016-2017 Code of Student Conduct." Francis Howell School District. Web. May 1, 2017. Page 11.

Bock, Jessica. "Francis Howell Students Welcome Normandy Transfers." *St. Louis Post-Dispatch*, August 8, 2013. Accessed May 1, 2017. https://www.stltoday.com/news/local/education/francis-howell-students-welcome-normandy-transfers/article_e33f18f1-80d7-5278-bc41-dddc66667340.html.

Crouch, Elisa. "Missouri Appeals Court Upholds Transfer Rights of Normandy Students." *St. Louis Post-Dispatch,* June 8, 2016. Accessed May 1, 2017. https://www.stltoday.com/news/local/education/missouri-appeals-court-upholds-transfer-rights-of-normandy-students/article_6d32ed59-2b44-545b-a7ea-27517ee31422.html#:~:text=In%20a%20unanimous%20ruling%2C%20the%20Eastern%20District%E2%80%99s%20three-member,2014%20voted%20to%20send%20them%20back%20to%20Normandy.

Crouch, Elisa. "A Senior Year Mostly Lost for a Normandy Honor Student." *St. Louis Post Dispatch*, May 4, 2015. Accessed March 22, 2017. https://www.stltoday.com/news/local/education/a-senior-year-mostly-lost-for-a-normandy-honor-student/article_ce759a06-a979-53b6-99bd-c87a430dc339.html.

"Lunch Menu-All Middle Schools." Francis Howell School District. N.p., n.d. Web. May 3, 2017. http://fhsdfhn.sharpschool.net.

McDermott, Kevin, and Jessica Bock. "After Normandy District Refuses to Pay Transfer Tab, Legislators Pressure State Board to Take Over." *St. Louis Post-Dispatch*, October 26, 2013. Accessed March 22, 2017. https://www.stltoday.com/news/local/education/after-normandy-district-refuses-to-pay-transfer-tab-legislators-pressure-state-board-to-take-over/article_b1a723c6-88a5-5405-86f2-cdb7aeec78a4.html.

"Normandy Schools Collaborative Data." Missouri Department of Elementary and Secondary Education. N.p.,n.d. Web. 15 Apr. 2017. https://apps.dese.mo.gov/MCDS/Visualizations.aspx?id=22.

Phillips, Camille. "The St. Louis Heroin Epidemic: Who Is Addicted and Where Is It Coming From?" STLPR, March 3, 2014. Accessed March 3, 2017. https://news.stlpublicradio.org/show/st-louis-on-the-air/2014-03-03/the-st-louis-heroin-epidemic-who-is-addicted-and-where-is-it-coming-from.

"School Clubs." Francis Howell School District. N.p., n.d. Web. May 3, 2017.

Sultan, Aisha. "Aisha Sultan: 'Lunch Shaming' Should Shame Us All." *St. Louis Post-Dispatch*, April 14, 2017. Accessed May 1, 2017. https://www.stltoday.com/news/local/education/aisha-sultan-lunch-shaming-should-shame-us-all/article_d3c50a2a-054c-5559-abee-ccd311fdcc23.html.

Yamashiro, Nikki, and Rinehart, Jen. "America After 3PM: Afterschool Programs in Demand." *Afterschool Alliance*, 2014, 6. Wallace Foundation, 2014. Accessed March 3, 2017. https://www.wallacefoundation.org/knowledge-center/Documents/America-After-3PM-Afterschool-Programs-in-Demand.pdf.

John from Pasadena Hill's story

"After School Activities." *St. Ann Catholic School*. N.p., n.d. Web. Accessed Apr 4, 2017. https://sacs-stl.org/extra-curricular-activities/.

"Eco Club." *St. Ann Catholic School*. N.p., n.d. Web. Accessed April 4, 2017. https://sacs-stl.org/garden-club/.

"Faculty and Staff." St. Ann Catholic School. Accessed April 4, 2017. https://sacs-stl.org/faculty-and-staff/.

Fleck, Alissa. "How Junk Food Affects Children." Weekand.com, December 29, 2018. Accessed July 10, 2023. https://www.weekand.com/healthy-living/article/junk-food-affects-children-18014193.php.

"Morning and After Care." *St. Ann Catholic School*. N.p., n.d. Web. Accessed Apr. 2017 (no link).

Owen, Lauren. "A Comparison of Public and Private School Teaching." *Teaching Community*. Monster, n.d. Web. Accessed May 9, 2017 (no link).

Reft, Jacob. *April 28 Parent Newsletter (*April 28, 2017): n. pag. *St. Ann Catholic School.* April 28, 2017. Web. Accessed May 9, 2017. Page 2 (no link).

"School Data." School Data | Missouri Department of Elementary and Secondary Education. Accessed April 15, 2017. https://dese.mo.gov/school-data.

"Science." *St. Ann Catholic School.* N.p., n.d. Web. Accessed April 4, 2017.

3.2.15 | Charter schools

"About Our Organization." The Opportunity Trust, August 29, 2022. Accessed July 9, 2023. https://theopportunitytrust.org/about/.

Davis, Chad. "Planned Charter School in St. Louis County Renews Debate over Public School Funding." STLPR, March 15, 2022. Accessed March 2023. https://news.stlpublicradio.org/education/2022-03-15/planned-charter-school-in-st-louis-county-renews-debate-over-public-school-funding.

Delaney, Ryan. "St. Louis Education Nonprofit, The Opportunity Trust, Has Plenty of Skeptics." STLPR, May 19, 2021. Accessed July 9, 2023. https://news.stlpublicradio.org/education/2021-05-12/untrusted-st-louis-ed-nonprofit-the-opportunity-trust-has-plenty-of-skeptics.

Delaney, Ryan. "St. Louis County May Get Its First Charter School." STLPR, November 20, 2020. Accessed July 9, 2023. https://news.stlpublicradio.org/education/2020-11-19/st-louis-county-may-get-its-first-charter-school.

Delaney, Ryan. "St. Louis Public Schools Will Close 8 Schools, Sparing 3." STLPR, January 12, 2021. Accessed July 9, 2023. https://news.stlpublicradio.org/education/2021-01-12/st-louis-public-schools-will-close-8-schools-sparing-3.

Erickson, Kurt. "Senate Cuts Funding for 'Controversial' St. Louis School Program." *St. Louis Post-Dispatch*, April 19, 2021. Accessed July 9, 2023. https://www.stltoday.com/news/local/education/senate-cuts-funding-for-controversial-st-louis-school-program/article_a0bd2aed-351e-538a-8699-82b758c353fc.html#tracking-source=in-article education/2022-03-15/planned-charter-school-in-st-louis-county-renews-debate-over-public-school-funding.

Gordon, Colin. "Closing Doors: Race and Opportunity in St. Louis Schools." *Dissent Magazine*, January 6, 2021. Accessed March 2023. https://www.dissentmagazine.org/online_articles/closing-doors-race-and-opportunity-in-st-louis-schools.

Robertson, Brett, education policy analyst, conversation with the author, July 14, 2023.

"What We Do." The City Fund. Accessed July 10, 2023. https://city-fund.org/what-we-do/.

3.2.16 | Empowerment centers

"2022-2023 Board of Directors (09/30/23)." Community Action Agency of St. Louis County, Inc., June 12, 2023. Accessed July 10, 2023. https://www.caastlc.org/home-2/board-of-directors/.

Google maps search "empowerment," "youth," "boys."

Niche St. Louis school district ratings, 2022-23: "2023 Best Public High Schools in St. Louis County." Niche. Accessed July 10, 2023. https://www.niche.com/k12/search/best-public-high-schools/c/st-louis-county-mo/.

IMAGE Beyond empowerment

Jan, Tracy. "Four Years after Michael Brown Was Shot, the Neighborhood Where He Was Killed Still Feels Left Behind." *The Washington Post*, June 21, 2018. Accessed July 10, 2023. https://www.washingtonpost.com/graphics/2018/business/is-racial-discrimination-influencing-corporate-investment-in-ferguson/.

3.2.17 | Higher education / Summer melt

"ACS 2020 (5-Year Estimates)." Social explorer, 2020. Accessed July 10, 2023. https://www.socialexplorer.com/tables/ACS2020_5yr/R13170318.

Addo, Koran. "Summer Is Risky Time for College-Bound Students." *St. Louis Post-Dispatch*, June 15, 2015. Accessed July 16, 2023. https://www.stltoday.com/news/local/education/summer-is-risky-time-for-college-bound-students/article_84dbb369-7c80-55e5-a239-bd5962922044.html.

"Census Bureau Releases New Educational Attainment Data." United States Census Bureau, February 24, 2022. Accessed July 16, 2023. https://www.census.gov/newsroom/press-releases/2022/educational-attainment.html.

"Cost to Attend University of Missouri St Louis." CollegeCalc. Accessed July 16, 2023. https://www.collegecalc.org/colleges/missouri/university-of-missouri-st-louis/.

"Ferguson-Florissant R-II School District." Public School Review. Accessed July 16, 2023. https://www.publicschoolreview.com/missouri/ferguson-florissant-r-ii-school-district/2912010-school-district.

3.M.01 | *Mobilize* Public schools and libraries

hooks, bell. *Teaching to Transgress: Education as the Practice of Freedom*. New York: Routledge, 1996.

3.M.02 | *Mobilize* Taxes directed at common wealth

3.M.03 | *Mobilize* School lunch

"Clayton High School." High Schools. Accessed July 16, 2023. https://high-schools.com/directory/mo/cities/clayton/clayton-high-school/290972000275/.

"Food Access Research Atlas Documentation." USDA Economic Research Service, 2022. Accessed July 2023. https://www.ers.usda.gov/data-products/food-access-research-atlas/documentation/.

"Go to the Atlas." USDA Economic Research Service, 2023. Accessed July 2023. https://www.ers.usda.gov/data-products/food-access-research-atlas/go-to-the-atlas/.

Jyoti, Diana F., Edward A. Frongillo, and Sonya J. Jones. "Food Insecurity Affects School Children's Academic Performance, Weight Gain, and Social Skills." *The Journal of Nutrition* 135, no. 12 (2005): 2831–39. https://doi.org/10.1093/jn/135.12.2831.

"Normandy High School." High Schools. Accessed July 16, 2023. https://high-schools.com/directory/mo/cities/st-louis/normandy-high-school/292265001248/.

04 Politics

4.1.01 | Governmental units

"Regional Profile." Go to East-West Gateway Council of Governments. Accessed February 2020. https://www.ewgateway.org/about-us/who-we-are/regional-profile/.

4.1.02 | Governmental multiplicity

Jones, Endsley Terrence. *Fragmented by Design: Why St. Louis Has So Many Governments*. St. Louis, MO: Palmerston & Reed Pub., 2000.

MetroMayorsSTL, website. Accessed June 2021. https://metromayorsstl.org/mayors/ (Link no longer valid).

4.1.03 | Weak-mayor government

"Episode 2: Mayor Reggie Jones (City of Dellwood) - 'Getting Stuff Done.'" Episode. St. Louis, MO: Speak Up St. Louis, 1AD. November 1, 2020. Accessed July 11, 2023. https://www.audible.com/pd/Episode-2-Mayor-Reggie-Jones-City-of-Dellwood-Getting-Stuff-Done-Podcast/B08L29V7VG?clientContext-t=135-7433837-7394224&showAuthLoginBanner=true.

"General Administration #2." Better Together Saint Louis, December 2015. https://www.bettertogetherstl.com/wp-content/uploads/2015/12/Better-Together-General-Administration-Report-2-FINAL-.pdf.

"General Administration #3." Better Together Saint Louis, January 2016. https://www.bettertogetherstl.com/wp-content/uploads/2015/12/General-Administration-Report-Study-3-Final.pdf.

Missouri Municipal League, *Forms of Government for Missouri Municipalities*. Jefferson City, MO: Missouri Municipal League, 2007.

O'Dea, Janelle, David Hunn, and Josh Renaud. "Municipal Government Salaries in the St. Louis Region." *St. Louis Post-Dispatch*, September 23, 2021. Accessed July 11, 2023. https://graphics.stltoday.com/apps/payrolls/salaries_2021/group/2/.

Salter, Jim. "The Embattled Mayor of Ferguson, Missouri Makes Just $4,200 a Year." *Business Insider*, March 14, 2015. Accessed July 11, 2023. https://www.businessinsider.com/the-embattled-mayor-of-ferguson-missouri-makes-just-4200-a-year-2015-3.

4.1.04 | City managers

"City Departments - Administration." Ferguson, MO - Official Website. Accessed July 2021. https://www.fergusoncity.com/58/Administration.

Harris, Taylor Tiamoyo. "Ferguson City Manager Resigns, This Time Permanently." *St. Louis Post-Dispatch*, January 26, 2023. Accessed July 11, 2023. https://www.stltoday.com/news/local/govt-and-politics/ferguson-city-manager-resigns-this-time-permanently/article_6bbfd770-0a4c-5a9d-9f45-f039626b8113.html.

Harris, Taylor Tiamoyo. "Ferguson's City Manager Speaks out on Why He Chose to Stay after Sudden Resignation." *St. Louis Post-Dispatch*, October 6, 2022. Accessed July 11, 2023. https://www.stltoday.com/life-entertainment/local/wellness/ferguson-s-city-manager-speaks-out-on-why-he-chose-to-stay-after-sudden-resignation/article_dabded76-f64b-5cbf-b7ba-be76178491a4.html.

Missouri Municipal League, *Forms of Government for Missouri Municipalities*. Jefferson City, MO: Missouri Municipal League, 2007.

4.1.05 | Muni maneuvers

"Ferguson Extends Contract of Jeff Blume, a Villain of DOJ Report." *St. Louis American*, February 27, 2020. Accessed July 11, 2023. https://www.stlamerican.com/news/political_eye/ferguson-extends-contract-of-jeff-blume-a-villain-of-doj-report/article_6598f7be-5906-11ea-811b-9754bcf2294b.html.

Harris, Taylor Tiamoyo. "Ferguson City Manager Resigns, This Time Permanently." *St. Louis Post-Dispatch*, January 26, 2023. Accessed July 11, 2023. https://www.stltoday.com/news/local/govt-and-politics/ferguson-city-manager-resigns-this-time-permanently/article_6bbfd770-0a4c-5a9d-9f45-f039626b8113.html.

4.1.06 | Polling places

"Ferguson Ward Map." 2023. City of Ferguson. https://www.fergusoncity.com/DocumentCenter/View/5234/Ferguson-Ward-Map.

Montes, Amaris, and Zack Avre. "How Ferguson's Black Majority Can Take Control of Their City." In These Times, November 3, 2014. Accessed July 1, 2023. https://inthesetimes.com/article/the-lesson-from-ferguson-about-why-you-should-vote.

Zoning Map - Ferguson. n.d. City of Ferguson. https://www.fergusoncity.com/DocumentCenter/View/603/Ferguson-Zoning-Map.

Ferguson city council members

"Council Members," Ferguson, MO - Official Website. Accessed July 6, 2023. https://www.fergusoncity.com/171/Council-Members.

Area of 80% or more Black population

Strether, Lambert. "Ferguson in Context on the Eve of the Grand Jury Decision." naked capitalism, November 24, 2014. Accessed July 6, 2023. https://www.nakedcapitalism.com/2014/11/ferguson-context-eve-grand-jury-decsion.html.

Sample ballot and polling place

"Polling Place and Sample Ballot Look Up." Saint Louis County Open Government, October 15, 2021. Accessed February 2023. https://data.stlouisco.com/datasets/polling-place-and-sample-ballot-look-up.

4.1.07 | Voter participation

"Ferguson in Focus." The Thurgood Marshall Institute at LDF. 2017. Accessed July 12, 2023. https://tminstituteldf.org/wp-content/uploads/2017/08/Ferguson-in-Focus_4.pdf.

"General Administration #4." Better Together Saint Louis, January 2016. https://www.bettertogetherstl.com/wp-content/uploads/2016/01/General-Administration-Study-4-Final.pdf.

4.1.08 | Mixed public-private civic sector

24:1 Initiative 2017 Impact Report, Beyond Housing. Accessed June 2018. https://www.beyondhousing.org/uploads/files/beyondhousing-impactreport-2017.pdf (Link no longer valid).

Meet the Commissioners, St. Louis Positive Change website. Accessed June 2018. https://stlpositivechange.org/about-us (Link no longer valid).

"Promise Zone Resource Brochure." St. Louis Economic Development Partnership, November 27, 2017. Accessed July 11, 2023. https://stlpartnership.com/resources/promise-zone-resource-brochure/.

Rosenbaum, Jason. "Is Smaller Better? Multitude Of Municipalities Plays Into City-County Merger Debate." STLPR, April 23, 2014. Accessed July 2023. https://news.stlpublicradio.org/government-politics-issues/2014-04-23/is-smaller-better-multitude-of-municipalities-plays-into-city-county-merger-debate.

"St. Louis Promise Zone." St. Louis Economic Development Partnership, January 18, 2023. Accessed July 11, 2023. https://stlpartnership.com/who-we-are/our-teams/st-louis-promise-zone/.

University of Missouri St. Louis, Student of Service website. Accessed June 2018. http://umsl.edu/~umslsos/partners.html (Link no longer valid).

4.2.09 | State & federal development incentives

"About the New Markets Tax Credit Coalition." New Markets Tax Credit Coalition, May 25, 2021. https://nmtccoalition.org/coalition-highlights/.

"EEZ Locations." Missouri Department of Economic Development. Accessed July 11, 2023. https://ded.mo.gov/eez-locations.

Goshorn, Julie A. "In a TIF: Why Missouri Needs Tax Increment Financing Reform." *Washington University Law Review* 77, no. 3 (1999). https://openscholarship.wustl.edu/cgi/viewcontent.cgi?article=1485&context=law_lawreview.

Heyda, Patty. "The Facade of Redevelopment." Essay. *In The Material World of Modern Segregation: St. Louis in the Long Era of Ferguson*, 277–90. St. Louis, MO: Washington University in St. Louis, 2022.

"Local Incentives." St. Louis Economic Development Partnership, September 29, 2017. Accessed July 11, 2023. https://stlpartnership.com/who-we-are/our-teams/business-development/incentives/local-incentives/.

"Missouri State Auditor's Office." The Office of Missouri State Auditor Scott Fitzpatrick. Accessed July 11, 2023. https://auditor.mo.gov/.

"New Markets Tax Credits Archives: Financing Distressed Communities." St. Louis Economic Development Partnership. Accessed July 11, 2023. https://stlpartnership.com/what-we-do/new-markets-tax-credits/.

"St. Louis Midtown 353 Redevelopment Plan." Development Strategies, November 9, 2016. Accessed July 11, 2023. https://cdn.nextstl.com/wp-content/uploads/20220627114459/SAINT-LOUIS-MIDTOWN-353-REDEVELOPMENT-PLAN.pdf.

"State Supplemental Tax Increment Financing (TIF)." Missouri Department of Economic Development. Accessed July 11, 2023. https://ded.mo.gov/programs/community/state-supplemental-tax-increment-financing.

St. Louis Economic Development Partnership, Infographic pdf. Accessed July 15, 2023. https://stlpartnership.com/wp-content/uploads/2018/07/Promise_Zone_Infographic_2018_071218.pdf.

"Tax Increment Financing (TIF)." City of St. Louis. Accessed July 11, 2023. https://www.stlouis-mo.gov/government/departments/sldc/economic-development/tax-increment-financing/index.cfm.

Wilson, Joe. "Given a Hammer: Tax Increment Financing Abuse in the St. Louis Region." *Saint Louis University Public Law Review*: Vol 34: No. 1, Article 8, (2014). https://core.ac.uk/download/pdf/234184118.pdf.

4.2.10 | Local & regional development incentives

Allen, Michael R. "Never Mind Mckee, Start Empowering Impacted Communities." *NextSTL*, June 20, 2018. Accessed July 2023. https://nextstl.com/2018/06/never-mind-mckee-start-empowering-impacted-communities/.

"Community programs," Missouri Department of Economic Development. Accessed October 2022. https://ded.mo.gov/programs/community/local-tif (Link no longer valid).

"Local Incentives." St. Louis Economic Development Partnership, September 29, 2017. Accessed July 11, 2023. https://stlpartnership.com/who-we-are/our-teams/business-development/incentives/local-incentives/.

No author, "NorthSide St. Louis Redevelopment Map," Google maps. Accessed June 2023. https://www.google.com/maps/d/viewer?mid=1Fi7wGYnsRhMDxmO6hDJ3FL6Yh-U&hl=en&ll=38.6346055986781%2C-90.22236215356445&z=14.

"St. Louis Promise Zone." St. Louis Economic Development Partnership, January 18, 2023. Accessed July 11, 2023. https://stlpartnership.com/who-we-are/our-teams/st-louis-promise-zone/.

Wallingford, Wayne, and Mike Parson, 2022 Tax Increment Financing in St. Louis. Pg 177 § (2023). https://dor.mo.gov/taxation/business/tax-types/sales-use/local-increment-financing/documents/2022_Local_Tax_Increment_Financing.pdf.

4.2.11 | Tax Increment Financing (TIF)

"Downtown Strategic Development Plan." City of Ferguson, December 2008. Accessed July 11, 2023. https://www.fergusoncity.com/DocumentCenter/View/387/Downtown-Strategic-Development-Plan-2008?bidId=.

"Ferguson in Focus." The Thurgood Marshall Institute at LDF. 2017. Accessed July 12, 2023. https://tminstituteldf.org/wp-content/uploads/2017/08/Ferguson-in-Focus_4.pdf.

Harvey, David. "The 'New' Imperialism: Accumulation by Dispossession," *Socialist Register,* 2004.

Herscher, Andrew. ""Blight," Spatial Racism, and the Demolition of the Housing Question in Detroit," *Housing After the Neoliberal Turn,* Stefan Aue, et al., eds. Spector Books, 2016.

Heyda, Patty. "Façade of Redevelopment," *Common Reader: Material World of Modern Segregation* St. Louis: Washington University, 2022.

The active creation of conditions of blight is also at play in areas of disinvestment. See, for example, on "desertification" in Kinloch, MO:

Heyda, Patty "Food Desert: Feeding the Regional Economic Imaginary," *Journal of Architectural Education* 77:2 (fall, 2023).

Johnson, Walter. *The Broken Heart of America: St. Louis and the Violent History of the United States.* New York, NY: Basic Books, 2021.

Keenoy, Ruth, and Karen Baxter. "National Register of Historic Places Multiple Property Documentation Form." St. Louis: Missouri Department of Natural Resources, October 15, 2008. Accessed July 16, 2023. https://mostateparks.com/sites/mostateparks/files/HistoricResources-Ferguson.pdf.

Metzger, Molly. "'What Is TIF?' Presentation - Team TIF St. Louis." Team TIF St. Louis. Accessed July 13, 2023. https://www.teamtifstl.com/resources/what-is-tif-presentation/.

Missouri Department of Revenue website, "Local Tax Increment Financing," n.d. Accessed October 2023. https://dor.mo.gov/taxation/business/tax-types/sales-use/local-increment-financing/.

"A St. Louisan's Guide to SLDC." Team TIF St. Louis. Accessed July 12, 2023. https://teamtifstl.com/resources/a-st-louisans-guide-to-sldc/.

IMAGE Tax Increment Financing (TIF) district edge, Kinloch, MO, historic center

Heyda, Patty. "Quality Urbanism: We Got What We Wanted but We Lost What We Had." *Conditions,* no. 5/6 (2010): 51–53.

IMAGE The writing on the wall on TIF policy

Heyda, Patty. "Quality Urbanism: We Got What We Wanted but We Lost What We Had." *Conditions,* no. 5/6 (2010): 51–53.

Heyda, Patty. "Erasure Urbanism," eds. Marrikka Trotter, Esther Choi, *Architecture is All Over.* New York, NY: Columbia Books on Architecture and the City, 2017.

4.2.12 │ Annexation

"Board Meeting Minutes." City Of Bel-Ridge. Accessed 2016. https://www.bel-ridge.us/board_meeting_minutes_and_agendas/index.php.

City of Webster Groves Finance Department. "St. Louis County Municipalities by Pool Sales Tax Designation." Webster Groves Parks and Recreation, September 1, 2022. Accessed July 16, 2023. https://wgparksandrec.com/DocumentCenter/View/11103/St-Louis-County-Sales-Tax-Pool ---City-Designation-List.

"Natural Bridge Road TIF District." The Office of Missouri State Auditor Scott Fitzpatrick, 2017. Accessed July 12, 2023. https://auditor.mo.gov/TIF/ViewTIF/5243.

Rosenbaum, Jason. "Is Smaller Better? Multitude of Municipalities Plays into City-County Merger Debate." STLPR, April 23, 2014. https://news.stlpublicradio.org/government-politics-issues/2014-04-23/is-smaller-better-multitude-of-municipalities-plays-into-city-county-merger-debate.

Snider, Patricia. "Motion Filed to Add Unincorporated Areas to Map." Village of Bel-Ridge: St. Louis County Boundary Commission, June 8, 2006. https://boundarycommission.com/wp-content/uploads/2021/02/bel-ridge-transmittal-letter.pdf.

4.2.13 │ Commission stacking

Arnstein, Sherry R. "A Ladder of Citizen Participation." *Journal of the American Planning Association* 85, no. 1 (1969, published online 2019): 24–34. https://doi.org/10.1080/01944363.2018.1559388.

"Boards and Commissions." City of St. Louis. Accessed July 2018. https://www.stlouis-mo.gov/government/boards/.

Case study: *Erasure suburbanism*

4.C.14 │ Missouri's "first Black city" / Mundane violence

Heyda, Patty. "Erasure Urbanism," eds. Marrikka Tortter, Esther Choi, *Architecture is All Over.*New York, NY: Columbia Books on Architecture and the City, 2017.

Parish, Norm. "Kinloch Protests Polling Site in Berkeley," *The St. Louis Post-Dispatch*, Metro Section, March 2, 2006, B1.

Schuessler, Ryan. "Kinloch Connection: Ferguson Fueled by Razing of Historic Black Town." *Al Jazeera America*, August 20, 2014. http://america.aljazeera.com/articles/2014/8/20/kinloch-town-blackmissouri.html.

Wright, John A. *Kinloch: Missouri's First Black City*. Chicago: Arcadia Publishing, 2000.

4.C.15 | Airport expansion / Noise mitigation / Runways

Ahmad, Ishmael. "Kinloch Sues St. Louis to Halt Home Buyouts near Lambert; Redevelopment Deal Was Broken, Community Says," *The St. Louis American*, March 9–15, 2000. Accessed 2012. http://www.awj-law.com/news.php?article=2.

Heyda, Patty. "Erasure Urbanism," eds. Marrikka Tortter, Esther Choi, *Architecture is All Over*. New York, NY: Columbia Books on Architecture and the City, 2017.

4.C.16 | Airline hub

Dummit, Ralph. "County Tries to Block Expansion of Lambert Field Airport in St. Louis, Missouri," *St. Louis Post-Dispatch*, October 2, 1998. http://www.nonoise.org/news/1998/sep27.htm.

Goldsmith, Steve. *Missouri Town Files Suit to Overturn Expansion at Lambert-St. Louis International Airport,* The Bond Buyer, October 2, 1998. https://www.nonoise.org/news/1998/sep27.htm.

Mihalopoulos, Dan. "Economic Developers See Benefits if Missouri's Lambert Field Expands," *St. Louis Post-Dispatch*, October 1, 1998. https://www.nonoise.org/news/1998/sep27.htm.

Schlinkmann, Mark. *Bridgeton Files Suit After FAA OK's Lambert Expansion; Various Factions Speak Out,* The Bond Buyer, October 1, 1998. http://www.nonoise.org/news/1998/sep27.htm.

Schoenewies, Jamie Desy. 56 Houses Left, October 12, 2007. Accessed 2015. https://56housesleft.com/.

United States Department of Transportation Federal Aviation Administration, Environmental Impact Statement: Record of Decision; Lambert–St. Louis International Airport; City of St. Louis, St. Louis County, Missouri (September 30, 1998): 22.

Woodburn, Amber. "Investigating Neighborhood Change in Airport-Adjacent Communities in Multiairport Regions, 1970–2010." *Transportation Research Record: Journal of the Transportation Research Board* 2626, no. 1 (2017): 1–8. https://doi.org/10.3141/2626-01.

Flight operations per year

Lambert Masterplan Draft Aviation Activity Forecasts PDF, 2009. Accessed in 2010. Link no longer available.

Missouri government House and Senate past legislation database

"Bills from 1995 to 2011," Missouri House of Representatives. Accessed October 2010. https://house.mo.gov/.

Missouri Senate, SB 100 Creates a tax credit for contributions to developmental disability care providers and modifies provisions of the residential treatment agency tax credit program § (2011). https://www.senate.mo.gov/11info/BTS_Web/Bill.aspx?SessionType=R&BillID=4074446.

"Past Session Information." Missouri Senate 2022. Accessed July 12, 2023. https://www.senate.mo.gov/22web/pastsessions/.

IMAGE Suburban subtraction

Easterling, Keller, Nikolaus Hirsch, and Markus Miessen. *Subtraction*. Berlin: Sternberg Press, 2014.

Schoenewies, Jamie Desy. "Pandemics and Setbacks." 56 Houses Left, October 12, 2007. Accessed 2015. https://56housesleft.com/.

4.C.17 | Regional investment

"Keep the Momentum Building." NorthPark: NorthPark, 2011. Accessed July 2023. http://www.northparkstl.com/links/files/keep_the_momentum_building.pdf.

"Kinloch, Missouri." City Data. Accessed July 12, 2023. https://www.city-data.com/city/Kinloch-Missouri.html.

"Northpark Advantage." NorthPark. Accessed June 22, 2022. http://www.northparkstl.com/.

"Northpark Incentives." NorthPark. Accessed 2017. http://www.northparkstl.com/incentives.

Wallingford, Wayne, and Mike Parson, 2022 Tax Increment Financing in St. Louis. Pg 177 § (2023). https://dor.mo.gov/taxation/business/tax-types/sales-use/local-increment-financing/documents/2022_Local_Tax_Increment_Financing.pdf.

2020 population figure

Harvey, David, "The New Imperialism: Accumulation by Dispossession," *The Socialist Register,* 2004.

"Kinloch, Missouri Population." World Population Review. Accessed July 2020. https://worldpopulationreview.com/us-cities/kinloch-mo-population.

IMAGE Accumulation vs. Congregation

Lipsitz, G. "The Racialization of Space and the Spatialization of Race: Theorizing the Hidden Architecture of Landscape." *Landscape Journal* 26, no. 1 (2007): 10–23. https://doi.org/10.3368/lj.26.1.10.

4.C.18 | Big box / basements

Heyda, Patty. "Erasure Urbanism," eds. Marrikka Tortter, Esther Choi, *Architecture is All Over.* New York, NY: Columbia Books on Architecture and the City, 2017.

Heyda, Patty "Food Desert: Feeding the Regional Economic Imaginary," *Journal of Architectural Education* 77:2 (fall, 2023).

"Keep the Momentum Building." North Park: North Park, 2011. Accessed July 2023. http://www.northparkstl.com/links/files/keep_the_momentum_building.pdf.

"Northpark Advantage." North Park. Accessed June 22, 2022. http://www.northparkstl.com/.

"Northpark Incentives." North Park. Accessed 2017. http://www.northparkstl.com/incentives.

4.C.19 | Food desert

Brennan, Vince, "Schnucks keeps the community in mind with Kinloch distribution center," *St. Louis Business Journal*, Sep 21, 2017. Accessed July 15, 2023. https://www.bizjournals.com/stlouis/news/2017/09/21/schnucks-keeps-the-community-in-mind-with-kinloch.html.

Cloud, Kristen. "Schnucks Building New DC in Kinloch, Missouri." The Shelby Report, May 28, 2015. Accessed December 2022. https://www.theshelbyreport.com/2015/05/28/schnucks-building-new-dc-in-kinloch-missouri/.

Hampel, Paul. "Urban Farmers Working Vacant Kinloch Property Get Surprise When Land's Rightful Owner Shows Up." *St. Louis Post Dispatch*, February 9, 2015. Accessed December 2022. https://www.stltoday.com/news/local/metro/urban-farmers-working-vacant-kinloch-property-get-surprise-when-lands-rightful-owner-shows-up/article_a69bbb45-2cc1-542d-b7c0-51e6205c8e2c.html.

Heyda, Patty "Food Desert: Feeding the Regional Economic Imaginary," *Journal of Architectural Education* 77:2 (fall, 2023).

"Schnucks Set to Begin Construction for New Distribution Center." Progressive Grocer, May 6, 2015. Accessed December 2022. https://progressivegrocer.com/schnucks-set-begin-construction-new-distribution-center.

"United States Department of Agriculture Food Access Research Atlas." USDA Economic Research Service. 2019. Accessed December 2022. https://www.ers.usda.gov/data-products/food-access-research-atlas/go-to-the-atlas/.

Additional sources for case study maps 4.C.14–4.C.19

History and development

Barbour, Clay. "County Seeks Expansion of Business Park Project." *St. Louis Post-Dispatch*, August 5, 2005.

Census profile: Kinloch, MO. Census Reporter. Accessed 2021. http://censusreporter.org/profiles/16000US2938972-kinloch-mo/.

City of Kinloch, Missouri. Accessed July 13, 2023. https://kinlochmo.org/.

Hamilton, Keegan. "A Video Tour of Kinloch, the Saddest City in St. Louis County." *Riverfront Times*, March 23, 2010. https://www.riverfronttimes.com/news/a-video-tour-of-kinloch-the-saddest-city-in-st-louis-county-2579924.

"Hazelwood Logistics Center." St. Louis Regional Freightway, 2015. Accessed July 13, 2013. https://www.thefreightway.com/portfolio/hazelwood-logistics-park/.

Heyda, Patty. "Erasure Urbanism," eds. Marrikka Tortter, Esther Choi, *Architecture is All Over*. New York: Columbia Books on Architecture and the City, 2017.

Heyda, Patty. "Quality Urbanism: We Got What We Wanted but We Lost What We Had." *Conditions*, no. 5/6 (2010): 51–53.

Ishmael, Ahmad, "Kinloch Sues St. Louis to Halt Home Buyouts near Lambert; Redevelopment Deal Was Broken, Community Says," *The St. Louis American*, March 9–15, 2000.

"Keep the Momentum Building." NorthPark: NorthPark, 2011. Accessed July 2023. http://www.northparkstl.com/links/files/keep_the_momentum_building.pdf.

Schuessler, Ryan. "Kinloch Connection: Ferguson Fueled by Razing of Historic Black Town." *Al Jazeera America,* August 20, 2014. http://america.aljazeera.com/articles/2014/8/20/kinloch-town-blackmissouri.html.

St. Louis Lambert International Airport website, Noise Mitigation and Land Management Section, Acoustical Area map (2005). The documents have since been removed from the website; Accessed September 2009. http://www.lambert-stlouis.com/flystl/about-lambert/noise-land/.

St. Louis Lambert International Airport website, Noise Mitigation and Land Management Section, Eligible Sound Mitigation Areas map (1999). The documents have since been removed from the website; Accessed September 2009. http://www.lambert-stlouis.com/flystl/about-lambert/noise-land/.

St. Louis Lambert International Airport website, "Baseline Mitigation Eligibility Areas" map (September 12, 2005). The documents have since been removed from the website. Accessed September 2009.

Steinbach, David, Lynn Schenck, and David Branding. "Industrial & Office Build to Suits." NorthPark, 2012. https://images4.loopnet.com/d2/-c-vp_3WtjefR4Y3z4EXYjCI2QpVhuyim-huLZ7d5l3A/document.pdf.

US States News, "Gov. Blunt Announces State Tax Credits for NorthPark Redevelopment," *The Missouri Department of Economic Development News Release*, November 13, 2006.

Woodson, Alana Marie. *The Kinloch Doc*, 2021.

Woodson, Alana Marie. *The Kinloch Doc*, 2018. https://www.facebook.com/thekinlochdoc/videos/the-kinloch-doc-official-short/2321713108042867/.

Wright, Gwendolyn. *Through the Eyes of a Child Oral History Project Transcripts*. Missouri Historical Society Library and Research Center. Kinloch, 1998.

Wright, John A. *Kinloch: Missouri's First Black City*. Chicago: Arcadia Publishing, 2000.

IMAGE Cultivation

Hampel, Paul. "Urban Farmers Working Vacant Kinloch Property Get Surprise When Land's Rightful Owner Shows Up." *St. Louis Post Dispatch*, February 9, 2015. Accessed December 2022. https://www.stltoday.com/news/local/metro/urban-farmers-working-vacant-kinloch-property-get-surprise-when-lands-rightful-owner-shows-up/article_a69bbb45-2cc1-542d-b7c0-51e6205c8e2c.html.

Heyda, Patty. "Food Desert: Feeding the Regional Economic Imaginary." *Journal of Architectural Education* 77: 2 (fall 2023).

IMAGE Reclaim Space

Daher, Natalie. "Project Backboard Turns Urban Basketball Courts into Public Art." Bloomberg.com, February 7, 2018. Accessed July 13, 2023. https://www.bloomberg.com/news/articles/2018-02-07/project-backboard-turns-urban-basketball-courts-into-public-art.

Hayden, Dolores. *The Power of Place: Urban Landscapes as Public History*. Cambridge: MIT Press, 1997.

4.M.01 | *Mobilize* Fellowship / Local planning

Heyda, Patty. "Dispatch from the Moral Border." *ThinkSpace: Moral Borders Competition and Exhibition*. Zagreb, 2011.

4.3.20 | Fortune 500

Fortune's 500 Companies, Accessed June 2018. http://fortune.com/fortune500/list/filtered?statename=Missouri (Link no longer valid).

4.3.21 | Concentrated wealth

"AQI Calculator." AirNow. Accessed July 13, 2023. https://airnow.gov/index.cfm?action=airnow.calculator.

City Data. 2016. Accessed July 12, 2023. https://www.city-data.com/city/.

Community Facts, Census.gov, Accessed June 2018. https://factfinder.census.gov/faces/nav/jsf/pages/community_facts.xhtml (Link no longer valid).

Cool Valley profile, DataUSA, Accessed June 2018. https://datausa.io/profile/geo/cool-valley-mo/ PST045218 (Link no longer valid).

"Crime in the U.S. 2010." FBI, 2010. https://ucr.fbi.gov/crime-in-the-u.s/2010/crime-in-the-u.s.-2010/tables/table-8/10tbl08mo.xls.

"Explore Air Pollution in Missouri." America's Health Rankings. Accessed July 13, 2023. https://www.americashealthrankings.org/explore/annual/measure/air/state/MO.

"Ferguson City, Missouri; United States." U.S. Census Bureau, July 1, 2022. https://www.census.gov/quickfacts/fact/table/fergusoncitymissouri,US/PST045222.

Johnson, Walter. "Ferguson's Fortune 500 Company." *The Atlantic*, April 27, 2015. Accessed 2018. https://www.theatlantic.com/politics/archive/2015/04/fergusons-fortune-500-company/390492/.

4.3.22 | Company town

"Emerson Company History." Emerson US. Accessed July 13, 2023. https://www.emerson.com/en-us/about-us/company-history.

Johnson, Walter. "Ferguson's Fortune 500 Company." *The Atlantic*, April 27, 2015. Accessed 2018. https://www.theatlantic.com/politics/archive/2015/04/fergusons-fortune-500-company/390492/.

Poe, Ryan. "Walmart Black Friday Jubilee." LAWCHA, November 16, 2012. Accessed June 27, 2022. https://www.lawcha.org/2012/11/16/walmart-black-friday-jubilee/.

Rubbelke, Nathan. "Emerson's Monser on Bolstering the Region's STEM Education." *St. Louis Business Journal,* June 21, 2018. https://www.bizjournals.com/stlouis/news/2018/06/21/emersons-monser-on-bolstering-the-region-s-stem.html.

Sassen, Saskia. *The Global City*. Princeton, NJ: Princeton Univ. Press, 2001.

4.3.23 | Jobs

Community Facts, Berkeley, MO, Census.gov, Accessed October 2016. https://factfinder.census.gov/faces/nav/jsf/pages/community_facts.xhtml (Link no longer valid).

Salary information: www.payscale.com/. Accessed Nov 13, 2018.

Boeing Industries website. Accessed June 2018. https://www.boeing.com/features/2014/09/bds-st-louis-09-25-14.page (Link no longer valid).

"Boeing in Brief." The Boeing Company. Accessed July 16, 2023. https://www.boeing.com/company/general-info/.

4.3.24 | Corporate land use

Barker, Jacob. "Boeing: St. Louis Reimagines Aerospace for 75 Years and Counting." Aviation Pros, January 27, 2021. http://boeing.com/features/2014/09/bds-st-louis-09-25-14.page.

St. Louis Lambert International Airport website, "Future (2015) NEM/NCP Noise Exposure Contour," map. https://www.flystl.com/uploads/documents/noise-program/2015-STL-Noise-Contours-Map.pdf (The link is no longer valid).

2021 Boeing revenue

"Boeing Revenue 2010-2023: BA." Macrotrends. Accessed July 2021. https://www.macrotrends.net/stocks/charts/BA/boeing/revenue.

4.3.25 | Property tax assessment / Boeing and Express Scripts Corporate campuses

City of Berkeley, Comprehensive Annual Financial Report, General Revenue, 2018. Accessed 2018. https://www.berkeleymo.us/.

St. Louis County Open Data Property Look up GIS Web Application. Accessed 2018. https://data-stlcogis.opendata.arcgis.com/apps/e70f8f1814a34cd7bf8f6766bd950c68/explore.

St. Louis County Assessor. Accessed 2018. https://stlouiscounty-mo.gov/st-louis-county-government/county-assessor/.

4.3.26 | Property tax assessment / Emerson Corporate campus

City of Ferguson, Missouri, Comprehensive Annual Financial Report, 2018 Accessed 2018.

City of Ferguson, Missouri, Annual Operating Budget Fiscal Year 2017 – 2018. Accessed 2018. http://www.fergusoncity.com/DocumentCenter/View/2854/2018-COFM-Budget-Main-SMALL?bidId=.

City of Ferguson, Missouri, Comprehensive Annual Financial Report for the Year Ended June 30, 2017. Accessed 2018. https://www.fergusoncity.com/Archive/ViewFile/Item/822.

City of Ferguson, Missouri, "CITY OF FERGUSON MISSOURI ANNUAL OPERATING BUDGET FISCAL YEAR 2018 - 2019." City of Ferguson, 2018. https://www.fergusoncity.com/DocumentCenter/View/3118/FY2019-FINAL-BUDGET.

Johnson, Walter. "Ferguson's Fortune 500 Company." *The Atlantic*, April 27, 2015. Accessed 2018. https://www.theatlantic.com/politics/archive/2015/04/fergusons-fortune-500-company/390492/.

St. Louis County Open Data Property Look up GIS Web Application. Accessed 2017. https://data-stlcogis.opendata.arcgis.com/apps/e70f8f1814a34cd7bf8f6766bd950c68/explore.

St. Louis County Assessor. Accessed 2018. https://stlouiscounty-mo.gov/st-louis-county-government/county-assessor/.

4.3.27 | Philanthropy

Berger, Henry. "Ferguson and Emerson Electric." LAWCHA, December 19, 2014. Accessed July 13, 2023. https://www.lawcha.org/2014/12/19/ferguson-emerson-electric-paradox-imperial-reach/.

Buchanan, Larry, Ford Fessenden, K.K. Rebecca Lai, Haeyoun Park, Alicia Parlapiano, et al., "What Happened in Ferguson?" *The New York Times*, August 13, 2014. Accessed July 13, 2023. https://www.nytimes.com/interactive/2014/08/13/us/ferguson-missouri-town-under-siege-after-police-shooting.html.

Horrigan, Kevin. "Horrigan: Ferguson's Global Giant, and Those Left Behind." *St. Louis Post-Dispatch*, August 24, 2014. Accessed July 13, 2023. https://www.stltoday.com/opinion/columnists/horrigan-fergusons-global-giant-and-those-left-behind/article_54cf78a2-c735-5488-8fcd-c366ee36e132.html.

Jan, Tracy. "Four Years after Michael Brown Was Shot, the Neighborhood Where He Was Killed Still Feels Left Behind." *The Washington Post*, June 21, 2018. Accessed July 13, 2023. https://www.washingtonpost.com/graphics/2018/business/is-racial-discrimination-influencing-corporate-investment-in-ferguson/.

Johnson, Walter. "Ferguson's Fortune 500 Company." *The Atlantic*, April 27, 2015. Accessed 2018. https://www.theatlantic.com/politics/archive/2015/04/fergusons-fortune-500-company/390492/.

Kukuljan, Steph. "Emerson CEO on Ferguson: 'This Was a Wake-up Call.'" *St. Louis Business Journal*, August 8, 2017. Accessed July 13, 2023. https://www.bizjournals.com/stlouis/news/2017/08/09/emerson-ceo-on-ferguson-this-was-a-wake-up-call.html.

4.3.28 | Nonprofit index: Better Together (2021)

"Home." Better Together Saint Louis. Accessed 2021. https://www.bettertogetherstl.com/.

Hunn, David. "Better Together Pulls St. Louis City-County Merger Proposal." *St. Louis Post-Dispatch*, May 7, 2019. Accessed July 13, 2023. https://www.stltoday.com/news/local/govt-and-politics/better-together-pulls-st-louis-city--county-merger-proposal/article_c71a51d2-998b-5e95-9926-ad3707671690.html.

4.3.29 | Nonprofit index: Forward Through Ferguson (2022)

"A Path Towards Racial Equity." Forward Through Ferguson. Accessed 2022. https://forwardthroughferguson.org/report/executive-summary/next-steps-2/.

"Next Steps." Forward Through Ferguson. Accessed 2022. https://forwardthroughferguson.org/report/executive-summary/next-steps-2/.

4.3.30 | Nonprofit index: Greater St. Louis Inc. (2021)

Greater St. Louis, Inc. website, Accessed 2021: https://www.greaterstlinc.com/leadership/ (Link no longer valid).

4.3.31 | Nonprofit index: Show Me Institute (2021)

"2020 Annual Report - Show-ME Institute." Show Me Institute, 2020. Accessed 2021. https://showmeinstitute.org/wp-content/uploads/2021/07/2020-Annual-Report-Elec.pdf.

"Board of Directors: Show-ME Institute." Show Me Institute, January 7, 2021. Accessed 2021. https://showmeinstitute.org/show-me-institute-board-of-directors/.

4.3.32 | Nonprofit index: United Way of Greater St. Louis (2021)

"2020 Annual Report to the Community." United Way of Greater St. Louis, 2020. Accessed 2021. https://helpingpeople.org/wp-content/uploads/2021/01/2020-Annual-Report_v7_2.pdf.

"Leadership Team & Board of Directors." United Way of Greater St. Louis. Accessed 2021. https://helpingpeople.org/who-we-are/board-of-directors/.

4.3.33 | Nonprofit index: Urban League of Metropolitan St. Louis (2021)

"Board of Directors." Urban League of Metropolitan St. Louis. Accessed 2021. https://www.ulstl.com/board-of-directors.html.

4.M.02 | *Mobilize* Nonprofits that rebuild root systems of democracy

"Freedom Requires Action." Action St. Louis. Accessed July 14, 2021. https://actionstl.org/.

4.M.03 | *Mobilize* Nonprofits that hold power accountable

"Board of Directors." ArchCity Defenders, Accessed 2021. https://www.archcitydefenders.org/about-us/board-of-directors/.

05 Justice

5.1.01 | Police patrols

Bose, Richard. "As Wealth and Residents Flee, St. Louis County Munis Turn to Fines and Fees." *NextSTL*, November 10, 2014. Accessed July 13, 2023. https://nextstl.com/2014/11/wealth-residents-flee-st-louis-county-munis-turn-fines-fees/.

5.1.02 | Municipal courts

Freivogel, William H. "St. Louis-Area Lawyers Are Still Trying to Fix the 'Muni Court Shuffle.'" *St. Louis National Public Radio* (STL NPR), August 9, 2016. Accessed 2023. https://news.stlpublicradio.org/government-politics-issues/2016-08-09/st-louis-area-lawyers-are-still-trying-to-fix-the-muni-court-shuffle.

Harvey, Thomas, Sophia Keskey, John McAnnar, Michael-John Voss, Megan Conn, and Sean Janda. *ArchCity Defenders: Municipal Courts White Paper*. St. Louis: ArchCity Defenders, 2014. Accessed 2016. https://www.archcitydefenders.org/wp-content/uploads/2019/03/ArchCity-Defenders-Municipal-Courts-Whitepaper.pdf.

5.1.03 | Municipal borders

5.1.04 | Lawyer doubling

"Missouri Courts Home." Missouri Courts Judicial Branch of Government. Accessed 2016. https://www.courts.mo.gov/.

"Missouri Volunteer Movement." Facebook. Accessed 2016. https://www.facebook.com/missourivolunteermovement/.

IMAGE #UnWarranted

Harvey, Thomas, and Kim Norwood. "St. Louis County Municipal Courts, For-Profit Policing, and the Road to Reforms." Essay. *In Ferguson's Fault Lines: The Race Quake That Rocked a Nation /* Edited by Kimberly Jade Norwood, edited by Brendan Roediger. American Bar Association, Section of State and Local Government Law, 2016.

5.1.05 | The muni shuffle

Balko, Radley. "Opinion | How Municipalities in St. Louis County, Mo., Profit from Poverty." *The Washington Post*, September 4, 2014. Accessed 2016. https://www.washingtonpost.com/news/the-watch/wp/2014/09/03/how-st-louis-county-missouri-profits-from-poverty/.

Bolden, Nicole. "Debtors Prisons Are Illegal in America. Missouri Locked Me up in One Anyway." *The Guardian*, February 12, 2015. Accessed July 2023. https://www.theguardian.com/commentisfree/2015/feb/12/debtors-prisons-illegal-america-ferguson-missouri-incarcerated.

Case: 4:16-cv-01693 Doc. #: 1. *The City of Florissant vs. Thomas Baker, Sean Bailey, Nicole Bolden, Allison Nelson, Meredith Walker*. Courthouse News, October 31, 2016. Accessed July 2023. https://www.courthousenews.com/wp-content/uploads/2017/12/DebtorComplaint.pdf.

Heyda, Patty. Conversation with Nicole Bolden, April 21, 2023.

Sources

5.1.06 | Traffic stops

"About the Data." *The Stanford Open Policing Project.* Accessed 2021. https://openpolicing.stanford.edu/data/.

"Justice Department Announces Findings of Two Civil Rights Investigations in Ferguson, Missouri." Office of Public Affairs, March 4, 2015. Accessed July 2023. https://www.justice.gov/opa/pr/justice-department-announces-findings-two-civil-rights-investigations-ferguson-missouri.

"U.S. Police Traffic Stop Data by City & State 2020 V4 - State of Missouri." Stanford Libraries. Accessed 2021. https://searchworks.stanford.edu/view/yg821jf8611.

5.1.07 | Pretrial rights

"Pre-trial arrest" visual, Prison Policy Initiative, Accessed April 2020. https://www.prisonpolicy.org/.

Pretrial Justice Institute, Glossary of Terms and Phrases Relating to Bail and the Pretrial Release or Detention Decision, PDF, 2015. Accessed April 2020.

"ProSeGuides," ArchCityDefenders. Accessed April 2020. https://www.prosestl.org/courts-jails-police-guides.

5.1.08 | Public safety

Eagle, Haley, Ellie Zimmerman and Ethan Chiang. Interviews with Jocelyn Garner, Washington University, 2019.

Heyda, Patty. Conversation with Jocelyn Garner, May 2023.

"Liberty and Justice for All." ArchCity Defenders, Accessed 2021. https://www.archcitydefenders.org/

5.2.09 | Health insurance

"Health Data Map." PLACES: Local Data for Better Health. Accessed July 14, 2023. https://experience.arcgis.com/experience/22c7182a162d45788dd52a2362f8ed65.

Rep. *A Report on the Health and Well-Being of African Americans in St. Louis and Why It Matters for Everyone.* Washington University and Saint Louis University, May 30, 2014. Accessed 2018. https://forthesakeofall.files.wordpress.com/2014/05/for-the-sake-of-all-report.pdf.

St. Louis Community College Workforce Solutions Group. *2021 State of the St. Louis Workforce.* Accessed December 11, 2023. https://stlcc.edu/docs/st-louis-workforce/state-of-st-louis-workforce-report-2021.pdf.

Tutlam, NT, Kelsey, D, Hutti, E , Adams, C, and Wang, E. Rep. *Leading Causes of Death Profile, St. Louis County Missouri.* Chronic Disease Epidemiology (CDE) program profile, no 13. St. Louis County, MO: Department of Public Health. October 2021. Accessed 2022. https://stlouiscountymo.gov/st-louis-county-departments/public-health/health-data-and-statistics/chronic-disease-reports/leading-causes-of-death/leading-causes-of-death-report-2020/.

Life expectancy sources

"Explore Census Data." United States Census Bureau. Accessed July 14, 2023. https://data.census.gov/cedsci/.

"Life Expectancy." Missouri Department of Health & Senior Services. Accessed July 14, 2023. https://health.mo.gov/data/lifeexpectancy/.

"Life Expectancy 2018–2020." Think Health St. Louis. Accessed July 14, 2023. http://www.thinkhealthstl.org/indicators/index/view?indicatorId=8195&localeId=1649.

"U.S. Life Expectancy at Birth by State and Census Tract - 2010-2015." Centers for Disease Control and Prevention. Accessed July 14, 2023. https://data.cdc.gov/NCHS/U-S-Life-Expectancy-at-Birth-by-State-and-Census-T/5h56-n989.

"U.S. Life Expectancy at Birth by State and Census Tract - 2010-2015." Centers for Disease Control and Prevention. Accessed July 14, 2023. https://www.cdc.gov/nchs/data-visualization/life-expectancy/index.html.

Causes of Death

Benchaabane, Nassim. "Covid-19 Third Leading Cause of Death in St. Louis County in 2020, Report Says." *St. Louis Post-Dispatch*, October 5, 2021. Accessed July 14, 2023. https://www.stltoday.com/lifestyles/health-med-fit/coronavirus/covid-19-third-leading-cause-of-death-in-st-louis-county-in-2020-report-says/article_1f143450-5207-5283-b856-597102d0d982.html.

"Leading causes of Death Profile." St. Louis County. Accessed July 14, 2023. https://st.stlouiscountymo.gov/st-louis-county-departments/public-health/health-data-and-statistics/chronic-disease-reports/leading-causes-of-death/leading-causes-of-death-report-2020/.

5.2.10 | Public trust

COVID

"Leading causes of Death Profile." St. Louis County. Accessed October 2021. https://st.stlouiscountymo.gov/st-louis-county-departments/public-health/health-data-and-statistics/chronic-disease-reports/leading-causes-of-death/leading-causes-of-death-report-2020/.

Tutlam, NT, Kelsey, D, Hutti, E , Adams, C, and Wang, E. Rep. *Leading Causes of Death Profile, St. Louis County Missouri*. Chronic Disease Epidemiology (CDE) program profile, no 13. St. Louis County, MO: Department of Public Health. October 2021. Accessed 2022. https://stlouiscountymo.gov/st-louis-county-departments/public-health/health-data-and-statistics/chronic-disease-reports/leading-causes-of-death/leading-causes-of-death-report-2020/.

Vasquez Reyes, Maritza. "The Disproportional Impact of Covid-19 on African Americans." Health and Human Rights Journal, December 2020. 22(2): 299–307. https://www.ncbi.nlm.nih.gov/pmc/articles/PMC7762908/.

IMAGE Waiting for a shot

5.2.11 | Health / food

"Health Data Map." PLACES: Local Data for Better Health. Accessed July 14, 2023. https://experience.arcgis.com/experience/22c7182a162d45788dd52a2362f8ed65.

McDonald's

Cutolo, Morgan. "Here's Why All Sizes of McDonald's Soft Drinks Are Only $1." *Reader's Digest*, July 16, 2021. Accessed July 16, 2023. https://www.rd.com/article/mcdonalds-dollar-soft-drinks/.

Jones, David R. "Supersized Sugary Drinks Target the Poor." Community Service Society of New York, July 26, 2012. Accessed December 2022. https://www.cssny.org/news/entry/supersized-sugary-drinks-target-the-poor.

5.3.12 | Land use

"Living near Highways and Air Pollution." American Lung Association. Accessed July 14, 2023. https://www.lung.org/clean-air/outdoors/who-is-at-risk/highways.

Particulate matter (2018 data)

"EPA's Environmental Justice Screening and Mapping Tool (Version 2.2)." Environmental Protection Agency. Accessed July 14, 2023. https://ejscreen.epa.gov/mapper/.

The Nature Conservancy in Missouri. "The St. Louis Ecourban Assessment." The Nature Conservancy, October 26, 2021. Accessed July 14, 2023. https://storymaps.arcgis.com/stories/1fa2d6b75d8740cd82dd0583bf44833a.

"Overview of Environmental Indicators in EJScreen." Environmental Protection Agency. Accessed July 14, 2023. https://www.epa.gov/ejscreen/overview-environmental-indicators-ejscreen.

"Particulate Matter (PM) Basics." Environmental Protection Agency. Accessed July 14, 2023. https://www.epa.gov/pm-pollution/particulate-matter-pm-basics.

"Map of Power Plants in Missouri." PowerPlant Maps. Accessed January 24, 2024. https://www.powerplantmaps.com/Missouri.html

5.3.13 | Air use

St. Louis Lambert International Airport, Lambert Workshop, "14 CFR Part 150 Study, West Flow Radar Tracks" and "14 CFR Part 150 Study, East Flow Radar Tracks" maps (2010). The documents have since been removed from the website. Accessed December 2010.

5.3.14 | Commercialized floodplain

Barker, Jacob. "Levee Districts, Many Controlled by One Law Firm, Charge Millions to Taxpayers. and Bills Keep Rising." *St. Louis Post-Dispatch*, November 22, 2020. Accessed July 14, 2023. https://www.stltoday.com/business/local/levee-districts-many-controlled-by-one-law-firm-charge-millions-to-taxpayers-and-bills-keep/article_9fb024f0-c785-5ad8-aae4-d9bf37d5c72f.html.

Prairie duPont and Fish Lake

Hoelscher, Gary, and Bryan Martindale. "PRAIRIE DU PONT LEVEE REHABILITATION INITIATIVE." Illinois Floods, 2009. Accessed July 14, 2023. https://www.illinoisfloods.org/content/documents/hec_leveemodeling.pdf.

MESD 500 years

"About Us." MESD Online. Accessed July 14, 2023. http://mesdonline.org/about_mesd/index.php.

Chain of Rocks 500 years

Petersen, Mike. "Corps of Engineers Completes Full Restoration of Chain of Rocks Levee." US Army Corps of Engineers, March 23, 2015. Accessed July 14, 2023. https://www.mvs.usace.army.mil/Media/News-Releases/Article/581222/corps-of-engineers-completes-full-restoration-of-chain-of-rocks-levee/.

Wood River 100 years

"Impaired Waters and Total Maximum Daily Loads (TMDL) GIS Viewer." Missouri Department of Natural Resources. Accessed July 14, 2023. https://modnr.maps.arcgis.com/apps/webappviewer/index.html?id=35beafa2d4614f18b1857ba574a8d4a4.

Rep. *2022 Annual Water Quality Report, St. Louis County / St. Charles County.* Missouri American Water, 2022. Accessed July 14, 2023. https://www.amwater.com/ccr/stlouisregion.pdf.

Wood River Drainage and Levee District. Accessed 2021. https://wrleveedist.org/public-notices/about-us/.

5.3.15 | Deregulation

Impaired Waters and Total Maximum Daily Loads (TMDL) Viewer

"Impaired Waters and Total Maximum Daily Loads (TMDL) GIS Viewer." Missouri Department of Natural Resources. Accessed July 14, 2023. https://modnr.maps.arcgis.com/apps/webappviewer/index.html?id=35beafa2d4614f18b1857ba574a8d4a4.

Gustafson, Bret. "Coal Ash in the Missouri River Flood Plain Is a Bad Idea." St. Louis Post-Dispatch, March 4, 2019. Accessed 2019. https://www.stltoday.com/opinion/columnists/coal-ash-in-the-missouri-river-flood-plain-is-a-bad-idea/article_76ea25b8-72e9-5398-b6e3-94c0f26429c8.html.

St. Louis Metropolitan Sewer District GIS sewer data, Washington University Libraries Geospatial Data Collection (2014).

IMAGE Public health

5.3.16 | Externalized costs

Agency for Toxic Substances and Disease Registry, Evaluation of Community Exposures Related to Coldwater Creek St Louis Airport/Hazelwood Interim Storage Site (HISS)/Futura Coatings NPL Site North St Louis County, Missouri (n.d.). Report, Accessed July 12, 2023. https://coldwatercreekfacts.com/wp-content/uploads/2022/10/St_Louis_Airport_Site_Hazelwood_InterimSto_PHA-508-1.pdf.

Cammisa, Rebecca. *Atomic Homefront*, 2017. Accessed July 2023. https://www.atomichomefront.film/.

Coldwater Creek-2015: 2725 Reported Illnesses from Survey Respondents: North St. Louis County. n.d. *Just Moms St. Louis West Lake Landfill.* Accessed January 29, 2016. http://www.stlradwastelegacy.com/north-county-coldwater-creeksites/coldwatercreek-2015-2725_reportedcases/.

"Coldwater Creek (North County)." Just Moms St. Louis West Lake Landfill. Accessed July 14, 2023. http://www.stlradwastelegacy.com/north-county-coldwater-creeksites/.

Coldwater Creek Factsheet, 2015. http://www.stlradwastelegacy.com/north-county-coldwater-creeksites/.

"Damn Lies." The First Secret City, July 4, 2017. Accessed July 14, 2023. https://firstsecretcity.com/tag/slaps/.

Formerly Utilized Remedial Action Program (FUSRAP). Missouri Department of Natural Resources. (n.d.). https://dnr.mo.gov/env/hwp/fedfac/fusrap/index.html. (Link not active).

Freshwater, Lori. "Casualties of War." *Earth Island Journal*, 2016. https://www.earthisland.org/journal/index.php/magazine/entry/casualties_of_war/.

Friedman, Ryan, and Kayla Hannon. "Recap: ENVIRONMENTAL JUSTICE WITH JUST MOMS STL." Washington University ProSPER, May 15, 2022. Accessed July 14, 2023. https://sites.wustl.edu/prosper/recap-environmental-justice-with-just-moms-stl/.

Hartmann, Ray. "We Wrote about Poisons in Coldwater Creek 37 Years Ago. Guess What the Feds Just Confirmed?" Riverfront Times, May 15, 2019. Accessed July 14, 2023. https://www.riverfronttimes.com/stlouis/we-wrote-about-poisons-in-coldwater-creek-37-years-ago-guess-what-the-feds-just-confirmed/Content?oid=31592561.

Kite, Allison. "Records reveal 75 years of government downplaying, ignoring risks of St. Louis radioactive waste," *Missouri Independent*, July 12, 2023. Accessed July 2023. https://missouriindependent.com/2023/07/12/st-louis-radioactive-waste-records/.

North County Inc. (2017). Economic Development Profile: North St. Louis County, Missouri, 3–20. https://doi.org/May 13th 2021.

"Our History." Coldwater Creek Facts, October 25, 2022. Accessed July 14, 2023. http://www.coldwatercreekfacts.com/.

Rep. *Health Consultation: Evaluation of Exposure to Landfill Gases in Ambient Air.* Missouri Department of Health and Senior Services. Bridgeton, MO: Agency for Toxic Substances and Disease Registry, September 21, 2018. Accessed July 14, 2023. https://www.docdroid.net/hgFw0aY/bridgeton-healthconsult-pdf#page=4.

Yun, Shumei, Schmaltz, Chester Lee, Sherri Homan, Philomina Gwanfogbe, Sifan Liu, Jonathan Garoutte, Noaman Kayani, Analysis of Cancer Incidence Data in Coldwater Creek Area, Missouri, 1996-2004 Report. Accessed July 12, 2023.

Yun, S., Schmaltz, C. L., Gwanfogbe, P., Homan, S., & Wilson, J. Rep. *Analysis of Cancer Incidence Data in Eight ZIP Code Areas Around Coldwater Creek.* Missouri Department of Health and Senior Services, September 22, 2014. Accessed July 14, 2023. https://health.mo.gov/living/healthcondiseases/chronic/cancer/pdf/ccanalysisSept2014.pdf.

5.3.17 | Spatial maneuvers

Kutik, William M. "Mallinckrodt Gift Funds Six Chairs: News: The Harvard Crimson." News | The Harvard Crimson, March 16, 1968. Accessed July 2023. https://www.thecrimson.com/article/1968/3/16/mallinckrodt-gift-funds-six-chairs-ppresident/.

Mann, Brian. "Drugmaker Mallinckrodt May Renege on $1.7 Billion Opioid Settlement." NPR, June 12, 2023. Accessed July 14, 2023. https://www.npr.org/2023/06/12/1181684340/drug-maker-mallinckrodt-may-renege-on-1-7-billion-opioid-settlement.

"Welcome to the Edward Mallinckrodt, Jr. Foundation." Edward Mallinckrodt, Jr. Foundation St. Louis, Missouri. Accessed July 14, 2023. https://emallinckrodtfoundation.org/home-page.

Tax inversion

"How Corporations Avoid Paying Their Fair Share." Public Citizen, May 1, 2019. Accessed July 14, 2023. https://www.citizen.org/news/how-corporations-avoid-paying-their-fair-share/.

Mallinckrodt history

Fentem, Sarah. "St. Louis-Based Mallinckrodt Files for Bankruptcy, to Pay Billions to Settle Lawsuits." STLPR, October 14, 2020. Accessed July 14, 2023. https://news.stlpublicradio.org/health-science-environment/2020-10-12/st-louis-based-mallinckrodt-files-for-bankruptcy-to-pay-billions-to-settle-lawsuits.

"Mallinckrodt." Wikipedia. Accessed July 14, 2023. https://en.wikipedia.org/wiki/Mallinckrodt.

Robbins, Brian. "Mallinckrodt Company That Remains in St. Louis Faces Big Threats." *St. Louis Business Journal*, December 7, 2018. Accessed July 14, 2023. https://www.bizjournals.com/stlouis/news/2018/12/07/mallinckrodt-company-that-remains-in-st-louis.html.

5.3.18 | Cleanup

Cammisa, Rebecca. *Atomic Homefront*, 2017. Accessed July 2023. https://www.atomichomefront.film/.

"Coldwater Creek (North County)." Just Moms St. Louis West Lake Landfill. Accessed July 14, 2023. http://www.stlradwastelegacy.com/north-county-coldwater-creeksites/.

"Damn Lies." The First Secret City, July 4, 2017. Accessed July 14, 2023. https://firstsecretcity.com/tag/slaps/.

"EPA's Environmental Justice Screening and Mapping Tool (Version 2.2)." Environmental Protection Agency. Accessed July 14, 2023. https://ejscreen.epa.gov/mapper/.

Fentem, Sarah. "Residents Say Coldwater Creek Report Lacks Answers to Cancer Questions." STLPR, June 26, 2018. Accessed July 14, 2023. https://news.stlpublicradio.org/health-science-environment/2018-06-26/residents-say-coldwater-creek-report-lacks-answers-to-cancer-questions.

Hartmann, Ray. "We Wrote about Poisons in Coldwater Creek 37 Years Ago. Guess What the Feds Just Confirmed?" *Riverfront Times*, May 15, 2019. Accessed July 14, 2023. https://www.riverfronttimes.com/stlouis/we-wrote-about-poisons-in-coldwater-creek-37-years-ago-guess-what-the-feds-just-confirmed/Content?oid=31592561.

Just Moms STL website, Accessed July 12, 2023. http://www.stlradwastelegacy.com/supporters/organizations/.

"Mallinckrodt Pharmaceuticals (MNK) - Revenue in 2022." CompaniesMarketCap Global Rankings, 2022. Accessed July 14, 2023. https://companiesmarketcap.com/mallinckrodt-pharmaceuticals/revenue/.

"Our History." Coldwater Creek Facts, October 25, 2022. Accessed July 14, 2023. http://www.coldwatercreekfacts.com/.

"West Lake Landfill – Bridgeton, Missouri." Just Moms St. Louis, January 9, 2019. Accessed July 14, 2023. http://www.stlradwastelegacy.com/.

5.3.19 | For-profit public utility

U.S. and Missouri fossil fuel and coal statistics

Gaug, Andrew. "Missouri among states most dependent on fossil fuels." NewsPressNow. August 21, 2021. Accessed January 2024. https://www.newspressnow.com/missouri-among-states-most-dependent-on-fossil-fuels/article_90c7127e-ffa7-11eb-ad56-5f13161e991a.html.

"Missouri State Profile Quick Facts." U.S. Energy Information Administration (EIA). July 20, 2023. Accessed January 2024. https://www.eia.gov/state/?sid=MO .

"Sources of Greenhouse Gas Emissions." U.S. Environmental Protection Agency. November 16, 2023. Accessed January 23, 2024. https://www.epa.gov/ghgemissions/sources-greenhouse-gas-emissions .

Other sources

"Ameren Missouri Facts." Ameren Missouri, April 2023. Accessed March 2021. https://www.ameren.com/-/media/missouri-site/files/aboutus/amerenmissourifactsheet.pdf

Ameren Electric. "Connecting Missouri". Ameren Missouri, 2011. Accessed March 2021. https://www.ameren.com/-/media/missouri-site/Files/Community/CommunityConnectionsBrochure.pdf.

"Ameren Net Income 2006-2020: AEE." Macrotrends. Accessed March 2021. https://www.macrotrends.net/stocks/charts/AEE/ameren/net-income. Ameren Net Income 2006-2020 | AEE | MacroTrends.

"Ameren Financial Statements 2009-2023: AEE." Macrotrends. Accessed March 2021. https://www.macrotrends.net/stocks/charts/AEE/ameren/financial-statements.

Associated Press. "Ameren Announces New Plans to Emphasize Renewable Energy." 5 On Your Side, September 28, 2020. Accessed March 2021. https://www.ksdk.com/article/news/local/ameren-renewable-energy-plan/63-67059b8e-b5ab-4d8c-be5c-1eb6bf54340e.

"Ch 4. Existing Supply-Side Resources - Ameren." *2020 Integrated Resource Plan*, Ameren Missouri, 2020. Accessed March 2021. https://www.ameren.com/-/media/missouri-site/files/environment/irp/2020/ch4-existing-supply-side-resources.ashx.

"Ch 6. New Supply-Side Resources - Ameren." *2020 Integrated Resource Plan*, Ameren Missouri, 2020. Accessed March 2021. https://www.ameren.com/-/media/missouri-site/files/environment/irp/2020/ch6-new-supply-side-resources.pdf?la=en-us-mo&hash=CC821CB2A220FAE2DBB-1B2A09FD087771255DD6A.

Clifford, Catherine. "60 Largest Banks in the World Have Invested $3.8 Trillion in Fossil Fuels since the Paris Agreement." CNBC, March 24, 2021. Accessed March 2021. https://www.cnbc.com/2021/03/24/how-much-the-largest-banks-have-invested-in-fossil-fuel-report.html.

"Coal." U.S. Energy Information Administration (EIA). May 22, 2022. Accessed March 2021. https://www.eia.gov/coal/data.php#transrate.

"Coal Explained." U.S. Energy Information Administration (EIA). November 16, 2022. Accessed March 2021. https://www.eia.gov/energyexplained/coal/coal-and-the-environment.php.

"Energy and the Environment Explained." U.S. Energy Information Administration (EIA). December 21, 2022. Accessed March 2021. https://www.eia.gov/energyexplained/energy-and-the-environment/greenhouse-gases-and-the-climate.php.

"Funding Success." Foundation Search - Best Funding Services In North America. Accessed March 2021. AMEREN CHARITABLE TRUST 2008 436022693.PDF

Gray, Bryce. "With Coal's Dominance in Missouri, Prospects of Clean Energy Transition Remain Uncertain." *St. Louis Post-Dispatch*, May 20, 2019. Accessed March 2021. https://www.stltoday.com/business/local/with-coals-dominance-in-missouri-prospects-of-clean-energy-transition-remain-uncertain/article_81b48f73-8b1c-59cc-8571-86e18576edec.html.

Hinman, Pip. "Scientists Say Net Zero by 2050 Is Too Late." MR Online, November 16, 2020. Accessed March 2021. https://mronline.org/2020/11/16/scientists-say-net-zero-by-2050-is-too-late/#:~:text=Climate%20scientists%20argue%20that%20net,the%20countries%20of%20the%20South.

"How Renewable Energy Credit Prices Are Set." *EnergySage*, June 7, 2019. Accessed March 2021. https://www.energysage.com/other-clean-options/renewable-energy-credits-recs/renewable-energy-credit-prices/.

John, Jeff St. "Ameren Sets Goal of Net-Zero by 2050, Plots Major Wind and Solar Expansion in Midwest." Greentech Media, September 29, 2020. Accessed March 2021. https://www.greentechmedia.com/articles/read/ameren-sets-net-zero-by-2050-goal-plots-major-wind-and-solar-expansion-in-missouri.

Maidenberg, Micah, and Chris Wack. "Arch, Peabody Aim to Keep Utility Coal Competitive with New Venture." *The Wall Street Journal*, June 19, 2019. https://www.wsj.com/articles/arch-coal-peabody-energy-to-form-coal-joint-venture-11560948644.

"Mayors of 12 Major Cities Commit to Divest from Fossil Fuel Companies, Invest in Green and Just Recovery from Covid-19 Crisis." C40 Cities, September 22, 2020. Accessed March 2021. https://www.c40.org/news/cities-commit-divest-invest/.

"Meramec Power Plant Retention Pond." Global Energy Monitor, April 30, 2021. Accessed March 2021. https://www.gem.wiki/Meramec_Power_Plant_Retention_Pond.

"Missouri State Profile and Energy Estimates." US Energy Information Administration, June 15, 2023. Accessed March 2021. https://www.eia.gov/state/data.php?sid=MO#EnergyIndicators.

Nussey, Bill. "How Much CO2 and Pollution Comes from Burning Coal?" Freeing Energy, September 9, 2021. Accessed March 2021. https://www.freeingenergy.com/how-much-co2-and-other-pollutants-come-from-burning-coal/.

Place, Eric de, and Laura Feinstein. "Playing Monopoly; or, How Utilities Make Money." Sightline Institute, June 14, 2022. Accessed March 2021. https://www.sightline.org/2020/05/18/playing-monopoly-or-how-utilities-make-money/#:~:text=The%20utility%20business%20is%20not%20like%20most%20other%20businesses.&text=That's%20right%2C%20utilities%20do%20not,used%20to%20provide%20the%20service.

"Map of Power Plants in Missouri." PowerPlant Maps. Accessed January 24, 2024. https://www.powerplantmaps.com/Missouri.html.

"Pure Power: Ameren Missouri." Ameren Missouri - Ameren Missouri. Accessed March 2021. https://www.ameren.com/missouri/company/environment-and-sustainability/pure-power.

"Renewable Energy Standard." DSIRE, November 3, 2022. Accessed March 2021. https://programs.dsireusa.org/system/program/detail/2622.

"Renewable Portfolio Standards." NREL Transforming Energy. Accessed March 2021. https://www.nrel.gov/state-local-tribal/basics-portfolio-standards.html#:~:text=A%20renewable%20portfolio%20standard%20(RPS,as%20a%20renewable%20electricity%20standard.

Rep. *Committed to Clean: Transformational Changes Toward Net-Zero, 2022 Climate Report.* Ameren Electric, 2022. Accessed March 2021. https://www.ameren.com/-/media/corporate-site/files/environment/reports/climate-report-tcfd.pdf.

Rep. *Renewable Energy Standard Compliance Report 2019.* Ameren Electric, April 15, 2020. Accessed March 2021. https://www.ameren.com/-/media/missouri-site/files/environment/renewables/compliance/res-compliance-report.pdf.

Rep. *Building a Brighter Energy Future.* Ameren Electric, 2018. Accessed March 2021. https://www.annualreports.com/HostedData/AnnualReportArchive/a/NYSE_AEE_2018.pdfa.

St. Louis Clean Energy Advisory Board Technical Committee. Rep. *Pathways to 100% Clean Energy.* October 26, 2019. Accessed March 2021. http://apps.stlpublicradio.org/documentcloud/document.html?id=6552038-St-Louis-Pathways-to-100-Clean-Energy-Report.

"Saint Louis Electricity Rates." Electricity Local. Accessed March 2021. https://www.electricitylocal.com/states/missouri/saint-louis/.

"Strings Attached: How Utilities Use Charitable Giving to Influence Politics and Increase Investor Profits." Energy and Policy Institute, December 10, 2019. Accessed March 2021. https://energyandpolicy.org/strings-attached-how-utilities-use-charitable-giving-to-influence-politics-increase-investor-profits-ameren/.

"Vital Signs - Arctic Sea Ice Minimum Extent." NASA, March 2, 2023. Accessed March 2021. https://climate.nasa.gov/vital-signs/arctic-sea-ice/.

What is FERC and its Natural Gas Pipeline Application Process. Federal Energy Regulatory Commission, 2016. https://www.youtube.com/watch?v=N3mXjH1J4TU.

5.M.01 | *Mobilize* Public transit

Schlinkmann, Mark. "Bi-State Reveals Possible North County Metrolink Routes." *St. Louis Post-Dispatch*, February 18, 2023. Accessed July 14, 2023. https://www.stltoday.com/news/local/business/bi-state-reveals-possible-north-county-metrolink-routes/article_e08ec4b8-2f51-53b7-a297-d9755e31bf9f.html.

5.M.02 | *Mobilize* Public open space

East West Gateway Council of Governments, Open Space data set (2013).

Greenway Project Map. Great Rivers Greenway, 2019. Accessed July 14, 2023. https://greatriversgreenway.org/wp-content/uploads/2020/07/Greenway-Project-Map-2019.jpg.

"Greenway Plans and Projects." Great Rivers Greenway, Accessed June 14, 2023. https://greatriversgreenway.org/plans-and-projects/.

Threatened or Endangered Species, St. Louis Metropolitan Area map, East-West Gateway Council of Governments. November 2018. Accessed January 24, 2024. https://www.ewgateway.org/wp-content/uploads/2018/11/TorE_Species_MOM_NOV_2018.pdf

Underwood, Angela. "Cities with the Most Green Space per Capita." Stacker, July 26, 2019. Accessed July 14, 2023. https://stacker.com/environment/cities-most-green-space-capita.

5.M.03 | *Mobilize* Local knowledge

Coldwater Creek Facts website. Accessed July 2023. https://coldwatercreekfacts.com/.

"EPA's Environmental Justice Screening and Mapping Tool (Version 2.2)." Environmental Protection Agency. Accessed July 14, 2023. https://ejscreen.epa.gov/mapper/.

Kite, Allison. "Records reveal 75 years of government downplaying, ignoring risks of St. Louis radioactive waste," *Missouri Independent*, July 12, 2023.

"West Lake Landfill – Bridgeton, Missouri." Just Moms St. Louis website, January 9, 2019. Accessed July 14, 2023. http://www.stlradwastelegacy.com/.

Yun, S., Schmaltz, C. L., Gwanfogbe, P., Homan, S., & Wilson, J. Rep. *Analysis of Cancer Incidence Data in Eight ZIP Code Areas Around Coldwater Creek.* Missouri Department of Health and Senior Services, September 22, 2014. Accessed July 14, 2023. https://health.mo.gov/living/healthcondiseases/chronic/cancer/pdf/ccanalysisSept2014.pdf.

5.M.04 | *Mobilize* The just transition

Transition quote

Brower, Derek. "An energy editor's farewell reflections, The energy transition will be volatile," *Financial Times*, June 29, 2023. Accessed June 30, 2023. https://www.ft.com/content/86d71297-3f34-48f3-8f3f-28b7e8be03c6.

Alternate energy existing and potential

"Mapping Clean Energy: Missouri," E2 website, June 6, 2018. Accessed June 2022. https://e2.org/reports/mapping-clean-energy-missouri/.

U.S. Energy Administration Information Maps website. Accessed July 2022. https://www.eia.gov/maps/.

Energy burden

"Environmental Justice: Environmental Racism in St. Louis." East-West Gateway, 2021. Accessed 2023. https://www.ewgateway.org/wp-content/uploads/2021/12/2021-Aug-AQACPres-Env-Racism.pdf.

Additional references

Associated Press. "Ameren Announces New Plans to Emphasize Renewable Energy." 5 On Your Side, September 28, 2020. Accessed March 2021. https://www.ksdk.com/article/news/local/ameren-renewable-energy-plan/63-67059b8e-b5ab-4d8c-be5c-1eb6bf54340e.

Gray, Bryce. "With Coal's Dominance in Missouri, Prospects of Clean Energy Transition Remain Uncertain." St. Louis Post-Dispatch, May 20, 2019. Accessed March 2021. https://www.stltoday.com/business/local/with-coals-dominance-in-missouri-prospects-of-clean-energy-transition-remain-uncertain/article_81b48f73-8b1c-59cc-8571-86e18576edec.html.

Hinman, Pip. "Scientists Say Net Zero by 2050 Is Too Late." MR Online, November 16, 2020. Accessed March 2021. https://mronline.org/2020/11/16/scientists-say-net-zero-by-2050-is-too-late/#:~:text=Climate%20scientists%20argue%20that%20net,the%20countries%20of%20the%20South.

Interstate Renewable Energy Council (IREC) website. Accessed January 2024. https://irecusa.org/about-irec/.

Shelor, Jeremiah. "FERC Approves Midwest Spire Pipeline in Another Split Decision." Natural Gas Intelligence, August 7, 2018. Accessed July 14, 2023. https://www.naturalgasintel.com/ferc-approves-midwest-spire-pipeline-in-another-split-decision/.

St. Louis Clean Energy Advisory Board Technical Committee. Rep. *Pathways to 100% Clean Energy*. October 26, 2019. Accessed March 2021. http://apps.stlpublicradio.org/documentcloud/document.html?id=6552038-St-Louis-Pathways-to-100-Clean-Energy-Report.

"Vital Signs - Arctic Sea Ice Minimum Extent." NASA, March 2, 2023. Accessed March 2021. https://climate.nasa.gov/vital-signs/arctic-sea-ice/.

Acknowledgments

This book has been a long time in the making. It was inspired by my interest in mapping, social justice and design politics, interests that were fueled by work in the urban design and architecture studios I taught at Washington University in St. Louis over many years. My 2016 studio, *The Problem of the Suburb*, in particular, laid groundwork for ideas and drawings that inspired this atlas.

I am indebted to Casey Ryan's incredible design and research leadership in that first studio. Her graphic clarity and aesthetic palate still resonate in drawings throughout this book. I've been privileged since then to continue work with some of the best graduate and undergraduate research assistants in the world. Tuoxin Li and Sheng Yan helped me compile and update an early set of maps and topics. And Tim Buescher stuck with it on the other end, helping create new maps over lots of Zoom calls outside of another full-time job. Andrew Tsuei and Andy Entis took on politics research assignments with the depth, exceptional competence and enthusiasm of our stellar undergrads. And Celine Haddad supported parts of the final book-preparation processes with her consistency and rigor. Thank you also to the design talents of Martine Kuchner, Elaina Echevarria, Weicong Huang and Madison Dugar, who contributed to key drawings at the right times. Thank you also to Ethan Miller, Lige Tan, Yijin Zhao, Yu Liu, Ryan Treacy, Nakesha Newsome, Boya Wang, Max Posen, Carmen Chee, Avni Joshi, Fatimah Alsaggaf, Micah Floyd, Madeleine Starr, Elliott Boyle, Chloe Kelley, Meredith Busch and Connor Merritt; along with Casey, Tim, Celine, Elaina, Madison, Andy and Andrew listed above, whose contributions from various other classes with me informed the book or appear in drawings throughout the atlas. The interactions with curious, committed students are what make my job at Washington University so enriching and rewarding.

I thank my colleagues at Washington University in St. Louis for years of fellowship and intellectual inspiration. I'll start with Jesse Vogler and Micah Stanek, whose landscape studio neighbored my suburbs studio at the Lewis Center in 2016, and who were always willing to talk about politics in design. Michael Allen's sharp writing, and our conversations and studio critiques, are a constant inspiration. And thank you, Bob Hansman, for sharing the beauty of St. Louis and its people with me. I am grateful for conversations with Linda Samuels and Jenny Price on all things mapping and for their important questions of the project. In my Washington University seminar, *Radical Mapping*, Petra Kempf, Jonathan Stitelman, Eric Ellingson, Gia Daskalakis, Irene Compadre, Ian Trivers, Geoff Ward, Jake Rosenfeld, special guest Jordan Weber and many others made invaluable contributions to our thinking on what a radical practice might actually entail. Thank you to Molly Webb and Bill Winston at the Washington University Libraries geospatial data services for hours of troubleshooting in and outside of the *Radical Mapping* and studio classrooms. I'm indebted to Winifred Elysse Newman for our early collaborations in mapping, art and speculative thinking at Washington University, and for the ongoing conversations across time and institutions. And thank you, Gavin Kroeber, Derek Hoeferlin, Ila Sheren and our *Laboratory for Suburbia* team, along with the project's extended family of designers and scholars across intuitions. The *Lab for Suburbia* conversations and sprawl sessions motivated me to keep going with this compendium. I also thank Eric Mumford, Zeuler Lima, Catalina Freixas, Heather Woofter, Bruce Lindsey, Audrey Treece, Ellen Bailey, Enrique Von Rohr and Chad Henry for support of this project and for camaraderie across the decades.

I am lucky to have valued colleagues across campus who welcomed me into the Departments of Sociology, Anthropology, Urban History, African and African American Studies, along with the American Culture Studies program and the Centers for the Humanities, and for Race, Equity and Ethnicity (CRE2). Thank you David Cunningham, Caity Collins, Shanti Parikh, Geoff Ward, Heidi Kolk, Iver Bernstein, Tila Neguse, Adrienne Davis, Billy Acree, Hank Webber and many others.

This project was supported by several Washington University grants at different stages of development: a Sam Fox School Creative Activity Grant and Faculty Research Award; a Center for Race, Equity and Ethnicity (CRE2) Scholar Grant, and a Mellon Foundation-funded Divided Cities Faculty Collaborative Grant. Thank you to Washington University and CRE2 colleagues, including Molly Metzger, Gerald Early, Bryce Robinson, Johnny Gabbert and many others, who saw the book in raw form at an early workshop and provided feedback and questions.

In St. Louis, I'm indebted to Z Gorley and Blake Strode at Arch City Defenders for their encouragement and collaboration with Z's helpful eyes on the project at different times. And Jocelyn Garner and Nicole Bolden for their enthusiasm and trust. I thank many people in Ferguson public institutions who opened the doors to me and students during visits, or who came as guests to reviews over the years. This book is for those in North County who live the contradictions of public-private business as usual—and those who mobilize every day to make things right. Any errors are my own, but my hope is for this book to support the important conversations already underway in our region. Thank you to my visual-storyteller colleagues who have been willing to share their work and passions for North County: Alana Marie, for our conversations on Kinloch, and Jami Desy Schoenweis, for your generosity to share Carrollton's story through your lens with me over the years.

In Boston, a shout-out to David Gamble, my collaborator on American cities and sounding board for all things urban design, teaching and the necessary next steps. And to Alex Krieger for leading our way. Thank you Jen Lee Michaliszyn, for decades of ongoing provocations and for providing generous feedback and encouragement at the right time for this atlas. I'm grateful for Walter Johnson's endorsement of the maps early on, Rahul Mehrotra's support and Diane Davis and Dan d'Oca, who all shared a willingness to ask hard questions of St. Louis, a place we all love and try to understand. Just beyond Boston, thank you, Brett Robertson, for pointed feedback on the state of privatizing public education. On the West Coast, I am thankful for Fonna Forman and Teddy Cruz, who generously agreed to write the foreword of this book. There is an even larger group of scholars in and outside of my field who I continue to learn from, including the team at Interboro, Jodi Rios, Colin Gordon, Kimberly Norwood, Amanda Kolson-Hurley, James Corner, John Robinson, Christopher Mele, David Harvey, Samuel Stein, Wendy Brown, John A. Wright, Sr., Jason Hackworth, Todd Swanstrom, Richard Rothstein, June Williamson and Ellen Dunham-Jones, Peter Rowe, Delores Hayden, George Lipsitz, the late Michael Sorkin, and numerous others.

At Belt, thank you, Anne Trubek and the editors, for your willingness to take on a radical atlas, and for your confidence, encouragement and patience in the process. And to Isabella Levethan, graphic designer for the book's system, who stuck with the project across time and distance and devised a flexible layout with great fonts and potential for nuance.

There are a few special colleagues and friends whom I've lost but whose views on urban design and history will forever inform my thinking of cities, St. Louis and my approach to teaching, questioning and communicating to the world. I really miss the lucid voices of Jacqueline Tatom and Maggie Garb, along with their generosity and warm collegiality. Outside of academia, Herb McCray had an infectious curiosity that we all benefitted from. I am sorry he never got to test drive this book that he loved before he even got to see it. And Sharon Gustafson. I miss them all.

Lastly, my family motivates me to demand a better world. I am grateful for my East Coast family and sister Karen Heyda Jackson who is always there to listen and lend support no matter what. And for my Texas family, for bringing the humor when we all needed "grilled possum" comic relief. My mom Ivana Heyda is a guide and inspiration, who keeps me going at the right times. Her help during the last weeks of atlas production was invaluable—and nourishing. Beyond those weeks, I'm grateful for a lifetime of energy and love. Thank you Thomas, Jack and Bridget Gustafson for tolerating so much (too much) work at home, and for reminding me how incredible the midwestern landscape and cities are when you get out in them. You three model jollity, learning as freedom, and trust. Bridget and Jack are also pretty great research assistants. Thank you finally to Bret Gustafson, who has been through it all with me and stuck through these projects. He inspires me each and every day, with lessons on writing, scholarship and politics; thinking on justice—and acting on it. In life, he models what love means and how it should manifest in everything we do. This book is for him and my family. Thank you.

About the author

Patty Heyda is professor of Architecture and Urban Design at Washington University in St. Louis. She is the coauthor of *Rebuilding the American City* and *Rebuilding the American Town*.